INSIGHT GUIDE

SYRIA & LEBANON

D0905943

Discovery
CHANNEL

APA PUBLICATIONS

L

Part of the Langenscheidt Publishing Group

ABOUT THIS BOOK

Editorial

Editor
Dorothy Stannard
Editorial Director
Brian Bell

Distribution

UK & Ireland
GeoCenter International Ltd
The Viables Centre, Harrow Way
Basingstoke, Hants RG22 4BJ
Fax: (44) 1256-817988

United States
Langenscheidt Publishers, Inc.
46–35 54th Road, Maspeth, NY 11378
Fax: (718) 784-0640

Worldwide
Apa Publications GmbH & Co.
Verlag KG (Singapore branch)
38 Joo Koon Road, Singapore 628990
Tel: (65) 865-1600. Fax: (65) 861-6438

Printing

Insight Print Services (Pte) Ltd
38 Joo Koon Road, Singapore 628990
Tel: (65) 865-1600. Fax: (65) 861-6438

©2000 Apa Publications GmbH & Co.
Verlag KG (Singapore branch)
All Rights Reserved

First Edition 2000

CONTACTING THE EDITORS
Although every effort is made to
provide accurate information, we
live in a fast-changing world and
would appreciate it if readers
would call our attention to any
errors or outdated information
that may occur by writing to:
Insight Guides, P.O. Box 7910,
London SE1 1WE, England.
Fax: (44 20) 7403-0290.
e-mail:
insight@apaguide.demon.co.uk

www.insightguides.com

This guidebook combines the interests and enthusiasms of two of the world's best known information providers: Insight Guides, whose titles have set the standard for visual travel guides since 1970, and Discovery Channel, the world's premier source of nonfiction television programming.

The editors of Insight Guides provide both practical advice and general understanding about a destination's history, culture, institutions and people. Discovery Channel and its popular website, www.discovery.com, help millions of viewers explore their world from the comfort of their own home and also encourage them to explore it first hand.

Insight Guide: Syria and Lebanon is carefully structured to convey an understanding of the region and its diverse cultures as well as to guide readers through its sights and activities:

◆ The **Features** section, indicated by a yellow bar at the top of each page, covers the history and culture of the countries in a series of informative essays.

◆ The main **Places** section, indicated by a blue bar, is a complete guide to all the sights and areas worth visiting. Places of special interest are coordinated by number with the maps.

◆ The **Travel Tips** listings section, which has an orange bar, provides a point of reference for information on travel, hotels, shops, restaurants and more. An index to the section appears on the back cover flap.

The Writers

This book was edited by **Dorothy Stannard**, a long-standing managing editor at Insight Guides, specialising in North Africa and the Middle East. Like all Insight Guides, it is the work of many hands, and Stannard enlisted writers and photographers with a special knowledge of the region.

Husband and wife team **Sylvie Franquet** and **Anthony Sattin** covered most of the Syria places chapters, as well as the features on the Rich Cultural Mix, Daily Life and Lebanese and Syrian Cuisine. They also wrote the picture stories on arts and crafts, shrines, souks and desert life and the short piece on the Hejaz Railway. Franquet is an Arabic scholar who spent many years living and working in the Middle East, and Sattin is a regular writer on the Middle East for London's *Sunday Times*.

The remaining Syria places chapters, on the Orontes Valley and the Desert Steppe and the Northwest, are by archaeologist **Pamela Watson**, with input from Dorothy Stannard.

When it came to Lebanon, the editor commissioned the BBC correspondent in Lebanon, **Christopher Hack**, who has been writing and broadcasting from Beirut for several years. Hack wrote the four Places chapters on Lebanon and supplied information boxes on a range of topics – the hostage-taking of the 1980s, the rebuilding of Beirut, Lebanon's wine and skiing industries, the myths and reality surrounding Hizbollah, and the famous cedar trees of the Lebanon.

The complex history of both countries was covered by regular Insight historian **Rowlinson Carter**. Carter believes that history should be about people as much as dates, as his very readable chapters show.

Lastly, the fact-packed Travel Tips section was split between **Brian Briank**, who lives and works in Damascus, and **Peter Grimsditch**, who edits the *Beirut Daily Star*.

The Photographers

Most of the images in this guide were supplied by **Alan Keohane**. Keohane, who lives in Morocco, specialises in photographing and writing about North Africa and the Middle East. Among his acclaimed photographic books are *The Berbers of North Africa* and *The Bedouin*, based on his experiences of living with these fascinating peoples.

Among the other photographers with work in this guide are **Lyle Lawson** and **Gonzalo M. Azumendi**.

Proof-reading and indexing were completed by **Penny Phenix**.

Map Legend

—··—	International Boundary
————	Province Boundary
—•—	National Park/Reserve
✈ ✈	Airport: International/Regional
🚌	Bus Station
P	Parking
❶	Tourist Information
✉	Post Office
✝ ✝ ✝	Church/Ruins
✝	Monastery
☾	Mosque
✡	Synagogue
🏰	Castle/Ruins
∴	Archaeological Site
∩	Cave
𝟏	Statue/Monument
★	Place of Interest

The main places of interest in the Places section are coordinated by number with a full-colour map (e.g. ❶), and a symbol at the top of every right-hand page tells you where to find the map.

CONTENTS

View over
the Euphrates

Travel Tips

Insight on ...

Information panels

Places

◆ **Full Travel Tips index
is on page 321**

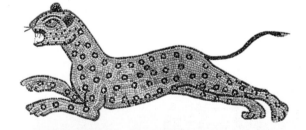

ARMIES AND IDEAS

In Syria and Lebanon east meets west, capitalism rubs shoulders with socialism, and Christianity and Islam coincide

Modern Syria and Lebanon are 20th-century entities, created in the wake of World War I and the break-up of the Ottoman Empire. Previously, the name Syria had referred to the whole area covered by Lebanon, Syria, Palestine and Transjordan, a unit whose frontiers were the Taurus Mountains, the sea, the Euphrates, and the deserts.

Historical Syria was located geographically between the great civilisations of the east (Mesopotamia and Persia), the West (Europe), the north (Anatolia) and the south (Egypt). Syria, in the middle, was a true crossroads of civilisations and cultures, the natural battleground not only of armies but also of ideas. The result was a magnificent heritage of people, cultural expressions and monuments that has drawn the most eminent explorers and Orientalists of recent times, from Johann Burckhardt and Richard Burton to extraordinary women travellers such as Lady Hester Stanhope and Gertrude Bell, not to mention a swathe of eminent surveyors and archaeologists. All were attracted by the region's fabulous ghosts, but they soon became intrigued by its present.

The arbitrary sub-division and isolation of Greater Syria as a French Mandate sidelined the major trading cities of Damascus, Homs and Aleppo. In more recent times, development was inhibited by Lebanon's civil war and Syria's alliance with the Eastern Bloc countries, isolation from the West and frosty relations with neighbouring Arab countries such as Iraq and Jordan. In addition, a limited touristic infrastructure tended to discourage all but the bravest travellers.

But now, with the end of Lebanon's civil war, the breakdown of Cold War alignments and the progress being made towards peace in the Middle East, the whole region is transforming itself economically and culturally. Tourism is certainly benefiting, with Syria and Jordan in particular joining forces to improve tour organisation and site development. If long-term peace with Israel eventually becomes a reality, growth in the region could be dynamic.   ❑

PRECEDING PAGES: drawing water from a well is a long haul, northern Syria; a shepherd leads the way, northwest Syria; friend and family, near Beirut; a nightclub in Jounié, near Beirut.
LEFT: facing a bright new future.

Decisive Dates

8000–4000 BC Neolithic period. Settlement along the Euphrates and development of agriculture. Ugarit, Tell Halaf and Mureybit date from this time.

3000–2000 BC Early Bronze Age. Establishment of "cities", including Ebla, Tell Brak, Kadesh and the Mesopotamian city of Mari. In southern Mesopotamia King Sargon founds the Akkadian Dynasty, whose empire eventually extends to the Mediterranean.

2000 BC Amorite invasion. Amorite power centres on Mari, from where it spreads through the

establish port cities in Sidon, Tyre and Byblos, found trading posts throughout the Mediterranean. In 814 BC they found Carthage.

612 BC The Assyrians are defeated by the Babylonians, who assume control of Syria.

540 BC The Persian army under Cyrus the Great defeats the Babylonians.

334 BC Alexander the Great begins his conquest of Asia, introducing the Graeco-Roman period.

3rd century BC Local powers start to re-establish themselves, as Seleucid power declines.

1st century BC Rise of the Nabataeans based in Petra, in modern Jordan. Their influence spreads throughout southern Syria.

Euphrates region. Canaanites settle the coastal strip; they develop the world's first alphabet.

1500 BC Tuthmosis I of Egypt invades Syria, followed by the Hittites.

1285 BC The Battle of Kadesh between the Hittites and the Egyptians at Homs. The Hittites gain control of large areas of Syria.

1100 BC The Arameans establish various city-states, including Damascus. The Aramaic language spreads far and wide.

900 BC The Assyrians, whose power has waxed and waned in northern Syria, conquer most of Syria. They commit terrible atrocities, but also introduce a brilliant culture.

900–800 BC On the coast, the Phoenicians, who

64 BC Pompey annexes Syria, bringing Rome into conflict with the Parthians in Persia.

AD 106 Collapse of Petra forces trade routes north. Rise of the magnificent Arab state of Palmyra at the new crossroads of east–west trade routes. Though a protectorate of Rome, Palmyra retains a great deal of independence.

269 Queen Zenobia of Palmyra defeats the Roman general Heraclianus and conquers the whole of Syria. In 272 Roman supremacy is restored when Zenobia is captured and sent to Rome.

300–600 The Byzantine period. Christianity takes hold and becomes the empire's official religion in 392. Fall of the Roman Empire in the West in 476.

6th century Repeated incursions by the Persians.

632 Death of the Prophet Mohammed.
640 The Arab conquest of Syria is complete.
660–750 Umayyad Dynasty. Damascus is the seat of the caliphate. The Umayyad Empire spreads from Spain to Central Asia.
750–mid-10th century Abbasid Dynasty. Caliphate moves to Baghdad. Arabic gradually replaces Greek and Aramaic as the *lingua franca* in the region.
10th century As Abbasid power disintegrates, a variety of smaller powers takes hold, including the Hamdanids in Aleppo and the Shi'ite Fatimids in the south. Sunni and Shi'ite divisions become increasingly sharp; complex off-shoots flourish.
11th century Seljuk Turks seize both Aleppo and Damascus.
1098–1124 Series of Crusades to reclaim the Holy Land. Crusaders seize cities and build fortresses.
1176–1260 Ayubbids introduce a new golden age. They try to re-establish Islamic orthodoxy, building *madrasas* (theological schools).
1187 Saladin, founder of the Ayubbids, defeats the crusaders at the Battle of Hattin, though the Christians later regain parts of the coast.
1260 Mongols invade Syria and sack Aleppo. They are curbed by the Mamlukes of Egypt, efficient rulers who embark on public works and encourage trade in the region.
1516 Mamlukes are defeated by the Ottoman Turks, who rule Syria for the next 400 years.
1789–1840 Emir Bechir rules Lebanon.
18th century Ottoman power begins its slow process of decay.
1860 The Druze massacre of Maronites in Lebanon is followed by a Muslim massacre of Christians in Damascus. The French intervene and establish the semi-autonomous district of Mount Lebanon under a Christian Governor.
1909 Revolt by the Young Turks in Istanbul inspires nationalism in populations under Ottoman rule.
1914–19 World War I. The Ottoman Empire joins the war at the end of 1914, siding with Germany.
1916 The Arab Revolt. Emir Feisal, son of the Sherif of Mecca, takes up leadership of the Arab Pan-nationalist Movement. It joins forces with the British to drive out the Ottoman Turks.
1920 San Remo Conference. Victorious Allied powers carve up the old Ottoman Empire. Syria and Lebanon come under the mandate of France.
1927 The French put down a Druze revolt.

PRECEDING PAGES: the Siege of Antioch.
LEFT: mosaic at Ma'aret an-Numan, Syria.
RIGHT: young PLO supporters in Lebanon, 1987.

1939 Antioch and Alexandretta are ceded to Turkey.
1944 The Druze area in Syria loses its autonomy.
1945 Syria and Lebanon gain independence.
1948 Creation of the State of Israel.
1958 Syria and Egypt, under President Nasser, form the United Arab Republic, though this is later dissolved. President Camille Nimir Chamoun in Lebanon fears Nasser wants to destroy Christian domination of Lebanon. Civil War in Lebanon.
1962 Baathists party is elected.
1967 Six-Day War between Israel and the Arab states. Syria loses the Golan Heights to Israel.
1971 General Hafez al-Assad becomes president of Syria.

1975–89 Second civil war in Lebanon between Maronite-led Lebanese Forces and the National Movement spearheaded by the PLO. In 1976 Syria occupies most of Lebanon; in 1978 Israel invades southern Lebanon.
1980s Westerners are taken hostage in Beirut.
1985 Israel withdraws to a buffer zone in southern Lebanon.
1991 Syrian-Lebanese Treaty grants Syria special privileges in Lebanon.
1990s Lebanon recovers from the war, though regular attacks by Israeli forces continue against Hizbollah in southern Lebanon.
2000 In Syria, President Assad dies. In Lebanon, Israeli forces withdraw from the south. ❑

EARLY INVADERS

From the Phoenicians to the Persians and the Greeks, Syria sustained many changes of rule in its early history, and they've all left their mark

Phoenicians who settled along the Syrian coast some 5–6,000 years ago worshipped their supreme god Baal by flinging live children into a roaring furnace. The goddess Astarte was more pleasantly appeased. It was encumbent upon one and all – human, animal and vegetable – to perpetuate their species by emulating Astarte's coupling with the handsome Adonis, and temples specifically for the purpose sprang up everywhere. Women would gather at these temples, available to any man that came along.

In the 5th century BC, a long way down the line, the Greek historian Herodotus found the practice still current at the temple at Byblos (Jebeil). "Many rich women are too proud to mix with the rest," he reported. "They drive to the temple in covered carriages with a whole host of servants in tow and stay in their carriages, waiting. Most women, however, wear a plaited string around their heads and sit in the temple precincts. A great crowd they are, what with some sitting there, others arriving, others going away. Through them all are gangways along which men pass, making their choice. Tall, handsome women are soon done with and go home, but the ugly ones return day after day for three or four years with less and less hope of ever fulfilling the condition which the law demands." Herodotus, who could take most things in his stride, considered this ancient practice "wholly shameful".

Phoenician traders

Nevertheless, these worshippers of Baal and Astarte were the same people who invented the phonetic alphabet, sailed to the Baltic and down the west coast of Africa, and built a vast commercial empire trading in everything from their famous purple cloth (the dye extracted from the shellfish murex), to precious metals, horses, wine and ostrich eggs.

If, as Homer observed, the Phoenicians – a branch of the Semitic Canaanites – were "skilled at all things", their overwhelming preoccupation was business, and from the outset they were perfectly positioned to function as middlemen between the powerful Egyptian and Mesopotamian civilisations. If fighting was

TOOL OF TRADE

Not the first of its kind, the Phoenician alphabet was nevertheless more popular than its North Semitic predecessors by virtue of being a tool of trade in Phoenicia's vast commercial empire. Earlier forms of writing like Egyptian hieroglyphs were virtually private languages between professional scribes.

The alphabet consised of 22 consonants without any vowels, and text read from right to left. Regional variations developed in colonies such as Cyprus and Sardinia, and Carthage in North Africa produced the "neo Punic" cursive form. It was eventually subsumed by its Greek and Roman descendants in the 3rd century AD.

LEFT: Baal holding a thunderbolt. This 17th–13th century BC limestone stele came from Ugarit.
RIGHT: 9th–8th century BC Phoenician mask.

unavoidable, they hired mercenaries to do it.

Phoenicia was not a single state but a necklace of independent ports – Byblos, Berytus (Beirut), Sidon, Tyre, Tripoli and Aradus (Ruad) – nestling beneath a ridge of mountains generally known in the singular as "The Mountain" or, later, Mount Lebanon. The region was therefore narrower than modern Lebanon, which includes a parallel ridge farther inland, the Anti-Lebanon. These ridges, separated by the Bekaa "valley" – strictly speaking a plain – are high enough to be tipped with snow even

ANCIENT AUTOGRAPHS

Those who have left their names engraved on the rocks on their way through the Dog River bottleneck have included, among many others, Rameses II and Nebuchadnezzar.

god Anubis (he of the dog's head on a human body) whose job was to show the condemned to their seats for infinite agony. The god's howl when the wind blew in a certain direction could be heard, it was said, in Cyprus.

Another river, only a few kilometres away, turned red in spring and discoloured the sea in a huge arc. Rich earth brought down by floods perhaps? Of course not. It was the blood of Astarte's consort Adonis, who was killed by a wild boar while hunting in a grove upstream.

when the coast and hinterland are frying. Instead of dropping down to the sea, some streams from these heights headed inland on a suicide mission against endless desert. They went down in glory, however, their graves blossoming as the fantastic oases that gave birth to Damascus and other Syrian halts on the caravan road.

Gateway to the underworld

The Dog River, on the other hand, vanished into an abyss of caverns before resurfacing lower down for its final descent to the sea near Beirut. This, the ancient world decided, must be the gateway to the underworld and was accordingly graced by a colossal statue of the

Modern Syria is only part of antiquity's "Greater Syria", a region whose natural boundaries appealed to Napoleon Bonaparte's aesthetic and military sensibilities when he contemplated re-drawing the map. He liked the complement of Taurus mountains to the north, the Euphrates river in the east, the Sinai desert to the south, and the Mediterranean sea to the west, the whole representing, for imperial purposes, the link between the continents of Africa, Europe and Asia.

Bonaparte's designs did not get very far, but like scores of military predecessors and successors in the region, he was aware that the Syrian corridor narrowed into three lanes on a line drawn between Beirut and Damascus: the coast road, the middle road along the Bekaa valley, and the caravan road between Anti-Lebanon and the desert. The northern terminus of the caravan road via Damascus, Homs and Hama was Aleppo, from which roads fanned out to Europe and Asia.

Human traffic

The flow of peoples along the Syrian corridor was heavy in both directions. The entire cast of the Old Testament seems to have strolled by at one time or another: not only Hebrews going to or from Egypt, but Hittites, Perizzites, Gir-

2150 BC by the Amorites. With their backs against a wall, the Phoenicians saw their future across the Mediterranean, and they were incomparably equipped to exploit it. Past-masters of navigation, they had forests on their doorstep which provided cedar so finely grained that it almost did away with the need for caulking.

Tyre was trading as early as 2759 BC and the other ports were not far behind. Competition was fierce. Egyptian buyers routinely turned up looking for 40 shiploads of timber. According to Homer, Paris popped over from Troy to shop for clothes for his mother.

gashites, Amorites, Jebusites and all. The commanders of armies squeezing through the Dog River bottle-neck on the coast road – the entrance to hell – made a habit of signing the inviting rock faces. These marks remain in a variety of forms, including heiroglyphs, cuneiform, Greek, Arabic and Latin.

This constant traffic was dangerous to the cities and communities along the route. Byblos, for example, was razed to the ground around

LEFT: this 3,000 BC ivory and mother-of-pearl Sumerian mosaic came from Mari, northern Syria.
ABOVE: alabaster relief showing wood being unloaded from Phoenician ships.

The Ebla tablets

In the interior, over the mountains, Sumerians and Hurrians moved in from Iran about 3000 BC and were joined, or perhaps supplanted, by Canaanites around 2300 BC. Excavations during the 1970s uncovered a Canaanite city, Ebla, destroyed in 1600 BC, whose inhabitants used a script that had not been seen before. On being decrypted, no fewer than 15,000 surviving clay tablets revealed an army of bureaucrats obsessed with red tape.

These dedicated public servants were sacked, in both senses, when the Hyksos charged in with the unprecedented advantage of horse-drawn chariots and iron weapons. Having gone on to conquer Egypt, the Hyksos made an early attempt at one of history's most elusive goals, a union between Egypt and Syria.

The Egyptians themselves were more successful than most. The celebrated Amarna tablets record the correspondence on diplomatic and other matters between Egyptian governors in Syria and the pharaohs of the 18th Dynasty back at base.

The introduction of the camel in around 1000 BC revolutionised trade routes. Previously, oriental imports were brought up the Persian Gulf by ship and transferred to mule trains for the long haul along the Euphrates. Camels could cross deserts on little water, and carry heavy loads of around 200 kg (440 lbs), and that made feasible a short cut that began at Yemen, at the foot of the Red Sea, and proceeded via Mecca (whose future role at the centre of Islam was not unconnected with its traditional commercial importance) to the Syrian corridor, the back door to the Phoenician ports.

> ### DROMEDARY POWER
> The introduction of the camel in around 1000 BC had the same revolutionary impact on regional trade as the opening of the Suez Canal had in the 19th century.

As a result, Phoenician trade boomed, as may be judged by the fact that in 1000 BC Tyre founded a commercial colony at Utica in North Africa. In short order the Mediterranean basin was ringed with Phoenician colonies, including Carthage, reputedly founded by Elissa, the sister of the King Pygmalion of Tyre, who had fled Tyre after the murder of her husband.

David and Solomon

In Syria, meanwhile, David slew Goliath during the Israelites' campaign to wrest control of Palestine from the Philistines. David formed an alliance with Tyre but remained at odds with Damascus, against whose forces he fought a number of battles. His son King Solomon not only maintained warm relations with King Hiram of Tyre but apparently aped the Phoenicians too closely for his own good. He was criticised for spending money like water and keeping a harem stocked with exotic beauties.

Unlike the Assyrians *(see box, left)*, Cyrus the Great, arriving with a Persian army in the 6th century BC, was pleased to strike an alliance with Tyre, and this was continued by his successor, Darius I. The Phoenicians provided the fleet that dropped off Darius and his army for an expedition against Greece that ended in a shocking defeat at Marathon in 490 BC. His son Xerxes made amends by destroying Athens, but it was during this campaign that the Persian fleet – mostly Phoenician ships and crew – was crushed by the Greek navy at Salamis.

These defeats spelled the end of Persian rule over Syria. In the following century, the Greeks would arrive in force. ❏

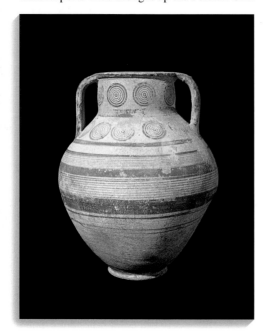

> ### SYRIAN SLAUGHTER
> The Assyrians swooped on Syria like a wolf on the fold. They, like others before them, took the coast road and, held up at the Dog River bottleneck, King Esarhaddon left not only a signature but also his portrait on one of the rocks. His stern expression and pursed lips were a crystal ball: he exterminated the Egyptian governors who had conscientiously been filing reports to the pharaoh and killed tens of thousands of their Syrian subjects. The prince of Tyre made a dash for Cyprus but was overtaken. Esarhaddon, according to an Assyrian inscription, "fished him like a fish out of the sea, brought him back, and cut off his head".

ABOVE: 8th-century BC Phoenician vase from Tyre.
RIGHT: two statuettes of gods, possibly Baal, from 1550 to 1200 BC.

GREEKS AND ROMANS

Graeco-Roman rule in Syria lasted a thousand years, from the invasion of Alexander the Great to the spread of Christianity and the coming of Islam

A t the age of 23, Alexander the Great pulled on the same kind of lion skin cap worn by his idol Achilles and set off from Macedonia in 330 BC with 50,000 men to conquer the world. When Egypt's turn came, it was completely predictable that Darius III, the Great King of Persia, would be waiting to put an end to this impertinent dream. As Alexander approached the Syrian corridor, he found the way barred by 400,000 Persian troops. Even against these odds, however, he managed to break through, and although Darius escaped to fight another day, the battle of Issus, now on the Turkish side of the disputed border with Syria, marked the start of a Graeco-Roman era in Syria that was to last 1,000 years.

Alexander's advance

While Alexander commemorated his victory by naming a nearby port after himself – Alexandretta – one of his generals raced ahead to seize Damascus before Darius re-grouped. Rifling through the Great Palace produced 2,600 talents of coin and 500 pounds of silver – more than Macedonia's annual national budget – as well as "329 female musicians, 306 different cooks, 13 pastry chefs, 70 wine waiters and 40 scent makers". Advancing down the Phoenician coast, Alexander's reception at various ports depended on how they had been getting along with the Persians. Sidon was still reeling from a dreadful massacre 12 years earlier, so Alexander was greeted there as a hero and asked to nominate a new king. No one raised an eyebrow when he chose a local gardener.

Tyre, in contrast, had profited enormously from commercial ties with Persia. An island fortress surrounded by a man-made harbour, Tyre had defied long sieges by the Assyrians and by Nebuchadnezzar's Babylonians. Lesser armies took one look at the sheer walls rising from the sea and moved swiftly on. Not

LEFT: doorway from the Temple of Bacchus at Baalbek, painted by David Roberts.
RIGHT: Alexander the Great.

Alexander. He introduced himself by asking for permission to enter the fortress to pray at the tomb of an ancestor – he seemed to have them everywhere – only to be told he could pray as much as he liked but only from the distance of Old Tyre on the mainland. Alexander withdrew to Old Tyre not to pray but to rip the place

apart, collecting the stone to build a causeway to the island and the timbers for siege machinery. Under a hail of boulders and flaming arrows from the fortress, completion of the causeway took seven months. Crouched under a leather canopy, the Macedonians were then able to bring two towers up against the walls and go over the top. They found King Azemilcus of Tyre praying, ironically, over the tomb of Alexander's questionable ancestor. He and visiting dignitaries from Carthage were spared, but 7,000 soldiers and sailors were executed and 30,000 civilians sold into slavery.

Alexander continued through Palestine and was welcomed in Egypt as a liberator. After an overwhelming victory over Darius at Arbella, almost the whole of the Persian empire fell into his lap. But he pressed on and was deep into India, his army having marched 27,000 km (17,000) miles in all, when the dream ran out of steam. Drinking heavily and behaving erratically towards the end, he died at 33, leaving an empire to be parcelled out among various heirs.

Syria was divided between two generals, Seleucus I (Seleucus Nicator) and Ptolemy Soter, whose headquarters were in Macedonia and Egypt respectively. As neither side was satisfied with this arrangement, it was a case of all-or-nothing when the Seleucid Antiochus III met

than 700 "Dead Cities" stand as a monument to their industry. The greatest of the Greek cities, Antioch, is still very much alive, although these days in Turkey rather than Syria.

New towns

Greek rather than Aramaic was spoken in the new towns and life was steeped in Hellenic culture. Politically, however, the settlers were as aggressively divided in Syria as they had been in the Greek city states at home, which was rather a case of doing what the natives did. The Phoenician ports had never got along, and small wars were the national pastime of nomadic

Ptolemy IV in battle in 198 BC and triumphed.

The Seleucids soon realised that running Macedonia and Syria at the same time was too much for them. Of the two, they preferred Syria, and, as many of their Greek subjects were of the same mind, cities like Athens and Corinth, for all their recent greatness, were virtually depopulated by the stampede for better opportunities in the Syrian new world. Damascus promptly bolted its gates against them, and as the Greeks were neither suited to life in the desert nor inclined to compete with the wily Phoenicians along the coast, they invested their energy and hopes in building a string of new towns along the Orontes. The ruins of no fewer

Arab tribes. With the whole region heaving with malice, outsiders couldn't resist trying their luck. The Ptolomies were forever mounting raids from Egypt and the Persians from across the Euphrates. Nabataeans dashed in from Petra and seized Damascus. In these unruly circumstances, the Roman general Pompey appeared in 64 BC as a potential saviour: Syria badly needed some Pax Romana.

Civilised invasions

The Romans, great admirers of the Greeks wherever they found them, were inclined to build on the status quo rather than destroy it and start again. No one was forced to speak Latin, and in general the Romans retained Greek place-names like Heliopolis for what had been Phoenician Baalbek, a combination of the god Baal and the location, Bekaa. Heliopolis was a religious centre, and apparently both Greeks and Romans took wholeheartedly to some of the more interesting ancient rites, whatever the historian Herodotus thought of them. In AD 300, the early Christian historian Eusebius, who had read Herodotus, was disappointed to find no real improvement in the vast temple complex which the Romans

HELIOPOLIS IN AD 300

Like Beirut, Heliopolis became a retirement colony for veterans of the Roman army and was therefore one of very few places where Latin was commonly spoken.

the Ptolemies in Egypt. Once Julius Caesar had the Ptolemies under control, the Romans sank wells at intervals of 38km (24 miles), no matter how deep they had to go. To deter Arab robbers they created the Roman Camel Corps and their caravans grew to as many as 3,000 animals at a time, with toll-collectors waiting at every stage to receive them.

Petra prospered beyond belief until the Nabataeans made the mistake of conspiring with the Parthians against Rome, at which point the emperor Trajan closed it down.

added. In the temples, men still encouraged their wives and daughters to take part in "shameless fornication", while castrated priests rolled round in female dress.

Nevertheless, the Romans characteristically knitted Syria together with a network of roads built to exacting standards. Their next undertaking was to re-commission the caravan route from Yemen, which the Seleucids had been forced to abandon because of interference by

LEFT: carving from the Temple of Bel at Palmyra. The Romans built on old Phoenician sites.
ABOVE: David Robert's painting of the Circular Temple at Baalbek.

Diverted traffic then went through Palmyra, an oasis known to the Assyrians as Tadmor, where the local dynasty turned the windfall into a premonition of Las Vegas and Hong Kong rolled into one. Temples, colonnaded avenues and private palaces shot up in what might have looked like the middle of nowhere but was in fact the point at which the outer limits of the Roman and Persian empires touched. Palmyra became the conduit for their commercial dealings, so it suited both parties to recognise – or at least play along with – Palmyra's neutral independence.

When the Sassanians overthrew the Parthians in Persia and declared war on Rome, Odenathus, the ruler of Palmyra, was ready to sacrifice neutrality and join the winning side. After the Roman emperor Valerian was captured at the battle of Edessa in 260, Odenathus sent a camel train loaded with presents to the Persian commander with his congratulations. "Who is this Odenathus?" the Persian sniffed as he gave orders for the whole lot to be dumped in the Euphrates. Affronted, Odenathus ordered his army to attack Persian outposts, and he was delighted when one bagged a bevy of the Great King's most desirable beauties.

These human prizes notwithstanding, it was Zenobia, a local woman, who ruled Odenathus's heart. She was, wrote the historian Edward

Gibbon, "perhaps the only female whose superior genius broke through the servile indolence imposed on her sex by the climate and manners of Asia". When Odenathus was murdered in a foolish argument over the etiquette of hunting, Zenobia took over as regent with ambitions that would have taken even his breath away. She was determined to conquer Rome, and to begin with her army enjoyed astonishing success against Roman forces in Egypt. It was too good to last. When Zenobia eventually entered the imperial capital, it was as a prisoner in chains.

Having lost patience with Palmyra, the Romans closed it down by the simple expedient of cutting off the water supply.

Imperial disgrace

In spite of the upset at Palmyra, Syria continued to send a stream of professors, philosophers and lawyers to Rome, and the province had its first taste of the purple when the emperor Septimius Severus married Julia Domna, who came from Emesa (Homs). Cultivated and beautiful, she presided over a salon in Rome unembarrassed by her poor grasp of Latin. Among the sniggers behind her back were accusations that she had no notion whatsoever of marital fidelity. But if she was open to criticism, her son, the emperor Caracalla, was without question "the common enemy of mankind". The imperial court, if not mankind, trembled when it became widely known that the emperor's aunt, Julia's sister, was carrying his child.

Born Varius Avitus Bassianus in Homs, the child was revolting in the cradle and grew steadily worse. He changed his name to Elagabalus (Heliogabalus), a variation on Baal, the god to whom he was high priest. Proclaimed emperor at 15 by the Roman legions in Syria, he entered Rome wearing a tiara, collars and bracelets studded with precious stones, and make-up which blackened his eyebrows and gave him red and white spotted cheeks. The Roman senate looked at this apparition and sighed. "Having long experienced the stern tyranny of their own countrymen," Gibbon wrote, "Rome was at length humbled beneath the effeminate luxury of Oriental despotism". Elagabalus was a disgrace in every imaginable way for three years before the Praetorians dragged his body through the streets and dumped it in the Tiber.

Christian persecution

By then, however, the empire was trapped in religious turmoil that could not so easily be disposed of. Roman governors in the Syrian province routinely silenced the most persistent agitators by nailing them to a cross or by some other form of capital punishment. St John the Baptist, for example, lost his head for refusing to condone King Herod's affair with his sister-in-law. Pilate's execution of Jesus of Nazareth might have seemed unremarkable at the time, but the repercussions were of course timeless.

Paul of Tarsus, a rabbi and tent-maker, was on the road to Damascus to deal with some of Christ's troublesome followers when he experienced a vision that turned him into a fervent believer. Under Paul's influence, the new religion went beyond trying to reform wayward Jews and aimed instead at converting pagans. This met with immediate success in Syria, where the term Christian was coined and the cross adopted as a symbol. Antioch, the greatest of the Greek-built cities, ranked with Rome and Alexandria as a capital of Christendom.

The legalisation of Christianity

The Christian revolution was well under way when a second Syrian, Philip the Arab, was elevated to the imperial throne, again by military proclamation. Philip drained the treasury to lay legalised Christianity and took measures to stamp out the more grotesque forms of paganism. At Heliopolis, he was told, sacred virgins were now being disembowelled and fed to pigs.

On the other hand, many Christian Graeco-Syrians had been schooled in the subtleties of Aristotle and Plato, and it was they who intellectualised Christianity – not that philosophy staunched the flow of blood. The infamous Monophysite question raised such passions that monks were dragged out of monasteries and murdered in their hundreds by those who took the opposite view. In spite of what amounted to a religious civil war, the secular administra-

on the most lavish entertainments seen in Rome since Nero and to transform his Syrian birthplace, Chahba, into a showpiece along the lines of Palmyra. But his attempts to ingratiate himself with the Romans could not disguise the fact that Germanic hordes were hovering over the empire's northern border and a resurgent Persia was again threatening from the the east.

Constantine the Great's grand strategy to save the empire was to move the capital from Rome to Constantinople. At the same time, he tion in Syria sailed on, attracting growing numbers of Arabs into the cities and towns, where most turned Christian.

The coming of Islam

Some tribes remained on the fringes of the desert, where they formed statelets whose independence Byzantium recognised as a buffer against Persian incursions. But in keeping a watch on the Persians in the east, the emperors failed to appreciate the implications of a new force in the rivalry between Mecca and Medina for the caravan trade. The turning point was the leader of the Medina faction, Mohammed, proclaiming himself the Apostle of God.   ❑

LEFT: Zenobia of Palmyra.
ABOVE: *The Conversion of St Paul* painted by Pieter Brueghel the Elder.

ISLAM

With Arab invasion and the spreading of the Prophet's word, Syria became a victim of the great schism between the Sunnites and the Shi'ites

Between the Archangel Gabriel telling Mohammed in 610 that he had been chosen to lead the Arabs, and his death in 632, tribes who had been fighting tooth and claw were united, albeit temporarily, under the banner of Islam. The new religion preached an almighty God and prescribed a new way of life based on that belief, but it retained an outstanding feature of paganism, the worship of a meteorite enshrined in the Kaaba in Mecca.

The rock moved seamlessly into Islam and continued to attract large numbers of pilgrims, a prestigious asset in Mecca's long-standing struggle with Medina for control of the desert caravan road. The amazing speed of the Arab conquest, let alone the modest number of troops involved, was unparalleled in history, and there seemed little to stop them outdoing Alexander the Great's stunted attempt to rule the world until critical questions emerged over who would succeed Mohammed.

The Prophet's succession

In spite of marrying 11 times, including to a girl named Aisha when she was nine and he was 53, the Prophet Mohammed died without a male heir and without stating who should succeed him or even the criteria for so doing. The elders of his tribe, the Quraish, got together and, after heated debate, finally chose little Aisha's father, Abu Bakr. The title he assumed, caliph, was in Western terms "emperor" rather than "pope". Abu Bakr swiftly mobilised the tribal armies for a three-pronged attack on Byzantine territory to the north, one of the main objectives being Damascus.

At Jabel Druze, however, the Arab cavalry found themselves in a cul-de-sac of jagged lava, the legacy of extinct volcanoes. The only exit was down the precipitous course of the Yarmuk River, through the so-called Deraa gap, and this the Byzantines had heavily fortified against just such an eventuality.

LEFT: a 16th-century depiction of Aleppo.
RIGHT: proclaiming the faith.

Anyone who has seen the film *Lawrence of Arabia*, or indeed read T. E. Lawrence's *Pillars of Wisdom*, may recall that the forces of the Arab Revolt ran into the same predicament of having to take Deraa before advancing on Damascus. After fighting like furies in 633 to take Deraa, the Arabs saw the walls of Damas-

cus as an even tougher nut to crack. Untouchable in the difficult terrain of the desert on their camels and horses, they as yet knew nothing about concerted siege warfare.

The taking of Damascus

The unexpected solution at Damascus was provided by the perplexing issue of the nature of God the Father and God the Son. Were they one and the same or merely related? Orthodox Damascus subscribed to the dualist line, but there was a solitary Monophysite bishop in the city who took the opposite view and was prepared to betray his fellow Christians. He lent the Arabs two ladders and promised to let them know when the guard on the walls was changing. Accordingly, a handful of men went over during the night and opened the gates from the inside. By morning, the Byzantine governor was ready to surrender on two conditions: firstly, a reduction in the new taxes which Mohammed had decreed non-Muslim subjects must pay, and secondly a partition of the cathedral so that Christians could still worship in half of it. Damascus changed hands without reprisals or looting.

Damascus was governed with exemplary

DAZZLING DAMASCUS

Mohammed once proclaimed that the city of Damascus undermined the delights he anticipated only in heaven. It was indeed a showpiece of Byzantine architecture.

tab as his successor before he died. That worked well enough, but when Umar was stabbed by a Persian slave in the Medina mosque, he saved his dying words to name not a successor but a selection committee. All were members of the Prophet's tribe, but it was split between two hostile factions, the Hashims and Umayyads.

The former expected to win the contest. The Prophet had been one of them and their candidate, Ali, was both his cousin and son-in-law, having married the Prophet's daughter Fatima. To the amaze-

efficiency by the Byzantines, and the Arab conquerors had reason not to rock the boat. Islam, they believed, belonged to the Arabs and no one else, so there was no question of trying to win non-Arab converts. Even voluntary conversion was unwanted because it would reduce the number of non-Muslims liable for the new tax. Above all, perhaps, the Arabs saw themselves as warriors with a long list of unfinished imperial business. If the management of Damascus, not least the collection of tax, could be entrusted to the existing administration, so much the better.

Having masterminded the first wave of Arab conquests, Abu Bakr nominated Umar ibn Khat-

ment and anger of the Hashims, however, the chairman's nod went to Othman, who was a 70-year-old Umayyad.

Hashimite caliphate

Othman was still caliph at 82 years of age when a mob broke into his house, found him sitting on the floor over the Qur'an, and hacked him to pieces. Ali, the Hashim who had lost out to Othman, was immediately proclaimed caliph. Muawiya, the Umayyad leader then acting as the governor of Syria, called him a murderer. Collecting an army of 50,000, Ali set off for Syria to deliver his riposte, and after two days of battle, Muawiya was on the brink of defeat when he sent his cavalry forward with Qur'ans swinging from the tips of their lances and a cry of "Let the word of God decide". In the minds of Kharijite fundamentalists who made up the bulk of Ali's army this made perfect sense, so they laid down their arms. Protracted negotiations between the two commanders were going nowhere when a Kharijite saw Ali taking a break in the doorway of a mosque and lunged at him with a knife, ending the short-lived Hashimite caliphate. Muawiya took over, with one important difference: under the Umayyads, the caliph would sit in Damascus.

Muawiya ruled unchallenged and with a light

years of Umayyad rule was the language of official correspondence changed from Greek to Arabic, mainly because the empire had reached parts where Greek was unknown. Letters went hither and thither by carrier pigeon.

Cosmopolitan Damascus

As the capital of an empire stretching across both Mediterranean shores to the Atlantic and eastwards almost to China, Damascus became vibrantly cosmopolitan. Among the new arrivals were thousands of fair-haired Goths taken as slaves in Spain. The cathedral which Muslims and Christians had agreed to share

touch for 19 years. Like the Arabs who had conquered Damascus, he and his Umayyad successors initially saw no need to tamper with the long-established Graeco-Christian administration in the Syrian capital. St John the Damascene, an Aramaic-speaking Syrian, ran the city's finances, as had his father and grandfather before him, and for a time the Homs district had a Christian governor. Only after 50

LEFT: in this depiction from a Persian manuscript, all religions of the world set sail on the sea of eternity, but only one comes back – Shi'ism.
ABOVE: *The Arrival of the Caravan, Khan Asa Pash, Damascus*, by Charles Robertson.

was demolished to make way for the Great Mosque – built with Byzantine help – while in Jerusalem, the Dome of the Rock was intended to woo Muslim pilgrims away from Mecca.

While presiding over all this as patrons of poetry and music festivals, the Umayyad princes were not inclined to cut their desert roots. Kast el-Heir is the best surviving example of a host of desert palaces where they kept their hands in at desert sports, one long-distance horse race attracting 3,000 runners. Muawiyas's son and heir, Yazid I, sent hawks circling overhead to spy out game while he rode out at the head of a column of trotting slaves, each holding a seluki dog adorned with jewels and gold anklets. The *tour de force*, though, was crouched on the horse's rump behind him – a cheetah trained to pounce on quarry on command.

The great schism

The sporting caliph's nickname, "Yazid of Wines", was self-explanatory but not derogatory. What did concern the Muslim establishment, especially those in Medina and Mecca, was that he had inherited the caliphate by virtue of being his father's eldest son. In Arab tribal custom, inheritance went to the most able son, not necessarily the eldest, and if none of the brothers was thought up to scratch, a cousin or

perhaps an uncle would do. The Hashim now argued that in the case of the caliphate the descendants of previous caliphs should be given equal consideration. Proceeding on this assumption, they proposed one of their own, Hussein, the son of the murdered Ali. As the Umayyads rejected the proposal and there seemed no immediate prospect of dislodging them, Hussein was encouraged by his kinsmen to set up an alternative caliphate in Iraq.

Hussein was on his way, crossing the desert with relatives and retainers, when the small convoy was intercepted by 4,000 cavalry at a place called Kerbela and butchered. The Umayyad governor of Kufa, where Hussein was expected

to set up the caliphate, ordered the massacre, but Yazid was held responsible. This, and the destruction of Medina two years later by an Umayyad army acting on Yazid's orders, led to a schism in Islam that to this day has not healed. Sunni Muslims are those who do not accept the Shi'ite contention that the only legitimate line of descent from the Prophet begins with his son-in-law, Ali, who married Fatima.

While Shi'ites subscribed to a narrow definition of the Prophet's true heirs, they believed that Islam should be thrown open to all races and that converts were as good Muslims as those born into the religion. As Sunnites, the Umayyads stuck to the view that Islam was exclusively an Arab birthright. The paradox emerging from this was that Shi'ites who believed their religion was for everyone were inclined to use force on those who did not wish to join it, while the narrow-minded Sunni, in this respect, had no objection to non-Arabs practising any religion they liked.

Umayyad policy ran into difficulties when Arabs became a shrinking minority in their empire. They were outnumbered by North African Berbers, Persians and others who converted to Islam whatever Damascus said and naturally preferred the Shi'ite doctrine.

Abdul Malik: caliph of all Islam

With Arabia in rebellion over Yazid's destruction of Medina and converts elsewhere unwilling to accept the status of second-class Muslims, the Umayyad caliphate to which Abdul Malik succeeded in 685 was reduced to Syria, Palestine and Egypt. Determined to shepherd the defectors back to the fold, he sent the Syrian army to reclaim Mecca from the rebel Abdulla ibn Zubair. The city was bombarded with rocks for eight months before Abdulla emerged, waving a sword and apparently ready to continue the fight single-handed, only to be bowled over by a torrent of arrows. Against opposition of this calibre, it was 12 years before Abdul Malik could plausibly claim to be the caliph of all Islam.

Sensitive to any allegations of Umayyad immorality, Abdul Malik took pains to appear pious. He enjoyed a drink in private, he said, but got drunk only once a month. That could not be said of Walid II, who became caliph in 705 and filled his swimming pool with wine. Where his Muslim subjects drew the line, however, was using the Qur'an for target practice, and sending concubines to the mosque to lead prayers in his place. He had been in office for little more than a year when his head came off and was paraded on the point of a lance.

Such falls from grace fuelled a Shi'ite propaganda war against the Umayyads. It was masterminded by Mohammed ibn Ali ibn Abdulla ibn Abbas, whose name proclaimed descent from Abbas, the Prophet's uncle. This did not meet the Shi'ite criterion for succession but he was supported by Kharijites in Iraq and by Persian Muslims. Merwan, the Umayyad caliph, raced backwards and forwards trying to con-

Syria's decline

Baghdad became the richest city in the world, and when the Byzantine emperor Nicephorus wrote to Harun demanding money supposedly owing to Constantinople, war inevitably broke out. Syria was reduced to a backwater and was helpless when the Byzantines returned a century later, sacking Homs, Hama and the whole coast from Tripoli to Tarsus. The emperor John Tzimisces followed this up with devastating attacks on Damascus, Sidon and Beirut. At this stage Syria was part of the Fatimid caliphate in Cairo, but no help could be expected from that quarter because it, too, was in a mess.   ❏

tain rebellions, to no avail. The conclusive battle was fought at the River Zab in 750. After an overwhelming defeat, Merwan fled through Syria and into Egypt with Abbasids in hot pursuit before he was overtaken and killed.

The price exacted by the Persians for their leading role in overthrowing the Umayyads was to establish the Abbasid caliphate in their territory, first in Kufu and later in Baghdad. Nevertheless, the early Abbasid caliphs were Arabs, and it was under Harun al-Rashid, that the Abbasids reached their zenith.

LEFT: mosaic from the Umayyad Mosque, Damascus.
ABOVE: Harun al-Rashid, Caliph of Baghdad.

THE GREAT ESCAPE

After Merwan, the Umayyad caliph, was killed by the pursuing Abbasids in AD 750, all members of his family in Syria bar one were also put to death. The survivor, Abd-al-Rahman, donned a disguise and, accompanied by one servant, managed to make his way across Palestine, Egypt and the forbidding Atlas Mountains to reach the relative safety of the Straits of Gibraltar.

Syrians who had settled in the port of Ceuta after the Arab conquest of North Africa welcomed this fugitive prince and helped him found a new Umayyad state in mainland Spain, which later became the caliphate of Cordova (Córdoba).

la cité dimas. Qui la fondi. de
fruitz et iardins asemuon. De
sordre que tindnt ses princes a
lassieger. Comment les iardins
fuirent prins. Du grant coup
que fist sempnur. Et de la tni
hison pour laquesse fut le siege
seue. la cite estant prce de pren
dre.

·VSVII·

Amas est la p
issant Cite de
la terre de la
mendre Suric
qui par austre nom est apr
lee. La plume de siban et a
ceste occasion dit le prophete
parlant de ceste Cite de dam
Chief de Suric. Luin des se
riteurs de abrasim apresse di
mas la fondi z fut par ce

THE CRUSADES

Heeding a call from Pope Urban II, waves of zealous Christians took up arms against their Muslim enemies – not just to reclaim lost territories but to gain new ones

At the dawn of the second millennium, the Muslim world had broken up into a patchwork of troubled caliphates. Egypt and Syria, including Palestine, were all that remained of the Fatimid Empire under a caliph, Al-Hakim, whose sanity was called into question when he condemned all dogs to death to stop them barking, made shops stay open all night in case he – but no one else – wanted to do some shopping, and banned the sale of shoes to put street-walkers out of business.

In Baghdad, the Abbasids were in danger of being overwhelmed by Seljuk Turks, originally employed as mercenaries to defend them. Rome, meanwhile, was a run-down slum next to Byzantine Constantinople, but western Europe was bursting with Christian zeal.

A fatal edict

The first threat to peaceful coexistence between Muslims, Christians and Jews in Abbasid Syria – the north being part of the Byzantine Empire – was a new edict by the unstable Al-Hakim requiring Christians and Jews to wear distinctive dress and to ride donkeys rather than horses, among other measures. On 4 October 1009 he ordered the destruction of the Church of the Holy Sepulchre in Jerusalem, a place of pilgrimage for Muslims no less than Christians and Jews. Al-Hakim then went out on one of his customary nocturnal rides, perhaps to do some shopping, but in any case to check that no one else was breaking the curfew he had imposed. Nothing more was ever seen of him except a tuft of bloodied hair.

His more tolerant successor rebuilt the church, and pilgrimages from Europe grew to contain as many as 11,000 pilgrims at a time, each paying one gold piece (three for a horse) as they passed through Constantinople.

In 1055, however, the Seljuk Turks took over

Baghdad completely and soon demonstrated imperial ambitions. Having decisively defeated the Byzantine army at Manzikert in 1071, their gradual conquest of both Byzantine and Abbasid territory in Syria was crowned in 1085 by the capture of Antioch, Byzantium's last possession in the region, and of Jerusalem.

With the former uppermost in his mind, the Byzantine emperor Alexius Comnenus appealed to the West for help. His greatest concern was the recovery of lost territory, but in the West his appeal sounded more like an opportunity to take up arms against the Muslim infidel and rescue Jerusalem. The response to Pope Urban II's encyclical calling for a crusade was instantaneous, joyful and enormous.

Alexius envisaged experienced volunteers who would recover the lost territories under his direction and then go home. The first arrivals in Constantinople were the last thing he wanted, a horde of peasants under Peter the Hermit (a French evangelist) and Walter the Penniless,

LEFT: 15th-century book illumination depicting the Siege of Damascus during the Second Crusade.
RIGHT: the crusader depicted as a Christian hero by an unnamed artist.

who had poured out of Germany and robbed and pillaged their way across Hungary.

Rather than have them loitering in Constantinople until proper soldiers turned up, Alexius shipped the peasants across the Bosphorus and pointed them in the direction of Jerusalem. First reports said they had taken to roasting Turkish babies on spits; the next, that they had been ambushed by Turkish troops and wiped out.

Some 30,000 knights and infantry who turned up at Constantinople that summer were supposedly under the orders of a papal legate, but it was immediately apparent that no one took any notice of him. Feeling the pressure of

Bohemund if he would mind staying outside the city walls until he left for the Holy Land.

Painful progress

Once on the move, the crusaders began to wonder whether the guides provided by the emperor were deliberately leading them into Turkish ambushes, and they soon learned that heat, hunger and thirst were as deadly as Turkish scimitars. Turkish scouts kept ahead of them, poisoning the wells as they went along. In the meantime, more Turks were pouring in from the north and Egyptians captured Jerusalem in 1098. On the other hand, Jews, Armenians and

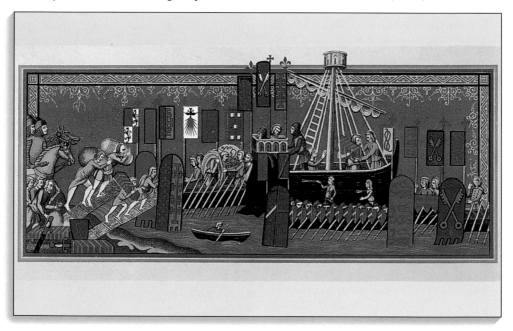

feudal land hunger in Europe, some knights were thinking of settling in Syria and agents of the Italian maritime states made no secret of their desire to gain greater access to oriental trade by taking over the Phoenician ports. To add to the emperor's worries, his daughter Anna seemed unable to take her eyes off Bohemund, a Norman knight from Sicily. "Like no other man ever seen in the Byzantine Empire, whether barbarian or Greek," she gushed. "He was narrow in the belly and flanks, broad in the chest and shoulders and strong in the arms. His whole stature could be described as neither constricted nor over-endowed with flesh, but blended as perfectly as possible." The emperor asked

Christian Arabs living in towns welcomed the crusaders as liberators and invited them to take Edessa under their wing as an independent state. The emperor was horrified.

The siege of Antioch

Antioch also had a largely Christian population, but it was in the firm grip of a Turkish governor and garrison. The crusaders besieged the city for nine months before they found an Armenian breast-plate maker named Firouz who would take a bribe to open one of the gates. As 500 knights charged in to a fanfare of trumpets, the Turkish governor, Yaghi Siyan, sat up in bed and asked what was going on.

Within minutes he was out of another gate at top speed and did not slow down until he reached the nearby mountains. Three Syrian Christians spotted him catching his breath and sent his head back to Antioch in a bag. "The head was of enormous size," Albert of Aachen reported, "the ears very wide and hairy. His hair was white and he had a very long beard which flowed from his chin to his navel.

But the crusaders had barely dismounted in Antioch before they were themselves besieged by Turkish reinforcements, including an army from Damascus. They were in desperate trouble when a certain Peter Bartholomew reported that

an ordinary Arab sword when he saw one and remarked, not for the first time, that Bartholmew was "born to be hanged at the crossroads". Grabbing an authentic Viking sword, he led a ferocious counter-attack which put the surrounding Arabs to flight. Antioch was now secure, but the emperor had nothing to celebrate. Instead of being returned to him, Antioch became the second independent crusader state. To add to his despair, its proclaimed prince was Bohemund.

The recovery of Jerusalem

The road to Jerusalem, after Raymond of Toulouse made a quick detour to reduce the

St Andrew had informed him in a dream that the Holy Lance used to pierce Christ's side at the crucifixion was buried in a local church. Frantic digging produced nothing until Bartholomew went off by himself and immediately struck lucky – or so he said – as he waved a rusty weapon in the air.

"The people led the lance in procession with hymns and songs," a chronicler wrote, "loading Peter with gifts and rolling him in gold." But Bohemund, the giant whose perfect proportions had so impressed the emperor's daughter, knew

LEFT: embarking for the Crusades.
ABOVE: Knights of St John charge the Saracens.

Greek-built towns along the Orontes, retraced Alexander the Great's march down the Phoenician coast. The Shi'ites of Tripoli handed over buckets of gold and hundreds of horses to be left in peace, but in any case the crusaders hoped to avoid battle with the ports in order to reach Jerusalem as soon as possible.

They were at the walls five weeks later on 7 June 1099. "If you want to know what was done to the enemies we found in the city," a communique to the pope stated, "know this: that in the portico of Solomon in his Temple, our men rode in the blood of the Saracens up to the knees of their horses."

With the recovery of the holy city of Jerusalem,

most of the knights couldn't wait to get home, but others stayed on to consolidate the independent states collectively known as Outremer. The Franks had two priorities: to secure the coast against the attentions of the Egyptian navy, and to hold the mountain passes leading to the coast from a hinterland still dominated by the Turks. The castles built to do this exceeded anything in contemporary Europe. Beaufort castle appeared to hang in the air over the Litani River, and Markab, north of Tortosa, was a solid

A LEARNED LEADER

Nour ad-Deen brought the Second Crusade to an end and installed himself in Damascus. Learned, pious and polo-mad, he spent lavishly on new colleges, mosques and parks.

Syrian corridor that ran along the edge of the desert. So the road from Cairo to Baghdad was still open, and there was little the Franks could do to prevent enemy armies from picking the time and place to attack. Inland Edessa was the most vulnerable Frankish state, and it fell on Christmas Eve, 1144 to Imad ad-Deen Zanghi, the Turkish governor of Aleppo, in scenes of such unremitting carnage that the pope called for an immediate Second Crusade.

European princes and knights again rushed to

block of black basalt against a background of white chalk. In all cases, knights and men-at-arms patrolled the walls day and night.

The mountain castles were built from scratch, whereas the coast had been fortified since Phoenician times, and several of the new castles rose on the ruins of some ancient acropolis. As ever, Tyre resisted and had to be taken by force, the siege lasting as long as Alexander the Great's – seven months. Once in Frankish hands the island fortress repulsed countless attacks for almost two centuries.

Solid as the Frankish defences were along the coast and in the mountains, they did not extend far enough inland to close the well-travelled

take up the cross. Irreversibly sworn to carry the fight to the accursed infidel, many decided that their obligation could more conveniently be discharged by killing Jews in Germany, Muslims in Spain and Portugal, or Slavs in the Baltic. While they went to this task with a vengeance, the minority who undertook the arduous journey across Asia to the Holy Land were surprised to find the expatriate Franks in Outremer in good spirits and not much bothered about the loss of Edessa. They had married local women, often wore Eastern costume and got on well with their Muslim neighbours, in particular the Turks in Damascus, with whom they had even gone to war against other Turks in places such as Aleppo.

The resident Franks were therefore disgusted to learn that the crusaders were planning to attack their friends in Damascus instead.

The crusaders hoped to ambush Damascus by approaching under cover of orchards on one side. So dense were the orchards, however, that the crusaders were trapped when Nour ad-Deen materialised with an army from Aleppo. "The stench from their corpses was so foul that it almost overcame the birds in the air," the Damascene chronicler Ibn al-Qalanisis wrote.

CHANGED MEN

To their great surprise, many of the Outremer Franks were seduced by the east. "We who had been occidentals have become orientals." observed Fulcher of Chartres.

cenary, initially in the Frankish army. Having sent his former employers packing from Egypt, it was time to apply the *coup de grâce* to the ailing Fatimid caliphate. Molanus, the elderly caliph was reputedly worn out by the demands of his harem – "the same number of concubines as the days of the year" – and could scarcely lift an arm as Saladin approached with sword drawn. With Egypt in his grasp, Saladin then heard of the death of Nour ad-Deen in Damascus. Hurrying back to marry his

Enter Saladin

Having brought the Second Crusade to an ignominious end, Nour ad-Deen installed himself in Damascus. His next thought was the conquest of Egypt, but the Franks beat him to it. The lieutenant whom Nour ad-Deen then despatched to dislodge the Franks was destined to become a hero, even in Western lore.

A point sometimes overlooked in Western lore was that Saladin, a Kurd, was a brothel-keeper in Damascus before he became a mer-

LEFT: Richard the Lionheart and the Master of the Knights of St John at Acre in 1191.
ABOVE: a treaty is made with Saladin.

widow, Saladin eliminated any children who stood in the way in order to become the undisputed ruler not only of Syria and Egypt but of Mesopotamia and "recesses of India" as well.

A truce between Saladin and the Franks in Outremer was broken when Reynald of Chatillon, the lord of Transjordan, attacked a caravan on its way from Cairo to Damascus. Tit-for-tat reprisals culminated in a full-scale battle at the Horns of Hattin. The Franks were not only comprehensively beaten but lost possession of the True Cross, the holiest relic in Christendom, which Saladin paraded through the streets of Damascus. On learning that Jerusalem was also lost to Saladin on 2 October 1187, Pope

Urban III dropped dead. His successor, Gregory VIII, called for the Third Crusade.

The start did not bode well. Frederick I (Barbarossa), the geriatric Holy Roman Emperor (1220–50), lost his footing while crossing a shallow river in Asia Minor and drowned. Philip Augustus, the French dauphin, retired in a huff when Richard I of England challenged his presumption that he would be the next "King of Jerusalem". The first major battle with Saladin, at Acre, was a resounding victory for the crusaders, but Richard then learned that his brother was conspiring to seize his crown and rushed off to tackle the problem. Henry VI, the new Holy

Roman Emperor, took up the reins and captured Beirut and Sidon only to catch fever and die. At that point, his army packed up and went home.

The Fourth Crusade

Subsequent crusades didn't prove to be any more edifying. With none of the European kings willing to put up money for the Fourth Crusade, it became a commercial gamble, with Venice providing the ships in exchange for half the booty. The crusaders first sacked Zara, a port which happened to belong to the Christian King of Hungary and a former crusader himself, and then looked at the incomparable wealth of Constantinople and could not restrain themselves. If many still regard the 1204 sacking of Constantinople – for nine centuries the capital of Christendom – as the greatest armed robbery of all time, the Children's Crusade which followed eight years later is high among the greatest follies.

Tens of thousands of French and German children, none over 12 years of age, set off on foot to conquer the infidel through the power of piety. Many began crying when the sea failed to divide before them. In Marseilles, a couple of merchants, Hugh the Iron and William the Pig, offered to take them across the sea in ships – not to the Holy Land, however, but to the slave markets in North Africa and hence, in some cases, to Egypt and Syria. Their fate was unknown until one escaped 18 years later.

Growing doubts

In spite of growing doubts about the efficacy of the crusades, King Louis IX of France, later St Louis, rose from his supposed deathbed – the sheet was already over his head – on learning that Kipchak Turks had retaken Jerusalem in 1244. Landing in Egypt five years later, Louis went on to defeat the Saracens at Mansourah but was captured after the battle and held in irons while the colossal ransom of one million marks was being raised. Although the Franks hung on to Beirut and Acre until the end of the century, a conversation between Louis and one of his captors at this juncture was a reasonable epitaph to the crusades as a whole.

"How did a man of your majesty's character, wisdom and good sense ever conceive the idea of embarking on a ship, riding the waves of this sea and journeying to a land so full of Muslims and warriors, assuming that you could conquer it and become its king?" an emir asked. Louis laughed but said nothing. "In our land," the emir continued, "when a man voyages on the sea, exposing himself and his worldly goods to such risks, his witness is not accepted as evidence in any court of law." "Why not? asked Louis. "Because such behaviour implies to us that he is lacking in sense, and such a man is unfit to give evidence." Louis again laughed and declared: "By God, whoever said that was right; whoever ruled thus was not in error." ❏

LEFT: engraving of Saladin.
RIGHT: crusader Louis IX of France (St Louis) in a painting by El Greco.

MAMLUKES AND OTTOMANS

The élite regiments of the fearsome Baybars I – Sultan of Syria and Egypt –

founded an empire that would last for 250 years

While the battle of Mansourah in 1250 wound up King Louis IX's campaign in the east, it also marked the end of the Ayubbid dynasty which took the field against him. Sultan Al Salih Ayub, ruler of Egypt and Syria, died three days after the battle, but his Armenian-born widow, Spray-of-Pearls, kept his death a secret and took up the reins in collusion with the eunuch in charge of the palace. She arranged the succession of her stepson, Turanshah, but the deputy commander of the army, a Mamluke named Baybars, took exception to his drunken behaviour and swiped at him with a sabre.

Turanshah ran for his life, taking shelter in a wooden tower next to the Nile, but soldiers had spotted him and set it on fire. As he leapt into the river and swam for the opposite bank, Baybars went in after him, presumably with his sabre between his teeth, and came back alone. Impressed by the way Spray-of-Pearls had handled affairs after her husband's death, he led the troops in proclaiming her queen.

A power vacuum

The Syrians would have none of it. They unilaterally seceded from Egypt and put Saladin's great-grandson, Malik al Nasir Yusuf, on their throne. The Abbasid caliph in Baghdad felt much the same way. "Unhappy is the nation which is governed by a woman," he wailed. "If you need a man," he wrote to Spray-of-Pearls, "I'll send you one." Instead, she married the Mamluke commander-in-chief of the Egyptian army and soon regretted it. A couple of eunuchs walked in while he was in the bath and reached for his throat. A few days later, Spray-of-Pearls herself sailed over the battlements of the Cairo citadel and was picked up dead in a gutter.

Piles of corpses accompanied the scramble among Mamluke army officers to fill the vac-

LEFT: *Mamluke from Aleppo,* painted by William Page (1794–1872).
RIGHT: *The Great Khan, Damascus,* 1866, painted by Richard Phene Spiers (1838–1916).

uum left behind, but these paled next to a simultaneous tornado of genocide from the east. Syria and Egypt had been spared the first Mongol invasion a quarter-century earlier, but Genghis Khan's grandson, Hulagu, was back, his army supported by Armenian and Georgian allies. It was reported from Baghdad that the

city's entire population of 80,000 had been butchered. In Aleppo, all men were killed and 100,000 women and children taken into slavery. The newly created king of Syria, Saladin's great-grandson, was caught trying to flee from Damascus and got no further.

Genghis Khan's own invasion had ended abruptly with his departure to deal with family matters in Mongolia. Hulagu, too, suddenly dropped everything for the same reason, but he left behind in Damascus a formidable Mongol garrison. Qutus, who had eventually won the power struggle in Cairo, arrived at the city with a Mamluke army bedecked, as always, in fine silks and satin, their saddles glistening with gold and precious stones. Seeing only the vanguard led by Baybars, the Mongols charged out, were surrounded by the main army on all sides, and trounced. Qutus entered Damascus to tell the Syrians their declaration of independence was null and void, and with that set off on the return journey to Cairo.

He was asleep in his tent in the Sinai desert when Baybars, whose request to be appointed governor of Damascus had been turned down, lifted the flap and went in. Baybars emerged to announce that he was now the sultan of Egypt and Syria, and would be taking Qutus's place of honour for the triumphant entry into Cairo.

A huge man with a deafening voice, Baybars is regarded as the founder of a Mamluke empire which lasted 250 years, in spite of bad patches when, for instance, six successive Mamluke sultans lasted on average six months each. Born into a Kipchak Turkish tribe on the Russian steppes, he was captured in the Crimea by slavers when he was six or seven, shipped to Syria and offered for sale to the emir of Hama. He was altogether too tough, even at that age, for the emir's taste, but that made him ideal material for the sultan's Mamluke Guard. He joined other boys of the same age for several years of intense military training. Promotion was strictly by merit.

Mamluke regiments

A Mamluke's loyalty to his owner was absolute during the latter's lifetime but it was customary thereafter for him to start his own regiment by buying boys – "mamluke" meant slave – and training them. He might by then have had children by local women, but only boys brought up in the same conditions he had known were considered suitable for a Mamluke regiment. Apart from anything else, they had no family ties to compromise loyalty to their owner. A self-perpetuating cycle of slavery it might have been, but the system produced an élite fighting force.

As the Mongols at Damascus discovered, fabulous outfits did not impair a Mamluke's deftness with bow or cold steel. The disruptive element in the system was the fact that the reigning Mamluke was balanced precariously on the tip of a pyramid of other Mamlukes whose own private armies might be as powerful as his. When an ambitious underling fancied his chances at the sultanate, his first move set off a race with other Mamlukes hoping to get there first.

Baybars' demise

Having consolidated the reunification of Syria and Egypt, Baybars wanted a word with the rulers of the two remaining Outremer states, Antioch and Tripoli. "The kingdom of Syria and other places now belong to me," he roared, "and I do not need your help." To show that he meant business, he had one baron murdered and sent an Assassin, one of an Ismaili sect whose original notoriety was enslavement to hashish, to run amok in the chapel in Tyre. The Franks were seriously thinking of inviting the Mongols back to lend a hand when Baybars invited an Ayubbid prince who was a bit too popular for his liking to join him at the palace for drinks. When the waiter came round, Baybars reached for the wrong glass and within minutes was flat on the floor, clutching his stomach.

Obviously unsure of their tenure, Mamluke sultans did not dally before commissioning the mosques and works of art by which they hoped to be remembered. The results in Egypt, less so in Syria, would have thrilled the pharaohs. Lesser Mamlukes served as governors of provinces of Syria, Damascus being regarded as something of a sinecure because, as in the time of the Umayyads, everything was done by professional civil servants. Even so, one governor of Damascus lost his job because, a contemporary noted, "he had long held power and his prestige had increased".

Baybars' absent-mindedness when the drinks came round merely postponed what he had intended to do about the remaining Franks in Outremer, whose position was not helped by the Knights Templar and the Hospitallers of St John fighting one another and unsportingly burying their captives up to their necks to die slowly of sunstroke and starvation. In 1291, Baybars' Mamluke successors mobilised what was

TAMERLANE THE GREAT

The late, great figure of Tamerlane was in fact a sheep-stealer and bandit from Uzbekistan, previously known as "Timur the Lame" due to a permanent limp caused by a wound early in his decadent career.

a Turkman tribe of refugees from central Asia who had done well as mercenaries in the tangled web of Balkan politics. Known as Ottomans after their chief, Othman, they were an independent state in their own right when he was succeeded by Murad I, who racked up victories over the Serbs, Bulgarians and Hungarians before being killed by a Serb in 1389. His son and successor, Bayazid the Thunderbolt, took revenge on the Serbs on the Field of Blackbirds in Kosovo, a defeat which still haunts the Serbs today.

said to be the largest siege train ever seen against Acre, by then the crusaders' last bastion, and smashed through its walls. The survivors reached Cyprus and began building a navy to attack the Phoenician ports that had been their homes. The Mamlukes had no answer to crusader ships whose white sails bore a large red cross, so they resorted to scorched earth tactics, destroying even Tyre and evacuating the coastal population.

With the former crusaders resorting to piracy, a new power emerged in the region in the form of

LEFT: Mamluke soldier in battle dress.
ABOVE: caricature of Mamluke pursuing a Frenchman, 1799.

The coming of Tamerlane

European powers were so alarmed by the apparently unstoppable Ottomans that they hoped to form a pact with a mysterious army, reputedly Christian, that was closing in from the east. There had been stories before of Prester John and a Christian nation living in the outer reaches of India or China. The man on whom these hopes were pinned, however, was a bandit from Uzbekistan known as Tamerlane.

His trademark, as he laid waste to Asia, was to make mountains out of the skulls of his victims. On storming into Aleppo, he put every man and child to death before the women were raped. After similar scenes at Hama, Tamerlane's arrival at Damascus coincided with the appearance of the Mamluke cavalry after a hard ride from Cairo. The city had been engulfed in furious fighting for several days when a courier turned up in the middle of the night and handed the Mamluke commander a note about an impending coup in Cairo. By morning he was gone and, with a collective shrug, his army followed.

Victory by default seemed to put Tamerlane in a conciliatory mood. He invited the notables of Damascus to a meeting to let them know that in the interest of "the Companions of the Prophet who dwelt there" he proposed to stay a day or two and then leave them in peace. The

gates were opened to let him in – and it was Aleppo and Hama all over again. He moved on to devastate Baghdad, crush the Ottomans at Ankara, and was planning his next move on China when he was taken ill and died. A letter arrived shortly before his death from King Martin I of Aragon congratulating him on his recent success against the Ottomans.

Having been given a terrible beating at Ankara, the Ottomans picked themselves up and caused apoplexy in Europe by capturing Constantinople in 1453. With his sights now set on Vienna, Mehmet II lost interest in Asia Minor and left it to his successor, Salim the Grim, to tie up loose ends. His Janissaries were

not unlike Mamlukes in that they, too, had been captured as boys and trained for battle, but they had no compunction about using firearms (which the Mamlukes considered effete) when the two armies met at Marj Dabiq to fight for Aleppo. The Mamlukes were mown down and, after claiming Aleppo, the Ottomans marched unopposed into Damascus.

Syria divided

After the Mamlukes' scorched earth policy on the coast and Tamerlane's destruction of the interior, Syria had little to offer the Ottomans, nor were they inclined to repair the damage. As no single group of the divided population seemed capable of raising a rebellion that could not be slapped down by Janissaries, Ottoman policy amounted to ensuring that the groups did not unite. To this end they believed that they had a perfect tool in the diminutive Fakr-ed-Din – a Muslim as far as they were concerned, because he never said otherwise – who was in reality a Druze, reared in secret by Christians after the death of his father at Turkish hands.

It is difficult to imagine how, other than by offering a share of the profits, Fakr-ad-Deen persuaded the Turks to let him throw open Sidon, where he lived, to European trading interests. The Italian maritime states and France were immediately off the mark, taking up residence in their own purpose-built *khans*, or hostelries, generously provided by Fakr-ad-Deen himself. In 1581, the English Levant Company chartered by Queen Elizabeth I set up its stall in Aleppo. In quiet moments this English contingent played cricket while Turkish pashas relaxed in the Azem Palace in Hama.

"It was in such settings," a diplomat observed, "that the Turkish governors and the great men reclined in their Damascene silks and upon their Damascene brocades, and in such an encouraging atmosphere, with their amber-lipped pipes at hand, that they cultivated the elaborate Turkish courtesies and the ritual of doing nothing with elegance."

In so doing, they failed to notice that Fakr-ad-Deen creating a commercial empire that gave him control of everything between Aleppo and Jerusalem or, more remarkably, that he had an army of 40,000 mercenaries. When the Turks finally woke up to reality – and it took 15 years – they arrested Fakr-ad-Deen and sent him to Constantinople to be ritually strangled by mutes.

Stagnation resumed until Mohammed Ali – an Albanian tobacconist who had worked his way through the Ottoman hierarchy to become the sultan's pasha in Egypt – broke away by declaring Egypt's independence. On his understanding of history, Syria was an annex of Egypt so he sent his son Ibrahim Pasha to reclaim it. Egyptian rule was no more than an interlude, 1832–4, but by attempting to impose a central administration on Syria it broke down the delicate fences between feudal warlords so that an argument

NEW WEAPONS

Mehmet II's successor, Salim the Grim, used artillery for the first time to smash the Safavid dynasty in Persia before turning this deadly weaponry on the Mamlukes.

pursuing Druzes climbing over the back wall. There were no survivors.

When the killing spread to Damascus, Western powers decided to intervene and asked for volunteers. Napoleon III, who had previously dabbled in Mexican and Chinese affairs and had written a book on the principles of sound government, was ready to go. His troops landed at Beirut and the French then put their heads together to devise a plan that would carry Syria into the 20th century, if not beyond it. ❏

between a Druze and a Maronite – over whose shot had brought down a partridge – was enough to start a small war. In 1860, the last semblance of co-existence was shattered when Druzes attacked Christians at Jezzine. In their attempt to flee, hundreds fell into a ravine and died. Those who got as far as Sidon found the gates locked and were massacred by Muslims. More than a thousand Christians were offered sanctuary in Deir al Kamar by the Turkish governor who, out of the other eye, could see the

LEFT: *General View of Tyre*, by David Roberts.
ABOVE: *View of Sidon towards Lebanon*, also by David Roberts.

NAPOLEON WAS HERE

On invading Syria, Napoleon III – Bonaparte's nephew – was impatient to add his name to the illustrious inscriptions on the steep cliffs at the Dog River (Nahr al-Kalb) bottleneck. Since antiquity, it had been a tradition for invading armies to leave a record of their successful crossings of the river *(see page 22)*. Not too bothered that the spot he fancied already had a commemorative inscription, in a rather boorish display of egotism he simply carved his name over it. The chap underneath, it transpired, was Rameses II.

These inscriptions can still be seen at Nahr al-Kalb, just outside modern Beirut *(see page 263 for details)*.

MODERN SYRIA

Betrayed by Europe, influenced by Arab nationalism and plagued by coups,
Syria lived with chaos until strongman Hafez al-Assad took control

France plotted the future of Syria after the 1860 Druze massacres with a sense of local involvement that went back to the Abbasid caliph, Harun al-Rashid, author of *Arabian Nights*, who had granted the protectorate of the Holy Places to Charlemagne (748–814). Crusaders were all "Franks", i.e. French, no matter where they came from (in some cases Hungary), and it was during the Crusades that Louis IX – the King of France and a saint – recognised at once a mystical bond with the Maronite Christians, the victims of the Druze massacres in 1860. "We are persuaded that this nation, which we find established here under the name of St Maroun," he intoned on being introduced in 1248, "is a part of the French nation, for its love of France resembles the love which Frenchmen bear one another."

Although guides provided by the Maronites seemed to deliver a worrying number of French crusaders into the jaws of hidden Turks, the relationship survived and the key to French plans for modern Syria was the creation of a semi-independent sanctuary for their spiritual kinsmen in the Lebanese mountains.

Rising nationalism

The Ottoman sultanate, widely diagnosed as being seriously ill, was stoical about a part of its Syrian territory being detached for grooming as the future Lebanon because it was more concerned about a dangerous and rising level of nationalism in its European, and particularly Balkan, possessions. When nationalist sentiments surfaced, albeit slowly, in the Middle East and the Arabian peninsula, no small part of the momentum was provided by the introduction of Arab studies in two foreign institutions in Beirut – the French Jesuit college and the Syrian Protestant college founded by American Presbyterians, later the American university.

The laying of a railway through Syria to Medina in Arabia, which began in 1906, was a tacit acknowledgement of changing circumstances.

Although its name, the Hejaz railway, stressed improved facilities for Mecca-bound pilgrims, quiet thought had also been given to Ottoman troop movements should the need arise.

A few years later, Kaiser Wilhelm II offered to finance a line from Berlin to Baghdad – linked to the Hejaz railway – in exchange for a con-

cession to prospect for oil along its course. As its construction progressed, European nations were entangled in a growing Gordian knot of mutual defence pacts. The Baghdad railway partners, Turkey and Germany, also shared grave misgivings about Russia's undisguised imperial designs. Against this backdrop, T. E. Lawrence arrived in Syria with a secret brief to see how the German railway engineers were getting along and to plot a route north for the British army based in Egypt, should the need arise. When the Archduke Franz Ferdinand was assassinated by a Serb in Sarajevo in 1914, all such pretences went by the board.

Arab leaders saw the outbreak of World War I

LEFT: Arab forces on the march in the Arab Revolt.
RIGHT: Lawrence of Arabia.

as their opportunity to throw off Ottoman rule, and the proposal put to British representatives in Egypt was that they would raise an armed rebellion in exchange for the creation of a post-war independent Arab kingdom. Sir Henry McMahon, the High Commissioner in Cairo, spoke about having to exclude an unspecified area "west of Damascus" because in reality Britain, France and Russia had already reached broad agreement on the dismemberment of the Ottoman empire after the war. The Balfour Declaration subsequently clarified McMahon's muted reservations by stating the case for a Jewish homeland in Palestine, and the Sykes-

Taking Damascus

"Damascus went mad with joy," Lawrence wrote of the Allies' entry into the city. "The men tossed up their tarbushes to cheer, the women tore off their veils. Householders threw flowers, hangings, carpets, into the road before us: their wives leaned, screaming with laughter, through the lattices and splashed us with bath-dippers of scent."

After setting up an administration to run the city, beginning with the formation of a police force, Lawrence asked to be relieved of further duties and returned to Cairo. In the meantime, the allied campaign rolled on to Aleppo, which

Picot agreement between Britain and France outlined respective "spheres of influence" which left little or no room for a wholly independent Arab kingdom.

Nevertheless, the Arab Revolt commenced on 5 June 1916 when Hussein, the Sherif of Mecca, leant out of his bedroom window and fired at Turkish barracks opposite. His sons, the Emirs Ali and Feisal, rode out of Medina at the head of a column of 30,000 determined but rather ragged Arab irregulars with Lawrence acting as their British liaison officer. Having captured Aqaba, they were joined by a British army under General Sir Edmund Allenby for the next major objective, Damascus.

the Turks abandoned without a fight. On 29 October 1918, the junction of the Baghdad and Syrian railways was taken. Two days later, Turkey was out of the war, and on 11 November, Germany capitulated.

The Versailles peace conference which followed was littered with misunderstandings, broken promises and accusations of treachery. France insisted that its claim to Syria went back to the Middle Ages. Emir Feisal, the Sherif of Mecca's son who had played a leading part in the Arab Revolt, arrived at the conference carrying the crown, as it were, to the anticipated Arab kingdom. France would have no truck with it, and Feisal interrupted a minister who was discussing France's crusader pedigree with the retort: "Pardon me, monsieur, but which of us won the Crusades?" A few months later, his brother Hussein explained to Bedouin sheikhs where matters stood: "I have come to remark a great change-round of the Allies, and especially of France, in favour of Turkey. Asia Minor, comprising Armenia, will remain Turkish, Syria is given to France in spite of our protests; our possession of Damascus is strongly disputed." The English, he added, had been proven "faithless".

PROMISES, PROMISES

Britain was caught between contradictory promises given to France under the Sykes-Picot agreement and to the leaders of the Arab Revolt that they could keep any land they conquered.

This was soon modified to include two extra self-governing units, Latakia and Jabal Druze, as homelands for Shi'ite Muslims and Druzes. The Shi'ites in question were the Alawi; the Jabal Druze, a mountainous area notorious in Roman times as the haunt of outlaws, was the adopted home of Druzes who fled their traditional home on the Lebanese Mountain to avoid reprisals after the 1860 massacres.

If this hinted at good old divide-and-rule tactics, Latakia was the joker in the pack. The

Arab nationalists took matters into their own hands in 1920 and proclaimed Feisal king of Syria, an action repudiated by both Britain and France with the result that a French army under General Gouraud occupied Damascus and Feisal fled to Iraq. Granted a League of Nations mandate to govern Syria, France envisioned Syria and Lebanon, predominantly Sunni Muslim and Christian respectively, as separate countries, perhaps in some kind of federation, progressing towards self-government under its supervision.

LEFT: Turks marching in Damascus as part of the Turko-German alliance in World War I.
ABOVE: General Allenby in his car in Damascus.

Alawis of Latakia were wretchedly poor and still locked in serfdom. "Agricultural exploitation is linked with compulsory services of various sorts, and forms the basis of the most extreme social and political dictatorships on the part of the landlord," an observer commented. According to the point of view, a French policy of giving Alawis an enormous boost into the armed forces was either on humanitarian grounds or to build up a counterweight to the Sunni majority. Either way, the policy caused such resentment that the whole country, except Latakia, rose in open revolt in the 1920s, and at one stage the French brought in artillery to suppress rioting in Damascus.

To jump ahead of the story, it was this policy

which ushered a 16-year-old Alawi from a peasant family of nine children into the air force. Changing his name from the Arabic word for "boar" to another meaning "lion", Hafez al-Assad rose through the ranks to become head of the air force and thence to defence minister, prime minister and finally president.

To return to the 1920s, another French idea with long-running repercussions concerned the province of Alexandretta, which included the eponymous port and Antioch, the greatest of the Greek-built cities. In the dismemberment of the Ottoman empire after World War I, the new Turkish government made a special plea to have

the province, which they called Hatay, as part of Turkey. The eventual compromise was that Alexandretta would fall under France's Syrian mandate but would have an independent administration. In 1936, however, France announced further steps towards Syria's self-government, and Turkey, suspecting that Alexandretta's independence would soon be subsumed, asked to have the province back. France agreed, and such was the storm among Syrian nationalists that the proposals for Syrian self-government were suspended, as was – temporarily – the transfer of Alexandretta/Hatay to Turkey.

The map of Syria which emerged from the horse-trading at Versailles and French adjust-ments on the ground was a far cry from the natural boundaries of Greater Syria. To begin with, France had expanded Lebanon to include most of the Phoenician ports, thus cutting off much of Syria's direct access to the sea. Instead of the Taurus mountains, a stretch of the northern border was a single-track railway across the desert. If most of this was the legacy of World War I, Syria entered World War II in constitutional disarray, the French parliament having refused to ratify treaties aimed at self-government.

In Syria, the fall of France early in World War II resulted in a kind of auction between Germany's Vichy French vassals and Free French forces waiting to step in from the wings. The Vichy tried to buy calm with the promise of qualified self-government "in the near future". The Free French outbid them with an offer of immediate independence, albeit with a continuing French military presence.

With the expulsion of the Vichy, the Free French delivered their promise of independence in September 1941. Its powers, however, did not cover the French armed forces or the Troupes Specialies, who were Syrians and Lebanese serving in the French forces. Great Britain made the arrangements to evacuate the French troops and to turn the Troupes Specialies into the nucleus of the Syrian and Lebanese national armies.

Arabs against Zionism

The enlarged Syrian army was soon in action, joining other Arab forces in 1948 against Zionism. Its defeat piled on the misery of intractable economic disputes with Lebanon and grave internal differences over the best political alignment in a volatile Arab world. Talk of a union with Iraq did an about-turn and became an alliance with Jordan, Egypt and Saudi Arabia against Iraq. The choice between Egypt and Iraq polarised affairs, and colonels leaning one way or the other hurtled through revolving doors in a series of coups and counter-coups, while the KGB, probably as confused as anyone, tried to dig itself into the only Arab state where Communism was legal.

At the time of the Suez crisis, Syria was negotiating a union with Egypt that envisaged a joint command in Damascus. One contribution to the war effort was to sabotage a pipeline carrying Saudi and Iraqi oil to the Mediterranean, infuriating both owners, followed by a refusal after the war to let anyone repair it until Israel withdrew its troops from Gaza and Aqaba. Repair gangs went to work when Israel withdrew from the disputed areas in 1957, but the American Sixth Fleet was then standing offshore demanding an immediate withdrawal of Syrian troops from Jordan, where they were supporting Palestinians trying to force Jordan into a union with Egypt. The United Arab Republic, a union of Syria and Egypt without Jordan, was approved by the National Assembly later that year.

At that stage, Syrian Baathists would have preferred a union with Iraq rather than Egypt because of common socialist ideals, while conservative land-owners wanted nothing to do with Egypt, Iraq or socialism. The army developed doubts about sending officers to Egypt or playing host to Egyptian officers in Syria, and the union with Egypt was severed by a military coup in 1961. Syria asked if it could reclaim its separate seat at the United Nations.

The "Revolution of 1963" put the Baathists in charge and resulted in wholesale nationalisation, a purge of the non-Baathists, and preparations for a union with like-minded Iraq (the Baathists were swept out of Iraq by a coup before union could be effected).

With Baath socialism proving a huge drain on the treasury and its adherents wondering what to try next, the Alawi in Latakia were diligently consolidating the grip on the military which France had bestowed before independence. In the meantime, radical Baathists perceived a panacea in the construction of a great dam on the Euphrates. A quick coup gave them a prime minister ready to fly to Moscow to ask for a loan of $100 million to build the dam. On his return, he negotiated a mutual defence treaty with Egypt

in time for the start of the Six-Day War. The Israelis were within 65 km (40 miles) of Damascus when Syria signed the UN ceasefire, saying it would oppose any concessions over Palestine.

Air Force General Hafez Assad then emerged as a Minister of Defence who, while giving away nothing on Palestine, was prepared to experiment with pragmatism instead of ideology. When a clampdown on Communists resulted in a warning from Moscow that all Soviet aid including military spare parts might cease, his right-hand man was on the next plane to Peking. He seized the premiership to frustrate hard-liners planning to send in tanks to help Palestinian guerrillas take over Jordan, but pragmatism then

LEFT: French military commanders saluting during a rendering of the "Marseillaise", at their garrison in Damascus, 1950.

ABOVE: poster linking Assad to Nasser's heritage.

allowed Syrian tanks and artillery to fire at Jordanian positions when King Hussein cracked down on guerrillas. .

President Sadat of Egypt's treaty with Israel was greeted with contempt. Syria's alternative was to continue supporting the Palestinians without provoking Israel into war. Nowhere was this more difficult than in Lebanon, where the Palestinians were apparently bent on making up for what they had failed to accomplish in Jordan. The Maronite Christians opposing them were supported and in some cases armed by Israel, but eventually it looked as if the Palestinians would win. This put a cat among the pigeons. Nothing disturbed Syria more than the thought of a massive Israeli invasion of Lebanon and, Damascus reasoned, this was bound to happen to deny the Palestinians victory. So it was to prevent their nominal allies from winning that 30,000 Syrian troops crossed the border to prop up the Christians in 1976. Syria's military presence in Lebanon cost $70 million a month, but neither that nor the logic behind it prevented President Assad from being returned for a second term of office.

> ### SECOND SON FIRST
>
> Bashar was Assad's second son. His charismatic eldest son, Basil, was killed in a car crash in 1994. An ophthalmologist by profession, Bashar was perceived as shy and studious compared to his brother.

The death of Assad

Assad's presidency went from strength to strength. Syria enjoyed a long period of stability, and, unlike other Arab states in the region, steadfastly refused to compromise with Israel, which won it enormous respect in the Arab world. Though Syria was vilified by the West for long periods of Assad's rule – for its links with the Soviet Union and its support of terrorism in the shape of Hizbollah – relations eventually softened. During the Gulf War of 1990–91 Syrian troops joined Allied forces against Saddam Hussein, Assad's arch-rival, and during the late 1990s Syria joined peace talks with Israel.

On 10 June 2000 the increasingly frail-looking Assad died of a heart attack. Though his death had been anticipated for some time, it was still an enormous shock for the nation. He had designated his son Bashar to succeed him, and within a month Syria duly elected him president in a national referendum (parliament having hastily lowered the minimum age at which a presidential candidate could stand in order to accommodate the 34-year-old Bashar).

How Bashar will cope with the presidency in the long term remains to be seen. His success depends on his retaining the support of Syria's powerful military, but like other members of the new generation of Arab leaders – King Abdullah in Jordan and Mohammed VI in Morocco – he must also modernise his nation. ❏

> ### THE DESTRUCTION OF HAMA
>
> Hafez al-Assad's suppression of opposition was often brutal, but never more so than during uprisings against his regime in the Hama region in the early 1980s. To an outlawed group of Sunni reactionaries calling themselves the Muslim Brotherhood, Assad personified two evils: heretical Shi'ism and the secular socialism of Baathism. In 1982, the Brotherhood seized the Great Mosque in Hama, killing as many Shi'ites and Baathists as they could find. In response, the army, under the control of Assad and with a hierarchy of Alawi officers, wheeled in artillery and blew the city centre to pieces. The unofficial death toll was between 10,000 and 30,000.

LEFT: Assad stands alongside former enemies at the funeral of King Hussein in 1999.
RIGHT: Assad was rarely seen in public, but his image was everywhere.

MODERN LEBANON

Despite its turbulent past as a land of warring factions, Lebanon is poised
for recovery. The Israelis have departed from the south and Beirut is booming

Alone in a bellicose Middle East, Beirut "swung" through the 1960s as if to repudiate the conventional wisdom of Ottoman sultans that unity among the Lebanese was a pipe dream. What seemed to have done the trick was the "National Covenant", a gentlemen's agreement to abide by an obtruse power-sharing formula originally devised by France in 1926.

As the country sailed along apparently oblivious to the Six Day War of 1967, Beirut took on the appearance of Monte Carlo, challenging tourists to swim in the sea, ski in the mountains and catch a casino floorshow on one and the same day. Everything worked, and oil sheikhs flew in for no other purpose than to make international phone calls, or so they said. Nevertheless, there was always the unsettling thought that if for any reason the National Covenant ceased, the consequences could be civil war.

History of division

History lent substance to this gloomy scenario. At the very beginning, the Phoenician commercial empire reached parts of the world no one else had even dreamt of, but it was the aggregate of individual efforts by ports such as Tyre, Sidon, Tripoli and Beirut itself. Although squeezed into just 160 km (100 miles) of coastline, they never formed a single state, and Nebuchadnezzar discovered he could pick them off one by one. Many centuries later – from the 7th century onwards – the population on the "Mountain", the ridge running parallel with the shore, was no different in this respect. Ethnic groups arrived at various times as refugees, but their common pedigree of persecution was not enough to form a bond. Between them and the Phoenicians, every port, peak and valley in Lebanon flew a different flag.

The 17th century produced an odd exception to this rule. The Ottoman sultan of the day had his head in his hands over what do about

LEFT: proclamation in Beirut, 1920, giving Syria and Lebanon separate status.
RIGHT: General Henri Gouraud.

Lebanon when a local emir, Fakr ad-Deen, offered a large sum of money and implicitly a share of the profits if the sultan would close his eyes and let him experiment with a few ideas of his own. The emir looked harmless: so small in stature that it was said an egg could fall from his pocket without breaking, and so cautious

that he reputedly did nothing without first consulting his mother.

Fakr ad-Deen, it transpired, was a complex character. Born a Druze, he was brought up in secret by Maronite Christians, whose religion was a cross between Byzantine Orthodoxy and Roman Catholicism, after his father was poisoned, or perhaps starved to death, by the Turks. The Druze knew him as one of their own, the sultan thought he was a fairly orthodox Muslim, and he wore a concealed Christian crucifix.

When the sultan opened his eyes 15 years after accepting the bribe, Fakr ad-Deen had stolen the whole country between Aleppo and Egypt, repudiated Ottoman policy by throwing it open to European trading interests, and amassed a fortune which enabled him to guard his assets with a private army of 40,000 mercenaries. Here was a man whom the Phoenicians would have saluted, but the sultan took the opposite view. Fakr ad-Deen was dragged to Istanbul and ritually executed by strangulation.

The Druze, Fakr ad-Deen's people, were responsible for the massacre of Maronites in 1860, which prompted France's intervention on behalf of the Western powers. As recounted in the previous chapter,

> **POWER OF THE PEOPLE**
>
> To accommodate all the minorities, the new Lebanese Republic, with a population of less than 1 million, came into being somewhat top-heavy with government.

The boundaries of new Arab states were generally influenced by historical considerations, but in some areas resorted to arbitrary features such as railway lines. Given a League of Nations mandate over Syria and Lebanon, France decided that the Maronite enclave needed some additions to make it a viable autonomous state. These included most of the Phoenician ports, the Bekaa and two Muslim areas. Syria was outraged by the loss of its most convenient access to the sea, but if these additions made economic sense for

France felt a mystical attachment to the Maronites, including speculation in crusader times that they were a lost tribe of the French nation. The first step, therefore, was to draw a line around the "Mountain" to create a Maronite sanctuary, the Druze by then having departed to the south. The Maronite sanctuary had a Christian governor approved by the Ottoman sultan and, with French economic input, it prospered until World War I.

French intervention

The map of the Middle East more or less as it exists today replaced the Ottoman empire brought down by Turkey's defeat in the war.

a Greater Lebanon they also sacrificed the original idea of a homogenous Christian land reminiscent of the crusader states of Outremer. The Lebanese Republic, as it was named, included a mixed bag of minorities whose feelings towards the Maronites, and one another, were not reliably warm.

It was in this context that France devised the National Covenant. By consensus, the president would be a Maronite Christian as they were the majority, the prime minister a Sunni Muslim as they were the second biggest group, the parliamentary speaker a Shi'ite Muslim, and so on. Government ministries and parliamentary seats were to be doled out according to the same criterion. At the bottom of the scale, minorities such as Protestants, Jews and Nestorians would have to take turns in a single parliamentary seat.

Coexistence

The Maronites assured of the presidency were more likely to have been of Greek origin than to have been a lost tribe of France, if only because they first came to light in the Orontes Valley, the region favoured by Greek immigrants under Alexander the Great's Seleucid heirs. They caught the eye of the Byzantine emperor Heraclius because they seemed to have found a middle way between God the Father

theological compromise eventually produced a cross between Eastern Orthodoxy and Roman Catholicism. It was also on the Mountain that the Maronites first met the Druze, who originated from Arabia and were now on the run from Egypt due to their religious beliefs. Based on Ismailism, a branch of Islam, their religion had gone its own way in such secrecy that only a small circle of elders were privy to the finer points. Ordinary followers, known as *juhhal*, were said to perform rites regarded as blasphemous by the Egyptians.

The Druze's difficulties in Egypt arose because one of their beliefs concerned Al-

and God the Son being one and the same or merely related, the lethal difference between Monophysite and Orthodox Christians. But his successor, Justinian II, decided in 680 that their compromise was heretical and drove them out of the valley, forcing them to abandon the tomb of their inspiration, the hermit St Maron, and take refuge on the Lebanese Mountain.

On the Mountain, the Maronites' senior bishop was still known as the patriarch of Antioch, the greatest of the Orontes cities, and their talent for

LEFT: doing "the fish" at the Acapulco beach disco in Beirut in the 1960s.
ABOVE: a car is held up by Druze rebels in 1958.

Hakim, the 11th-century Fatimid caliph widely regarded as mad. The Druze, on the other hand, saw him as God-incarnate, their equivalent of Jesus Christ, and when he was murdered they fled to the Lebanese Mountain in part to await his Second Coming, scheduled for 1996.

The Sunni Muslims, accorded second place in the National Covenant, were an overflow from the majority in Syria. The Shi'ites in third place comprised two groups, Alawis in the north and Metawilleh in the south along the border with Israel and in Tyre, which they occupied after the Mamlukes had used the biggest battering ram ever seen to breach its walls and eject the last of the crusaders.

The National Covenant mollifed Muslims who would rather have been in Syria and the republic got off to a promising start. Beirut prospered as a trade centre, there was an improvement in public utilities, communications and education, and an urban middle class emerged. All of this contributed to a sense of national identity and a desire for greater autonomy.

France had agreed in principle to independence before the onset of World War II. With the fall of France, however, this was suspended until a tug of war between the Vichy and Free French was resolved in the latter's favour by British intervention. Independence was duly pro-

claimed, but lost credibility when the elected president and government were arrested for presuming to interfere with the way the country was run. It only became wholly convincing with the withdrawal of French and British troops after the end of the war, and membership of both the United Nations and the Arab League.

Lebanon side-stepped the 1948 Arab-Israeli war by declaring itself on the side of the Arabs while quietly negotiating a separate armistice with Israel. The Suez Crisis of 1956, however, tested the National Covenant to the hilt, as did the Lebanese general uprising which followed in 1958. Parliament backed Egypt while President Camille Chamoun refused to break diplo-

matic relations with France and Britain. Ominously, Palestinian refugees from the 1948 war, not in the reckoning when the covenant was drawn up, seized Sidon, as well as Tripoli, parts of Beirut and Muslim rural areas. President Chamoun had American friends who had secretly funded his election campaign against pro-Nasserites and they provided US Marines to restore his authority.

The next uproar came from the Christians, when the incoming prime minister turned out to be Rashid Karami, the leader of a Muslim insurrection in Tripoli. But the National Covenant kept a lid on the situation and Lebanon entered the 1960s in fine fettle.

Warning shots

The golden decade had no sooner ended, however, when the National Covenant was tested by developments unforeseeable at the time of its inception. On one afternoon in 1970, the streets of Beirut were suddenly rattled by automatic fire from thousands of Kalashnikovs. Guests lounging around hotel pools collected their towels and dived for cover, but things were not as dangerous as they sounded. The sky took a beating that afternoon, but the only injuries were caused by spent bullets returning to earth. Significantly, however, the trigger-happy demonstrators were Palestinian refugees, unrepresented in the Covenant, who wished to register their dismay at the death of General Nasser, the Egyptian president in whom they had seen their best and possibly only hope of regaining Palestine.

Nasser's death coincided with King Hussein's "Black September" onslaught, which drove the Palestine Liberation Organisation (PLO) guerrilla army out of Jordan. Lebanon was the only country willing to take them in, the understanding being that the PLO would have a free hand in the Palestinian refugee camps around Beirut and along the border with Israel, as long as they did not interfere in Lebanese politics and held their fire until they had actually crossed into Israel.

At that point, the Maronites were still the biggest single group in Lebanon but, with Palestinians now accounting for a tenth of the population and a higher birth-rate among Muslims, they were no longer the majority. Moreover, the Maronites were a mosaic of neo-feudal clans and it didn't take much to make the fault-lines show.

In 1975, the Palestinian forebodings – demonstrated so noisily when Nasser died – were realised, it seemed to them, by his successor President Anwar Sadat reaching a provisional peace agreement with Israel. Uncertain of their future in Lebanon, PLO guerrillas turned their Kalashnikovs on the Lebanese security forces.

Tangled webs

Lebanese army commanders were reluctant to engage the PLO for fear of alienating the Muslims in their ranks. Suleiman Franjieh, now president, was hamstrung by the Muslims in parliament, who had fallen behind Kamal Jum-

Christian town of Damour, which obstructed communications between the Muslim strongholds in west Beirut and Sidon, Fakr ad-Deen's capital in the 17th century. The carnage in both cases was a declaration of civil war.

In the space of a few months, it looked as though the Palestinians were going to win, and this set off a remarkable chain reaction. In Syria, the mainsheet of President Assad's foreign policy was to stand fast on Palestine and the Palestinians by any means except another war with Israel.

Damascus now believed that Palestinian victory in Lebanon would inevitably attract a mas-

blatt, the head of the Druze party. With no confidence in the Lebanese government's ability to rein in the PLO, Israel attacked the camps in the south and at the same time encouraged the Christian private militia to come off the Mountain and deal with the guerrillas in the Beirut camps. Dany Chamoun, son of the former president, duly emerged with the National Liberal Party's "Tigers" and a fleet of 13 elderly tanks, provided by Israel, to attack the Tel al Zaatar camp on the road between the Mountain and Christian east Beirut. Conversely, the Palestinians attacked the

LEFT: Druze leader Kamal Jumblatt.
ABOVE: Yasser Arafat in Tripoli, 1983.

sive Israeli invasion, and Syria in turn would be forced into the war it wished to avoid. Therefore, to make sure that its Muslim allies, the Palestinians, would be denied the chance of victory in Lebanon, 20,000 Syrian troops crossed the border to prop up the Christian forces.

The bubble bursts

That was the end of "Monte Carlo"; in its place, Stalingrad. Opulent corniche hotels disintegrated under artillery fire, anti-tank rockets screamed head-high down side streets, and gangs helped themselves to the contents of pulverised bank vaults.

Amazingly, shops in west Beirut went on

offering a good deal on almost anything unless, or until, they took a direct hit. Moments of light relief, such as the sight of a tank in a queue of cars waiting to fill up at a garage, did not last long: other cars were towing prisoners through the streets at the end of ropes tied round their ankles, horns blowing to invite anyone with a gun to take a pot shot. Sharp eyes recognised some of the crews of such cars who, having dumped the bodies off a bridge, went home to change into their snappy suits and chunky gold jewellery for a night out on what was left of the town.

> **HEAVY TOLL**
>
> By 1976 the civil war had resulted in 45,000 dead, 100,000 injured, and 500,000 emigrants.

In reality the fighting never stopped; the only difference was that both sides, Christian and Muslim, broke up into factions and fought a seemingly mindless war of attrition in every possible permutation. Scarcely a day passed without a street battle or a car-bombing incident. In 1982, however, the attention of all parties concerned was suddenly focused on the south where 60,000 Israeli troops invaded with orders to destroy the PLO and force Lebanon into a peace treaty with Israel along the same lines as Egypt.

The Green Line

The war supposedly ended in October 1976 with the arrival of an Arab League peacekeeping force, mostly Syrians, and the subsequent partition of the country along a "Green Line", which ran past the Beirut Museum and along the road to Damascus. East Beirut was the Christian "capital" with its port, Jounié, providing a shuttle service with Cyprus.

A leftist coalition of Muslims, Druze and Palestinians under Druze leader Kamal Jumblatt was based in West Beirut. When Beirut airport was closed by rocket-fire, as it often was, the only way in from abroad was to fly to Amman in Jordan and take a taxi through Syria.

The invasion was successful in so far as the PLO guerrillas boarded ships for various destinations in North Africa, but they did so on the strength of an American guarantee that the Palestinian civilians left behind would be safe. The Christian factions got together and elected Bashir Gemayel as their president, only to see him assassinated before inauguration. In revenge, the Israeli army and Christian militias began moving into West Beirut. Members of one militia, the Lebanese forces, were then sent into the Sabra and Shatilla refugee camps where they slaughtered hundred of civilians – precisely what Washington had promised wouldn't happen.

Mediation and escalation

France had intervened after massacres in 1860 and French troops were again sent in as part of a multinational peace-keeping force which took up positions in Lebanon. Against this backdrop, Christian, Muslim and Druze leaders broke precedent by meeting, in Geneva, to attempt to work out a solution. The meeting was chaired by Amin Gemayel, the brother of the assassinated president-elect and himself now president. After acknowledging that the National Covenant was outmoded because Muslims were now a clear majority in Lebanon, he reminded delegates that half of the country was occupied by foreign troops and proposed that they all leave. Israel replied that it would if the Syrians went at the same time. Syria declined, and so on...

It was, in fact, the multinational force that left after a series of bombings, the first of which blew up the US embassy, resulting in 63 deaths. This was followed six months later by two massive suicide bomb attacks which killed 241 American and 57 French servicemen. As the UN forces withdrew, Druze artillery opened fire on the Christians in east Beirut, and the Christians replied by firing on the Shi'ite suburbs in south Beirut. National reconciliation was clearly going nowhere, but if it looked like the same story all over again there was, in fact, a change of emphasis brought about by the withdrawal of the PLO and, belatedly, by the Shi'ite revolution that overthrew the Shah of Iran.

The Lebanese Shi'ites, long the poorest community in the country, now saw the dawn of a new era for Shi'ites around the world, and they were ready to take their turn as sword-bearers.

The hostage snatchers

Anonymous spokesmen for groups who took it upon themselves to lead the Shi'ite renaissance in Lebanon at first used an archaic form of Arabic to disguise their regional origins when telephoning news agencies to claim responsibility for some action or other. But components of the Islamic Jihad soon had recognisable names, if not faces, as their activities focused on the particular business of snatching hostages off the streets of Beirut for political ends dictated by the regime in Tehran.

Various splinter groups linked to Hizbollah

LEFT: living on the Green Line.
RIGHT: guerrilla fighters in war-torn Beirut.

("The Party of God") bundled hostages into cars at gunpoint, with many facing years of captivity in squalid hide-outs in the southern suburbs of Beirut. One of the first victims, the American diplomat William Buckley, died in detention, as did one of the four Soviet diplomats taken prisoner for the purpose of exerting leverage on Syria. Otherwise, the rest of the Western hostages were teachers, journalists and, curiously, the Archbishop of Canterbury's emissary Terry Waite, who arrived in Beirut hoping to negotiate the release of the hostages and then became one himself. The largest number were American, mostly working at the American Uni-

versity in Beirut (AUB). But there were also British, French and Germans, among others.

Several hostages never made it to freedom. In 1986 the UK government allowed American warplanes based in Britain to be used to bomb Libya. Three British hostages were murdered by Abu Nidal – a Palestinian group with close links to Libya which had been offering $7 million for any British citizens. Several years later an American was murdered in retaliation for the Israeli detention of a Hizbollah leader.

Hizbollah fights on

The gradual release of the hostages, in some cases after more than five years in captivity, mirrored another trend. With the PLO out of the picture, the Shi'ite groups who assumed the leadership of the campaign against Israel positioned their forces in traditional Shi'ite territory in the south for what amounted to a permanent rocket and artillery duel inside the borders of Lebanon.

The occasional more northerly thrust apart, Beirut was now removed from the regular grind of the war. The Syrian army was still around, at a reputed cost to Damascus of $70 million a month, but they dismantled their road blocks and withdrew to the background. Comparative tranquillity revived the entrepreneurial instincts of Christians and Muslims alike, notably the Sunni Muslims who felt less sympathy for the Shi'ite militia than they had for the Palestinians. Bulldozers moved in to clear a path to the Beirut Museum through the wreckage of cars that had failed to run the gauntlet of the Green Line crossing between east and west Beirut. Tel el Zaatar, the Palestinian camp where in 1975 the civil war had started, was razed to make way for office blocks, and the mountainous graves of dead hotels made way for a race among their replacements to meet the millennium deadline.

But Hizbollah continued to attack the Israelis in southern Lebanon and the occupation became

THE SOUTH LEBANON ARMY

Israel's ally in the occupation of southern Lebanon was the 2,500-strong South Lebanon Army, a mainly Christian organisation set up in 1978 when Saad Haad, a Lebanon Army officer, defected. Trained, armed and paid by Israel, the SLA served as a buffer for Israeli soldiers. It was required to man the most dangerous positions and charged with the most difficult tasks, such as running the notorious Al Khiam prison, where Palestinians and Lebanese were imprisoned in appalling conditions.

With the Israeli withdrawal from southern Lebanon in July 2000, many members of the SLA fled to Israel. Those caught by the Lebanese were tried for collaboration.

increasingly unpopular with Israel's electorate. As a result, in March 2000, the Israeli cabinet voted for the complete withdrawal from southern Lebanon, and by July its forces had gone.

The tricky job of re-establishing the international border between Israel and Lebanon fell to the United Nations, which has also deployed a peace-keeping force along the border. Whether the fragile peace will hold is difficult to say. Syria would like Hizbollah to keep up pressure on Israel until the return of the Golan Heights. Hizbollah, meanwhile, may have its own agenda – wider power and influence in Lebanon. ❏

LEFT: Syrian soldiers in Beirut in the 1980s.

The Hostages

Thousands of Lebanese were abducted during the civil war by various militiamen at checkpoints or from their homes. Some were released for money or swapped for rival detainees, but most were killed, and 17,415 people remained officially missing. Most Lebanese are therefore hardly aware of the 44 westerners held hostage during the 1980s. Yet for the rest of the world, the word "hostage" is synonymous with Lebanon and grainy pictures of Terry Anderson, John McCarthy, and Jean-Paul Kauffmann.

The taking of foreign hostages began in July 1982, when Christian militiamen kidnapped four Iranian diplomats. In retaliation, Islamic Jihad – a militant Muslim group linked to Hizbollah, and therefore Iran – kidnapped David Dodge, president of the American University in Beirut (AUB). After a year, Iran learned that its diplomats were dead, and quietly released Dodge. But the precedent was set.

Two years later, in February 1984, 17 men were sentenced to long jail terms in Kuwait for a series of pro-Iranian bombings. One was closely related to a leader of Islamic Jihad. In a bid to free the prisoners, Islamic Jihad began to seize westerners in Beirut, hoping to make an eventual swap. But the strategy didn't work because the Kuwaiti government refused to budge. However, others in Beirut, seeing the reaction of the west, began to see hostage taking as a useful weapon for a variety of political purposes. They sought the release of Arab prisoners held in the west or Israel, or a halt to western support for Iraq in the Iran-Iraq war, or an end to support for the Lebanese Christians in the civil war. "Freelance" hostage takers emerged, picking up westerners, then trying to sell them on to the highest bidder.

The journey into captivity typically began outside the hostages' homes when they were forced into the back of a Mercedes at gunpoint. They were pinned to the floor, and driven at speed to the southern suburbs of Beirut, interrogated, then thrown into cells blindfolded. But there were exceptions. In January 1987 police officers arrived at the Beirut University College and asked to see any American teachers. Four were produced, and were informed there was a kidnap threat. The police officers said they were there to teach the Americans how to react in case of kidnapping. They were told

RIGHT: British hostage John McCarthy, freed in 1991.

not to panic, and were tied up and carried to a truck outside under the eyes of college security. Only later did college authorities realise the police officers were bogus. The teachers joined the growing list of those detained.

The time hostages spent in captivity had much to do with the approaches of their governments. The Soviet government was the most direct. After four diplomats were seized in 1985, it commissioned a rival group to free them. The group kidnapped the kidnapper's brother, and sent one of his fingers back every day until the diplomats were free. No more Russians were taken.

Initially the hostages' various governments agreed

not to "negotiate with terrorists". But faced by increasing domestic pressure, most secretly caved in. France bought the release of its hostages in 1988 with political and financial promises to Iran. A trickle of Americans were released after US administration official Oliver North secretly sold weapons to Iran. Britain and West German stuck dogmatically to the no-negotiations agreement, and consequently their hostages were the last to be released.

In 1990, a stroke of luck befell the remaining hostages when Iraq invaded Kuwait, inadvertently releasing the pro-Iranian prisoners. With the principal cause of the hostage taking out the way, a UN diplomat came to Beirut, and quietly negotiated freedom for the remaining hostages. ❑

THE RICH CULTURAL MIX

The cultural diversity of Syria and Lebanon has been at the heart of the countries'
many conflicts, but it is also one of the reasons they are so fascinating to visit

The region of Syria and Lebanon has produced several significant empires in its long history, but more often it has been a meeting place where people from the near East, Asia and the West have exchanged goods, ideas and blows. Here, too, Christianity, Judaism and Islam were nurtured. As a result, and despite their modest size, Syria and Lebanon are home to an amazing variety of different ethnic and religious communities.

Light and dark

Sit outside a café in Damascus, Beirut or one of the region's other cities and you will be struck by the variety of features passing by, from the palest milky-white skin with blue or green eyes to the darkest shade of brown skin and eyes, with raven black hair. The Bedu, with their long faces and prominent noses and chins, are clearly related to Arabs of the Arabian peninsula. People of the towns may have Hittite, Aramean, Philistine, Mesopotamian, Phoenician, Greek, Roman, Persian, Arab, Turk or European characteristics, but the large majority of them can also be ethnically defined as Arabs.

In the biblical sense "Arabs" were nomads who inhabited the deserts of northern and central Arabia. From the 7th century onwards they conquered a vast empire which, over many centuries, underwent "arabisation". Even today, there are many similarities between Arab countries all over the world, from North Africa to the Middle East and the Arabian Gulf.

A Muslim majority

Twenty or 30 years ago, under the umbrella of pan-Arab nationalism, many Syrians prided themselves on being Nasserites, communists or Baathists, but since the collapse of the pan-Arab ideal many now define themselves by religion: Alawi, Sunni, Shi'ite, Druze, Armenian,

PRECEDING PAGES: coffee and a game of dominoes, Hama, Syria; along the Corniche, Beirut.
LEFT: a student entertains friends, near Damascus.
RIGHT: Lebanese boy caught by the camera.

Maronite and so on. Unlike some other Arab countries, Syria does not have a state religion – the original constitution did not even mention Islam, although a clause stating that the Head of State should be a Muslim was later added by popular demand. While the President remains firm about keeping religion out of politics, the

Syrian ideal is of a state held together by Islam but with a tolerance towards minorities. In Lebanon, where pan-Arab nationalism never took root, parties have traditionally been based on religious or ethnic affiliation.

Most Syrians and a majority of Lebanese are Muslims, believers in Islam. Muslims believe that there is only God – Allah – and that Mohammed was his prophet or messenger. The Qur'an is Islam's holy book, believed to be the word of God delivered in Arabic directly to the Prophet Mohammed. The Prophet, who could neither read nor write, recited the 114 *suras* or chapters over 22 years to his followers (Qur'an means recitation). Mohammed is considered the last in a line of prophets beginning with Adam and including Abraham, Moses and Jesus. Muslims revere Jesus not as God's son, but as an important prophet who came to deliver the same message as Mohammed.

Sunni and Shi'ites

In both Syria and Lebanon, Sunnis are the largest religious group, comprising around 75 percent of the population in Syria and over 50 percent in Lebanon. The Shi'ites are fractured into several groups.

> **BOOK PEOPLE**
>
> Muslims regard Christians and Jews as *Ahl al-Kitab* (People of the Book), who received the divine message of one true God but who, through weakness and corruption, failed to stay true to it.

Among the most important are the Ismailis, known as the "Seveners" because they recognise only seven principal caliphs after the death of the Prophet Mohammed. When the sixth imam died in 765, the caliphate should have passed to his oldest son Ismail, but most Shi'ites supported his younger brother Musa al-Kazim. The Ismailis opposed this and chose Ismail as their rightful seventh Imam. They also scandalised other Muslims by nurturing a cult around the descendants of Ali.

> **THE PILLARS OF ISLAM**
>
> The Five Pillars of Islam are considered obligatory to every believer. The *shahada* is a public declaration that "there is no God but Allah, and Mohammed is his prophet". *Salaat* or prayers should be performed five times a day at appointed times (facing Mecca, but not necessarily in a mosque). During Ramadan Muslims should fast *(saum)* and abstain from drinking, smoking and sex from sunrise until sunset. Giving alms to the poor *(zakat)* is also compulsory, although no longer a tax levied by the government. At least once in a lifetime, circumstances permitting, Muslims should perform the *hajj*, the pilgrimage to Mecca.

The Aga Khan, the spiritual head of the Ismailis, claims direct descent from the Prophet Mohammed and Ali. In 1094, more divisions were created when the Fatimid caliph al-Mustansir's older son Nizar was disinherited in favour of his younger brother al-Mustali. Of the two sects which grew out of this division, the Mustalians (now known as the Boharis) are mainly found in India. The other, the Misaris, who later produced the Assassins, form the largest Ismaili group in Syria and live mainly around Hama and in the coastal mountains *(see page 194)*.

ABOVE: Shi'ite worshipper at Bab as-Saghir, Damascus.
RIGHT: veiled in Aleppo.

The Alawis

Another Shi'ite sect, the Alawis, also known as Nusayris, has risen to prominence recently, as it counted among its number the late President Assad. The sect's origins are obscure, but it is believed that Mohammed Ibn Nusayr an-Namiri founded the sect in the 9th century. At that time Alawis were considered heretics, mainly because they elevated Ali in the same way Christians elevated Jesus. Alawi theology, a mixture of Islam, Zoroastrianism and Christianity, with pagan and gnostic elements, is fully understood by only a few initiates.

Hated by Muslims and Crusaders alike and persecuted throughout their history, Alawis took refuge in the harsh Jabal Ansari or Nusayri mountain region of Syria. Once a poor rural minority, they are now a strong political force representing nearly 12 percent of Syria's total population and with a power base in Latakia.

The secret beliefs of the Druze

The Druze *(Duruz* or *Darazi* in Arabic)*, another Shi'ite sect, an off-shoot of the Ismailis, have clung to their identity throughout their turbulent history. They took their name from their founder Mohammed bin Ismali ad-Darazi, but the faith is based on the teachings of Hamza

SUNNIS VERSUS SHI'ITES

When the Prophet Mohammed died in 632, he did so without leaving an heir or appointing a successor. Abu Bakr, the Prophet's companion, was made Khalifa Rasul Allah, Caliph or Successor to the Prophet of God, but Ali, the Prophet's son-in-law and cousin, considered himself the natural heir. Ali did eventually become the fourth caliph but both he and his son Hussein were murdered by their rivals.

This led to a major division in Islam which continues today. Shi'ites recognise Ali as the first legitimate caliph and believe that only his descendants have a right to inherit the caliphate. The majority of Shi'ites, particularly in Iran, are known as "Twelvers" because they accept the succession of the 12 caliphs or imams. They also believe that the last caliph, who disappeared in 873, will return as the Mahdi or Messiah on the Day of Judgement.

Unlike the Shi'ites, Orthodox Sunnis, who make up the majority of the world's Muslims, recognise the first three democratically elected caliphs but do not acknowledge any of the Prophet's descendants as legitimate caliphs. In theory, they do not recognise any intermediary in man's relationship with God and no organised clerical hierarchy. Sunnis divide themselves into four schools of Muslim law – the Maliki, Shafi, Hanafi and Hanbali – with the Shafi and the more liberal Hanafi schools dominating in Syria.

ibn Ali, who amalgamated the many strands of spiritual thinking then current in the Middle East, including reincarnation and utopianism.

The Druze declared the Fatimid Al-Hakim "bi-Amr Allah" (Ruler by the Order of God), caliph from 996–1021, the divine representative of Allah. Al-Hakim, a bizarre character *(see page 39)*, mysteriously disappeared in 1021; his followers await his return as the Messiah.

The Druze are considered heretics, even by the Ismailis, mainly because their creed denies

> **A SECRETIVE SOCIETY**
>
> One cannot convert to the Druze faith and intermarriage is strictly forbidden. Their *hikmah* or religious doctrine and the full extent of their rituals are known only to very few initiates *(uqqal).*

true figure may be as high as 20 percent, with large communities in Damascus and Aleppo. Damascus has always had a special significance amongst Christians, because it is was here that St Paul converted to Christianity, and that the important Roman Temple of Jupiter was replaced by a Basilica of St John the Baptist.

But the majority of the city's Christians only came to the city after their co-religionists were massacred in the Syrian countryside and in Lebanon in 1860. The Christian community in

two of the Seven Pillars of Islam, forbidding them to fast during Ramadan or to make the pilgrimage to Mecca. Traditionally, they tended to live in isolated mountain areas, originally in the Lebanese mountains, although many of them moved to Syria in the late 19th century. Today the Druze inhabit the Chouf Mountain in Lebanon and the southern Hauran mountains in Syria; important communities also survive in Israel, around Haifa and in the Golan Heights.

Christians

According to official figures, Christians of various denominations today account for about 10 percent of the Syrian population, although the

Syria flourished under the French Mandate (1920–46), but their political representation in the government has now shrunk dramatically. Only two or three Christian ministers remain in the government and Christians hold few important posts in the army, although several of the president's inner circle of advisors are said to be Christians. In schools, religious education, which is mandatory, is divided into Muslim and Christian classes.

None of this has stopped Christians from getting the best education or from becoming wealthy. Some 20 percent of Syrian doctors are Christian and Christians are found in many other intellectual and liberal professions. But while many Christians enjoy a better standard of living, the increase of Islamic fundamentalism has left them fearful for their safety and prosperity. Some have left Syria while others have sent their children to school in the United States, in the hope of eventually obtaining for them the much desired Green Card.

Christian sects

Much of the early development of the Christian Church took place in what is now Syria and Lebanon. Although the Romans

LAWS UNTO THEMSELVES

Though civil law is common to all religious communities in Syria, Christians and Muslims have their own religious courts to settle matters of personal status, such as divorce and inheritance.

insisted he was solely divine. A middle way was offered by the Monothelites who suggested that Christ had two natures but only one will, a view that was backed by the 7th-century Byzantine Emperor Heraclius. Out of this dispute separate sects and creeds developed, including the Coptic church in Egypt, the Armenian or Gregorian church, the Nestorean church, the Maronites and the Monophysite Syrian or Jacobite church, founded in Syria by Jacobus Bardaeus, a 6th-century monk.

persecuted early Christians, in AD 313 the Roman Emperor Constantine, himself recently converted to Christianity, passed an edict allowing them to practise their beliefs. In 380 the emperor Theodosius went further and made Christianity the official religion of the Roman Empire. But official recognition exacerbated profound theological differences between the growing Christian communities.

The main dispute was over the nature of Christ. While the Orthodox believed that Christ was both human and divine, Monophysites

LEFT: nightlife is reviving in Beirut.
ABOVE: a Lebanese trader gestures.

A SMALL JEWISH COMMUNITY

Jews have lived in Syria at least since Roman times. They are Arabic-speaking and hardly distinguishable from Muslim and Christian Arabs. With the establishment of the State of Israel, however, their position was made difficult and by 1968 most of them had left. In an attempt to improve Syrian-American relations, President Assad in 1992 granted the remaining few thousand Jews permission to leave the country. Most emigrated to the USA and now only a few hundred remain, mainly in Damascus and Aleppo. They are barred from government employment and are the only nationality whose religion is included on their passports and identity cards.

By the 11th century the theological differences had become confused by political considerations and the Church was split by the Great Schism of 1054, after which the Eastern church refused to recognise the legitimacy of the Roman Pope and elected instead their own Patriarch of Constantinople.

Later, several independent churches elected to return to Roman Catholicism. As a result, many independent churches have both a Catholic and an Orthodox branch. The major-

SEEKING NEW HORIZONS

By some accounts as many as a quarter of the entire Christian community of Lebanon has emigrated, mainly to the USA, Europe, Australia, West Africa and South Africa.

Lebanon's Maronites

About 35 percent of the Lebanese population is Christian and by far the largest group, some 20 percent of the total, are Maronites. The Maronite faith centres upon an obscure 4th-century hermit called Maron, who lived in the ruins of a pagan temple near Cyrrhus. After his death, Maron was buried somewhere near Hama, probably in Apamea, where during the 5th century a monastery and place of pilgrimage developed around his tomb.

ity of Syrian Christians belong to either the Greek Orthodox Church or the Greek Catholic Church, Syria's largest Uniate Church (meaning with its own liturgy but recognising papal authority), although there are important Armenian communities in Damascus and Aleppo. In the same Christian quarters there are also communities of Syrian Orthodox, Syrian Catholics, Roman Catholics, Protestants and Anglicans. The Greek Orthodox have their liturgy in Arabic, while Syrian Orthodox and Catholics use Syriac, a language closely related to Aramaic.

The small Chaldean Catholic community, which has largely preserved the ancient East Syrian liturgy, also practise in Syriac.

One account of Maronite history suggests that the Church flourished after the AD 680 Council of Constantinople, at which John Maron of Sarum, the head of St Maron's monastery, was appointed bishop of Antioch and representative of the Roman Orthodox Church in the East. However, another account has it that at the same Council of 680, the Maronite Church was condemned for its Monothelite heresy.

During the 10th century continuing Muslim persecutions of the Maronites drove them out of Syria into the isolated valleys of northern

ABOVE AND RIGHT: celebrating a Kurdish wedding, northern Syria.

Lebanon, where Bcharré became the seat of their patriarch *(see page 294)*. The Maronites helped achieve the safe passage of the first Crusaders to Jerusalem, and in 1180 they officially declared their union with the Pope and the Roman Catholic Church.

Over the centuries, recognised by Rome and the West – by France in particular – as a useful ally in a very divided region, Maronite power and influence gradually increased, spreading from Bcharré into the Chouf and Metn mountains. And it was partly because of the special relationship between the Maronites and France that the province – and later the state of Lebanon – was created *(see page 62)*. The French aim was to produce a sufficiently strong power base to guarantee the survival of Christian communities in a predominantly Muslim environment.

The second largest group of Christians in Lebanon are Greek Orthodox, with smaller communities of Greek Catholics, Syrian Catholics and Orthodox, Armenian Catholics and Orthodox, Roman Catholics, Protestants and Nestorians. Traditionally the Christians had a small majority in the country (at times only 51 percent), but even before and particularly during the civil war many Christians emigrated.

FACTION UPON FACTION

Nothing showed up the problems of this multi-cultural region more clearly than the Lebanese civil war. The various groups had lived in relative harmony until the Great Powers intervened in 1860. British support for the Druze and French support for the Maronites were significant contributing factors to the start of the civil war.

After World War II, the French created "Greater Lebanon", twice the size of the former Ottoman province, where the Maronites no longer had an absolute majority. Nonetheless the Maronites remained in control and the newly incorporated Sunni and Shi'ite Muslims and the Druze had no power whatsoever. During the economic crisis of the early 1970s many unemployed Lebanese depended for an income on the various armed militia, based on religious or ethnic affiliations. The more radical Palestinians joined the leftist Lebanese National Movement (LNM), a coalition of Druze, Shi'ite and Sunni groups under the leadership of Kamal Jumblatt. By 1975 various Maronite organisations had joined forces with Pierre Jumayyil's Maronite Populist movement of Kata'ib or Phalange. In December of that year both Muslim and Christian militia committed atrocities; in January 1976 the Phalange attacked Palestinian refugee camps and Beirut was divided into a Muslim West and Christian East.

The Armenian community

The Armenian Orthodox church was founded by the Armenian King Tirdate in AD 301, making Armenia the first Christian nation in the world. Armenians have lived in Syria for centuries but the majority of the current population is descended from survivors of the World War I massacre of Armenians by the Turks, in which as many as 2 million people died. Aleppo saw the greatest influx of Armenians: before World War I it had just 300 Armenian families while by 1943 there were more than 400,000 Armenians. Many of these immigrants left for Soviet Armenia in the 1960s, when anti-Christian feel-ings became strong. Nevertheless, they have maintained a considerable presence in Aleppo, Damascus and Beirut, mostly as traders in textiles and fabrics. Both the Armenian Catholic and Orthodox churches hold their liturgies in classical Armenian and strongly guard their Armenian traditions and identity.

Kurds

Kurds are the largest minority group in Syria, now representing approximately 10 percent of the total population. After World War I the Kurds were not granted their promised homeland and today they remain a people without a country, spread over Syria, Turkey, Iraq and Iran. They have little freedom to express their political views in Syria, where they live north of Aleppo and in the Jazira, but with the government's consideration for minorities they tend to fare better than their brethren in neighbouring countries.

Several acts of terrorism in Syria – as elsewhere in the region – have been accredited to Kurds as part of their fight for an independent state. But most of their activities have been concentrated in Turkey where Kurdish guerrillas have been fighting a civil war with the Turkish army. Turkey has often blamed Syria for giving shelter to Kurdish guerrillas.

Other minorities

There are still as many as 300,000 Palestinians in Syria, mainly in Damascus, while Lebanon remains home to 350,000 mostly Sunni Muslim Palestinians. They arrived after the 1947–49 Arab-Israeli War and later in the 1960s and '70s. In Lebanon, only a few have obtained Lebanese citizenship and most live in poor conditions in southern Lebanese refugee camps. The influx of Muslim Palestinians is one of the main reasons that Muslims now outnumber Christians in Lebanon.

Among other minorities, a number of Turks are settled east of the Euphrates. Aramaic-speaking Christians live in and around Ma'lula, near Damascus. There are also small communities of Circassians, Russian refugees who fled their country during the 19th and 20th centuries. ❑

DEVIL WORSHIP?

The Jazira, in northeastern Syria, contains one of the most intriguing of Syria's religious minorities, the Yazidis, a Kurdish-speaking people that originated in southern Iraq. Like the Druze, they are highly secretive about their faith, which combines elements of Islam, Judaism, Christianity and Zoroastrian but is most famous for what is sometimes referred to as "devil worship".

In fact, Yazidis do not believe in evil and reject the notion of hell, but they revere the fallen angel Lucifer, called Malak Ta'us and symbolised by a peacock. They believe that when Lucifer repented he was pardoned and restored to his role as leader of the angels.

LEFT: Bedu boy on the Sryian plain.
RIGHT: studying Islam in one of Damascus's many *madrasas* (theological schools).

DAILY LIFE

*Water shortages and electricity failures may be common discomforts, but renewal
in Lebanon and signs of a new openness in Syria are cause for optimism*

Images of the Middle East often conjure up ideas of terrorism, Muslim fanatics, veiled women without voice or rights and Arabs against Israelis. It is these and other negative images that first-time visitors bring to Syria and Lebanon, as to elsewhere in the region. But after magazine or television images have been replaced by personal experience – especially after contact with the Syrians and Lebanese, visitors tend to take away with them a very different impression.

Divided we stand

There's nothing new about this bad press. One Arab legend has it that long ago, when God divided men into nations, he also gave each a positive and a negative quality. Iraqis received pride and hypocrisy, desert Arabs were given excellent health counterbalanced by the harsh demands of their environment, while the Syrians were blessed with intelligence but cursed by foolishness. Another local legend attempts to explain why Damascenes are famous for being ardent liars. Shortly after the Creation, it maintains, Satan visited Earth with seven bags of lies, which he planned to distribute evenly over the world. However, he fell asleep in Syria and while he slept his bags fell open near Damascus, spilling the lies.

Other Arabs say of Syrians, *"Shami shoumi"*, meaning Syrians are a wicked lot. Syrians, of course, have another spin on this story. Ask about it and you may be told, " If you think we are liars then you must not have met an Iraqi – they are the worse. And the Lebanese! They will cheat and steal from you without you noticing. And possibly worse than both the Iraqis and the Lebanese are the Egyptians. Do not believe a single word they say."

More than dispelling the myth of Arab brotherhood, these legends go a long way towards confirming the region's long-standing tribal lines and bring to mind another famous saying: "Me

against my brother; me and my brother against my cousin; me, my brother and my cousin against the world."

However, there are other social obligations which are binding, and hospitality is one of them: most people travelling through Syria and Lebanon, particularly through the countryside,

DESERT ROOTS

Many of the customs of urban Arab society are rooted in the culture of the nomadic Bedu, whose difficult but noble way of life was often idealised by the sedentary Arab city dweller. The code of hospitality to strangers, for example, stems from the desert tradition of welcoming a guest for exactly three and a half days – the time it took for all traces of the host's food to pass through the body of a stranger – while the desire for news stems from the days when Bedu encampments were few and far between and news from friends or strangers was the only way of keeping in touch with a wider world.

LEFT: a quiet smoke in a café in Damascus.
RIGHT: gift-wrapped.

are struck by the friendliness and generous hospitality of the people. In rural towns, you may find yourself being dragged into a café or shop where the primus stove will be lit and coffee duly brewed and served – all part of an intricate social code which deems it an honour to entertain strangers. And don't make the mistake of thinking this is a one-way transaction. The code of hospitality dates to a time when news was passed by word of mouth. So while you are enjoying hospitality, your hosts will be satisfying their curiosity as to who you are and what you are doing and may have learned something about the place you come from. You will also have supplied them with conversational material for long after you have left.

This sort of open hospitality, often at odds with 21st-century global society, is becoming less common, but you still get offered a pot of tea or a coffee by almost every Syrian or Lebanese you meet.

Population growth

Syria's population has grown dramatically in the past few decades. With an annual growth rate for much of the 1990s of 3.6 to 3.8 percent – the highest in the region, and one of the highest in the world – the number of Syrians is estimated at

FEMALE FORTUNES

Like most Arab countries, Syria and Lebanon are conservative in their attitudes towards women. In spite of Syria's socialist ideology, many of its customs are derived from Qur'anic precepts. Meanwhile, although Lebanon, with its large Christian population, appears to be more liberal, with Western dress common and advertising billboards suggesting consumer-led lifestyles, in rural areas a very different image prevails. "Crimes of honour", when disgraced women are murdered by their male relatives, run at about 80 a year in Lebanon. It is also legal to employ children over the age of eight, which means that some very poor Lebanese families help to augment their family income by placing their young daughters in work as maids.

Nonetheless, the women of the region are far from meek and mild. Lebanese women played a crucial economic role during the country's civil war. And Syria has recently celebrated its most famous female figure, Queen Zenobia, the 3rd-century Queen of Palmyra (see page 30), in a 22-part television series in which Zenobia was played by the beautiful Arab film star Raghba. The words "Damn the crown on the head of the humiliated, and bless the chains on the hands of free and proud men", attributed to the real Queen Zenobia, have become a rallying cry of Palestinians today.

around 17 million. As a result, Syria is a young country and, with nearly half the population under the age of 14 and only around 3 percent over 65, it has a considerable amount of growing up to do. Urban areas, particularly Damascus and environs (population around 3 million) and Aleppo (population around 5 million), have seen the fastest growth, helped by a steady flow of people moving in from the country-side. Roughly 60 percent of these migrants are thought to have abandoned the countryside in

RETURN OF THE NATIVES

Since the end of hostilities, large numbers of Lebanese have returned home, although nearly 10 million, or about three times the resident population, continue to live abroad.

have neither the ability to build enough housing for everyone nor the power to oppose the massive amount of illegal building. The city's new *mukhalafat* (illegal suburbs) have risen like mushrooms and surrounded the well-planned inner city. The impact of these "illegal" quarters can be gauged from the statistics: they have twice the population density of the other quarters, account for some 31 percent of Damascus' surface and are home to around 47 percent of the city's inhabitants.

search of work, education and better living conditions. But Syrian towns and cities have also had to absorb the Palestinian and Syrian refugees who fled the Golan Heights after Israel's occupation in 1967. Some 50 percent of the country's total population now lives in towns and cities along the main Damascus–Aleppo highway and along the Syrian coast.

This influx has irrevocably changed the landscape, and towns and cities are now ringed by sprawling, rapidly-built and poor quality housing. In Damascus, for instance, the authorities

LEFT: comparing notes at a wine-tasting in Lebanon.
ABOVE: café in Beirut.

Not a drop to drink

The rural exodus and urban population explosion have resulted in other problems. Water in the cities is now at a premium and because supply cannot match the increasing demands some inhabitants have siphoned it illegally from the public canal system, lowering the flow of the entire network. The electricity grid is similarly failing to provide, and being illegally tapped, causing problems with the regularity and the tension of the electrical supply. Other social services, from public transport to state schools, are also overwhelmed by the sudden population growth.

A similar drift from the countryside to towns

has happened in Lebanon, a country that also had to contend with the arrival of some 400,000 Palestinian refugees fleeing Jordan and Israel. Although there has not been an official census in the country since 1932 (the complex mix of Christians and Muslims being too sensitive an issue to confront head on), in 1995 it was calculated that half of the estimated population of 3.7 million people were living in Beirut and its suburbs. While the number of Palestinians increased, the number of native Lebanese declined. Some

150,000 Lebanese died in the civil war, with nearly one in seven families losing their breadwinner; many others emigrated.

> ## BEHIND THE IMAGE
>
> One in two Lebanese women have sex before marriage, according to research presented at a conference on sexuality in the Middle East.

Break for the border

If you sit down with either Syrians or Lebanese for any length of time, one thing will become clear – they have a few preconceptions about each other. While many Syrians will never manage to forget their nostalgia at the passing of pre-civil war Lebanon, even the Lebanese are having to recognise that Syria is beginning

SMOKING COMPANION

If there is one aroma visitors take with them from Lebanon or Syria, it is of apple tobacco being smoked in a traditional *nargeileh* or hubble-bubble pipe. From cafés and street corners, to the tables of the most fashionable restaurants, men and women of all backgrounds can be seen puffing away thoughtfully, generating clouds of thick white smoke.

Tobacco is heated at the top of the tall *nargeileh* by glowing charcoal, smoke is drawn down through a vessel of cooling water, and out through a pipe to the mouth. The experience is cool, pleasant, and slightly intoxicating. Most smokers today charge their pipes with mild fruit-flavoured tobacco, while some continue to use traditional strong,

dark tobacco, often imported from Iran. During Lebanon's civil war, farmers in the Bekaa Valley took advantage of the lawlessness to grow hashish, with more than 1,000 tonnes produced each year. Some Lebanese took solace from the horrors of the war by adding a little hashish to their *nargeileh* tobacco, though the practice was brought to an end when the war finished.

A *nargeileh* is often offered to guests as a gesture of hospitality. It is generally not shared, but if it is, the pipe is passed with its head turned inwards. It is considered rude to light a cigarette from the coals of the *nargeileh*, as it is said to disturb the rhythm of the burning charcoal.

to change with the times. Before the war Beirut was the "Paris" of the Middle East, a boom city which happily mixed hard work with a lust for pleasure. A financial and banking centre for the region, it attracted billions of petrol dollars from the Gulf States, but at the same time was renowned for its restaurants and casinos. At the height of the pleasure-years, one statistician calculated that there was one bar per 140 inhabitants. Pre-war Lebanese were also renowned for their need to flaunt their wealth.

FLATTERY, FLATTERY

Even the late President Assad felt that the sycophants sometimes went too far. Shortly before his death he ordered the Syrian media to stop referring to him as the "eternal guide".

ished majority. Many expatriate Lebanese are now returning home and creating the sort of demands that ought to re-establish Beirut as one of the region's fashion and entertainment centres.

While wealthy Syrians visit Beirut to buy the luxury goods they cannot find at home, some Lebanese make the brief journey into Syria to buy cheaper consumer goods and clothes. Continuing peace – and the hope of a solution to the region's continuing tensions and, with it, of a Syrian pull-out from

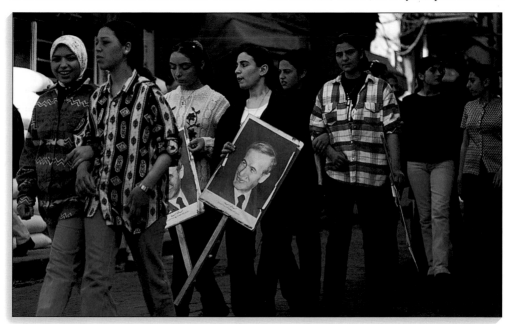

The war put an end to much of that, but not all: even during the heaviest fighting some of Beirut's bars and jazz clubs stayed open, race meetings took place during the lulls and even when things were at their bleakest, there were still more consumer goods available in Beirut than in Damascus, where the state and ideology exerted tighter controls on imports.

One of the casualties of the war was Lebanon's middle class, which suffered equally from death and emigration, leaving only a small, very wealthy elite and a large impover-

Lebanon – is helping to broker better relations between the two countries and Lebanon's more forward-looking people are having an influence on their more numerous neighbours.

Big brother

Until Hafez al-Assad's death in June 2000, everywhere you went in Syria your eye was met by gigantic portraits and statues of the president. Several buildings in the big squares of Damascus were covered by his portrait, virtually every car had a few stickers of the president on the back window, bearing slogans, such as "Hafez al-Assad for ever" or "Our beloved President Hafez al-Assad". Towards the end of

LEFT: school's out in Syria.
ABOVE: in support of the late President Assad.

his life images of the President were often joined by pictures of his two sons, Basil whom Assad had hoped would be his successor until his death in a car crash in 1994, and Bashar, who did indeed succeed him.

The purpose of this personality cult is to create an impression that the president is all-seeing, all-powerful, an icon of stability. Whether Bashar will try to bolster his own presidency in the same crude way remains to be seen.

Behind the veil

As Syria slowly changes behind its veil of conservatism, so does the role of the old social sup-

ports. You are still unlikely to meet a Syrian who will openly criticise the president, admit to being a non-believer, will allow his wife as much social freedom as her counterpart in France, or will allow his daughter to live with a boyfriend before marriage.

Many Syrians live with huge social pressures and restrictions, a fact that was perfectly captured in *The Extras,* a film by Syrian director Nabil Maleh, in which an unmarried couple try to find a place where they can be alone together: even in a friend's empty apartment, they are imposed upon – and kept apart – by the thought that they had been seen entering the building and by the sounds coming through the shutters and locked door.

And yet foreign television and music, new access to the internet and greater freedom of movement are having their effects in the city. People feel freer to speak their minds and there is less looking over the shoulder or dropping to hushed tones than there used to be. Culture often comes with surprisingly well-informed cosmopolitan overtones, and 20- and 30-something Syrians and Lebanese are unrecognisable as the children of the blood-stained people who stared into the lenses of the world's media during the 1970s and 1980s. As a result of that – and of the eroding of tribal lines and old traditions that tends to happen naturally in cities – you are less likely to be overwhelmed by hospitality there.

A slower pace

In the countryside, however, both in Syria and Lebanon, things are changing more slowly. The mosque or church remain at the centre of the community, identities and ambitions tend to remain inward-looking and often patriotic, women dress and behave more conservatively and families will get together at set times each day to eat and observe traditions. The only thing that is likely to break this routine is the arrival at the door of a passing stranger, an opportunity to show the sort of traditional hospitality that many visitors find hard to believe is without strings. And while the hospitality is being offered, Syrians and Lebanese indulge in their favourite pastimes, talking, joking and asking questions. ❏

TUNING IN AND WAKING UP

Though the urban Lebanese were early converts to the telecommunications revolution, the Syrians are only just nudging their way into the technological world. Almost until his death in 2000, former president Hafez al-Assad's tight control over the media included banning both internet access and mobile phones. But even Assad realised that he could not hold back world influences for ever and satellite television was eventually legalised (some 22 percent of television-owning households now own satellite dishes), and in the few months before his death some 20,000 people were estimated to be online. His son is reportedly keen to extend that number.

ABOVE: an Americanised lifestyle, Beirut.
RIGHT: in the gold souk, Aleppo.

HOLY LANDS AND SACRED PLACES

Syria and Lebanon are packed with pilgrimage sites, from the Shia shrines in Damascus to the simple chapels marking the footsteps of St Paul

▷ FEMALE MARTYRS
The Bab as-Saghir cemetery in Damascus contains the tomb of Fatima, daughter of the Prophet and wife of Ali, attracting Shia pilgrims.

The Islamic tradition mentions 124,000 prophets since Adam, of which Mohammed was the last one. Sites connected to them are considered sacred. Mount Kassion in Damascus, with its sanctuaries of hundreds of prophets *(see page 146)* is especially sacred. Many are still visited today, including Adam's cave, the cave where Cain killed Abel, the sanctuary of Abraham and the maqam al-Arbaeen, together known as the burial place of "40,000 prophets". The most recent saint is Sheikh Harun, a stone cutter but also a mystic and religious authority, who died in 1962.

The area of Salhiyeh in Damascus *(see page 145)* is also a place of pilgrimage, as many saints *(salihoun)* lived or were buried here. From the beginning of Islam the oasis of Damascus was considered a paradise on earth. Although the Prophet Mohammed never set foot in it, fearing that he would then not reach the heavenly paradise, many of his descendants lived and were buried there.

△ GREAT ESCAPE
St Paul's Chapel, Damascus, where the apostle was lowered in a basket to escape persecution by the Jews *(see page 140).*

TO BE A PILGRIM

Both Sunni and Shia Muslims perform regular pilgrimages to sanctuaries to ask favours from their favourite saints. Women, for example, ask for cures for infertility, help with childbirth, marriage difficulties or education. They knot strips of fabric to the grille of a saint's tomb *(see above)* to bind their contract with him. Water or oil is often put into tombs to receive a saint's *baraka* (blessing), after which it will be administered to the sick. Until recently local sheikhs would visit important shrines to ask for help during periods of war or drought.

◁ OLD FLAME
A lantern to St Charbel in the town of Zahlé in the Bekaa Valley, Lebanon. St Charbel was born in the Bekaa in 1828 and canonised in 1977.

△ REST IN PEACE
The Shia Hizbollah fighters, infamous for their deadly suicide missions and kidnappings, are considered martyrs of Islam when they die in combat.

CHRISTIAN DEVOTION

◁ **A POPULAR HERO**
The tomb of Basil al-Assad, the beloved elder son and intended successor of the former President Hafez al-Assad, has become a popular pilgrimage site.

▽ **RURAL SHRINES**
The countryside is dotted with small domed tombs of local Muslim saints, which are visited for their miraculous powers.

Syria and Lebanon are home to no fewer than 11 different branches of Christianity, all noted for their strong expressions of devotion. The countries' links with important religious figures also draw Christians from further afield. Damascus is associated with St Paul (he converted to Christianity on the road to Damascus and was lowered to the ground in a basket to escape the jews from a window in St Paul's Chapel) and John the Baptist, whose head is said to be entombed in the Ummayyad Mosque.

But the countryside is also well stocked with shrines. The 5th-century church of St Simeon, for instance, was once the largest church in the world and would accommodate thousands of pilgrims paying homage to the Stylite who had spent 30 years living on top of a stone pole. The village of Aqoura in the Adonis Valley, famous for its religious fervour, still has 40 churches and chapels, and thousands of pilgrims head for St Charbel's monastery, dedicated to Lebanon's most popular saint, when a local woman bleeds miraculously.

ARCHITECTURE

An account of the region's architectural achievements, from the magnificent

8th-century Mosque of Damascus to the modern-day reconstruction of Beirut

The ancient Phoenician, Roman and Byzantine cities and the Crusader castles of Syria and Lebanon are probably their most celebrated architecture, but the region also possesses many of the world's finest examples of Arab religious, military, commercial and domestic architecture. As well as the great Umayyad mosques of Damascus and Aleppo, and their attendant *madrasas* (religious colleges), there are several outstanding palaces, whose Damascene rooms epitomise a style of interior design that was all the rage among the wealthy bourgeoisie in the 18th and 19th centuries. There are also the great *khans* of Damascus and Aleppo, vast warehouses built during the Middle Ages when these cities were important hubs on east–west trade routes. The wealth created by trade was reflected in the architectural splendour of the *khans*, with their multi-domed roofs and often intricate wood carvings.

Mosques and madrasas

Shortly after the the Arabs conquered Syria, it became the seat of the Umayyad Dynasty, the administrative capital of an empire stretching from the Atlantic ocean across Asia. The arrogantly confident Umayyads loved luxury and their buildings were designed to appeal to the senses as well as impress. Their architects drew upon many different influences, but mainly Byzantine and Sassanian.

One of their most famous public buildings (along with Al-Aksa Mosque and the Dome of the Rock in Jerusalem), the Great Mosque of Damascus is among the most impressive Islamic buildings in the Middle East. Commissioned in the early 8th century by the Umayyad Caliph Al-Walid, it replaced the Byzantine Cathedral of St John. Though incorporating elements of its Christian predecessor as many other mosques did (square minarets, for example, drew their inspiration from Christian belfries) and following the basic outline of the cathedral, its design was dictated by the Prophet's courtyard house in Medina, the prototype for mosques all over the Arab and Islamic world, A *mirhab* was built in the south wall to reorientate the building towards Mecca.

INTIMATIONS OF PARADISE

One of the most surprising and impressive features of the Umayyad Mosque in Damascus are the beautiful green and gold mosaics covering the octagonal treasure house and the arcades of the court. These large expanses (in fact, just a fraction of their original extent) depict a paradisiacal garden with kiosks, palaces and running streams in a naturalistic style clearly derived from the Byzantine tradition and very different from the geometric motifs that dominated decoration in later centuries. However, even here, in line with the Islamic prohibition on depicting the human form, the mosaics do not include human figures.

In spite of their urbanity, the Umayyads were a desert people, and they built a host of desert palaces, fortresses and trading posts from where they could indulge in their favourite sports of falcony and hunting, and maintain contact with the Bedouin tribes, on whose loyalty they depended. They often rebuilt and expanded Byzantine buildings, adding bath houses, spacious courtyards and great halls for audiences or for entertainment, adorned with columns and carvings, mosaics and frescoes, some of which contain sensuous depictions of human figures. They were served by sophisticated hydraulic and heating systems, so that the stresses of a hard day's hunting or diplomacy could be soothed by fountains, pools and hot baths.

These buildings were often isolated in the desert, but at Aanjar *(see page 271)*, in modern-day Lebanon, an Umayyad city was built. At the crossroads of important trade routes, the city was wealthy, as the remains of houses, baths and some 600 shops testify. Its buildings

BUILDING ON THE PAST

Early Islamic buildings often recycled Roman and Byzantine stonework. Corinthian columns proved particularly useful for holding up prayer halls or supporting arcades.

IN DEFENCE

Though Arab warfare began in the wide open spaces of the desert, control of the growing cities quickly became crucial to military success, and by the Middle Ages every city had its stronghold that could withstand long periods of siege. Though these were often built upon the foundations of Roman forts, raised to defend the empire's crumbling frontiers, their design was dictated by Arab militarists, who spent many years refining the arts of warfare and defence, copying and adapting techniques learnt by the Byzantines as well as inventing their own.

Under the Ayubbids, wars against the crusaders saw a proliferation of castles (crusader and Muslim), especially in coastal regions, but it was under the Mamlukes, the dynasty responsible for ousting the powerful Mongols from Syria, that defensive architecture reached its zenith. One of the most formidable Mamluke strongholds is the citadel in Aleppo, rebuilt in the 15th century after Mongol attacks under Tamerlane had severely damaged the previous fortress. Crowning a rocky hill that rises at a 48° angle in the centre of the city, its mighty stone walls are punctuated by towers; its heavily defended entrance, which is large enough to be a citadel in itself, contains three gateways and five turnings and is reached by a causeway over a 22-metre (72-ft) deep moat.

are heavily influenced by classical architecture, but the delicately carved stonework of the palaces display the characteristically sensuous style of the Umayyads.

Mamluke architecture

After the Umayyads, the Abbasids shifted the caliphate to Iraq, and destroyed much of the architectural legacy of the Umayyads, decrying them as degenerate heretics. But a renaissance came during the 12th and 13th centuries under the Ayubbids and the Mamlukes, when Syria

TRADEMARK COLOURS

Characteristic of Syrian architecture is the use of contrasting coloured stone such as limestone and black basalt, especially to frame arches.

and including student lodgings) proliferated. Initiated a little earlier by the Zengids, who used them to reinforce the Sunni branch of Islam, they later became popular causes for members of the growing bourgeoisie. Funding their often lavish decoration was a way in which citizens could make a mark on society while expressing their piety. In the 13th century Mosques of Repentence *(tawba)* also sprang up in Aleppo and Damascus, often replacing brothels or drinking dens.

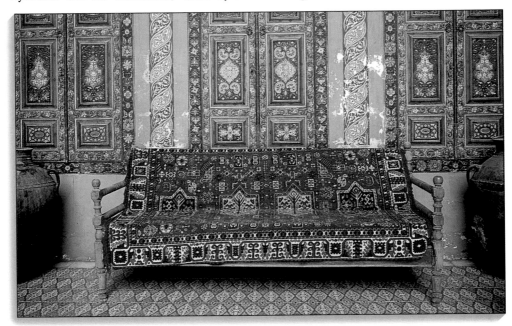

became important to the new centre of the caliphate, Egypt. Though the largest building work was reserved for Cairo, Syrian arts and crafts flourished, and Syrian artisans were considered among the most skilled and innovative in the Islamic empire. They excelled at woodwork, inlay, enamelled glass and stucco-work, all of which embellished the mosques, palaces and wealthy furnishings of the period.

It was around this time that *madrasas* (theological colleges, usually attached to mosques

FAR LEFT AND LEFT: exterior and interior of the Azem Palace, Hama.
ABOVE: a typical Damascene interior.

Domestic architecture

Mamluke influences later evolved into the Ottoman-Arab style displayed in the Azem palaces of Damascus and Aleppo and the Beit ed Dine south of Beirut. Such palaces also inspired the homes of the cities' merchants.

For the Arabs, the aesthetic role of buildings, so important in the West, has traditionally taken second place to the practical function of defining a space, a purpose emphasised by huge, dramatic gateways, enclosed courtyards and enormous defensive walls. Throughout the Arab world domestic architecture is governed by the importance of privacy, The traditional urban house was therefore designed to protect and hide the intimacy of the family (particularly the women. Exteriors were usually plain and uninviting, with anonymous-looking doorways opening onto blind passage-ways. The wealthiest houses, however, might incorporate *mashrabiya* balconies overlooking the street. Inset with finely carved latticework screens, these enabled the sequestered women of the house to look out on the passing scene without being observed. Such balconies can still be seen in the old quarters of Aleppo and Damascus today.

> ### LONG LABOUR
>
> A traditional Damascene room takes around five years to complete. Though the skills for creating such a room still exist, they rarely get called upon.

But the anonymous facades hid a very different interior. Impressions changed as soon as one entered the pleasant courtyard with its central fountain, lemon or orange trees, and vines and jasmin flowers perfuming the air. The noise of the old-city's streets and the hubbub of the souks suddenly seems far away, and life takes on a slower rhythm. The courtyard itself might be laid in geometrical patterns of contrasting coloured marble .

High-ceilinged rooms around the courtyard were usually lavishly decorated with inlaid and painted woodwork, as well as polychrome marble stone work. Thick walls kept the houses cool in summer and warm in winter, while on hot summer afternoons the family could rest in the shade in the sumptuous open *iwan*. Most houses had several quarters all with their own courtyard, the *salemlek* (a reception area for the men), the *haremlek* (the private quarters for the family) and a quarter for the servants.

Seating in such rooms was traditionally low and relatively simple, though upholstered in fine silks and brocades. Niches in the walls might hold porcelain ornaments or fine glassware. Blankets for warmth in winter were often neatly piled.

The passion for highly decorated interiors peaked in the 18th and 19th centuries with the so-called "Damascene Rooms", which drew their inspiration from a fusion of Turkish, Arabian and Persian influences. Wealthy families would commission the master craftsmen of the day to create splendid reception rooms (*madafah*) in which marble, stone, wood and textiles were integrated to dazzling yet powerfully ordered effect, using in infinite permutations the small repertoire of the geometric and floral motifs permitted in Islamic art and architecture. Every surface of the room was covered in intricate decoration. Variously coloured marble was used in geometric patterns on walls and floors, while finely carved doors, ceilings and panelling was inlaid or painted with beautiful garden motifs or Kufic script.

The modern home

Most modern architecture of the region appears to be a far cry from these traditional forms. The majority of new building comprises new flats and villas, which on the face of it are little different from other such properties around the Mediterranean. However, in spite of a rather different attitude towards privacy – windows are numerous, exteriors often ostentatious – inside, the bones of the traditional home can still be discerned. The layout will be similar and the most important room, the reception hall (*madafah*), will be as lavish as possible, incorporating traditional decorative techniques, such as stucco, wood carving, marble and ceramics, albeit on a less ambitious scale. ❑

LEFT: old techniques employed on a new mosque in Damascus.

Rebuilding Beirut

From the first days of the civil war to the last, fighting between rival armies and militia mostly took place in Beirut. As a result, the bloodshed and destruction in the city was much worse than elsewhere. The Green Line dividing Beirut between various militia in east and west ran right through the city centre. Shelling and small arms fire day after day for 15 years reduced much of the area to rubble. The heart was ripped out of the city, and almost no building was left unscathed.

When the war came to an end, rebuilding began. Appropriately enough, the man who came to office as prime minister in 1992 was Rafik Hariri, a self-made construction tycoon. Over the next six years he led efforts to rebuild the country, drawing on his experience in the construction industry in Saudi Arabia. His first government drew up Horizon 2000, an ambitious plan to reconstruct Beirut on a grand scale. With state-of-the-art infrastructure, it was thought, Beirut could recover its position as the financial and service centre of the Middle East.

Hariri put $130 million of his own money into the formation of a new government-mandated company, Solidere. He then engineered the passing of a law giving all property in the downtown area to Solidere, with original owners receiving shares in the company in exchange. The law was controversial to say the least. Many property owners complained that after protecting their buildings through 15 years of war, they had them stolen by Solidere.

In total about 1.8 million square metres of central Beirut was to be restored, including some 60 hectares of land reclaimed from the sea in a scheme to dispose of a huge mountain of garbage which had collected during the war. The coastal waste dump has progressively been ploughed into the sea, as the base for a new financial quarter. Downtown's crumbling infrastructure has gradually been replaced with state-of-the-art equipment, such as fibre-optic telephone lines to every building, and even chilled underground pipes to deliver cool water in summer.

Beyond central Beirut, Hariri built a new international airport bigger and better than many in Europe, and with a capacity far in excess of present use. Connecting the airport to downtown is a new six-lane highway, allowing arrivals to travel seamlessly to the futuristic city.

The reconstruction effort also tried to pay heed to

RIGHT: rising from the ashes.

the city's cultural heritage. While most downtown buildings were flattened, those that were retained (around the parliament building) were restored at great expense, with European stonemasons hired to replace damaged Ottoman facades. And as a by-product, the Solidere project allowed archaeologists to dig under the centre of the city.

But in 1998, Hariri was ousted from office, leading to a slowdown in the reconstruction as the new government tried to distance itself from his legacy. Many complained the plans were too ambitious, too expensive, and had directly led to the ballooning state debt. Others said the Hariri reconstruction had ignored all but central Beirut, high-profile high-

ways, airport and office complexes, with little concern for the needs of the poor. Supporters of Hariri say that the government had no choice – if Lebanon were to have any hope of revival, massive investment in infrastructure was essential.

At the beginning of 2000, Solidere completed its first phase of the reconstruction of downtown. The centre of the city is now unrecognisable from pre-war days. Most of the area is a vast expanse of open areas, awaiting developers. Elsewhere, there are shiny new office buildings, interspersed with carefully restored churches and mosques, and shops. It is clean, organised and modern. But the area is still a ghost town, especially at night, with few shops, and even fewer residents. ❑

HIVES OF ART AND INDUSTRY

When you wander off the main streets of the souks, you discover closely packed workshops where traditional artisans practise centuries-old crafts

Once upon a time Syrian arts and crafts were the most exquisite in the Islamic Empire, and Syrian craftsmen were employed on some of its greatest monuments, including India's Taj Mahal. Damascus, in particular, was noted for its artistry and was renowned for refined, high quality products, such as its famous silver swords. Damask (fine cotton embroidered with silk) and damascene metalwork (*see below*) take their names from the city that created them.

TRUE METAL

When the Prophet Mohammed banned the use of gold and silver eating vessels on the grounds that they were too extravagant, craftsmen developed clever ways of making ordinary metals look exquisite. A favourite technique was damascening, whereby softer metals such as copper, and later silver and gold, were applied to harder brass or bronze surfaces in elaborate filigree patterns. Even today, no souk would be complete without the lively sounds of hammers bashing away on metal, though it is usually only to apply the finishing touches to vessels and plates, as most brassware is industrially produced. But from time to time commissions from wealthy families enable copper-smiths to display their craftsmanship to the hilt.

Some traditional crafts have been encouraged by the growing tourist industry. The government is also taking steps to revive traditional crafts, for instance by installing workshops in the Takieh as-Sulaymaniyya in Damascus.

▷ **BY HAND**
Hand-loomed clothing has survived among nomads and farmers in rural areas.

△ **TEXTILES MATTER**
The manufacture of cotton and silk has been important in Syria since the Middle Ages.

◁ MUSIC MAKERS
Hand-made lutes from Damascus are renowned amongst connoisseurs as being the best you can buy.

△ HAND-MADE FURNITURE
Cheap and simple cane furniture, as well as more elaborate wooden dressers, abound in the souks.

▽ AN OLD TRADITION
Artisans produce fine hand-made multi-coloured inlay for everything from small boxes and chess games to large pieces of furniture.

△ THE LAST CEDARS
As the last cedars in Lebanon are protected, most wooden trinkets are carved from naturally fallen cedar or from other wood.

▷ MOTHER-OF-PEARL
The Fatimids are thought to have imported from Egypt the still popular tradition of decorating furniture with mother-of-pearl

THE GLORY THAT WAS GLASS

Ancient writers mention both Tyre and Sidon as having a fully developed glass industry at the beginning of the Christian era. As in Egypt and Mesopotamia, vessels were made by melting glass around a sand core. The Lebanese coast was ideal because of the fine quality of the sand and the rich supply of resinous pine, used to fuel the furnaces.

At around the same time the technique of glass-blowing originated in Syria. During the Mamluke era, Damascus was known throughout the Arab world for its fine enamelled and gilded hanging mosque lights. Nowadays, there are only two such glass-blowers left, who still quite magically blow exquisite objects from glowing lumps of molten glass and then swing them through the air to create the desired shape. These masters can make more than 100 types of vessel with a precision acquired through years of experience. In the 13th century the crusaders took the technique to Venice, since when Murano glass has become the most famous in the world.

LEBANESE AND SYRIAN CUISINE

There is much more to Lebanese food than its myriad forms of mezze.
Syria, meanwhile, is famous for its sweet sensations

With its exquisite subtlety and inventive variety, Lebanese food is the undisputed star of Middle Eastern cuisine, but Syrian kitchens also produce tantalising tastes, especially when it comes to honey and nut based sweets and pastries.

The rich variety of dishes on any Syrian or Lebanese table reflects these countries' long history at the crossroads of great civilisations. Shortly after the death of the Prophet Mohammed in AD 632, his followers, Bedouin Arabs from the Arabian Peninsula, established a vast Islamic Empire which stretched from Spain, Sicily and North Africa over to Asia. The first Bedouin rulers, who based their court in Damascus, ate once a day – a rudimentary diet of dates, bread, some mutton, goat or camel's meat and milk. But they were soon seduced by the often elaborate cooking of the peoples they conquered, the Persians, Byzantines, Egyptians, Asians and Greeks. The best of these kitchens were brought to the court.

Under the reign of the Abbasid caliph Harun al-Rashid (786–801), gastronomy was regarded as an art worth recording. In the 14th century the Ottoman sultans embraced this love of food and interest in culinary literature, and introduced yet more influences, including the European dishes cooked up by their Christian slaves.

The dishes of Lebanon and Syria have much in common, but you will probably notice differences on restaurant menus. The Lebanese have inherited from the Phoenicians the art of pleasure and enjoyment, and from the Arabs they learnt the rules of hospitality; their long association with the French taught them about refining their cuisine.

An abundance of fresh ingredients and a long established tradition of restaurants have made eating out very much part of family life. In Syria, on the other hand, daily life is generally harsher and, apart from in large cities such as Aleppo

and Damascus, it can be difficult to find anything but basic snacks outside hotels.

One of the delights of Arabic food is the wide selection of *mezze* or appetisers, usually served in a casual, unhurried way, often with wine, beer and especially *arak*. The variety of dishes is endless, and to make the most of *mezze* it

PRECEDING PAGES: for a sweet-toothed nation, Syria.
LEFT: bread for sale in Aleppo.
RIGHT: café comforts at Beit Jabri, Damascus.

BREAD OF LIFE

Aish, the Arabic word for bread, literally means "life", and all over the Arab world bread is treated with reverence. It accompanies every meal, and is traditionally used to scoop the food from the plate using the right hand. The senior male present will usually cut or break the bread and distribute it to those present; at the end of the meal any leftover bread is gathered up and recycled in home-made pastries. *Aish* (also called *khoubz*) are flat round discs, baked unleavened. Popular for breakfast or as a snack are *mankoushi*, flat round loaves of bread topped with *zaatar*, a mixture of cumin, oregano and *sumac* (grilled sesame seeds and olive oil).

helps to be with a few people to share a larger spread. *Mezze* can be simple – a small plate of roasted nuts, olives, cucumber or cheese – but usually makes a full meal with dips, salads, vegetable dishes, grilled cheese and small bites of fish or meat such as sautéed chicken livers dressed with lemon juice and garlic. The more popular *mezze*, also eaten as snacks on their own, are *baba ghanoush* or *mouttabal* (a dip of grilled and mashed eggplant with *tahina* (a sesame paste), lemon juice, olive oil and garlic, hummus (puréed chick peas with *tahina*, garlic and lemon), *taratour* (a thick mayonnaise of ground pine nuts, garlic and lemon), *muham-*

marah (a paste of ground nuts, chilli, cumin and olive oil) sometimes served with pomme-granate syrup, and *labneh* (a strained yoghurt).

Salads such as the zesty *tabbouleh* (cracked wheat, chopped parsley, tomatoes, onions and mint), crunchy *fattoush* (greens, tomatoes, carrots, cucumber, mint, onion and toasted pitta bread), *loubieh* (green bean salad) are dressed with olive oil and a generous squeeze of lemon juice. *Warak enab* or *warak dawali* (stuffed vine leaves) are often on the menu, as well as stuffed peppers, courgettes, aubergines, cabbage leaves and vibrant Swiss chard. In homes stuffed vegetables are usually

STREET FOOD AND SNACKS

Snack bars, cafés and street stalls are plentiful and ready to serve a variety of delicious snacks to overcome hunger pangs in between meals or indeed to eat as an inexpensive full meal. The most readily available are *falafel*, crisp patties of puréed chickpeas and broad beans, enlivened with fresh spices and herbs and served with pitta bread, salad and *tahina*. Another staple is *fuul*, a stew of broad beans served with oil, cumin and lemon for breakfast and in sandwiches all day long. The carbohydrate-loaded *kushari*, a bowl of warm rice, macaroni and lentils moistened with a topping of spicy tomato paste, cumin and crisply fried onions, is a favourite lunchtime snack. *Fattehis* is a rich mixture of *fuul*

or chick peas with yoghurt, pine nuts and melted butter, and sometimes (vegetarians should check) morsels of lamb's feet or head.

Meat lovers may prefer *shawarma*, layers of lamb or chicken roasted on a vertical spit, sliced and served in flat bread laden with salad, tamarind paste and garlic sauce, or *farouj* (crispy-skinned chicken); *shawarma* carvaries are found on every street corner. Specialised bakeries in both Syria and Lebanon sell wonderful *mankoushi (zaatar* bread, *see page 107)*, and delicious *fatayer*, small savoury pastries which come in different guises: stuffed with mint and mozzarella, meat, spinach or *zaatar*.

reserved for special occasions as they take several hours of painstaking preparation.

Meat dishes are either served as *mezze* or as a main course. The national dish of Syria and Lebanon is *kibbeh*, large balls of ground lamb and cracked wheat which are either fried or baked. Traditionally women pound the meat and wheat with a heavy pestle in a stone or metal mortar, and it is believed that some women are blessed with a special hand or extra long finger to shape the meatballs. Other popular variations are *kibbeh*

> ### COOL TREATS
>
> Ice-cream parlours *(booza)* are popular in Syria and Lebanon and often serve wonderful home-made ice-creams dipped in pistachio nuts.

(hamour) and tuna *(ballamida)* are usually grilled or fried and served with salad and a lot of lemon. *Sayyadieh*, fish with rice and cumin, is particularly good in Tripoli but also common as Friday's *plat du jour* in many coastal restaurants.

Sweets and preserves

Like the Prophet Mohammed and other Arabs, the Syrians and the Lebanese have a very sweet tooth, and the selection of sweet delicacies in pâtisseries is dazzling. Traditionally every household keeps

nayeh, eaten raw like steak tartare, or *kibbeh bi-saniyeh*, stuffed with pinenuts and chopped onion, and then baked. There is no shortage of kebabs, *kofta* (grilled minced meat) and *shish tawouk* (chicken grilled on skewers, often with a strong garlic sauce). Some restaurants in Aleppo serve cherry kebab, a welcome variation of the traditional dish.

Fish is expensive but widely enjoyed along the Syrian and Lebanese coasts. Red mullet *(sultan Ibrahim)*, sea bass *(lukos)*, sea bream *(farride)*, prawns *(gambari)*, Red Sea grouper

LEFT: *mezze*, the ultimate Lebanese feast.
ABOVE: barbecue in the Bekaa Valley.

stocks of home-made sweetmeats, pastries and jars of fruit preserves, ready to serve to passing visitors on beautiful silver or porcelain trays, with tea, coffee or a cold syrup. The most popular pastries are *asabeeh* or ladies' fingers (rolled filo pastry stuffed with pistachios, pinenuts and honey), *baklawa* (layered filo pastry stuffed with nuts and honey), *barazak* (crisp biscuits sprinkled with sesame seeds) and *basbousa*, a semolina cake soaked with syrup. During the fasting month of Ramadan, Kamar ed-Din, a sweet apricot preserve is often served to break the fast. Specialist shops in Damascus sell beautiful boxes of candied fruits.

Many pastries are made for specific religious

celebrations. During Ramadan, *katayef* or thick pancakes filled with cheese, cream and nuts and drowned in syrup, are served just after sunset to open the appetite. A favourite sweet of the Aid al-Fitr, the festival held to mark the end of Ramadan, is *konafa bi-jibn*, layers of angel hair, semolina and white cheese. Christians celebrate the Baptism of Christ on 6 January with *awamat*, flour and rice puffs, and aniseed macaroons. *Maamoul*, delicious biscuits stuffed with dates or walnuts, are now available all year round, but traditionally

> ### FINDING FAVOUR
>
> The Lebanese are proud of their wines. Despite the obsession with all things French, the wines on the tables at the most expensive restaurants are often local.

espresso and cappuccino, while upmarket hotels will sell American instant coffee, generically known as Nescafe.

Aseer or fruit juice stalls sell juices of the fruits in season: grapefruit, orange, lemon, watermelon or pomegranate and, with milk, banana or strawberry. Milk bars, on the other hand, sell *haleeb* (unpasteurised milk), *labhan* (yoghurt drink) and *ayran* (a salty yoghurt drink).

The Qur'an advises Muslims not to drink wine, and many restaurants do not sell it. The

they were made by Christians for Easter and for Aid al-Adha, the Muslim commemoration of Abraham's sacrifice of a ram instead of his son Isaac. Another favourite for this feast are *kaak*, gridle cakes made with milk or aniseed.

Fire waters or cooling juices

Though tap water is considered safe it is probably wise to stick to bottled mineral or spring water. Tea (*shai*) served in tiny glasses is prepared throughout the day, coffee (*ahwa*) comes in small doses but is very dark, strong and usually syrupy sweet. For less sugar ask for *ahwa mazbout* or *wassat*, for no sugar *ahwa saada*. Many cafés, particularly in Lebanon, serve

locally produced alcohol is inexpensive in the shops, but prices escalate in restaurants. Syria grows and produces wines around Damascus and Homs, but the wines of the Bekaa Valley in Lebanon are far superior, particularly Château Musar and Kefraya *(see opposite)*. The same applies to the beers: Syrian beers are quite drinkable when served icy cold, but Lebanese brews are preferable. *Mezze* are often served with a flowing supply of *arak*, the fiery spirit made from local grape and aniseed liquor, which is similar to Greek ouzo. It is often considered a good cure for upset stomachs. ❏

ABOVE: making coffee in Lebanon.

Lebanon's Wines

I n some of the more fashionable wine shops in New York, London and Paris, it is occasionally possible to buy the odd bottle of Lebanese wine. The leading brands – Musar, Kefraya and Ksara – are usually marked on the shelves as "new wines", alongside bottles from Australia and the Americas. But the truth is somewhat different. Some of the world's first wines probably came from the area now known as Lebanon, and it has been producing a few fine bottles ever since.

The first record of exported local wine dates from 1850 BC. A stone tablet discovered in Egypt depicts huge casks of wine being offloaded from Phoenician ships at Egyptian ports. Records from antiquity – from the Greeks to the Romans – make mention of wines from the region. Phoenician merchants are thought to have shipped the then rich sweet brews in amphora jars to all four corners of the Mediterranean, to be drunk by the elite classes of Athens, Carthage and Rome. Indeed, when the Romans took up residence in the Levant, they decorated a vast temple in Baalbek with carvings of grapes, reflecting the importance of the industry.

In the early Christian era, wine continued to play an important role, notably in the Biblical story of the wedding of Cana (one of three modern villages claiming to be the Biblical Cana is just down the road from the modern vineyard of Kefraya.) The arrival of the crusaders, some 1,000 years later, gave a boost to the wine industry, as wine was used for liturgical rites. When they were finally driven out in the 13th century, some crusaders are said to have taken vines back to France.

Several hundred years later, the process was reversed. In 1857 Jesuit priests brought cuttings from France, and purchased Château Ksara, in the Bekaa Valley, beginning to develop it as a winery. The priests introduced high-quality vines, and stocked the cave cellars with wine and brandy, some of which can be seen today and is said to be still drinkable.

The modern wine industry is still based in the Bekaa Valley, which according to specialists, is perfect wine growing terrain. The vast plateau is at an altitude of more than 1,000 metres, with average annual rainfall of 550 mm, average summer temperature of 25°C (77°F) and more than 300 days of sunshine a year. As a result of the fine weather,

Lebanese grapes develop a high sugar content, which means the wines can achieve an acceptable alcohol level without the addition of raw alcohol, as happens in many vineyards in cooler climates. And thanks to the dry growing season, the vines are practically free of diseases.

Despite the industry's long history, modern production only began in the 1950s, when the leading wineries began to invest in modern facilities, planting grapes such as Cabernet Sauvignon, Cinsault, Syrah, Chardonnay and Sauvignon Blanc. During Israel's 1982 invasion, Israeli tanks drove across the vineyards of Kefraya, but the château nevertheless managed to produce a vintage for the year, bottles of

which can still be obtained. Since the end of the war, the châteaux have intensified efforts to improve quality and increase their overseas marketing. Vineyards now cover some 30,000 hectares (74,000 acres), with about 40 percent of the 5 million bottle output exported. Most are open to visitors.

Château Musar is the most famous producer because it has long exported 90 percent of its production, even during the war. But other châteaux, such as Ksara and Kefraya are slowly winning international recognition. (Kefraya's young reds are a local favourite.) And if you want to take some back home with you, the duty-free shop at Beirut airport has a fine selection, from the cheapest plonk to the most expensive vintages. ❑

RIGHT: produce of the Kefraya vineyard, Lebanon.

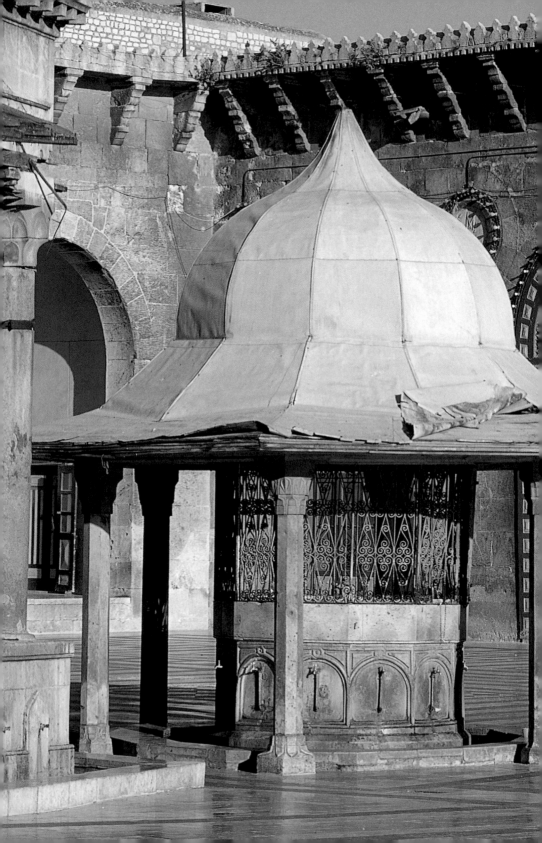

SYRIA

*A detailed guide to the entire country, with principal sites
clearly cross-referenced by number to the maps*

U nlike Lebanon, which is perfectly suited to gentle, day-long
excursions by hired car, Syria is a place for detailed exploration. Shielded from the outside world by the late President
Hafez al-Assad for so many years, it has only recently dropped its
veil, and travel here still has an exciting edge lacking in many other
countries of the Arab world.

A whirlwind tour should include Damascus and Aleppo, the two
great caravan cities of the Middle Ages; the fabulous desert oasis of
Palmyra, one of the most impressive classical sites in the world; and
a sampling of the great Arab and Crusader castles, such as Crac des
Chevaliers, guarding the country's western flank. But to confine
your tour to these highlights and not experience the grandeur of
Syria's landscapes, the semi-wild settings of its many other classical
sites, or life in cities such as Hama is to miss out on the full experience. Little visited by tourists, these are often the best places in
which to tune into the country's soul.

The geography of Syria is easy to grasp. In the south, near the border with Jordan, lies the brooding Haurun, littered with the black basalt
boulders spilled from Mount Bashan of the biblical *Psalms*; running
north just to the west is the castle-dotted Jabal al Nusayriya which
plunges sharply to the coast; in the northeast the Eurphrates snakes
through the mounds of ancient cities in the desolate Jazirah; and flowing through the centre on a north–south course, dividing the desert
from the sown, is the Orontes, on which is set the gracious town of
Hama with its medieval waterwheels and pleasure gardens. The Great
Syrian Desert runs east into Iraq, punctuated by palm oases, Bedu
encampments and remote classical remains, including Palmyra.

Any journey here follows in illustrious footsteps, such as those of
Rameses II, Alexander the Great, St Paul and Saladin, and Syria's
placenames resonate with history. Pondering on the clash of the
Hittites and Egyptians at the Battle of Kadesh, St Paul's conversion
on the road to Damascus or Lawrence's spying missions during
World War I is made all the more thrilling by the refreshing lack of
commercial development. ❑

PRECEDING PAGES: homes of Damascus; *norias*, water wheels at Hama, Syria;
the Omayyad Mosque, Aleppo.
LEFT: welcome to Palmyra.

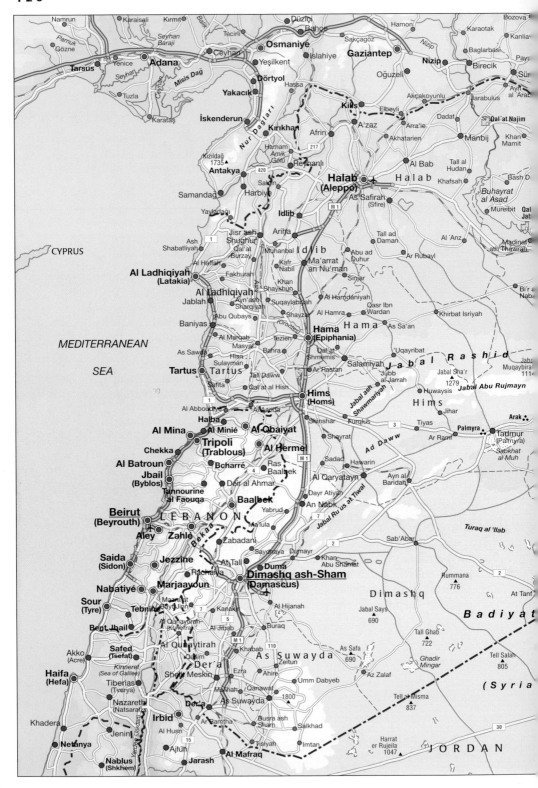

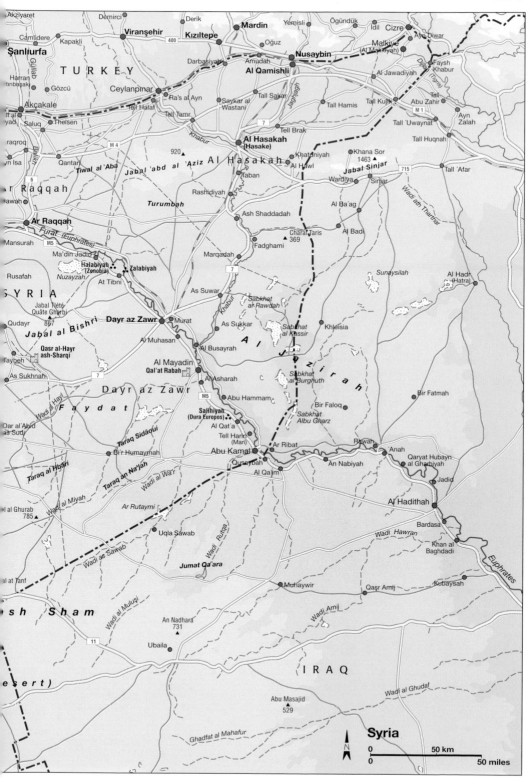

Akziyaret
Demirci
Derik
Mardin
Yemisli
Ögündük
Idil
Cizre
Çamlidere
Kapakli
Viranşehir
Kızıltepe
Oğuz
Ayn Diwar
Şanlıurfa
400
Darbasiyah
Amudah
Nusaybin
Malkiye
(Al Malikiyah)
Faysh
Khabur
T U R K E Y
Al Qamishli
Al Jawadiyah
Tall
Abu Zahir
Harran
Gözcü
Ceylanpınar
Ra's al Ayn
Saykar al
Wastani
Tall Sakar
Tall Hamis
Tall Kujik
M 1
tinbaşakı
Akçakale
Tell Halaf
Tall Tamr
Ayn
Zalah
Saluq
Theisen
7
Tell Brak
Tall 'Uwaynat
raqroq
Qantari
M 4
Al Hasakah
(Hasake)
Khatuniyah
Khana Sor
1463 ▲
Tall 'Afar
n Isa
Tiwal al 'Aba
Jabal 'abd al 'Aziz Al Hasakah
Al Hawl
Jabal Sinjar
715
r Raqqah
920 ▲
Taban
Wardiya
Sinjar
awah
Turumbah
Rashidiyah
Ash Shaddadah
Al Ba'ag
Wadi ath Tharthar
Ar Raqqah
Charaf Jaris
369
Al Badi
Al Hadr
(Hatra)
Furat (Euphrates)
Fadghami
Mansurah
M5
Ma'din Jadid
Marqadah
Sunaysilah
Halabiyah
(Zenobia)
Zalabiyah
7
Nuzayzah
At Tibni
As Suwar
S Y R I A
Jabal Tlété
Quâte Gharbi
897 ▲
Khabur
*Sabkhat
ar Rawdah*
Qudayr
Dayr az Zawr
Murat
As Sukkar
Khleisia
Bir Fatmah
Jabal al Bishri
Al Muhasan
Al Busayrah
Qasr al-Hayr
ash-Sharqi
Al Mayadin
*Sabkhat
al Kassir*
Taybeh
Qal'at Rabah
As Sukhnah
7
Al Asharah
*Sabkhat
al Burghuth*
Dayr az Zawr
M5
Abu Hammam
Bir Faloq
Bir Fatmah
Faydat
Salhiyah
(Dura Europos)
Al Qat'a
*Sabkhat
Albu Gharz*
Dar al'Abid
as Sud
Taraq Sidaoui
Tell Harin
(Mari)
Ar Ribat
Rawah
'Anah
Bi'r Humaymah
Abu Kamal
Qusaybah
An Nabiyah
Qaryat Hubayn
al Gharbiyah
Taraq al Hbari
Taraq an Na'jah
Al Qa'im
Jadid
Wadi al Miyah
Wadi al Hayl
Wadi al Wa'r
Al Hadithah
l al Ghurab
785 ▲
Ar Rutaymi
Bardasa
Khan al
Baghdadi
Wadi Hawran
at Tanf
Uqla Sawab
Wadi as Sawab
Kubaysah
Jumat Qa'ara
Wadi Amij
Muhaywir
Qasr Amij
Euphrates
sh Sham
An Nadhara
731 ▲
11
Ubaila
I R A Q
Wadi al Ghudaf
esert)
Abu Masajid
529
Syria
N
0 ___ 50 km
0 ___ 50 miles
Ghadfat al Mahafur

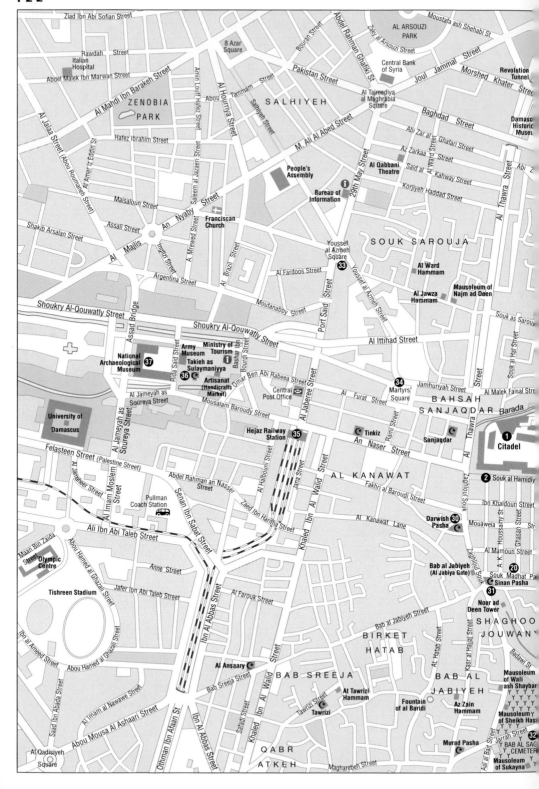

Ziad Ibn Abi Sofian Street

8 Azar Square

Rawdah Italian Hospital

Abdel Malek Ibn Marwan Street

Abou Tammam Street

Boukan Street

Pakistan Street

Moustafa ash Shehabi St

AL ARSOUZI PARK

Zaki al Arsouzi Street

Central Bank of Syria

Joul Jammal Street

Morshed Khater Street

Revolution Tunnel

AL MAHDI IBN ZENOBIA PARK

Al Mahdi Ibn Barakeh Street

Abdel Rahman Ghafiki St

Al Taireediya al Maghrabia Square

Baghdad Street

Damasc Historic Muse

Hafez Ibrahim Street

Amin Louf Hafez Street

Saleem al Jazaeri Street

M. Ali Al Abed Street

Abi Zar al Ghafari Street

Az Zarkaa Street

Said al Kahway Street

Al Thawra

Abi Z

SALHIYEH

Maisaloun Street

People's Assembly

Al Qabbani Theatre

Korjiyeh Haddad Street

Assali Street

Bureau of Information

SOUK SAROUJA

An Nyably

Franciscan Church

Youssef al Azmeh Square

Al Ward Hammam

Mausoleum of Najm ad Deen

Argentina Street

Al Fardoos Street

Youssef al Azmeh Street

Al Jawza Hammam

Shoukry Al-Qouwatly Street

Moutanabby Street

Port Said Street

Souk as Sarou

Assad Bridge

Shoukry Al-Qouwatly Street

Al Ittihad Street

National Archaeological Museum

37

Army Museum

Ministry of Tourism

Takieh as Sulaymaniyya

36

Artisanat (Handicrafts Market)

Central Post Office

Omar Ben Abi Rabeea Street

Al Jaberee Street

Al Furat Street

Martyrs' Square

34

Jamhuriyah Street

Al Malek Faisal Stre

BAHSAH

Al Jameyah as Soureya Street

Mousalam Baroudy Street

SANJAQDAR

Barada

University of Damascus

Hejaz Railway Station

35

Tinkiz

An Naser Street

Sanjaqdar

Citadel

1

Felasteen Street (Palestine Street)

Abdel Rahman an Nasser Street

Jana Street

AL KANAWAT

Fakhri al Baroudi Street

Souk al Hamidiy

2

Pullman Coach Station

Ali Ibn Abi Taleb Street

Al Kanawat Lane

Darwish Pasha

30

Ibn Khaldoun Street

Mouaweia Str

Maan Bin Zaida Street

Olympic Centre

Anne Street

Jafer Ibn Abi Taleb Street

Al Kanawat Lane

Al Mamoun Street

Bab al Jabiyeh (Al Jabiya Gate)

20

Souk Madhat P

Tishreen Stadium

Al Farouk Street

Sinan Pasha

31

Nour ad Deen Tower

SHAGHOO JOUWAN

BIRKET HATAB

Bab al Jabiyeh Street

Al Ansaary

Bab Sreeja Street

BAB SREEJA

At Tawrizi Hammam

BAB AL JABIYEH

Mausoleum of Wali ash Shaybar

Tawrizi Street

Tawrizi

Fountain of al Baridi

Az Zain Hammam

Mausoleum of Sheikh Hass

QABR ATKEH

Magharebeh Street

Murad Pasha

BAB AL SAC CEMETERY

32

Mausoleum of Sukayna

Mohamad al Boukhari Street

ila al Akheliya Street

MASJID
AL AQSAAB

Abdullah Ibn az Zoubair Street

Abdel Kareem al Khatabi Street

Abbasyyeen
Square

Morshed Khater Street

Abou Khalil al Kabbani Street

Al Mazniii Street

Halab Street

Al Akhtal Street

Ibn Koutaiba Street

Mausoleum
of Dahdaah

Ash Shaer Al Kourawi St

Al Kanawat Street

AL KASSAA

Ghafari Street

Ibn Zohar St

Zarkaa Street

AL DAHDAAH
CEMETERY

Baghdad Street

Al Farouk

Ibn Koutaiba Street

Souleiman Kredi St

Marcel Karame Street

George Khouri
Square

Okaibeh Street

Omaw Street

Al Kazzazen Street

At Tahrir
Square

Al Firdaus

Abdel Kasem Street

Fouad Saleem Street

Al Akhtal Street

Nahhasin

Badri al

At Katheeb

Naseef Bahra Street

Ibn al Bitar Street

OUKAIBEH

AMARA
BARRANIYAH

Al Rassam Street

Jawad Anzour Street

Gibran Khalil Gibran Street

Al Manama Street

Church of
the Cross

Manakh Street

Souk as Sarouja

Al Malek Faisal Street

al Faraj
of Deliverance)

Bardabak

Al Jawza
Mausoleum

As Sultan Hammam

Aqsab

BAB
AS SALAAM

Boutros al Boustani Street

Bab al Faradis
(Gate of the Orchards)

Bab as Salaam
(Gate of Peace)

AL JOURAH

Adeeb Izhak St

Al Kassaa Street

8

AMARA
JOUWANIYEH

Al Jourah Street

Madrasa
al Adiliyeh

6 Madrasa
az Zahiriyeh

7 Sayyida Ruqqiyeh

Hammam
Silsila

Madrasa Badraiya

AL QAYMARIYEH

Bab Touma
(Thomas's Gate)

10

Salah ad Deen's
Mausoleum

4 Madrasa Jaqmaqiya
5 (Museum of Epigraphy)

Bakri Street

As Satih
AyyuhTower

Reslan

Remains of the
emple of Jupiter

Propyleum

3 Umayyad

Al Qaymariyeh Street

Al Azaryeh

n al Jumrok

seum of
b Science
Medicine

BAB
AL BARID

9 Fatiyyeh

AL KHARAB

BAB TOUMA

Madrasa
Nuriya

17 Khan al Harir

14

11

Azem Palace
(Museum of
Popular Tradition)

Chapel of
St Ananias

27

Mahkama
Street

15 Madrasa
Abdullah
al-Azem Pasha

12

Dar el Hadith of Tinghiz

Maktab
Anbar

Al Maryam
(St Mary)

23

Khan al
Khayyatin

16

Hammam Nour ad Deen

21

Khan
Sulayman
Pasha

13

Khan Assad
Pasha

19 Bab Sharqi Street
(Street Called Straight)

Bab al Kanise
(Roman Arch)

24

Bab Sharqi Street

Bab Sharqi
(Eastern Gate)

26

adariya
drasa

MAZANET
ASH SHAHM

Beit Sibai

22 Beit Nizam

Dahdah
House

25

AL MIDAN

Ibn Assaker Street

Mausoleum
of Kaab

Al Ghouta Road

Bab as Saghir

Badawi Street

Badri al Kharat Street

Al Amin Street

Al Amin St

St Paul's Chapel

28

Bab Kisan

Ibn Assaker Street

Jarrah Street

SHAGHOOR
BARRANY

Shaghoor Street

Shaghoor Street

Hasan al Kharat
Square

Damascus

0   200 m
0   200 yds

DAMASCUS

*Associated with luxury and refinement since the Middle Ages,
the old city of Damascus fulfils every fantasy about the sensual east.
Its new city, on the other hand, is a vital modern capital*

Map
on pages
122–123

Damascus (Dimashq ash-Sham) competes with Aleppo, Jericho and a few other cities in the area for the title of the world's oldest continuously-inhabited city, but there is no disputing its antiquity. The American writer Mark Twain was hardly exaggerating when he wrote that Damascus "has seen all that has ever occurred on earth." Yet because people have always lived here, it has proved impossible to carry out any extensive excavations to verify the city's exact origins. The reasons for its existence are easier to find, for this is where the Barada River runs down from the Anti-Lebanon Mountains and greens the desert – Damascus is, in effect, an oasis.

Although there is evidence of settlement at least in the 4th millennium BC, and claims for earlier settlement, the name Dimashqa first appears in 2500 BC. The oasis was occupied by Amorites early in the 2nd millennium BC, came under Egyptian influence some 500 years later, and was subsequently taken by Arameans, Assyrians, the Chaldean king Nebuchadnezzar and Alexander the Great's general Parmenion. During the 700 years of Roman rule, it emerged as a significant city-state with a major temple at its centre, strong walls and an aqueduct to bring water from the mountains. Almost all of that, beyond the basic layout of the Old City, lies under your feet or in the city's museum.

LEFT:
courtyard of the
Umayyad Mosque.
BELOW:
an overview.

The modern city

Damascus has long outgrown its Roman walls and the historic centre is no larger than a navel in the urban body. Most of the city was built in the 20th century to meet the demands of one of the world's highest population growths that has driven the total number of inhabitants of the Damascus region up to 2¾ million of Syria's total population of 17 million. Where wood, stone and ceramics came to characterise the Damascus of old, concrete is the material of this newer city. The Damascus you see as you drive in, its houses without courtyards, its apartment blocks, multi-lane flyovers, advertising hoardings and industrial belt of small-scale businesses, is a city that took off in the 1950s.

Although some of this newer development – Sali-hiyeh and the other districts on the slope of Jabal Kassion, for instance – is well worth a visit, the most enchanting part of Damascus remains the old city with its many reminders of the glory years of the Arab empires, the madrasas and *khans*, intricate Damascene palaces, narrow souk lanes and, at the heart of it all, the grand 7th-century Umayyad Mosque, the most obvious – though by no means the only – link between the city's present and ancient past.

Most Islamic monuments and many old city shops are closed on Fridays. For much of the day the old city is quiet, providing a rare opportunity to wander

around and enjoy architectural details which otherwise are lost in the hubbub of the souks. Another good time for a stroll, perhaps en route to the Café al-Naw-farah *(see page 132)* is the early evening when the Umayyad Mosque is lit up.

THE OLD CITY

The most obvious starting point for a tour of the old city is the impressive **Citadel ❶** set in the city walls. A military base even before the Romans conquered Syria, the Romans developed it into a *castrum*. Although there are still stones from the Roman tower in the walls of the northeast tower, what remains is mostly 13th-century or later. The current citadel was built in 1079 by the Seljuk king Alsezin Adek and then enlarged in 1202 by Saladin's brother, the Ayubbid ruler al-Malik al-Adil, to strengthen the city against Crusader and Mongol attacks. The first Mongol invasion destroyed most of the fortifications, which were carefully rebuilt by the Mamluke Sultan Baybars between 1260–77.

In 1400, the Mongols returned under Tamerlane and again did not leave much of the citadel standing. The Ottomans used what was left as a military base, which the current regime used as a prison until 1985, when a massive restoration operation was undertaken.

Damascus citadel was built on flat ground rather than on a mound, which makes it less impressive than its counterpart in Aleppo. Its deep moat, once filled with water from the Barada River, has now disappeared. Its true grandeur lies in its interior, but unfortunately this remains closed to the public. The citadel is more or less rectangular in shape, 220 metres (720 ft) by 150 metres (490 ft), and is protected by 12 surviving towers. A heavily-restored tower on the western facade, visible from al-Thawra Street, gives an idea of

This "Holy" Damascus, this "earthly paradise" of the Prophet, so fair to the eyes that he dared not trust himself to tarry in her blissful shades – she is a city of hidden palaces, of copses, and gardens, and fountains, and bubbling streams.

— A. W. KINGLAKE
Eothen (1835)

BELOW:
statue of Saladin
near the Citadel.

the imposing Ayubbid architecture, using large rough-cut limestone blocks with fine machicolations and arrow slits. The large metal statue in the street outside the central entrance represents Saladin.

Just south of the citadel is the main entrance to the souks, the **Souk al Hamidiyah** ❷ which follows the main axis of the Roman city and leads straight to the Umayyad Mosque, built on the site of the great Temple of Jupiter/Haddad. The present 500-metre-long cobbled thoroughfare dates back only to the late 19th century, when it was widened and straightened by the governor Rashid Nasha Pasha. The corrugated iron roof was provided by the Ottoman Sultan Abdulhamid II, who gave it his name. The holes in the roof, which now create an interesting pattern of light and shade, were made in 1925 by French machine-guns. This souk appears to be more tourist-oriented than most, as well as being the main centre for black market money-changers, but late in the afternoon it is crowded with Damascenes buying fabrics, casual clothing and household goods.

The souk ends rather dramatically with the remnants of the *Propylaeum* (monumental gateway) to the 3rd-century AD Roman Temple of Jupiter, which gives way to a pleasant open square and a full view of the western wall of the Umayyad Mosque. To the left are a few arches of a Byzantine arcade which linked the outer and inner enclosure of the temple, now occupied by Qur'an sellers.

Umayyad Mosque

Tourists enter the **Umayyad Mosque** ❸ (daily from sunrise–sunset, except during Friday prayers 12.30–2pm; modest clothing covering arms and legs required, women must wear black-hooded cloaks, available at the entrance)

Maps:
City 122
Plan 128

TIP

No villager leaves the city without tasting Bakdash's famous *mahleya*, a rich milky cream with pistachios and almonds (winter only) or their delicious ice-creams rolled in broken pistachios. (Souk al-Hamidiyah; 8am–8.30pm).

BELOW: the Citadel's mighty walls.

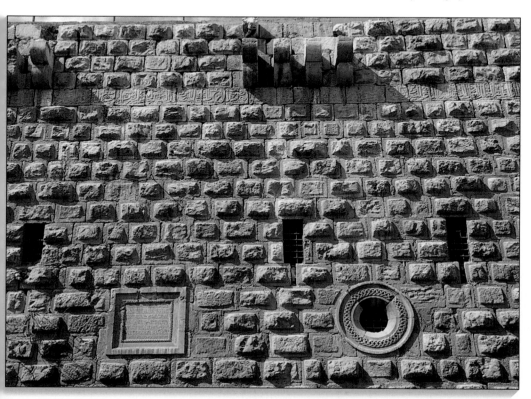

The arcade in the inner courtyard of the Umayyad Mosque.

from the ticket booth, to the left of the Bab al-Barid. Children can be seen chasing pigeons in the courtyard, women chatting away, hiding from the blazing sun, while men come and go from the souks for prayers or an afternoon nap.

The atmosphere in the mosque may be lively and relaxed, but this is one of the most sacred places in the Islamic world. The site has been an important religious cult centre for millennia. In the 10th century BC, Arameans built a temple dedicated to Haddad, the god of rain, storm and fertility, and his consort Atargatis. The Romans later identified these gods as Jupiter and Venus, and enlarged the temple. The present-day mosque more or less covers the inner enclosure (*temenos*) of the Temple of Jupiter, which would have been surrounded by a vast outer enclosure entered by four gateways. The Byzantines converted the temple into a Christian church during the 4th century AD and in the 7th century, in the early years after the Arab conquest, it was shared by both Christians and Muslims: Christians held their services in the western half of the building while the Muslims built a *mihrab* (prayer niche) in the eastern wall.

Khaled Al-Walid, who became the Umayyad caliph in 705, decided to put an end this co-operation and to expand the mosque into the church. He offered the Christians of Damascus several other sites in the city for them to build a new church, but they refused, warning him: "Our Holy Book says that anyone who destroys our church will die of strangulation." Al-Walid is reported to have answered: "If this is so, I shall be the first to destroy it", and then started to tear down the walls himself.

BELOW RIGHT: walking through the courtyard.

Al-Walid had his eye on posterity; the new mosque took nine years to complete, its construction costs consuming the empire's entire budget for seven years. When receipts were brought to him, carried on the backs of 18 camels,

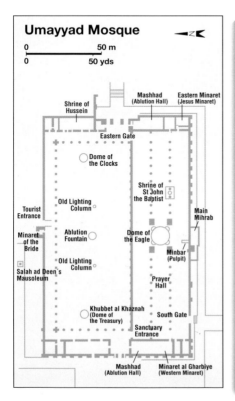

Umayyad Mosque

0   50 m
0   50 yds

Shrine of Hussein

Mashhad (Ablution Hall)

Eastern Minaret (Jesus Minaret)

Eastern Gate

Dome of the Clocks

Shrine of St John the Baptist

Old Lighting Column

Tourist Entrance

Main Mihrab

Minaret of the Bride

Ablution Fountain

Dome of the Eagle

Old Lighting Column

Minbar (Pulpit)

Salah ad Deen's Mausoleum

Prayer Hall

Khubbet al Khaznah (Dome of the Treasury)

South Gate

Sanctuary Entrance

Mashhad (Ablution Hall)

Minaret al Gharbiye (Western Minaret)

the caliph burned them without looking, because the mosque was built for Allah. The Great Mosque was one of the grandest Islamic monuments of that period. Over the centuries, the mosque suffered serious damage from invasions, earthquakes and fires and the splendour and beauty of the original mosque undoubtedly suffered. But in spite of many restorations and modifications, the mosque still inspires awe and wonder.

Maps:
City 122
Plan 128

Inside the mosque

Entering the marble-paved courtyard (50 metres/164 ft by 122 metres/400 ft) through the northern Bab al-Amara, you are immediately confronted by the magnificent central transept on the outer facade of the prayer hall. The superb golden mosaics may have been heavily restored – only the darker patches are original – but they still give an idea of what the mosque must have looked like when all the walls were completely covered with mosaics.

At the centre of the courtyard is an **ablution fountain**, flanked by columns with recently added metal globes. The **Khubbet al-Khaznah** (Dome of the Treasury), at the western end, is a rare domed octagonal structure, covered in mosaics, supported by eight fine Corinthian columns. The similar but smaller and undecorated structure at the eastern end of the courtyard is known as the **Dome of the Clocks**, having formerly housed the mosque's collection of clocks.

The courtyard is flanked on three sides by an **arcade**; the east and west sides still feature the original round columns interspaced with polychrome square pillars, but most of the columns on the northern side were replaced by heavy square pillars some time after the mosque was built. On the inner side of the western arcade is one of the highlights of the mosque, a stunning mosaic com-

The Umayyad Mosque in Damascus is regarded by some to be the fourth holiest place in Islam after Mecca, Medina and the Dome of the Rock in Jerusalem. The other contender for the title is Kairouan in Tunisia.

BELOW: detail from the Dome of the Treasury.

monly known as the **Barada panel**, depicting luxurious villas and palaces set in lush vegetation on the banks of a river, thought to represent either the Barada River in Umayyad times or possibly Paradise.

A door in the northeastern corner leads to the **Shrine of Hussein**, said to contain the head of the Shi'ite martyr Hussein, who was killed in the Battle of Kerbala. Despite the fact that several other places dispute the claim, including the Mosque of Hussein in Cairo, the shrine attracts large numbers of Shi'ite pilgrims. The courtyard is overlooked by three minarets.

Muslims believe that on the Day of Judgement Christ will descend from heaven and stand on top of the Eastern Minaret, also known as the Jesus Minaret, and slay the antichrist.

The main minaret, on the northern side, is known as the **Minaret of the Bride**, its name referring to the claim that a merchant's daughter, married to the caliph, paid for its construction. The upper part dates from a 12th-century restoration. The elegant **Minaret al-Gharbiye** (Western Minaret) in the southwestern corner is architecturally more interesting, being one of al-Walid's original towers, topped by a minaret built by the Mamluke Sultan Qaytbey in 1488. The tallest of the three is the **Eastern Minaret**, built in 1247, though the top was added during the Ottoman period.

The mosque's entire southern side is occupied by a vast **prayer hall** (136 metres/446 ft by 137 metres/446 ft) composed of three crossed naves and a crossed central nave which connects the *mihrab* with the courtyard. The central transept is topped by the impressive **Dome of the Eagle**, resting on four massive pillars and decorated with the names of the first four caliphs. It is thought that the dome and the transept represented the head and body of an eagle, while the prayer hall formed its wings. Beside the central *minbar* and *mihrab*, for the Shafi school, three other *mihrabs* are dedicated to the three other Sunni Islamic law schools, the Hanbalites, Hanafites and Malikites. The Malikite Mihrab in the

BELOW:
the Shrine of St John the Baptist.

eastern wall, erected when the Arabs first arrived in Damascus, is known as **as-Sahabat** (The Companions of the Prophet). Believers flock daily to the Ottoman **Shrine of St John the Baptist**, said to contain the saint's head, its hair and skin intact, found underground when Al-Walid's workers built the mosque. The prayer hall's original sumptuous decoration was damaged by fire in 1893, but the Ottoman renovations are still impressive with more than 70 coloured glass windows, polychrome marble decorations and a stained ceiling.

Madrasas and Mausolea

Beyond the mosque's Bab al-Amara is **Salah ad-Deen's Mausoleum** ❹ (daily 10am–5pm, same admission ticket as the mosque). Although Saladin was obviously buried in a prime location, his tomb reflects his lifestyle and is unassuming. Most of the Madrasa Aziziye in which Saladin's tomb was originally housed has disappeared, but the German Kaiser Wilhelm II, who passed through Damascus in 1898 on his way to the Holy Land, had the tomb chamber and tomb restored out of admiration for Saladin and in honour of the reigning Ottoman Sultan Abdulhamid II. The 19th-century sarcophagus is in white marble, while the original carved wood box stands crumbling beside it.

On the left, down from the Bab al-Amara, the **Madrasa Jaqmaqiya** ❺ houses a small Museum of Epigraphy (Al-Kallaseh al-Sadiriyeh; daily 9am–noon, Fri 9–11am). The Mamluke *madrasa,* built in 1418–20 by the governor Jaqmaq al-Argunsawi, has an impressive entrance and a wonderful polychrome marble *mihrab* with inlaid mother-of-pearl. The poorly-displayed collection of carved inscriptions and illuminated texts attempts to explain the development and diversity of Arabic writing.

Maps:
City 122
Plan 128

Like Christ, John the Baptist is holy to Islam as well as Christianity. He is revered as a prophet who foretold the coming of Christ.

BELOW:
Saladin's Tomb.

A left turn on Al-Kallaseh al-Sadiriyeh follows the northern wall of the mosque. Immediately beyond the little square is **Madrasa az Zahiriyeh** ❻ (Sat–Thurs 8am–5pm, or ask the guardian to open). Originally built as Bayt Akiki, the house in which Saladin's father Ayoub lived, the Madrasa az Zahiriyeh was converted by the Mamluke Baybars' son into a Qur'an school and mausoleum for his father. The black and yellow stone entrance is stunning, with fine marble inscriptions and a half-dome with cascading arches and shells. Beyond lies a small courtyard and the building which today is used as the National Library. The domed tomb chamber containing the tombs of Baybars and his son Mohammed Said is elaborately decorated with polychrome marble panels, a wide band of gold mosaic (similar in style to the Umayyad mosque) and an elegant *mihrab*.

Opposite is the 12th-century **Madrasa al Adiliyeh**, converted in 1218 into a mausoleum for Saladin's brother, Sultan al-Adil Saif ad-Din. The *madrasa* which now houses part of the National Library has a less impressive entrance than its neighbour and a simple unadorned tomb chamber to the left.

Returning along the same street past the Madrasa Jaqmaqiya and Hammam Silsila, head left towards the Bab al-Faradis. After all those fine medieval buildings, the glimmering modern **Mosque of Sayyida Ruqqiyeh** ❼ comes as a surprise. It was built in 1985 on the site of an older shrine to Sayyida Ruqqiyeh, daughter of the great Shi'ite martyr Hussein, who died in AD 680. The mosque clearly reflects Iranian tastes, with its generous use of marble and its onion dome, and it is unlike anything else in the neighbourhood. The place is particularly popular during the late afternoon when Shi'ites, mostly from Iran, come to pray. Of the 12th-century Ayubbid **Bab al Faradis** ❽ (Gate of the Orchards,

BELOW: doorway in the Madrasa az-Zahiriyeh.
RIGHT: enjoying a *narguileh* in Café al-Nawfarah.

also confusingly known as the Bab el-Amara) only the outer doorway and an arch of the inner doorway survives.

East of the Umayyad Mosque

Steps outside the eastern gate of the Umayyad mosque, known as the **Bab el-Nawfarah** or Gate of the Fountain, lead down to the ever popular **Café al-Nawfarah** with a high-ceilinged well-trodden interior and a terrace where you can watch people passing as you enjoy a coffee and *nargeileh* (water-pipe). Opposite is the slightly more expensive **Café al-Sham** in the former Hammam Nawfarah.

Further along the Badr ad-Din Street, lined with small antique and carpet shops, are the half-buried remains of the **Triple Gateway**, the eastern entrance to the outer compound of the Temple of Jupiter. Beyond it to the right is the elegant **Fatiyyeh Mosque ❾** (Qaymariyeh Street, daily at prayer times), built in 1742 by the Ottoman official and poet Fathy Effendi, with an interesting polychrome marble facade and a well-proportioned interior. Qaymariyeh street leads into the Christian quarter of Bab Touma. **Bab Touma ❿** (Thomas's Gate), the gate which gives its name to the quarter, is a 13th-century reconstruction of the Roman Gate of Venus.

South of the Umayyad Mosque

From the southwestern corner of the Umayyad Mosque, the Souk as-Silah (weapons market), now largely taken over by gold and jewellery shops, leads to the grand **Azem Palace ⓫**, home of the **Museum of Popular Tradition** (summer Wed–Sun 9am–5.30pm, in winter 9am–3.30pm, Fri closed noon–2pm in

Map on pages 122–123

TIP

For a vivid taste of old Damascus, visit Café al Nawfarah after evening prayer (around 7 or 8pm) when, on many evenings, a storyteller sings an episode from old Arab tales about love and bravery while men smoke or play backgammon.

BELOW: the Azem Palace.

Damascene houses look uninviting from the outside, but impressions change as soon as you enter the garden courtyard. The noise of the old city's streets suddenly seems far away and life takes on a slower rhythm. High-ceilinged rooms around the courtyard are usually lavishly decorated with inlaid and painted woodwork, as well as polychrome marble stone work.

BELOW: Hammam Nour ad-Deen.

summer, 11am–1pm in winter). This magnificent palace was erected in 1749 for Assad Pasha al-Azem, the governor of Damascus. An excellent example of Arab-Ottoman domestic architecture, it is divided into two separate parts, the *salamlek* or public part of the palace and the *haremlek* with the private family quarters. Most of the museum is housed in the latter, centred around a wonderful courtyard filled with fruit trees, jasmine creepers, fountains and bird song, evocative of the sumptuous life style of 18th-century Damascenes. The rooms are opulently decorated with painted and carved wood and filled with the museum's collection of crafts, household goods, costumes and fine 18th- and 19th-century furniture.

Coming out of the palace, turn left into the **Souk al Bzouriah** ⑫, the central market for spices and sweets. Pistachios, sugared chick-peas and pretty candied fruits are popular, but look out as well for the colourful *zuhurat,* a mixture of flowers including rose and camomile, boiled and drunk as infusions, and *za'atar*, a mixture of sesame seeds, ground cumin, oregano and sumac, delicious on pizza or bread. The first *khan* on the left, **Khan al Sawaf**, with more confectionery shops, has lost a lot of its character. Further to the left is one of the oldest *hammams* (bath houses) in Damascus, the **Hammam Nour ad Deen** or **Hammam al-Bzouriah** (daily 8am–midnight, for men only), founded in 1154 by Nour ad-Deen to generate funds for his nearby *madrasa*. The domed Ottoman-period reception room is particularly fine, with polychrome marble and a soothing fountain. On the same Souq al-Bzouriah, left again, the **Khan Assad Pasha** ⑬ is by far the most impressive of the old city *khans*. Built in 1752, by the same governor who built the Azem Palace, its massive central dome has now collapsed. Eight other side domes create an immense sense of space. The ground

LETTING OFF STEAM

There is a popular saying in Damascus that "a bath is the bliss of life" and although private bathrooms have become more common, particularly in the cities, the public bath, or *hammam*, retains its social significance. As a traditional part of wedding celebrations, for instance, the bride's mother invites all the women from both families for a hot bath and a meal before the wedding. For men, as in Roman times, the *hammam* is a social centre. Most baths are mainly reserved for men, although some hours or days may be dedicated to women. Spending a few hours being washed, massaged or steamed is a wonderfully relaxing experience.

The best *hammams* in Damascus are **Hammam Nour ad-Deen** (Souk Bzouriah, tel: 222 9513; daily from 8am–midnight, men only), **Hammam al-Khanji** (Souk Sarouja next to the Historical Museum; tel: 231 4192; a group of women can reserve the space in advance) and **Bakri Hammam** (near Bab Touma; tel:542 6606; men only, but a group of women can reserve the pleasant space). In Aleppo try the beautifully restored 14th-century **Hammam Yalbogha** (south of the Citadel; tel: 623 154; daily 9am–midnight, women on Mon, Thurs, Sat from 9am–5pm) for the full experience.

floor housed 23 warehouses, while the upper floor, reached by two sets of stairs, had more than 40 rooms looking down over the central courtyard with its polygon-shaped fountain. The overall effect is dramatic, accentuated by the black-and-white striped stonework of the walls. The *khan* is currently under restoration, with rumours that it will be turned into a craft or cultural centre. On the other side of the same street, the badly ruined 17th-century **Khan al Amud** is still used as a warehouse. Towards the end of the street, near Straight Street, are herbalists' shops stuffed with remedies for everyday illnesses, as well as jars with fox tails, dried lizards, tortoise shells and other supposed aids to sexual potency, home-made skin creams, love potions and *bukhur* (incense).

Wandering in the souks

Back at the Azem Palace, leave Souk al Bzouriah to the left and continue straight along A. Mounif Osmane Aidi Street (also known as Mouaweia Street). On the left-hand side is another remarkable *madrasa*, the **Madrasa Abdullah al-Azem Pasha ⑭**, built in 1779 by the governor Abdullah al-Azem, descendant of the man who built the Azem Palace. The *madrasa* is now signposted as the **Azem Ecole** and houses a tourist-oriented antiques and traditional crafts shop; the proprietors claim that their traditional hand-loom is the last one still weaving typical Damascene brocade. Even if you do not intend to buy anything, the small open courtyard surrounded by a two-storey arcade is worth a look and there are excellent views over the Umayyad Mosque from the roof. Back on the street, turn left and left again at the crossroads into Souq al-Khayyatin (Tailors' Market) where every possible item of haberdashery is sold, from glittery (mostly polyester) fabrics and colourful ribbons to buttons, sequins, fabric flow-

Map on pages 122–123

The fabulous Khan Assad Pasha has been fully restored. See also the painting on page 47.

BELOW: the coffee hour approaches.

ers and some of the world's most kitsch lingerie. To the right, the long stone wall belongs to the **Madrasa Nuriya** ⓯, last resting place of the great Arab ruler Nur ad-Deen, whose tomb is visible from the street through the window to the left of the entrance. The *madrasa* was founded in 1172, but only the front of the building and the mausoleum are original; the courtyard is surrounded by two modern mosques. The *iwans* from the mausoleum disappeared during restorations, but the honeycombed dome and marble cenotaph are intact.

Continuing along the same street, on the left hand side is the 16th-century Ottoman **Khan al Khayyatin** ⓰, its twin domes collapsed, but with a fine entrance of black and yellow striped stonework and elegant Arabic inscriptions. The *khan* now houses embroidery sellers and more fabric shops.

Return to the crossroads near the Azem Ecole, looking out for remnants of a Roman gateway which once led to the Temple of Jupiter, and follow Souk al-Hayyatin northwards. To the right is the beautiful entrance to the large 16th-century Ottoman **Khan al Harir** ⓱ (Silk Market) and about 30 metres/yards further to the left down a stone passage is the smaller 19th-century **Khan al Zafaranjiye**. The small souk more or less opposite this *khan* was once the changing room for the 16th-century **Hammam al Qishani**. Covered with six huge domes and entered by a striped gateway to the left is the L-shaped **Khan al-Jumrok** (Customs Khan), built in 1608 by Murat Pasha and now, like the rest of the area, occupied by fabric shops.

A medieval hospital

Returning south to the crossroads at Azem Ecole, turn right on A. Mounif Osmane Aidi Street, then take the second street to the right to the **Bimaristan**

Textiles have always been important to Damascus, which was particularly famous for its fine silks. The English word damask (silk or linen with a pattern woven into it) is derived from Damascus.

BELOW: verses from the Qur'an and religious literature on sale in Souk al-Miskiyeh, near the Umayyad Mosque.

Nour ad-Deen, which since 1978 has been used as the **Museum of Arab Science and Medicine**  (Wed–Mon 9am–2pm, Fri 9am–noon; closed for restoration at the time of writing). This remarkable hospital and medical college was founded in 1154 by Nour ad-Deen – tradition has it that he built it with crusader ransom money – and functioned as a hospital until the 19th century. The building was restored and expanded in the 13th century by the famous physician Badr ad-Deen, and again in the 18th century. The Bimaristan attracted the most capable physicians, who provided free medical care for rich and poor. The outer doorway is framed by a honeycombed semi-dome and a lintel recycled from a Roman building, while the original doors are inlaid with copper pins arranged in geometrical motifs. The entrance hall with the ticket booth has a spectacular honeycombed domed ceiling, flanked by semi-domes decorated with a cascade of stalactites and more honeycombs. An Arabic inscription runs around the room. The main courtyard has a pool with fountain, fruit trees and flowers and a large *iwan* or hall on every side. The museum's medical displays – astrolabes, mortars, 18th-century medical manuscripts, sponges, an anaesthetic solution of opium, hashish and belladonna, bottles with medical herbs and talismans – suggest that Arab physicians took a broad approach to healing.

The Street called Straight (Bab Sharqi Street)

Following the same street southwards leads to the **Street Called Straight** . This has been one of the city's main east–west thoroughfares since Roman times, when it was known as the Via Recta. Lined with shops and stalls, very much like the colonnaded streets discovered in Apamia and Palmyra, the Roman street was four times wider than the current one. The grand columns have long

Map on pages 122–123

Damascus is a faire city and full of good merchandise...In that city also dwell many physicians.

– JOHN MANDEVILLE
The Book of John Mandeville, 1360

BELOW: souvenirs of Damascus.

Keffiyas *(head-scarves for men) piled high in Souk Madhat Pasha.*

BELOW: detail, Maktab Anbar.

gone but this is still a bustling commercial axis in the old city, lined with many *khans*, shops and workshops. At its western end the street is known as **Souk Madhat Pasha ⓴**, its shops catering to villagers and Bedu by selling saddle bags, tent rugs, *keffiyas (see margin picture)* and *abayas* (big woollen cloaks). Some 200 metres/yards down the souk on the left hand side, the late 16th-century **Khan al Zait** was once an olive oil depot, and is now a pleasant courtyard in the shade of eucalyptus and orange trees.

A little further, again to the left, is the Mamluke **Khan Jaqmaq** of 1418 and across the street, through a striped entrance way, the 18th-century Ottoman **Khan Sulayman Pasha ㉑** is a wonderfully atmospheric place where the collapsed twin domes now frame the sky. Mouthwatering aromas come from coffee sellers at the crossing with Souk al-Bzouriah. Beyond, the street changes into **Bab Sharqi Street**. Take the second street to the right, at a black-and-white striped minaret; 100 metres/yards down, on the left, is the 18th-century Ottoman **Beit Nizam ㉒** (Naseef Pasha Street 42; Sat–Thurs 9am–2pm; knock on the door and the guardian will open) which served as the British Consulate during the 19th century. The house has three courtyards, the innermost one for the men being the most beautiful, with an *iwan* in black, white and yellow stripes. The richly decorated interiors are in typical Ottoman style.

Continuing down Straight Street, the next street to the left has (on the right) another splendid 18th-century Ottoman house, **Maktab Anbar ㉓** (courtyards Sat–Thurs), built by a Jewish merchant and now housing the offices for the restoration and preservation of the old city of Damascus. The first court is large and simple in decoration, but the next courtyard is more intimate and has been beautifully restored. From this point, Straight Street runs through what used to

be the **Jewish quarter** (Haret al Yahud), with the **Roman Arch** (Bab al Kanise) **㉔** vaguely marking the beginning of the Christian quarter. The arch was probably part of a triple arch, marking a major intersection on the *decumanus.* It was found below ground level during the French Mandate, buried under many layers of debris, and now stands somewhat forlornly in a patch of green by the side of the road. Just before the arch, turn right and then right again, following signposts for **Dahdah House ㉕** (usually open 10am–1pm and 4.30–6pm, ring the bell and the old man may open the door if he is in a good mood). This particularly beautiful 18th-century house, lavishly decorated in the typical Syrian-Ottoman style, has a peaceful courtyard with fountain and perfumed trees and an outstanding *iwan.* Beyond the arch, to the left, the church of **St Mary** (Al Maryam), the patriarchate of the Greek Orthodox Church, is thought to have been built over one of the city's oldest Byzantine churches.

Straight Street continues to the heavily restored **Bab Sharqi ㉖** (Eastern Gate), the Roman Gate of the Sun. This is the only gate in Damascus to follow the original Roman ground plan, with a triple passageway and two arcades leading out of the two outer ones. It was through Bab Sharqi that the Arab conqueror al-Walid entered the city in 636.

In the footsteps of St Paul

On the left just before Bab Sharqi, narrow, picturesque St Ananias Street is lined with antiques and crafts shops and a few old houses converted into restaurants or bars. A little way down, on the right, take a look into the elegant courtyard of **Nassam's Palace**, which has a small shop selling top-quality, hand-made silk brocade. At the end of the street steps lead down to the atmospheric Byzan-

Map on pages 122–123

The street called Straight is straighter than a corkscrew, but not as straight as a rainbow.

– MARK TWAIN
The Innocents Abroad
(1869)

LEFT: carrying lutes on the Street called Straight.
RIGHT: Bab Sharqi.

Insignia on the Chapel of St Ananias, one of the first followers of St Paul.

tine **Chapel of St Ananias** ㉗ (Wed–Mon 9am–1pm and 4.30–6pm), formerly known as the Church of the Holy Cross, built over the house of Ananias. Cartoon-like paintings in the right transept tell the story of how Ananias became one of the first followers of St Paul, after he was struck blind during his enlightenment on the road to Damascus. Returning to Bab Sharqi, turn right along the main road outside the city wall and take the entrance to the left of the next gate (Bab Kisan) to reach **St Paul's Chapel** ㉘. The modern chapel built against the 14th-century Mamluke gate incorporates some Roman stone blocks, but merits a visit more for symbolic than aesthetic reasons, for this, according to legend, was where Saul, later St Paul, was lowered from the walls in a basket whilst escaping from the Jews (The Acts of the Apostles, 9: 26).

Outside the city walls

Start at the Thawra bridge and walk west into Souk as-Sarouja, a pleasant tree-shaded street with a meat and vegetable market. Immediately to the left, before Hammam Khanji, the **Historical Museum of Damascus** ㉙ (No. 223 [no sign], open 8am–2pm, closed Fri) occupies the palace of former prime minister Khaled al-Azem. An unassuming gate leads into courtyards and public areas now housing offices; the museum occupies the more intimate *haremlek* at the back. Exhibits are rather dusty and badly labelled, but the house's decoration and furniture are magnificent and well preserved. Further along the street is the unusual **Tawba Mosque** (Mosque of Repentance), its name stemming from the fact that it was formerly a *khan* used as a brothel, its courtyard reminiscent of the Umayyad Mosque. On Thawra Street, walk south *past* the entrance to Souk a Hamidiyah. To the right is the 16th-century **Darwish Pasha Mosque** ㉚ with black and white stonework, a wonderfully worn wooden door and beautiful blue Damascene tiles covering the facade and the interior of the prayer hall. A small octagonal structure contains the tomb of Darwish Pasha, who built the mosque.

BELOW:
inside the Chapel of St Ananias.

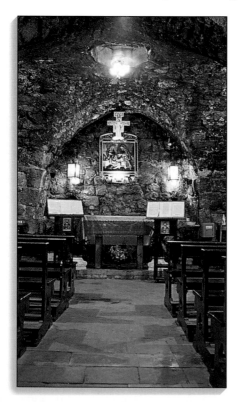

Just past the junction with Straight Street, on the left, is the **Sinan Pasha Mosque** ㉛, built in 1590 not by the famous Ottoman architect of the Takiyyah as-Sulaymaniyya, but by a governor of the same name. There are panels of Damascene tiling in the tree-shaded courtyard and a slender minaret, remarkable for its green-enamelled brick work.

Beyond the Sinan Pasha Mosque, Midan Street splits in two. The right-hand fork leads to the quarter known as **Midan**, its name a reminder that in the Middle Ages this was an exercise field (Midan al Akhdar). Later it was an area of souks, housing and schools for pilgrims as the caravan to Mecca assembled nearby. The area is riddled with mosques, *madrasas* and mausoleums, now squeezed between modern apartment blocks. Bear left into the covered **Souk Sinaniye**, where sheepskins and wool are sold. To the right is the **Al Ajami Mosque**, a rare cruciform *madrasa* and tomb, built in 1348 in memory of Afridun al-Ajami, a Persian merchant.

At the junction with al-Badawi Street lies the twin-domed, 14th-century **Mausoleum of Sayf ad Deen Bahadur al Mansuri** and, further along Midan Street to the left, the **Mausoleum of Sheikh Hassan**. After passing this mausoleum, take the first street to the left (al-Jarrah Street) and find, 150 metres/yards down on the left, the main entrance to the vast **Cemetery of Bab al Saghir ㉜**, covering both sides of this street. This cemetery contains many famous tombs. Among important places of pilgrimage for Shi'ites are the **Tomb of Fatima**, the Prophet Muhammad's favourite daughter and wife of Ali, the **Tomb of Sukayna**, great-grand-daughter of the Prophet and daughter of Hussein, the **Tombs of Umm Habiba and Umm Salama**, wives of the Prophet and the **Tomb of al Walid bin Abdul Malik**, the Umayyad Caliph who built the Great Mosque *(see pages 127–131)*.

THE NEW CITY

The main modern shopping areas are around **Place Youssef al Azmeh ㉝**, near the Cham Palace Hotel. In the late afternoon, the wealthier Damascenes can be seen strolling down the pedestrian end of Salihiyeh Street where shops selling casual clothes are interspersed with many jewellers. From the square, walk southwest on Youssef al-Azmeh Street and take the first street to the left, Souk as-Sarouja. This is the most atmospheric part of the modern centre, many of its narrow streets covered by vines, lined with old houses with balconies full of flowers, cobblers, bird shops and crumbling mausoleums. Just before the Thawra Bridge, turn right into the alley with the as-Saada Hotel, and cross over into a pleasant fruit and vegetable market.

Walk through the market in between modern office and apartment blocks coming to a dusty bird market where you turn right on Sharia Shohada towards **Place Marjeh ㉞** (Martyrs' Square). This messy square was the place to hang

Map on pages 122–123

TIP

Off Place Marjeh are some of the city's best pastry shops, selling mounds of Oriental pastries stuffed with pistachios.

BELOW: religious paraphernalia on sale in the Christian Quarter.

The interior of the Hejaz Railway Station. One of the old carriages left on the Damascus station platform has become a bar, popular with railway enthusiasts and young Damascenes.

BELOW: Takieh as-Sulaymaniyya.

out in 19th-century Damascus, but characterless apartment blocks now make it look rather shabby. The square's name refers to the victims of French bombardments in 1945, while the bizarre statue in the middle commemorates the first telegraph link between Damascus and Medina.

Walk southwest on Furat Street and then left on Said al-Jaberee Street to what was once another grand square, Saahat Hejaz (Hejaz Square), dominated by the **Hejaz Railway Station** ❸ *(see page 147)*. Return north along Said al-Jaberee Street and take a left on Barada Street. Continue along one of the city's main roads, Shoukry al-Qouwatly Street, following the tiny, rubbish-strewn Barada River, now a far cry from the river represented on the golden mosaics in the Great Mosque. Cross over the busy road and turn left into the street just before the Ministry of Tourism information office. An arch on the right, half way down, leads to a pedestrian street lined with crafts shops. Off here, to the left, is a small *madrasa* built by Selim II, now an Artisanat (closed Fri), an attractive handicrafts market with workshops. The **Selimiye Madrasa** is, in fact, a later addition to the main compound of the **Takieh as-Sulaymaniyya** ❸, reached from the entrance at the end of the pedestrian street. This grand mosque was built between 1554 and 1560 for Sultan Sulayman I, "the Magnificent", by his genius architect Sinan Pasha. The *takieh* (Hostel for Sufis) mixes typical Syrian black and white stonework and honeycombed domes with Turkish high domes and pencil-thin minarets. The compound was intended as an alternative departure point for the Mecca caravan and surrounding the courtyard are rooms for Mecca-bound pilgrims. The lovely gardens are now filled with battered aircraft and military equipment, part of the Army Museum (Wed–Mon 8am–2pm, closed on Tues) which now occupies the hostel.

The national treasure trove

From the Army Museum, turn right on Rida Said Street, and left along the river to find the entrance to the **National Archaeological Museum** ❿ (Shoukry al-Qouwatly Street; Wed–Mon 9am–4pm in winter, 9am–6pm in summer, closed all day Tues and Fri from 12.30–2pm). This is Syria's most outstanding museum, with world-class collections covering more than 11,000 years of history. Seeing the important and spectacular artefacts on display here will give an insight into the country's main archaeological sites.

Map on pages 122–123

Roman statuette of Venus on display.

BELOW: Roman sarcophagus.

The museum entrance is fronted by the facade of the Umayyad desert palace of Qasr al-Hayr al-Gharbi. The main hall is often used for temporary exhibitions, sometimes the new finds of European-Syrian missions. To the left, in the east wing, are the Classical and Byzantine collections, to the right, in the west wing, Arab-Islamic arts and Oriental antiquities, and upstairs a small collection of prehistoric artefacts as well as the rather dull modern art gallery. The first room in the east wing has interesting **mosaics from Shahba**, and in the next room is a finely sculpted 3rd-century AD **Roman sarcophagus** with a symbolic representation of the Trojan War. Busts of beautiful women adorn the **Palmyra Room**, as well as a mosaic of Cassiopia, who reveals herself, convinced she is the most beautiful of all. In the basement the early 2nd-century **Yarhai Hypogeum** came from the Valley of the Tombs at Palmyra, clearly illustrating the tradition of underground tombs for larger families. The **Synagogue of Dura Europos** is one of the museum highlights, its wonderfully-preserved frescoes found under rubble in 1931. The synagogue was built in 246 AD, just 10 years before Dura Europos was destroyed by the Persians, and its frescoes illustrate scenes from the Old Testament. As Jews rarely represented animals or humans,

A replica of a 13th-century BC stone tablet from Ugarit.

it is thought that they were influenced by Christian or pagan cults which dominated the city at the time. The sculptures in the Oriental Antiquities section are no less surprising. The **Ugarit Room** has some extremely fine ivory sculptures, delicate jewellery and 14th-century BC cuneiform tablets from the Court of Ugarit. Mari was at the height of its civilisation around 2350 BC, and the statues of big-eyed men with *konakas* (wool skirts) staring at eternity are hauntingly impressive. The Arab Section's **Manuscript Room** has some extremely rare manuscripts including a work by Ibn Sina, known in the west as Avicenna, whose *Canon Medicine* was significant in the development of modern medicine. The garden, littered with statues and architectural fragments, has a pleasant tree-shaded café.

Salihiyeh district

On the lower slopes of Mount Kassion, above the fashionable residential areas of Abou Romaneh and Malki, is the picturesque quarter of **Salihiyeh** or Mohi ad-Deen. The area was first settled around 1156 when Nur ad-Deen used it to house the first wave of Hanbalite refugees from Palestine fleeing crusader persecution. Nur ad-Deen who wanted to keep the Hanbalites separate from the Shafi school which ruled in Damascus, opened a new academy for them, known as the Omarieh School. The once barren area was watered by a canal fed by the Barada and Yazid rivers and soon turned into a flourishing place where rich townspeople built mausoleums, schools, bath houses and mosques. Many intellectuals, Mohi ad-Deen among them, were drawn to the academies in the area.

Take a taxi to Midan Al-Afif near the French embassy, walk uphill and take Madares Assad ad-Deen Street to the right at the end of the square. This street

LEFT: festooned with wires, flags and vines.
RIGHT: tea-time in the market.

contains most of the area's monuments. Do not be surprised if people offer you a little something to eat as this is in honour of the rich Andalusian Mohi ad Deen who ordered that after his death a daily meal should be offered to the poor. A little way along on the right is the 13th-century **Mausoleum of al Faranti**, and the 13th-century **Madrasa Murshidiya**, commemorating an Ayubbid princess, whose minaret is the only one in Damascus surviving from that period. To the left is the 14th-century **Mausoleum of Takritiya**, opposite which is the minaret of the **mosque-madrasa Atabikiya**.

Further to the left of the T-junction is the 13th-century **Madrasa Charkassiyeh**, but take the turning to the right. Immediately on your right is a gateway leading to the **Jami al Jadid** (New Mosque) and the lavishly decorated **Turba Khatuniye**, the mausoleum of Ismat ad-Deen Khatun, Nur ad-Deen's wife. Further to the right is the **Maristan Al Qaimari**, built in 1248 by the Emir Sayf ad-Deen Qaimari, whose mausoleum is on the other side of the street. The maristan follows the earlier plan of Nur ad-Deen's bimaristan in Damascus. Next, on the left, is the 16th-century **Imaret of Sulayman**, built by the famous Ottoman architect Sinan for the great Sultan Sulayman, to provide food for the poor and for pilgrims who visited the nearby tomb of al-Arabi. It is now used as a bakery.

Immediately to the right is the area's most important monument – the **Mosque and Mausoleum of Sheikh Mohyi ad Deen Ibn al Arabi**. The tomb of the famous 13th-century Sufi mystic (1165–1240) sits behind a silver grille in the basement of the mosque built by Sultan Selim in 1518. His two sons were also buried here, as well as his Egyptian son-in-law and Abd al-Kader, an Algerian patriot exiled to Damascus by the French in 1830. The mausoleum is still a centre for sufis and the tomb sees a continuous flow of women praying for fertility.

Map on pages 122–123

TIP

Most of the monuments in this area are closed to the public, but it is possible to admire their beautiful facades and enjoy the lively market area and tree-shaded streets.

BELOW: city in motion.

Map on pages 122–123

👁 TIP

There is no public transport to the top of Jabal Kassion, so a taxi is necessary. Discuss the price before starting, ensuring it includes waiting time and return to the centre.

BELOW: taking time out from the city centre.

Mount Kassion

Overlooking and protecting Damascus to the northwest is the bare and rocky **Jabal Kassion** (Qasyion). It rises 1,200 metres (3,900 ft) above sea level but only 600 metres (1,960 ft) above the city, whose houses seem to creep higher up its slopes every day. Its name probably derives from the Arabic word *qasw* meaning harshness or hardness, perhaps because the ground was so hard that no vegetation would grow on it. There are many legends attached to the mountain, which is considered sacred. Apparently, Adam stayed at Beit Abyat (House of Houses) at the foot of the mountain near **Turba Badrieh** and Cain slew his brother Abel nearby. The savage crime, the first on earth, so appalled nature that the ground opened to devour the murderer, thus forming the **Arbaeen Cave**, one of the mountain's many caves. The angels consoled Adam in the nearby **Gabriel Cave**. The Virgin Mary and Jesus stayed with her mother Hannah at a place called **Nayrab** near Rabweh.

On the eastern slopes just outside the village of **Barzeh**, a mosque has been built over a cave believed to be the place where Abraham was born. The popular saying 'Between Barzeh and Arzeh on the west lie buried forty thousand prophets' may be a slight exaggeration but the mountain's slopes are certainly dotted with holy shrines. It was from Kassion's summit that the Prophet Mohammed made his decision not to enter Damascus lest he would forfeit Heaven by having experienced paradise on earth.

There are several welcoming cafés on the summit of Jabal Kassion offering extensive views, cooler air and cold drinks in summer, and it is well worth coming here to escape the city's heat and dust. The views are best at sunset or at night, when the city lights twinkle. ❑

The Hejaz Railway

In May 1900, on the 25th anniversary of his accession to the Ottoman throne, Sultan Abdulhamid II announced the creation of two commissions for the construction of a railway line and telegraph link between Damascus and Mecca. The Sultan, a spiritual as well as a temporal leader, hoped that the line would ease the journey for the many pilgrims who made the annual *Haj* to Mecca. Before the line was built, pilgrims had to choose between travelling overland by caravan, which took up to 50 days and carried the risk of attack by Bedu, or else sailing to Jeddah across the Red Sea, on a voyage that lasted up to 20 days. The 1,600-km (1,000-mile) rail journey, on the other hand, was expected to take less than three days.

The Sultan also announced that the railway would be financed and run by Muslims. The job of one of the two committees appointed in 1900 was to collect funds for construction, which it did successfully and no foreign bank loans were taken out. But the hope that the line would be a purely Muslim undertaking, with everything from materials to manpower coming from Muslim lands, was misguided. In the end the rolling stock, rails and tyres were brought from Europe and the German engineer Heinrich Meissner was given responsibility for construction, with 26 of the other 43 engineers also coming from Europe.

By 1903 the line opened from Damascus to Amman and a year later it had reached Ma'an in southern Jordan, though it wasn't until 1908 that it reached Medina in Saudi Arabia. A Damascus–Medina service operated three times a week, with connections via Damascus and Aleppo to Istanbul and Europe as well as towards the Iraqi border, and via Haifa to Egypt and the Sudan. The Sultan never saw his dream fulfilled for he was deposed by the Young Turks in 1909 and after his departure, opposition by Bedouin tribes, who had lost the revenue they used to collect for allowing caravans safe passage, and by several religious leaders ensured that the line was never completed to Mecca.

Sultan Abdulhamid had also had a political motive for the construction. The Ottoman military had had great difficulty in controlling the rebellious Yemeni Imam Yahya in 1898 and the Wahhabi tribe of Arabia, with whom the Ottomans had fought bitterly in the early 19th century for control of the Holy Places, were once again threatening the Sultan's authority. The railway would make it possible to move troops into the area at speed. After the beginning of hostilities in 1914, the railway was put under the control of the Turkish military and was used to transport both Turkish and German troops. The British military was determined to disrupt services and a series of attacks on the line in the Ma'an area by T. E. Lawrence, Sherif Hussein and the Arab army was a prelude to the defeat of the Turks in the region.

After the war, there were reports of service being resumed. But Saudi opposition to the railway put an end to that, and the only service now in operation is a steam train that ambles from Damascus to Amman and back once a week.   ❏

RIGHT: an old steam train put to new use as a bar at the Hejaz Railway Station.

AROUND DAMASCUS

Old descriptions of Damascus portray a paradisal setting of orchards and bubbling streams. This rural idyll can still be sampled on day outings into the surrounding region

Map on page 152

Damascus

There are several options for escaping **Damascus ❶** (Dimashq ash Sham) for a day or an overnight to visit places with spectacular scenery and of historical or religious significance. The Barada, the river that created the oasis of Damascus, flows from a source northwest of the city and a journey up its valley is one of Damascenes' favourite outings – the road and scenic railway are both very busy on weekends and holidays. Elsewhere, in the hills due north of the city, there are several sites of great importance to Christianity, with early shrines and where the language spoken at the time of Jesus is preserved. Further east, at the beginning of the road to the desert city of Palmyra, the Roman remains of Dumeir continue to fascinate archaeologists and visitors alike.

Wadi Barada

The Barada River flows out of the Anti-Lebanon Mountains down a steep and narrow valley. One of the most unusual ways of seeing it is to take the small, Swiss-built steam train from the Hejaz Station in Damascus. The train visits all the major villages as far as Zabadani (and occasionally Sirghaya). In principle (not always in practice) there is a service up the line every Friday and Sunday morning, returning to Damascus late afternoon. The train taking some four hours to reach Sirghaya. In summer, there

PRECEDING PAGES: Deir Mar Taqla, Ma'lula. **LEFT:** summoned by bells, Saydnaya. **BELOW:** on Zar Zar Lake, Suq Wadi Barada.

should also be a daily service to **Ain al-Fijeh**, a village 22 km (14 miles) from the city, its name referring to the spring *(ain)* which now supplies the city with much of its clean water. This is the first main stop up the valley and there are several restaurants situated down near the river.

Suq Wadi Barada ❷, 6 km (4 miles) further up, is a small agricultural town of historical importance. It was built on the Hellenic settlement of Abila, one of the ancient *decapolis* (federation of 10 cities) of which Damascus and several cities in Jordan were also members. There is little of Abila to be seen in the Souq, although some ancient building materials have been reused, but 1.5 km (1 mile) out of town are the remains of the Roman road from Baalbek to Damascus and of Roman graves cut into the hillside. Legend has it that Abila took its name from Abel, who was buried here by his murdering brother Cain. The site, on the summit of Tell (Nabi) Abel, is marked by a Druze shrine. To visit any of these places requires a scramble up the rocks and over some perilous ledges.

Zabadani ❸, another 14 km (9 miles) up the valley, is one of the most popular day-trip and weekend retreats for middle-class Damascenes, particularly in summer when the city can be stifling. A considerable amount of construction has taken place here in recent years. The street running through the centre of town

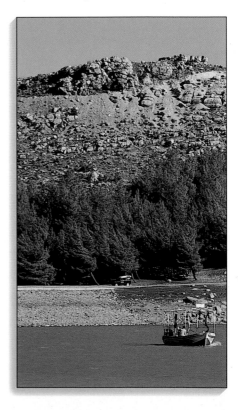

contains most of its shops and restaurants, while the older town, in the lower section, is more interesting for a walk. **Bludan** ❹ is 7 km (4 miles) from Zabadani, off the railway line and 1,400 metres (4,590 ft) above sea level. In winter it offers views across snow-clad Mount Hermon and the Anti-Lebanon Mountains; in spring its valley is filled with fruit blossom; in summer it offers relief from the heat of the plains. Here, too, is one of the sources of the Barada River, clad in concrete like everything else in town, and flowing down to irrigate the valley and provide water for Damascus. With some excellent restaurants, one relatively famous hotel, the Grand, and the homes of several ministers and well-known businessmen, Bludan is the most exclusive of Syria's hill towns.

An Orthodox nun in Saydnaya, the most important place of Christian pilgrimage in the East after Jerusalem.

Northeast of Damascus

The road northeast out of Damascus passes through some of its least picturesque districts before reaching the barren hills that attracted early devotees of Christianity. **Saydnaya** ❺, 26 km (16 miles) from the city, is an unprepossessing town in the middle of a housing boom, but it is also the site of one of the Middle East's most famous pilgrimage shrines – to the crusaders, **Notre Dame de Sardeneye** ranked second only to Jerusalem in terms of sanctity. The object of the pilgrimage, the Greek Orthodox convent and its Chapel of the Virgin, is a place clouded by legend, according to which the chapel's main icon – of the Virgin – was painted by St Luke. Scores of miracles are attributed to the icon. The proof of one of them can be seen on the steps up from the car park: an image of Jesus which apparently appeared after a man had rested his oil jar on that spot (the image is now preserved behind bars).

BELOW: Bludan, the most exclusive of Syria's hill towns.

It is difficult to make sense of the convent's jumble of architecture, but it is

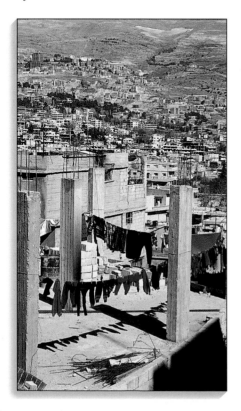

believed to have been founded during the 6th-century reign of Justinian. The inner chapel is a dark recess behind the main church, its altar hung with many lamps, icons and votive offerings for miracles and cures. The miracle-working icon is hidden behind a silver screen. The shrine is popular with Christian and Muslim pilgrims, especially during the Feast of Our Lady (8 September). Saydnaya contains several other shrines and churches, old tombs and the caves of hermits. A 2nd-century rock-cut tomb, above the first bend in the road leading from the convent car park, is a reminder of the site's enduring popularity. Coming down from the convent, to the right at the first roundabout, the Church of St Peter is housed in another ancient tomb, a cube of large masonry.

What Saydnaya lacks in terms of atmosphere and setting, **Ma'lula** ⑥ has in abundance. A charming village set against the austere rocks at the edge of the Qallamun Mountains, some 26 km (16 miles) from Saydnaya, Ma'lula was first settled in prehistoric times. During the early Christian era, its caves provided sanctuary for persecuted Christians. One of the village's most revered sites is the tomb of an early Christian martyr, St Taqla (Thekla), contained within a convent dedicated to her, **Deir Mar Taqla** (daily), situated just above the village. Legend tells of a Seleucid princess, a pupil of St Paul, persecuted by her father for her faith, who, thanks to prayer, found refuge in the cliffs. The convent is believed to be of Byzantine origin, but is of no architectural interest. The cave above the convent, venerated as the saint's tomb, is hung with silver lamps, votive offerings and icons – the saint is portrayed with a cross in her right hand and a document in her left.

More interesting is Ma'lula's other significant shrine, **Deir Mar Sarkis** (daily), the monastery of St Sarkis (also known as Sergius), most appropriately

Map on page 152

The nuns at Deir Mar Taqla exercise strict control over behaviour. Even the crossing of legs in the main church is frowned upon.

BELOW: view towards the snow-capped Anti-Lebanon from Bludan

THE GHOUTA

The name is Arabic, meaning a place where water collects between two mountains. The Ghouta was the garden of Damascus, fed by several sources, including the Barada River, which here provided the final flourish of its 80-km (50-mile) run from near Bludan *(see opposite)*. It was in the Ghouta that the Prophet Mohammed's comment that Damascus was a paradise on earth rang true. In the 10th century, the chronicler Al Muhallabi wrote of it: "In Damascus one finds a large number of colours of roses. Some are of bright yellow, others black, others are marbled red, or the distinguished rose *(muwajjah)* with petals in two colours, one on the inside, one on the outside. In no other country does one find as many flowers as in the garden of Damascus." No longer. Over the past hundred years, the population of Damascus has grown so much as to threaten the Ghouta, limiting its supply of water, turning its many villages into towns – the current population is well over a million – and encouraging the construction of factories in what was an entirely rural environment. The Ghouta is now at a critical stage and unless steps are taken to curtail further building and to guarantee adequate water supply, it could soon be no more than a concrete suburb and a pleasant memory.

reached by walking the steep path from the village, which passes through the cleft in the rocks for which Ma'lula earned its Aramaic name, "the entrance". Sergius, along with Bacchus, to whom the monastery is also dedicated, was a Roman soldier who served as a court official in the desert town of Ar Rusafah, on the route between the Euphrates and Palmyra. In 305, he was martyred for his faith, refusing even on pain of death to make a sacrifice to Jupiter. When Christianity was permitted just eight years later, following Constantine's conversion to the faith, Sergius became the focus of a popular cult and 200 years later Ar Rusafah had been renamed Sergiopolis and a large basilica been constructed in his honour *(see page 235).*

A Semitic language related to ancient Hebrew, Aramaic was the language Jesus used for his teaching and in which some of the scriptures were written. Although officially replaced by Arabic after the 7th-century Arab invasion, it survived as the lingua franca *of Ma'lula and several other villages, an indicator of the independent spirit of the villagers.*

His cult at Ma'lula has lasted longer – perhaps because of its more convenient location. The small **chapel**, reached through a low entrance, has a dome supported by four piers and a vault over the altar. The chapel is believed to be 4th-century, built on the site of an earlier shrine to Apollo. The central altar, a semi-circular stone table, is pre-Christian – its unusual rim and drainage channel being very similar to pagan sacrificial basins. The left-hand altar appears to have similar pagan origins and a beautiful painted wood canopy above it. The icons here are of interest: Christ the King and the Virgin hang on either side of the altar (19th-century works by Michael the Cretan); on the right-hand pier, Christ on the cross and the last supper (18th-century) while on the left hand pier, from the same period but very different in style, John the Baptist and St Taqla. Ma'lula is most famous, however, as a place where Aramaic, one of the languages current in the area at the time of Jesus, survived. It is now seldom heard outside some villages on the eastern side of the Euphrates.

Yabrud ❼, 19 km (12 miles) from Ma'lula and 8 km (5 miles) from the

BELOW:
Deir Mar Taqla.

main Damascus-Homs highway, is an agricultural town thriving off a small patch of fertile land. Although almost entirely modern in structure, Yabrud sits in the middle of an area that was first settled more than 12,000 years ago. The only building of interest is the **Greek Catholic Cathedral of Constantine and Helen** (daily). The cathedral, near the centre of town in a complex which also includes a school, could be of an early date, though there have been many additions which obscure its age, including the current entrance porch (1929). What is certain is that it was built using material taken from a Roman temple, believed to be that of Jupiter Yarbrudis, a deity of sufficient importance to merit an altar in Rome. The only interest inside the cathedral is a collection of icons kept in the sacristy, said to be of great age and impressive execution, but kept behind a grille and badly lit.

Towards Homs

Heading out of Damascus on the Homs highway and then taking the eastern turn-off towards Palmyra, leads after 43 km (27 miles) to **Dumayr** ❽. Originally the site of a Nabataean shrine to the god Baal on a major trade crossroads, what stands today is essentially a Roman temple of the 3rd century with Arab fortifications. The plan is unusual, having three entrances, a feature that some archaeologists have explained as a reflection of its strategic position; others have seen this as an attempt to satisfy the needs of a local cult, or of the fact that the building started out as a staging post or unusually large triumphal gateway. Whatever its origins, the heavily restored building was functioning as a temple to Zeus Hyposistos by AD 245 and was later used as a fortification by the Arabs, who closed up two of the archways and strengthened the walls. ❑

Map on page 152

TIP

If the gate to Yabrud's Cathedral of Constantine and Helen is locked, you should enquire about access at the school.

BELOW: trusty steed of the road.

SOUTHERN SYRIA

South of Damascus lies a striking landscape of sombre basalt boulders interspersed with fertile agricultural land. It is strewn with ancient sites and is home to the mysterious Druze

Map on page 160

South of the Damascus region the red soils of the Hauran plain stretch towards the border with Jordan, skirting the foothills of the Jabal al-Arab, known until recently as the Jabal Druze, after the principal inhabitants of the region (and also called the Jabal Hauran, or Mount Bashan of the biblical Psalms).In the far west, hard against Lebanon and Israel's Lake Tiberias (the Sea of Galilee), are the infamous Golan Heights, occupied by Israel since 1967, and formally annexed by it in 1981, but possibly seeing a return to Syria in the near future if current peace talks between Syria and Israel bear fruit.

The only town that can be visited on the Golan is the deserted shell of **Al Qunaytirah**, which was razed by Israelis following the Yom Kippur war of 1973, when Israel returned a few small parcels of the Golan. It lies in what is now the buffer zone administered by the United Nations. However, a special permit must first be obtained from the Syrian Ministry of the interior in Damascus. Once in Quneitra, you will be shown around by a member of the Syrian army.

The landscape

The Hauran (classical *Auranitis*) is littered with basalt boulders from the volcanic activity of the Jabal al-Arab. The *jabal* itself is not one but myriad volcanic cones which have spewed out lava in several phases over time. The accumulation of lava is sometimes more than 1,000 metres (3,300 ft) thick and the highest point on the *jabal* is 1,860 metres (6,200 ft). Describing the region in *East to West* in 1958, the author Arnold Toynbee wrote: "Imagine a very huge giant emptying out giant-size sackfuls of big basalt boulders, as a child might empty out paper-bagfuls of monkey nuts. Make the top of the heap rise five or six thousand feet above sea level, and sprinkle the higher altitudes of the boulder dump with dwarf oaks. That is the best notion that I can give you of the Jabal Druze. Here and there the cones of volcanoes stand up in the distance."

In winter the mountain is covered with snow and the higher rainfall catchment provides an important source of water for the Hauran settlements and for artesian basins to the south. Though it is a strange, bare and wild landscape, many sombre black villages dating back to Nabataean and Roman times perch on the edge of the desert to the east. On the eastern slopes, where nothing is grown today, the remains of ancient field systems are evident, attesting to a more populous and vital agricultural society in the past.

The use of black basalt building stone is typical of Hauran architecture. Lack of wood encouraged an idiosyncratic system of construction, whereby beams hewn out of basalt were placed on projecting corbels

PRECEDING PAGES: AND LEFT Bosra's magnificent theatre.
BELOW: Druze elder with characteristic beard and headdress.

to span the roofs, and transverse arches necessary to support them were placed at frequent intervals. Stone was also used for doors and window screens.

From Damascus the road south to the Jordanian border at Der'a (104km/65 miles) is fast and unexceptional. On the way, after some 75 km (47 miles) is the Byzantine church of **Ezra ❶**, dating from AD 515 and containing the purported tomb of St George, an early Christian martyr much revered by Christians in the Middle East *(also see page 197)*.

Der'a ❷, the Syrian border-point with Jordan, may ring bells in the minds of visitors familiar with the life of T. E. Lawrence. It was at Der'a that Lawrence was arrested while on a reconnaissance mission during the Arab Revolt. His account in his *Seven Pillars of Wisdom* of being led captive to the Turkish governor in order to be beaten and raped by his guards is so effusive in its language and detail that some scholars have suggested that the Der'a ordeal contributed to subsequent mental and emotional problems which occasionally made Lawrence suicidal.

One of the most important victories of the Arabs over the Byzantines happened at the Yarmuk River near Der'a in 636. It heralded the end of the Roman/Byzantine empire in the Middle East and the sweeping expansion of Islam.

Busra

East of Der'a lie the most interesting of the region's ancient cities. On the plain some 42 km (27 miles) east is the ancient town of **Busra ❸** (summer 10am–6pm; winter 9am–4pm; admission charge) still inhabited today, although the government is now relocating the population outside the city walls. Settlement dates from the early Bronze Age, but the town rose to pre-eminence in the late 1st century AD when the last king of the Nabataeans, Rabbel II, moved his capital from Petra to Busra, which was better placed to take advantage of changing international trade routes. When the Romans established direct control over

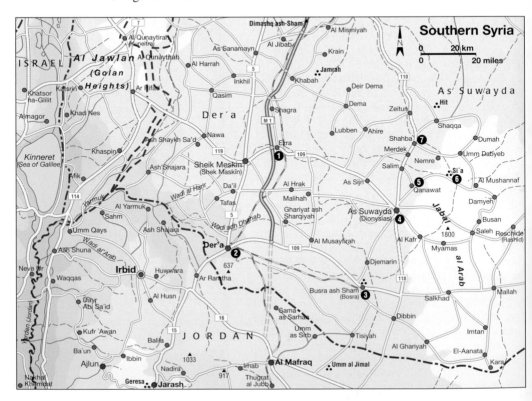

the region, Busra was made capital of the Roman province of Arabia. One can easily spend a whole day wandering through the extensive and well-preserved ruins dating from Nabataean, Roman, Byzantine and Islamic times, needing little imagination to picture the living city.

Map on page 160

The most surprising monument within this rich array is the **Roman Theatre**. Like a pearl within an oyster shell, it is completely hidden from view by the medieval citadel which fortified and surrounded it. Such protection has ensured its preservation as one of the most complete Roman theatres in the world. Clearance and excavation is ongoing, and the most recent discovery of note is an enormous Christian church of a centralised circular form, comparable in size to the great church of Hagia Sophia in Istanbul.

Museums are located in the citadel and in the Hammam Manjak (the restored Mamluke bath house). Other sites include impressive Corinthian columns and the Mosque of Omar. A new luxury hotel has made Busra the most attractive centre for exploring the Hauran and the Jabal.

The main regional centre of **As Suwayda ❹** is 32 km (20 miles) northeast of Busra, on the mid-western flanks of the Jabal al-Arab. The populous modern town has now overrun the classical city of Dionysias, but it does have an excellent regional museum, along the road out to Qanawat. Passing through the town, one is struck by the manner and dress of the local Druze population, where, as Robin Fedden, the author of *Syria and Lebanon*, observes, "even the poorest appear chieftains". A secretive religious minority, the Druze fled the Lebanon mountains in the mid-19th century after conflict with the Christians and sought refuge on the depopulated Jabal. They are noted for their beauty, courage and fiercely independent spirit. The latter has continually brought them into conflict

As Suwayda's excellent museum contains a stunning collection of mosaics, including this one of Aphrodite gazing into a mirror.

BELOW:
farmer at Qanawat.

Ploughing in the rich soil of the Jabal al-Arab. Crops of the region include wheat, chickpeas and barley. Vines are grown around As Suwayda.

BELOW:
cotton is loaded
for despatch.

with authority, as the Turks, the French, and even the modern regime can attest. Many still wear traditional costume and the turbaned men take pride in their magnificent moustaches waxed at the tips. The women wear sweeping patterned dresses bunched into a high waist and with a scooped neckline, striking quite a contrast to typical Arab attire.

A road northeast from As Suwayda leads to Qanawat through rising terrain and the remnants of oak forests which once flourished on the Jabal al-Arab. Perhaps the prettiest area in the Hauran, Qanawat commands expansive views westwards across the plain to Mount Hermon, also known as Jabal al-Shaykh on account of its year-round snow, which is likened to the flowing white beard of a venerable sheikh.

Qanawat ❺ was important from Hellenistic to Byzantine times and retains a charming but scattered collection of ruins. The main complex, the Seraya, is next to the central town square. It was originally a Roman temple and civic complex which was later appropriated to accommodate two Christian basilicas, with the addition of a monastery. Southwest of the town square are the remains of a small Temple of Zeus with a columned portico.

By following the road descending north from the front of the colonnaded courtyard of the Seraya access can be gained to the steep wadi on the right, containing a small theatre (odeon) and a nymphaeum set within a park of pine trees. Just off the road leading back to As Suwayda, in the northwest of the town, is a temple dedicated to the sun-god, Helios.

It is a short, 3-km (2-mile) drive southeast of Qanawat to the hilltop sanctuary of **Si'a ❻**. Set on a narrow ridge, this beautiful site was originally a Semitic "high place", which later, under the Nabataeans and then the Romans, was

embellished with temples and courts. An important place of pilgrimage for both urban and pastoral dwellers, even the Safaitic nomads have left their inscriptions there. The remains of the settlement, fortifications and a large gate spread along the ridge to the east.

Map
on page
160

The extraordinary product of a "local boy makes good" can be found at **Shahba** ❼ (the Roman Philippopolis), 26 km (16 miles) north of Qanawat. When Philip the Arab gained the imperial crown of Rome in AD 244, he decided to glorify his roots (and himself) by creating an Imperial Roman city at his birthplace. Unfortunately his reign was curtailed by his early and violent death and the most important monuments in Shahba can be dated to a few short years from AD 247–249, although a small Christian settlement lasted into the 4th century. Set beside black volcanic cones, the structures and streets that survived the 19th-century influx of Druze settlers are austere but beautifully built. A good little museum houses the best Syrian examples of late Roman (4th-century) mosaics, some of which are still in situ in the private house for which they were made.

Druze newlyweds.
The Druze normally
marry very early in
life – usually in their
mid to late teens.

To the northwest of Shahba lies a bizarre area of land called the Ledja., which is, in fact, a giant island of solid lava. A similar area of land (Safa, situated further to the east) was described by the indefatigable traveller Gertrude Bell as being "like a horrible black nightmare sea, not so much frozen as curdled." And yet the Ledja contains many villages, some still inhabited and with origins dating back to Roman times. From its time as the classical Trachonitis until the early 20th century, the Ledja has been notorious as a lair for brigands. The Romans tried to tame it by building a dual-carriageway across the middle of the lava. This highway is still visible today, and even the central reservation can be identified. ❑

BELOW: mother and child, in typical Druze dress.

THE ORONTES VALLEY AND THE DESERT STEPPE

Map on page 168

The vast desert steppe of Syria is the setting for the fabulous ancient city of Palmyra, while the fertile Orontes Valley offers the riverside cities of Homs and Hama

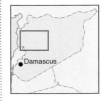

East of Damascus the Great Syrian Desert stretches all the way to Iraq and beyond. Characterised by rock and gravel steppe rather than undulating sand dunes, it is punctuated by a few small concrete settlements, occasional encampments of Bedu and a scattering of ancient remains, from isolated Byzantine churches and forts to Palmyra, one of the richest caravan stations of the ancient world and today one of the chief sights of the Middle East.

In contrast, the Orontes Valley is one of the busiest and most fertile parts of Syria, where sugar beet, cotton, wheat and fruit trees, particularly cherries, flourish. The Orontes River rises in the Bekaa Valley in Lebanon, flows into Syria, then runs north, eventually reaching Antakya (Antioch) in modern-day Turkey. Its unusual north–south course is believed to have earned it the name *Al Asi* in Arabic, meaning "the Rebel", though the explorer Richard Burton thought this to be an allusion to the turbulence of its upper streams.

In Syria, the most important towns along the Orontes are Homs (Hims) (population: 1.6 million) and Hama (population: 1.5 million), Syria's third- and fourth- largest cities respectively. After Hama, the river divides into many small branches as it flows through Al Ghab, a marshy region under the Jabal an Nusayriyah. The valley has been an important channel for the ebb and flow of civilisations, and includes interesting historical sites, among which are the Roman ruins of Apamia, and, near Homs, the site of the Battle of Kadesh, in which the Egyptians fought the Hittites. A more recent war was waged in Hama in 1982, when government forces brutally quashed an uprising organised by the Muslim Brotherhood; an estimated 5,000–10,000 civilians were killed and most of the city was flattened.

Transport in the valley is good. Trains and buses run between Damascus and Aleppo via Homs and Hama. Two fast highways, one from Damascus and another from Homs, strike east through the desert to Palmyra, with buses and microbuses running several times daily from both. There are few sights along either of these routes, though there is a Roman temple at **Dumayr**, north of the road from Damascus.

PRECEDING PAGES: the vast ruins of Palmyra. **LEFT:** classical setting for local life. **BELOW:** the Orontes.

Palm city

The oasis city of **Palmyra ❶** (summer 8am–1pm and 4–6pm, winter 8am–4pm; admission charge) rises like a mirage from the barren waste, 243 km (150 miles) northeast of Damascus. Strings of honey-coloured colonnades interspersed with elegant ruins march across the vast plain, partially enclosed by bare hills to the north and west, with a backdrop of brilliant

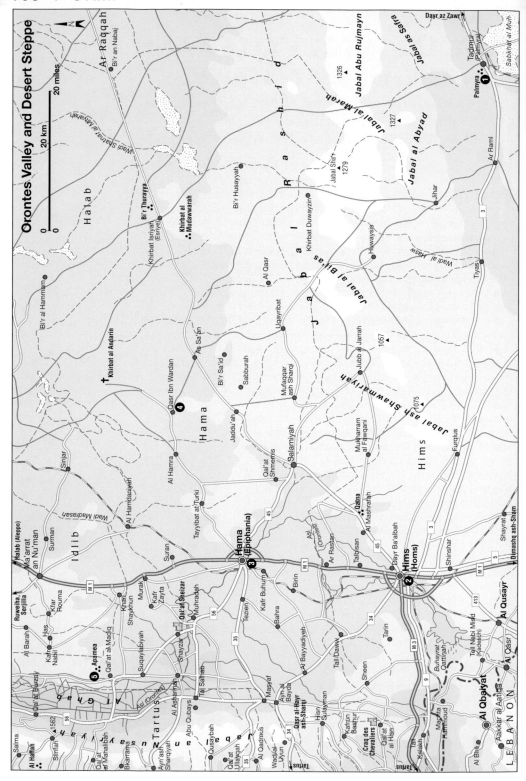

Orontes Valley and Desert Steppe

green from the palms and gardens of the springs to the south and east. As a source of water in the desert, midway between the coast and the Euphrates, Semitic Tadmur, as it was known, has been settled since Neolithic times.

Tadmur is thought to have come under Roman control during the reign of Tiberius, after which it was called "Palmyra", the place of palms, but the Romans allowed the city to carry on fairly independently. As a buffer between Rome and its successive arch-rivals in the east, the Parthians and the Sassanians, Palmyran troops proved to be successful campaigners. With the Roman annexation of the great Nabataean city of Petra in AD 106, coupled with the rise of Antioch as the main centre of Roman power in the east, Palmyra's fortunes soared. Needing a replacement for Petra, which had until then been the pre-eminent caravan station on east–west trade routes, the tribes of the desert organised to provide a safe route for traders, shipping goods up the Euphrates to the caravan city of Dura Europos and cutting the shortest way across the desert to Damascus and the great Levantine trading cities on the Mediterranean coast. The goods, from China and the Arabian Gulf, included aromatics, salt, ivory, pearls, copper, silk and agricultural goods.

By and large, the Palmyrenes were content to concentrate on trade. They benefited from the introduction of Roman knowledge and skills, but retained much of their own culture. In AD 129 Emperor Hadrian visited Palmyra and granted it the right to raise its own taxes. But, in the 3rd century, Roman power in the east faltered against the rising might of the Persian Sassanians, and in 260 a Sassanian army advanced as far as Antioch. Roused by the threat to Palmyra's wealth and status, a Palmyrene, Septimus Odainat, rallied the city's forces and drove the Sassanians out of Syria. But it was his wife, the remarkable Queen Zenobia (267–272), who exerted such power and independence that she took on the might of the Roman Empire itself, capturing Syria, Arabia, Egypt and Anatolia. This was the apogee of the city's fortunes, as the centre of an Arab empire.

However, it was all too brief – in 272 Zenobia was defeated by the Emperor Aurelian. She was taken prisoner and her chief supporters were put to death, including the philosopher Longinus, her political advisor. Zenobia herself was taken to Rome, where she lived out her days in a villa in nearby Tivoli.

Visiting Palmyra

The site is vast but the layout easily visible. From the major complex of the Temple of Bel in the east the main monuments of theatre, baths, agora and other temples are scattered on either side of the impressive main colonnaded street. At the western end lies the military camp of Diocletian, and a further climb up the northwestern hill leads to the later Arab castle of Qal'at Ibn Maan, from where a glorious panorama takes in the full extent of the tower, tombs stretching to the west and the southern cemeteries. The modern town of Tadmor spreads to the east of the site; its museum contains many of the sculptures and objects which adorned the site and the tombs.

Palmyra's largest complex, the **Temple of Bel** Ⓐ has been put to various uses since it was built to the

Maps:
Area 168
Site 170

Ripe dates in autumn. Palmyra means "Place of Palms", after the great palm oasis that surrounds the ruins.

BELOW: view from the Temple of Bel, Palmyra.

pre-eminent god Bel (ruler of the heavens) in the mid-1st century. It was converted into a church in the 5th century, fortified by the Arabs in the 12th, when a *mihrab* (niche indicating the direction of Mecca) was added, and more recently served as an enclosure for the homes of the local population. Excavations have also revealed evidence of earlier places of worship on the site, as far back as the Bronze Age. Inside the vast courtyard, which would have been surrounded by a double tier of Corinthian columns, is the sanctuary (cella), in which statues of Bel and fellow gods Yarhibol (the sun-god) and Aglibol (the moon-god), the Palmyrene triad, would have been worshipped by the priests of the temple. The chambers containing the statues are renowned for their decorated ceilings; the north chamber (where the main three statues were housed) has depictions of the seven planetary gods, with Jupiter in the middle, surrounded by the 12 signs of the zodiac; the ceiling of the smaller, less elaborate south chamber (thought to have housed a portable statue of Bel for use in religious processions) is decorated with rosettes and geometric figures.

Like much of Palmyra, and buildings elsewhere in the Eastern Roman Empire, the style of the cella differs from classical forms. Not only does the building mix the classical orders (Corinthian columns and Ionic columns) but its unusually tall entrance is reminiscent of the temples of Ptolemaic Egypt, and the spiral staircases leading to a flat roof are typically eastern, even today. The peristyle roof would have sat on huge stone cross beams, two of which can be seen outside the cella entrance; their reliefs depict veiled women following a camel carrying a booth, possibly containing the image of a god; Aglibol with a crescent moon on his shoulder and altars laden with offerings.

Also outside the sanctuary is an altar, for making sacrifices, and a pool for

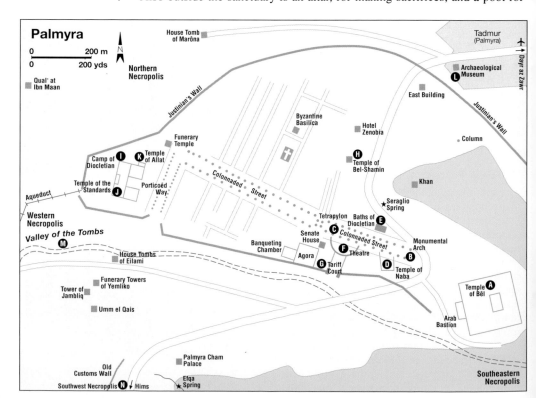

ablutions. Behind the temple complex are the remains of several 3rd-century patrician houses, whose rooms are arranged around central courtyards in typical Roman style, and a **museum of popular culture** (Wed–Mon 9am–1pm, closed Tues; admission charge) with displays of local costumes and crafts and recreations of a traditional Tadmor home and a Bedu tent.

Marking the start of the Cardo Maximus, the great colonnaded street bisecting Palmyra, is the triple-arched **Monumental Arch** ⓑ, though originally the route would have extended right up to the Temple of Bel. Decorated with carvings of acorns, vines and palm trees, it was built during the reign of Septimus Severus (193–211), as was the **Colonnaded Street** ⓒ itself. This impressive thoroughfare was built in several stages, beginning from its far (i.e. western) end. It is 11 metres (36 ft) wide and was flanked by the city's finest shops; the ornamental brackets projecting from the columns would have supported statues of the city's great and good, including its most influential merchants.

The remains of the 1st-century AD **Temple of Naba** ⓓ (the god of destiny) can be seen close to the arch on the south side of the street, and on the north the scant remains of the **Baths of Diocletian** ⓔ, identified by a portico of red granite pillars imported from Aswan in Egypt. Further along, on the south side of the street, is the 2nd-century **Theatre** ⓕ, accessed from a secondary colonnaded street that crosses the Cardo Maximus at this point. Nine tiers of seats have been restored, out of some 30 original rows.

The secondary thoroughfare leads to a gate in the south wall of the city, where merchandise would have been unloaded and inspected. Close by is the so-called **Tariff Court** ⓖ, named after a 5-metre- (16-ft-) long stone inscribed with information relating to the taxing of goods in AD 137, which was discovered in

Maps:
Area 168
Site 170

The ceilings of the chambers in the Temple of Bel were sketched by Robert Wood for his book Ruins of Palmyra, *published in 1753. These archaeological drawings helped Palmyra become something of a cult in Europe, inspiring everything from stage sets and ladies' fans to the ceilings of English mansions.*

BELOW:
Palmyra's Theatre.

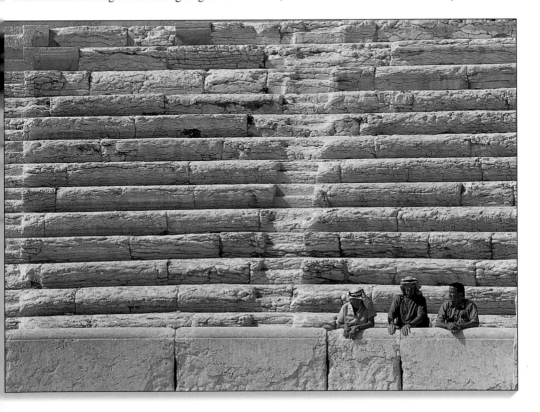

BELOW: richly decorated tomb.

the vicinity during the first excavations of the site, by the Russians, in the early 20th century. Also near here are the **agora** (market place), the supposed **senate** (identified by tiers of seating) and a **banqueting chamber**.

Back on the main colonnaded street, you can't miss the **Tetrapylon**. Consisting of 16 columns of Egyptian granite (only one of which is original; the others are of coloured concrete, erected by Syrian restorers) mounted in groups of four on four pedestals, the Tetrapylon marks a major intersection and also helps disguise a slight bend in the main Colonnaded Street. On the north side of the intersection, look for the well restored **Temple of Bel Shamin ⓗ**. Though dedicated to the Phoenician god of rain, two associated gods were also worshipped here: Aglibol, the moon god (also honoured in the the Temple of Bel) and Malakbel, the god of flocks and the fields. The temple was first built in AD 17 but converted to a church during the Byzantine era.

Beyond the Temple of Baal-Baal-shamin lie the northern walls, built by Diocletian in the early 4th century and reinforced under Justinian in the 6th.

Back at the Tetrapylon the western section of the Colonnaded Street ends at a 2nd-century family mausoleum with a six-column portico, known as the **funerary temple**. From here a street runs south to an oval plaza and the so-called Damascus Gate. To the right of this street as you face south is **Diocletian's Camp ❶**, an area mainly dating from the beginning of the 4th century, by which time Palmyra's trading days were over and its importance lay in its ability to defend the eastern flank of the crumbling Roman Empire. The **Temple of the Standards ❶**, where the legion's standards were housed, can be accessed by a sloping stairway. The camp area also includes the 2nd-century **Temple of Allat ⓚ**, marked by several fluted columns. Allat was identified with Artemis,

the Greek goddess of the hunt. It was here that archaeologists found the statue of a lion with an antelope between its paws, now restored and in the garden of Palmyra's Archaeological Museum *(see margin)*.

Maps:
Area 168
Site 170

Palmyra's tombs

As well as its fine temples and colonnaded streets, Palmyra's other highlight is its cemeteries, the Valley of the Tombs and the Southern Necropolises. It is worth visiting the tombs on a guided tour (some tombs can only be visited by guided tour) which leave four or five times a day from the **Archaeological Museum ❶** (Apr–Sept 8am–1pm and 4–6pm; Oct–Mar 8am–1pm and 2–4pm; Ramadan 8am–3pm; closed Tues) at the entrance to modern Tadmor. The museum contains many of the statues, grave goods, inscriptions and friezes discovered in the tombs, all worth seeing as a prelude to touring the cemeteries.

The desolate-looking **Valley of the Tombs ⓜ**, containing the most impressive of the city's famous tower tombs, stretches for 1km (½ mile) behind Diocletian's Camp. These tombs, some of which are up to five storeys high and can accommodate up to 500 bodies, are among the oldest remains in Palmyra. One of the largest tombs, still containing many of its statues and decoration, is the four-storey-high **Tower Tomb of Elahbel**, belonging to a prominent Palmyrene family, whose generous support of civic works included paying for the Temple of Naba. Built in AD 103, it had room for some 300 bodies, stacked in small chambers one on top of the other, each covered with a stone bearing a carved portrait of its occupant; a few of these reliefs can still be seen.

By the 2nd century, underground burials *(hypogea)* were more common than tower tombs, large complexes, often cross-shaped and accessed by a flight of

This lion, now in Palmyra's museum, was found near the Temple of Allat.

BELOW:
funeral statuary in Palmyra's museum.

stairs, with each wing containing numerous recesses. The most notable *hypogea* in the **southwest necropolis** is the 2nd-century **Hypogeum of the Three Brothers**, though many other bodies are also entombed here, as an inscription records that spaces in the 360-berth tomb were sold off to other families. The tomb is noted for its frescoes depicting symbolic scenes from Greek mythology, such as the abduction of Ganymede by Zeus disguised as an eagle.

The last sight of Palmyra is the 17th-century Arab castle, **Qal'at Ibn Maan**, thought to have been built by Fakr-ed-Din upon a 13th-century Mamluke fortress. Its chief attraction is the fabulous view over the ancient city below.

On to Homs

Pilgrims outside Homs' distinctive Mosque of Khalid Ibn al-Walid.

East of Palmyra, the only option is to cross the desert and link up with the Euphrates Valley or travel into Iraq. The only sight along the way is **Qasr al-Hayr ash-Sharqi**, a desert palace dating from the Umayyads,who built similar palaces in the desert east of Amman in modern-day Jordan. Finding the palace, which lies in the desert some 30 km (18 miles) off the road, is difficult and best not attempted by travellers driving without a local guide.

This chapter therefore returns to the main Damascus–Aleppo highway and the Orontes Valley, where the next stop is **Homs** ❷, the hub of the country's communications network. With rail lines running not only north and south but also west to the port of Tartus and east to Tadmur (Palmyra), it links the desert interior with the Mediterranean, just as it did in ancient times, when it was called Emesa and its great temple was said to rival the Temple of Bel in Palmyra. The ancient city was ruled by a series of priest-kings, who venerated a black stone representing the sun-god. A daughter of one of these priest-kings, Julia Domna, married the local Roman governor, Septimus Severus, who went on to become emperor, as did each of their sons, Caracalla and Geta. Under their grand-nephew, Emperor Elagabalus, who had formerly served as high priest at Emesa, the black stone was taken to Rome, where it was installed in a Temple of Baal. When Elagabalus's increasing signs of depravity led to his assassination by the Praetorian guard, the stone was returned to Emesa. However, its powerful reputation was restored by the Emperor Aurelian, who consulted it before his decisive battle against Zenobia in 272 *(see page 169)*, and the cult surrounding the stone didn't die out until the 5th century. Today, the **Great Mosque of al-Nuri** is thought to stand on the site of the temple.

BELOW:
the Mosque of
Khalid Ibn al-Walid.

Modern Homs bears little evidence of its early history. The most notable buildings are the early 20th-century **Mosque of Khalid Ibn al-Walid**, a popular place of pilgrimage built over the tomb of this 7th-century Arab conqueror; the Church of **Oum al-Zunnar** (the Virgin's girdle), whose main draw is a belt believed by some to have belonged to the Virgin Mary; and the Church of **St Elias**, where fine murals have been uncovered in the 6th-century crypt.

The region surrounding Homs has some important Bronze-Age sites. Twenty kilometres (12 miles) northeast lies the important Bronze Age kingdom of **Qatna**, where you can still see the earthworks of the

immense fortifications, spanning about 1km (½ mile) and standing up to 20 metres (65 ft) high. The same distance southwest of Homs, but with little to see, is **Kadesh** (Tell Nebi Mind), where Rameses II battled against the Hittites. The reason for the battle's fame is not so much its military significance as the propaganda created by Rameses II in the wake of the battle. Returning to Egypt, he set about adorning temples at Karnak and Abu Simbel with detailed accounts of the battle, in which he portrayed himself as a mighty conqueror. The battle was actually inconclusive and ultimately proved negative for both sides. Not only did it curb Egyptian expansion, but it also marked the beginning of the decline of the Hittites, whose preoccupation with fighting the Egyptians had left their eastern flank vulnerable to aggression by the increasingly powerful Assyrians.

Riverside Hama

A more attractive base for visiting central Syria is the river town of **Hama ❸**, straddling the curving banks of the Orontes 47 km (30 miles) north of Homs. Situated between desert and coast, it was an important caravan post from ancient times through the Middle Ages, when it became famous for silk production, an industry imported along the Silk Route from China. Its citadel, now just a mound in a bend in the river in the centre of town, has yielded finds from as early as the 5th millennium BC, and it is known that by the late 3rd millennium BC it was an important Bronze-Age kingdom, along with Qatna and Ebla. By 1100 BC it was known as Hamath, a prosperous Aramaean state, but was destroyed by Sargon of Assyria in 720 BC. The city was rebuilt and named Epiphania under the Seleucids, after which its fortunes remained fairly stable.

Today the town's chief landmarks are the picturesque wooden *norias (see*

Maps:
Area 168
Site 170

Fishing on the notoriously steep banks of the Orontes.

BELOW: Al-Azem Palace, Hama.

Lustrous decoration in Azem Palace, a fine setting for Syria's traditional arts and crafts.

picture on pages 114–115), enormous water-wheels introduced by the Byzantines as a means of lifting water over the river's steep banks. From the *norias* the water was fed into aqueducts for town and agricultural supplies. Today their function is decorative rather than useful, though local children like to hitch amusement rides on them. The biggest *noria*, the mighty 14th-century "Al-Mohammediyeh", is on the left bank of the river, downstream from the city centre.

Hama's garden image masks a violent recent past. In 1982 it was the scene of a bloody massacre, as government forces brutally quashed an uprising organised by the outlawed Muslim Brotherhood, who sought to harness the city's conservative Sunni opposition to the Alawite regime. Up to 10,000 people died in the episode, and much of the city centre was destroyed. Nevertheless a few of its mosques and *khans* survived and are being reconstructed, including some of the 17 waterwheels, the 12th-century **Mosque al-Nuri**, built in bands of yellow limestone and black basalt, and the **Khan of Rustam Pasha**. Besides the *norias*, however, the chief attraction is the **Beit al-Azem** (Azem Palace) (Wed–Mon 9am–6pm, closed Tues), built in the 18th century by the governor of Hama, Assad Pasha al-Azem, who also built the Azem Palace in Damascus, when he became governor there. Like the Damascus palace, it incorporates beautiful examples of Ottoman decoration, such as intricate inlay, wooden panelling and textiles. It also displays finds from archaeological excavations in and around Hama.

Around Hama

The desert east of Hama is punctuated by Byzantine churches and palaces, many of them apparently isolated. Chief of these is **Qasr ibn Wardan ❹**, a Byzantine outpost comprising palace, barracks and church, which, unusually, is built of brick rather than stone, in a style imported from Constantinople. It may be possible to visit this and one or two other such sites on an organised tour from Hama, which might also include a visit to a "beehive" house, a regional form of architecture dating from antiquity *(see page 237)*.

Far away to the west of Hama lies the Jabal an Nusayriyah, beneath which the Orontes flows through the marshy and, in summer horribly humid, Al Ghab, the setting for many conflicts between Arabs and crusaders in the late Middle Ages. One of the main fortifications of this castle-studded region was **Qal'at Sheizar** (28 km/17½ miles from Hama), which can be included on a trip to Apamia *(see below)*. Though this 11th-century Arab stronghold managed to repel crusader forces, it fell to an earthquake in 1157.

A little further on (56 km/35 miles from Hama) is the Hellenistic-Byzantine city of **Apamea ❺**. In contrast to the dramatic desert scape of Palmyra, its colonnaded streets, walls and citadel are beautifully set in lush farmland, overlooked by mountains to the west. A collection of superb mosaics have been recovered from the site and region, some of which are housed in the **museum** (Wed–Mon 9am–6pm, closed Tues; admission charge), a converted Ottoman caravanserai in the modern village of Qal'at Madiq.

Founded by Seleucus Nicator, who ruled Northern Syria after the death of Alexander the Great, Apamia was one in a network of trading cities, with Antioch at its hub, and was also an important garrison. It continued to prosper under the Romans from 64 BC, but when the Byzantine Empire began to crumble it fell into decline. It was revived under the Arabs and Ottomans, who exploited its strategic and trading advantages.

Much of this vast site is unrestored, consisting of little more than weeds and stones, but truly impressive are its colonnaded streets, chief of which is the north–south **Cardo Maximus**, which is even longer than the one at Palmyra. The main civic buildings worth seeing are along the Cardo north of where you join it as you walk into the site. On its west side are the **Agora** and **Temple of Zeus** and on the east a **nymphaeum**. Towards the northern gateway, the ancient exit for the road to Antioch, is a large column, marking an intersection with a secondary street. Near here, on the east side, are the remains of a **baths** complex built in AD 117 as part of a rebuilding programme following an earthquake two years before. The southern section of the site has the scant remains of a couple of Byzantine **churches**, one of them dedicated to the twin brothers and healers SS Cosmas and Damian, and, east of the Cardo, the outline of a large **cathedral**.

Towards Aleppo

North of Apamia is a scattering of so-called "Dead Cities" *(see page 225)*. Chief of these in terms of history if not remains is Ebla (covered in the chapter "The Northwest"), but the simple Roman towns of **Ruweiha** and **Serjilla** are well worth exploring. **Ma'arrat an Nu'man** is a modern town with little character, but its museum (9am–4pm, closed Tues; admission charge) in the Ottoman Khan Murad Pasha, contains a superb collection of mosaics and artefacts recovered from archaeological sites in the region. ❑

Map on page 168

On display in the museum at Ma'arrat an Nu'man.

BELOW:
mosaic at Ma'arrat an Nu'man.

THE LIVES AND TIMES OF SYRIA'S BEDU

Vast and barren, the Syrian Desert is seemingly inhospitable. Yet Bedu herdsmen have been surviving in these harsh conditions for millennia

Although some Bedu have given up their traditional life in the desert to resettle, many have remained true to their nomadic existence. Every Bedu is part of an extended family, which is itself part of a tribe. Tribal loyalty is all important, and each tribe has its own dress code, which is particularly observed by women, who cover their hair, though not always their face, and who often decorate the few visible parts of their body with intricate tattoos. Nowadays the Bedu are mainly herdsmen, who move around with their family and cattle, searching for viable grazing land. In the Syrian Desert, Bedu usually herd goats and sheep; camels are a rarer sight.

Hospitality is a matter of pride for the Bedu, who will automatically take care of any stranger that appears at their tents. Normally the men do not shake hands or sit with women, but foreign women will be treated as honorary males and made welcome with tea or coffee.

DESERT WANDERERS

The name Bedouin derives from *bedu*, Arabic for living in the desert. These nomadic tribes live in the deserts of Syria, Iraq, Jordan, the Arabian peninsula and North Africa. At the time of the great trans-Asia caravan trade, they were essential in guiding caravans across the desert. They also supplied pack animals to travelling traders and offered protection against the many raiders. Having been an essential link between Europe and Asia throughout their history, the Bedu have also played an important role in the exchange of culture and ideas between East and West. As herdsmen, they are now often considered primitive by city Arabs, though their heroic and romantic image continues to be celebrated by classical Arab poetry.

△ **DAILY BREAD**
A Bedu woman bakes flat bread *(shrak)* on the hot *saj*, a wide metal bowl turned upside down over a fire.

◁ **BORN TO BE A BEDU**
T. E. Lawrence wrote that "the Bedouin ways were hard even for those brought up in them."

◁ **THE COFFEE CEREMONY**
If you come across a Bedu tent in the middle of nowhere the first thing you are likely to be offered will be a shot of bitter black coffee.

△ **CRUCIAL COMMODITY**
The Bedu evolved as nomadic hersmen, living off the milk, meat, wool, hair and skins of their animals.

△ **LOOKING FOR PASTURE**
After the spring rains the Bedu pack up and drive their Nissan vans in search of green pasture, moving on again when that source of nourishment is exhausted.

▽ **DIVIDED WE STAND**
This tent divider, the largest decorated piece of textile made by the Bedu, separates the women's area from the men's. The "good" side always faces the men.

WHEN A DESERT SPRINGS TO LIFE

The Syrian Desert covering much of the eastern part of the country is a vast rocky limestone steppe, interrupted by mountain ridges. Only in the more distant desert do you find the more familiar image of shifting sand dunes.

Much of the region's once rich wildlife – gazelle, ostrich and antelope – was hunted almost to extinction in the 19th and early 20th centuries, and the fauna that remains comprises small mammals such as rodents, and reptiles.

For most of the year the inhospitable desert steppe is dry and barren, but when the slight rains fall each spring life returns and a variety of specially adapted wildflowers and grasses appear out of nowhere, transforming the desert with a light green carpet, attracting the Bedu and their herds. Their heat- and drought-resistant seeds will remain dormant until next year's rain falls.

When the rain does come it often arrives suddenly, washing some plants away. Like palm trees, oleander bushes, with their mass of pink flowers, and tamarisks climg on with their deep roots reaching far into the water table.

THE COASTAL REGION

Syria's western flank is separated from the rest of the country by the Jabal an Nusayriyah. Attractions include the resort of Latakia and hills bristling with crusader castles such as Crac des Chevaliers

Map on page 184

Syria isn't the sort of place that springs to mind when you think about beaches, but there are other wonderful attractions which enhance a trip along its Mediterranean coast and up into the mountains that separate the coast from the desert. For millennia this was one of the world's most vital trade routes and throughout antiquity armies fought for its control. During the Crusades the area again became of great strategic importance and both coastal towns and isolated mountain peaks were fortified with some of the world's most important castles. The mountains also offer some of Syria's finest scenery, especially in spring when the valleys are filled with wild flowers. Villages of the *jabal*, because of the difficulty in reaching them, became places of refuge for minorities, a tradition which continues today – the *jabal* is still home to Alawis, Christians and Ismailis.

The main Aleppo–Latakia road crosses the Orontes River at the agricultural town of **Jisr ash-Shugur**. This area between the Jabal an Nusayriyah and the more easterly hills was extremely fertile during the time of Alexander the Great, but returned to swampland until a recent World Bank-sponsored drainage project restored it to its fertile glory. Jisr's main attraction is its bridge over the Orontes. Built by the Romans, the variety of stonework is evidence of its many restorations.

Qal'at Salahidin

Some 51 km (32 miles) west of Jisr ash-Shugur on the Latakia road, a minor road leads back into the mountains through the village of Al Haffah to **Qal'at Salahidin ❶**, one of the region's great strongholds, which controlled the northern passage around the mountains. T. E. Lawrence, who tramped through the mountains in 1909, thought Qal'at Salahidin perhaps the finest castle in the country – Crac des Chevaliers was its only rival in his estimation. But where Crac impresses by sheer might, Qal'at Salahidin seduces by being in harmony with its surroundings, seeming to grow organically out of a ridge between two sharp ravines.

The Phoenicians recognised the site's importance, but serious fortification didn't start until the Byzantines took the hill in the late 10th century; their ruined citadel still occupies the higher ground. Most of what survives belongs to the 12th-century castle known to crusaders as Saône, after Robert de Saône, the local seigneur. The approach is the most impressive of all crusader castles, for the present road plunges down into a gulley some 30 metres (100 ft) below the castle. The sheer sides of the gulley, up to 20 metres (66 ft) wide and more than 150 metres (500 ft) long, were cut out by hand, a single needle of stone being left to

PRECEDING PAGES: beached at Latakia. **LEFT:** a leisurely beverage, Arwad. **BELOW:** River Khabur, between Latakia and Aleppo.

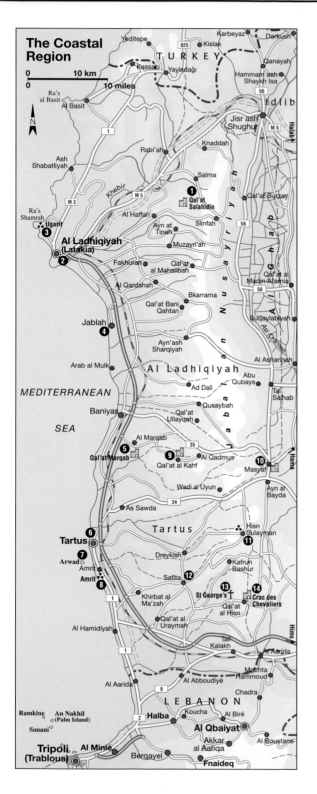

The Coastal Region

0   10 km
0   10 miles

support the drawbridge. Entrance is now through a modest doorway leading to the centre of the castle. Turn right, pass two towers and head for the main keep or **donjon**, a two-storey building with 5-metre (16-ft) walls, intended as a last line of defence. About 80 steps lead up to the roof, which has excellent views over the castle and the landscape it dominated. The original entrance to the castle was through the gatehouse beyond the donjon; from here, the excavation of the defensive gulley and the needle of rock left for the drawbridge looks an even more Herculean effort.

The castle's main **stables** lie to the south of the donjon and its water cistern beyond that. Passing the modern entrance, a path leads across the castle to the western walls, where one of the towers is used as a café (open daily for hot and cold drinks). The tower looks over a second ditch that was intended to protect the western walls. Unlike the gulley, this was never completed and when Saladin stormed the castle in 1188, after his victory at Hattin, it was near here that he broke through and forced the under-strength crusader garrison to surrender.

Opposite the castle's current entrance are the remains of a 12th to 13th-century palace complex, built after the defeat of the crusaders. The mosque dates from the reign of the Mamluke Sultan Qalawun (1280–90), but the entrance to the palace, with its stalactite decoration and elegant baths, is earlier.

Latakia

The road from Qal'at Saladin to **Latakia** (Al Ladhiqiyah) ❷ is more rural and interesting than the main Aleppo–Latakia route, connecting with the coastal highway just before the city. Latakia took its name from the mother of Seleucus I (Seleucus Nicator), although it was settled long before his 4th-century BC reign. The site flourished because of its safe anchorage, and today it is Syria's main port. Although it has little to show for its illustrious history, it does have an unmistakably Mediterranean and Levantine, rather than Arab character. Under the Roman Emperor Septimus Severus, Latakia was the capital of Syria and some of the original Roman street plan survives in the older part of town. A 2nd-century four-sided gateway, marking the eastern end of the ancient city centre, stands several feet below current street level near the junction of al Yarmuk and Bur Said streets, the victory or imperial visit that it was built to commemorate now forgotten. Nearby on Abdal Rahman al-Ghafiqi Street, several granite columns, perhaps from the Temple of Adonis, survive the traffic.

Map on page 184

There is equally little to see of the crusader city, sacked by Arabs and later by Christians and brought down by a series of earthquakes, but proof of its long-standing links with Christianity are found in the Greek Orthodox **Church of the Virgin**, in the souk on the corner of al-Quds Street. Its Byzantine origins are obscure, the heavily-carved marble iconostasis being an 18th-century addition. A couple of blocks away on the corner of Maysalun Street, the Church of **St Nicholas**, which houses a fine collection of 17th- and 18th-century icons, may also have early foundations.

The closest you can come to the past in Latakia is in its **museum** (on the Corniche, at its junction with al-Quds Street; Wed–Mon 9am–6pm; closed Tues), an Ottoman *khan* to which an upper floor was added during the French mandate, when it served as the governor-general's residence. The garden houses some large architectural pieces, including a good sarcophagus with cow's head decorations. An underground passage on the north side of the garden is said to have allowed the governor – and before him traders – to escape to the beach in times of trouble. The museum collection is neither as large nor as interesting as those in Damascus or Aleppo, but it does have several pieces from nearby

Latakia is Syria's main beach resort.

BELOW: the original entrance to Saladin's castle.

THE MIGHTY SALADIN

Of all the great Muslim commanders who opposed the crusaders, none can rival the accomplishments of Saladin. In 1169, Salah al-Deen, as he was properly known, a Sunni Kurd, ousted the Shi'ite Fatimid caliphs from power in Egypt. In 1176, on his uncle Nour al-Deen's death, he took power in Syria, creating a powerful new dynasty, the Ayubbids, named after his father. His consolidation of Muslim power was a crucial step in the loosening of the crusader grip on the Holy Land.

Saladin was a sharp tactician, as he showed at the Battle of Hattin in 1187, after which he took Jerusalem. In the following year he fought a dazzling campaign, storming up into Syria to attack the weak points of crusader defences, taking Tartus, Baniyas, Jablah and Latakia in July 1188 and capping a brilliant month by conquering the supposedly invulnerable Qal'at Saladin on the 29th. Four more castles fell the following month and, during the campaign, some 50 crusader fortifications were taken. As a consequence of his gains, the Third Crusade was launched in which he succeeded in defending Jerusalem against Richard I (the Lionheart) of England. On his death in 1193, Saladin was buried in a relatively simple tomb outside the Umayyad Mosque in Damascus *(see page 131)*.

Ugarit. The first room on the right houses displays of 14th-13th century BC pottery and (in cabinet 3) some early Ugarit texts. Ugarit stoneware and more pottery is shown in the second room, along with cylindrical seals. In the third room there is a very unusual terracotta coffin, in the shape of a cylindrical pot, 1.6 metres (5ft) long, discovered in Latakia in 1970.

Ugarit

The place-name Ugarit means "fennel", which grows abundantly hereabouts.

Some 14 km (9 miles) north of Latakia at Ra's Shamrah (Fennel Headland) lie the ruins of ancient **Ugarit ❸** (Wed–Mon 9am–7pm, closed Tues). Ugarit lacks the grandeur of Baalbek or Palmyra, but does bring to life conditions in a Bronze- Age city. As only some 25 percent of the site has been excavated, most statistics rely on educated guesswork. The site appears to have been settled as early as the 7th millennium BC. But most of what can be seen dates from the city's golden age, around 2000–1200 BC, when the eastern Mediterranean benefited from growing trade links between Egypt, Minoan Crete, Hittite Anatolia and the East, and when Ugarit was famous for its bronze and timber. Ugarit's end came around 1200 BC with the arrival of the Sea Peoples, an alliance of Libyans, Philistines and others who unsettled the entire region.

It went into such complete decline that the fact of its existence was forgotten, even among local villagers, until 1928, when a farmer called Mahmoud Mellah ploughed it up. Franco-Syrian excavations, patchy at best, have uncovered the foundations of some important buildings, but visitors are helped by neither signs nor explanations. With limited reconstruction of low walls and pillars, the site is low on spectacle, but some good views of the countryside and sea and wild flowers in spring add to its charm.

BELOW: loading up at Ra's al-Basit.

The site is entered over a small rise, above the oval-shaped entrance to the **royal palace enclosure**. The palace, believed to have had 90 rooms, was the centre of a community which flaunted its sophistications. Columns flanked the entrance (bases remain) to an **outer courtyard**. In the rooms to the left of here a series of clay tablets from the 14th and 13th centuries BC were found. Although the Egyptians and others had earlier writing, these wonderful treasures point to the Ugarites as the creators of the world's first alphabet where, as in Arabic and Hebrew, each symbol represents a single consonant.

The outer courtyard leads to a larger **inner court** where the pavement was cut through with water channels. These are found all over the site, for the control of water was another of the city's proud achievements. In one of the further rooms to the right (south) of the palace, an oven was found for baking clay tablets – the precursor to paper – many of which were found here.

The extent of the palace buildings is indicated by the end of the use of large stones. Elsewhere in town, smaller stones and rocks were used to build homes, although several houses near the palace were also palatial – the villa of a man called Rupanu, on the path between the palace and the acropolis, boasted some 34 rooms. More impressive today is an underground chamber, reached by steps, with a curved vaulted ceiling. Curved ceilings are also found in tombs. Beyond this residential area to the right of two hills, the acropolis housed the **Temple of Baal**, the city's patron (on the left), the **Temple of Dagon** (the underworld god) (to the right) and the **high priest's house** between.

Nearby excavation trenches reveal, through their many layers, the extent of settlement here. From the **acropolis** and its neighbouring rise you can see the ancient port (now a military area), a view which inspired the King of Ugarit to

An olive press, a relic of an ancient industry at Ugarit.

BELOW: wedding tributes at a flower shop in Latakia.

Well-covered local women bathing at Ra's al-Basit.

write his urgent plea for help on a clay tablet when he saw enemy ships arriving. The message was never sent and the plea only reached the outside world when the city was rediscovered.

Hills and beaches

The drive north of Ugarit leads through some beautiful country (though the road can be busy on summer weekends) to the hill-town of **Kassab**, which really only comes alive in the summer when Syrians come to escape the heat. Down on the coast near the border with Turkey (which Syria continues to dispute), Ra's al-Basit has one of Syria's cleanest beaches, notable for its black sand. The resort gets very busy in the summer.

Some 20 km (12 miles) south of Latakia along the fast coastal highway, a turn-off leads inland to **Al Qardahah**, a small town in beautiful hill country, where Basil al-Assad is buried. Basil was the elder son of President Hafiz al-Assad and widely accepted as his successor. A colourful character who was passionate about sport, particularly horses, Basil was killed in a car crash on the road to Damascus Airport in January 1994. Work continues, but his large tomb is open to visitors 24 hours a day and provides an insight into the ways of power and also into the genuine affection felt for the man many expected to be their ruler. Horse heads decorating the mourning area are a reminder of his equestrian prowess. A large hotel, clad with acres of marble, sits empty for most of the year but is fully booked each January for the commemoration service.

BELOW: exploring Ugarit.

The Phoenicians' eye for a good port is evident again a few kilometres further south at **Jablah ❹**, though the town's fortunes really rose under the Romans. The scale of its success can be gauged by the size of the **theatre** (Wed–Mon

8am–5pm, Tues 8am–2pm) which stands somewhat forlorn in the centre of town. Similar in plan if not extent of preservation to the theatre in Busra *(see page 160)*, the semi-circular auditorium could seat some 7,000 spectators (local estimates claim as many as 10,000). The stage has disappeared (the theatre was converted to a fortress by crusaders) but the soaring vaults beneath the seating area are worth the visit. A short walk across a public garden leads to the 8th-century **mosque of Sidi Ibrahim Ben Adham**, known locally as Sultan Brahim. The Sidi, a prince from Khorabagh, died here in AD 778 fighting the Byzantines and was buried over the ruins of a mid-7th century Byzantine church. The mosque has been much altered and extended since then. Note the seven-pointed Ugaritic star over the *qibla*. Across the courtyard, beyond a tree split by lightning, steps lead down to a run-down medieval *hammam*, still in use. Nearby, the Mamluke Hammam Tasawir has emerged from a thorough restoration.

Map on page 184

Qal'at Marqab

Continuing south along the coastal highway, the mountains close in and reduce the coastal plain to a mere strip. Just past **Baniyas** (drive into town and then look for a road that crosses the highway), the region is dominated from a spur by the massive **Qal'at Marqab** ❺ (daily 9am–6pm, until 4pm in winter). Although it controlled the coastal passage from Turkey to the Holy Land, the site wasn't fortified until 1062, when a local chief – believed to be Rashid al-Din Sinan – began work. The site was bought by the Knights Hospitallers in 1186, who immediately began work on the castle that still stands, using the local black volcanic basalt for its massive walls. The Hospitallers spent 17 years building up the castle, getting instant returns when Saladin left Marqab untouched as

BELOW:
the amphitheatre
at Jablah.

he swept up the coast after his crushing victory over the crusaders at Hattin. Marqab withstood almost another century of warfare, but suffered the same fate as many other strategic crusader castles because it lacked sufficient manpower to defend itself. Mamluke Sultan Qalawun delivered the final blow in May 1285. Recognising the strength of the site, Qalawun made Marqab the centre of his campaign to liberate the region from crusaders. The castle continued in use long into the Ottoman era.

The castle is entered through a **tower** in the west wall. Turn right here, as all of the important buildings are found at the southern tip, the castle's weak point. Some 30 metres (100 ft) in from the entrance tower a later crusader (1270) barbican gateway gives onto steps leading up to the central courtyard. Across the clearing is the northern door to the late 12th-century chapel, its main entrance facing west (the sea). Beautifully conceived and perfectly austere, the absence of pillars gives the relatively small chapel (23 metres/75 ft long and 9 metres/30 ft wide) a surprising sense of space. The west and north doorways have elaborate carvings and the remains of frescoes, which once covered much of the walls, can be seen in the northeast sacristy.

Buildings along the east and northeast sides of the courtyard were used as storerooms and, beyond them, as barracks. Southwest of the chapel are the remains of a two-storeyed building, most likely to have been the castle's Great Hall. T. E. Lawrence thought Marqab was "typical of the best period of French architecture." This seems especially so of the **donjon**, the three-storey tower of last resort to the south of the chapel, with walls up to 5 metres (16 ft) thick, rounded in places for greater protection. Ironically, it was Qalawun's sappers, digging under the walls, rather than bombardment, that led the defenders to

BELOW:
Qala'at Marqab.

THE HOSPITALLERS

The success of the First Crusade at the end of the 11th century, the taking of Jerusalem in 1099 and the subsequent creation of Christian kingdoms and principalities throughout the region give a distorted image, for the crusader forces were neither united nor particularly strong. In an attempt to create unified Crusader forces, the Order of the Knights of the Temple was created in 1118. Yet despite their specific brief – to protect the pilgrim routes to Jerusalem – the Templars became one of the key crusading powers. At the same time another order, the Knights Hospitallers, was created to care for sick pilgrims in Jerusalem. Both orders attracted sizeable grants of land and money in Europe, as well as many knightly volunteers.

Because of their growing wealth and manpower, both orders soon assumed political and military responsibilities. From the middle of the 12th century, many of the key crusader castles in Syria were handed over to one or other order, who built massive fortifications – the castles of Marqab and Crac des Chevaliers being their masterpieces. After the crusaders were forced out of the region, both orders continued to function in Europe, the Hospitallers maintaining most notably a formidable presence on the Greek island of Rhodes.

surrender. Returning to the main entrance gate and continuing north inside the walls reveals the ultimate fate of the castle, some of its blocks reused in the houses of a village which grew up here during the Ottoman period. Remains of an Ottoman *khan* fill the centre of this northern half of the castle.

Map on page 184

Tartus

For all its architectural magnificence, there is something stifling about Marqab and it doesn't take much imagination to believe how happy crusader knights must have been to find themselves another 40 km (25 miles) further south at **Tartus ❻**. Where Marqab is remote and overwhelming, Tartus has all the lightness and ease of a seaside town. It is also Syria's second port, after Latakia, and the beach has suffered as a result. Tartus, as with so many Syrian and Lebanese coastal settlements, was founded by the Phoenicians, who had a base on nearby Arwad Island. Alexander the Great took the city when he swept down the coast in 330 BC; Romans, Byzantines and Arabs followed his example. But Tartus owes its glory to the crusaders, particularly to the Hospitallers' rivals, the Knights Templar *(see opposite)*, who took control of the town in 1152 and began major construction work.

Tartus's classical name was Anti-Aradus, "against or near Aradus", Arwad's original name.

One of the things that sets Tartus apart from other crusader buildings is that its fortress has become part of the living city. Not just a vacant core, but a vibrant place whose medieval buildings have been adapted to make modern homes. The best thing here is just to stroll around and admire how this process has taken place. Before entering the old city from the seafront, try the door of the major building to your right, the entrance to a large crusader hall, remembering that 800 years ago the sea probably came up to the old city walls.

BELOW: cooling roasted coffee beans in Tartus.

Tartus's most remarkable attraction, however, stands outside the inner castle walls. The position of the Cathedral of **Our Lady of Tortosa** (Wed–Mon 9am–6pm; winter 9am–4pm, closed Tues) is reflected in its architecture, for it looks more like a fortress than a place of worship. This is understandable, since Saladin took the city for some months of 1188, after the battle at Hattin, and seriously damaged the cathedral. Apart from the austerity of its 13th-century reconstruction, it is of interest for housing the city museum. In the nave is a large 2nd-century sarcophagus, beautifully decorated, surrounded by other Phoenician coffins and a 12th-century fresco of the Virgin and St Simeon from Crac des Chevaliers. Elsewhere there are votive figures, more sarcophagi, pottery, glass and stoneware from ancient Amrit to Byzantine Tartus.

A Phoenican sarcophagus in the cathedral museum, Tartus.

Island visit

Just offshore (a 20-minute ferry ride from Tartus, if the sea is calm enough to cross) lies **Arwad Island** ❼, first settled by the Canaanites, but visited by everyone from Egyptian Pharaoh Tuthmosis III to St Paul. The crusader Knights Templar fortified Arwad along with Tartus; after the Christians abandoned their last mainland strongholds of Tartus and Athlit in 1291, they held out on Arwad for another 11 years before their inevitable defeat. Arwad today is a popular outing for Syrians, who stroll its narrow alleys and visit the Arab fort near the harbour (Wed–Mon 9am–4pm, closed Tues) which has a limited but eclectic display of antiquities, including some interesting mosaics. Several signs remind the inhabitants that their island is a tourist site and urge them to keep it clean, but money would be better spent on upgrading refuse clearance. The main pleasure to be had on Arwad, if the refuse situation is under control, is in its cafés, star-

BELOW: the Cathedral of Our Lady of Tortosa.

ing out to sea or, like the crusaders, back to Tartus, and strolling through the busy yard to watch fishing boats being made.

Map on page 184

Sacred Amrit

The only reminders of the area's early settlement are to be found 8 km (5 miles) south of Tartus at **Amrit ❽** (open access). Little of Amrit has been excavated, so as with Ugarit most pronouncements are speculation, but this is thought to have been a religious site established by the Arwadites. Remains cover an area of some 3 km (2 miles) by 2 km (1¼ miles) and while there is little above ground that is spectacular, what is to be seen proves that, even in antiquity, this was an area of mixed cultural influences. A cemetery on the southern part of the site contains two large *meghazils* or spindles. The taller, 7 metres (23 ft) high, is cylindrical, its base decorated with Persian-style lions; the other, 4 metres (13 ft) high, is topped with an obelisk. The most easily understood section of Amrit, however, is the northern temple complex, believed to be dedicated to Melqart. Its rock-cut lake was credited with healing properties and in it, now surrounded by tall grasses, frogs and the odd snake, stands a monument decorated with Egyptian motifs. Amrit is noted for the beauty of its setting, among wild flowers in spring and with great views of the nearby sea. Plans to exploit this, with a luxury tourist complex, appear to have been put on hold.

The two spindles rising over the cemetery at Amrit.

From Tartus, a number of roads lead up into the central Jabal an Nusayriyah, one of Syria's most beautiful regions, particularly in spring and autumn, and yet surprisingly little visited by foreigners. The road can be made difficult in winter by fog and snow. Thirteeen kilometres (8 miles) back up the highway from Tartus towards Latakia a good road leads off to the right towards Sheikh Badr.

BELOW: the citadel museum on the island of Arwad.

Following this road straight (as straight as is possible) leads to Masyaf, the Ismaili stronghold on the far side of the mountains *(see below)*, passing through the villages of Hussein al-Bahr, As Sawda, Dhar Matar and Shaykh Badr. If you have time, an adventurous spirit and a desire to see one of the most romantically ruined castles in the region, then at Sheikh Badr turn left (north) for Qal'at al-Kahf (pronounced *Ka-hef*), 6.5 km (4 miles) away along winding and mostly unsigned roads.

Qal'at al-Kahf ❾, the Castle of the Rock (open access), is set in wonderful rolling hills whose lower terraces are planted with olives, fruits and grain, the upper reaches with firs and pines. The villagers, all farmers and mostly still curious about foreigners, remain hospitable to passing strangers and will point you in the right direction. The castle, on a hilltop, has been mostly reclaimed by nature. Reached by a trail that winds up the right hand side of the hill and entered through a gate cut through the rock, there is little at the top – beyond some inscriptions and levelled surfaces – to indicate that this was one of the Assassins' strongholds, yet both the Regent of Jerusalem and an envoy of Louis XI of France visited the castle, hoping for an alliance with its leader. It took the Mamluke Sultan Baybars until two years after the fall of Crac to breach its defences. Even then, al-Kahf continued as a stronghold until the early 19th century, when an Ottoman force raided the castle at the request of Lady Hester Stanhope *(see page 310)* to release a French captive. When they withdrew they left nothing standing. Outside of winter, the view of the hills, the fresh air and perpetual winds are exhilarating.

The castle at **Masyaf** ❿ (officially 9am–3pm winter, until 6pm summer, but the caretaker may take some hunting down), some 50 km (30 miles) inland

BELOW: on the lookout at Crac des Chevaliers.

THE ASSASSINS

The Assassins, an Ismaili sect founded in Persia, rose to prominence in Syria during the 11th century. At a time of social and political unrest, the Shi'ite group began its own campaign to eliminate Orthodox Sunni leaders. Their style became apparent during the Muslim campaign against the First Crusade of the 1120s, when they plotted with the Crusaders against the Sunni majority. During the 1130s and 1140s, forced out of Aleppo, they established their mountain strongholds, including Masyaf and Qala'at al-Kahf, but waged attacks on the coast, including assaults upon the Count of Tripoli.

The Assassins went from strength to strength under their Iraqi leader Rashid al-Deen Sinan (1163–93), who was better known to the crusaders as the Old Man of the Mountain. During his lifetime the sect held 10 castles and a sufficiently large portion of the Jabal an Nusayriyah to be wooed by crusader leaders – even Saladin, according to one account, found himself confronted one night by the Ismaili killers. The Sunni Orthodoxy had tightened its grip on power by the time of Sinan's death in 1193 and the Assassins lost their main base in Iraq to the Mongols in 1260, though small Assassin communities still survive in the mountains today.

Map
on page
184

from the coastal highway, is a farming town famous as another stronghold of the Assassins, whose castle still dominates the town. The remains of Greek, Roman and Byzantine fortifications indicate the strategic importance of the site. Taken by crusaders in 1103, it fell to the Shi'ite Assassins in 1140 and became one of their main refuges against Sunni persecution. It was also, compared to places such as Qal'at al-Kahf, one of the most exposed. From here, as from several other strongholds in the hills, the Ismaili leader Rashid al-Deen Sinan, known in the West as the Old Man of the Mountain, terrorised both Saladin and his crusader adversaries in the turbulent years of the late 12th century. The vaulted entrance leads to a central keep and several passageways, as well as the caretaker's room. The castle is somewhat derelict inside, but there are good views on a clear day down towards the eastern plains.

Cult centre

Less than 30 km (18 miles) southwest of Masyaf, over winding and isolated mountain roads, **Hisn Sulayman** ⓫ is another of Syria's hidden treasures. The name is a misnomer for the place has nothing to do with Sulayman – either the Ottoman sultan or the Biblical Solomon – but is an early Semitic/Canaanite cult centre. The main attraction, the **temple of Zeus Baotocecian**, is a 2nd-century BC Roman construction. Zeus Baotocecian was a composite deity who assumed some characteristics of the local god Baal, who had been worshipped in these hills for millennia before the Romans arrived.

The temple (no gate, no opening hours) sits beside the road into a small village and local farmers graze their livestock in the precincts. This relationship between the temple, hillside and animal world seems appropriate. The temple

The name "Assassins" is a corruption of the Arabic hashashin – the hashish eaters. They were believed to be drugged before going on assassination operations.

BELOW: on the road, between Latakia and Hama.

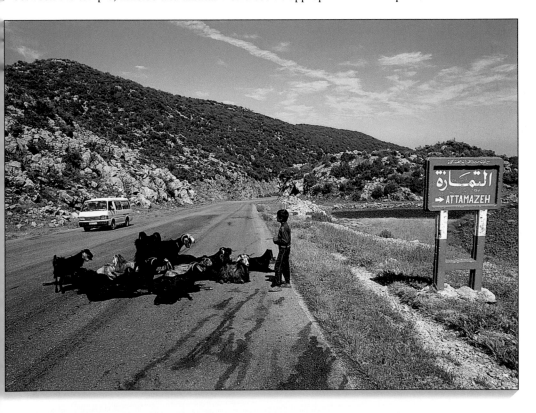

The Greek Orthodox Church of St Michael, which occupies the old Crusader keep at Safita.

BELOW: the interior of Castel Blanc.

is entered via its main entrance, a triple gateway (niches between the gates would have housed statues) in which the keystone hangs as perilously as at the Temple of Bacchus in Baalbek. There are other similarities with Baalbek, for Hisn Sulayman has been built from massive cut stones, some as large as 10 metres (33 ft) long. Inside the enclosure, smaller gateways can be seen in each of the other walls. The central *cella*, reached up massive steps, past water basins and early *trompe l'oeil* – massive blocks cut to look like pillars – is ruined. Decoration survives in places around the temple, particularly on the underside of the gate lintels. Across the road, in a building known as the **Deir** (Monastery), even more wonderfully ruined and with a Greek inscription, the roof has been replaced by the branches of a massive tree.

The hills here are criss-crossed with small roads. The main one out of Hisn Sulayman, heading back towards Tartus and the coast, passes through **Dreykish**, a town noted for its spring water, sold throughout Syria. It is possible and more rewarding, with time and patience, to cut across country to Safita – if you get lost, people will be happy to direct you. Otherwise, the easiest route to Safita is to head east, rejoin the main road running along the ridge south of Masyaf and then turn right (west) through the resort of Mashta al-Helou.

Safita ⑫, in the foothills of the jabal, is dominated by a crusader tower which T. E. Lawrence called "the most elaborate of the keeps of Northern Syria." The keep originally stood in the centre of a castle (crusaders called this place Castel Blanc, the White Castle), but most of this has disappeared – Lawrence reported that the local governor was using old masonry to build his house. The keep is unusual for having a chapel on the ground floor which now serves as the local Greek Orthodox Church of St Michael (the chapel and therefore also the

keep is usually open during daytime; if locked, ask at the neighbouring Al Bourj Restaurant). The iconostasis is modern, but some icons are old, while the cracks in the walls are a reminder of the earthquake of 1202. To the right of the door 55 steps lead to the first floor, once home to the garrison, the space divided in two by three massive piers which support the roof. Slits in the ground floor walls were purely to let in light, but the 11 slits here were for archers. 35 more steps lead to the roof from where, on a clear day, Tartus and the Crac des Chevaliers can be seen, a reminder of Safita's role as a look-out post. The old town around the keep has some fine old houses, while the rest of Safita, peopled by Greek Orthodox and Alawis, makes for a pleasant stroll.

Map on page 184

A visit to St George's.

Christian enclave

St George's ⓭, nestling in a valley below Crac des Chevaliers, some 30 km (18 miles) south of Safita, has been a Christian enclave since at least the 6th century, when the Greek Orthodox Monastery of St George was built on the orders of Emperor Justinian. Wadi Nasara, the Valley of the Christians, used to be a place of quiet refuge, but an ongoing building programme is rapidly robbing it of any remaining charm. The monastery has often been enlarged and rebuilt, its main church only dating to the mid-19th century. The older lower chapel, reached by steps from the courtyard, is medieval, perhaps 13th-century; nowadays it is only used for holy days and baptisms. Its elaborate ebony iconostasis is hung with good icons of Christ the King and Madonna and Child. The monastery is home to six monks and several volunteers, but comes alive on the feasts of St George (6 May) and the Holy Cross (14 September). It is sometimes also referred to as Marmarita, after one of the nearby Christian villages.

BELOW:
the Monastery of St George in Wadi Nasara.

Crac des Chevaliers

A couple of kilometres southwest of St George's stands one of the highlights of Syria and one of the greatest monument to the crusader era, the **Crac des Chevaliers** . Known locally as **Qal'at al-Hisn**, the Castle of the Citadel (the surrounding village is called al-Husn), the Crac (daily 9am–6pm, until 4pm in winter) sits on a rise above one of the region's key routes, the Homs Gap, a break in the hills which allows easy access between the coast and the interior of Syria – the Egyptian Pharaoh Rameses the Great recognised the area's importance when he fought his most famous battle against the Hittites at nearby Kadesh.

The Knights Hospitallers, builders of Qal'at Marqab, began their great work in 1170. The castle, state-of-the-art for its time, is defended by two enclosing walls separated by a moat dug out of the hillside. The castle is now approached via a late crusader **gateway** (the square tower to the left is a later Mamluke addition). A steep ramp leads up inside the castle; where it turns back on itself, continue straight on to reach the lower defences and the clearing between the walls. Among several flights of steps to the left of the clearing, a double staircase leads down to the Arab **baths**, laid out on traditional lines and with some surviving decoration. The first **tower** after the baths contains the remains of a gate, while outside is a stump of rock which once supported a drawbridge.

At the foot of this tower are vaulted **stables**, the loops to which horses were tethered still on the walls. At the opposite end of the stables, a small passage leads to a chamber with a massive inscribed pillar in its centre. Returning to the passageway, steps lead up to the wall. A broad walkway, restored in 1936, covers the long western wall and gives access, via steps in the base of the unusual Tower of the Princess, to the courtyard of the inner castle.

TIP

Spare at least half a day to see Crac – T. E. Lawrence, who called it "the finest castle in the world", thought he was skimming through by only spending three days there. A torch will be useful.

BELOW:
the famous Crac des Chevaliers.

One of the most remarkable buildings in the castle faces the entrance to the **upper courtyard**. The beautiful and relatively delicate loggia, classic Gothic, was built in the second half of the 13th century towards the end of the crusader period. Behind it stands the **Great Hall**, an earlier and more severe construction with fine vaulting. More interesting is the chamber beyond this hall, a 120-metre (400-ft) long curving space that served (to the right) as a lavatory with 12 latrines and (on the left) as kitchen (bread oven and larger general oven), well and store room (note the massive jars used for storing olive oil). It is here that the castle comes to life, for our homes contain these same spaces, as well as a place in which to eat (the huge pillared area beyond the store rooms is thought to have served as a dining room). Back across the courtyard, the chapel is from the first years of the Hospitaller project, a bare chamber with barrel vaulting, later converted into a mosque.

Stairs beside the chapel lead up to the **Tower of the Princess**, which has been converted into a café/restaurant serving cold drinks, Homs wine and basic Syrian food (such as kebabs, *mezze*, *kofta*) and with access, via a spiral staircase, to a flat roof. From here, on a clear day, you can see to the plains and over the hills to Safita.

Continuing along the upper level, the circular tower in the southwest corner contains a later addition, what is thought to be the Lord's room (1260), with the castle's finest decorated window. It was perhaps here, in 1271, that the Christian commander looked at his meagre army of 200 knights (Crac was built to hold a capacity of 2,000) and at Baybars' immense army which had broken through the outer wall, and agreed to the surrender which effectively ended Christian presence in the Holy Land. ❑

Map on page 184

Through the corridors of time at Crac.

BELOW: on the ramparts at Crac.

ALEPPO

*An important stop on ancient spice and silk routes, Aleppo has
always thrived on trade. Its fabulous* khans *and labyrinthine souks
still comprise the largest bazaar in the world*

Map
on page
204

T he northern city of **Aleppo** (Halab) challenges Damascus as Syria's commercial and cultural centre as well as for the right to call itself the world's oldest inhabited city. Its name is an indicator of its age, for as with Damascus it occurs on 2nd millennium BC records – tablets found in Mari and Ebla refer to *Halba*. Aleppo was created by trade and, although it no longer straddles a global trade route, the city is still involved in international trade, these days most visibly with Turkey and Russia. When Aleppo first appeared in historical records it was as capital of an Amorite kingdom that controlled much of northern Syria, but which fell to the Sea Peoples, as Ugarit on the coast had fallen, around 1200 BC. From the Assyrians to the Romans, the Arabs to the Ottoman Turks, Aleppo bowed to the same foreign powers as its southern rival. But perhaps more than Damascus, Aleppo has held onto its traditions and these days takes pride in what it perceives as its cultural superiority to Damascus. A cosmopolitan city, it remains one of the highlights of any trip to Syria.

THE OLD CITY

In the 1940s Aleppo still functioned in the way that its ancient planners intended, with the majority of its inhabitants living inside the city walls. Since then the city has expanded enormously and the historic core has been encircled – some say strangled – by new development. Declared a UNESCO World Heritage site for its architectural and cultural importance, the old city has been the subject of an extensive restoration plan, under the auspices of the mayor, since 1993. The intention is to encourage the continued use and traditions of the old city at the same time as taking action to restore the fabric of the city.

On a practical level, for visitors this means greater access to some of the old city's more spectacular buildings as some old houses are converted into restaurants and hotels and the medieval *hammams* are restored to their former grandeur.

The Citadel

The imposing **Citadel** ❶ (Wed–Mon 9am–5pm, 9am–4pm in winter), east of the main souk, built partly on a 50-metre (165-ft) high natural elevation, dominates Aleppo's long history as it does the skyline. The discovery of the remains of a neo-Hittite temple (10th century BC) and a later Greek temple suggest that its original use was religious rather than military, and no evidence has appeared to suggest that the Romans used it for anything other than religious cults. During the 10th century AD the Hamdanid ruler Sayf ad-Dawla fortified the hill to create a strategic post against the crusaders, although most of what

PRECEDING PAGES:
an attention-
grabbing cinema
poster.
LEFT: in Aleppo's
famous souks.
BELOW:
view of the old city.

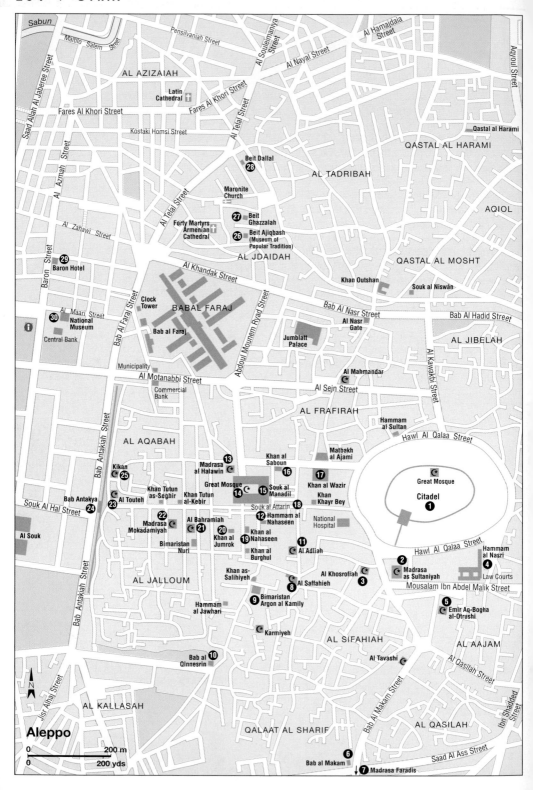

Sabun

Maitilo Salem Street

Pensilvaniah Street

Al Hamaidaia Street

Al Souleimaniya Street

Al Nayal Street

Aqyoul Street

AL AZIZAIAH

Latin Cathedral

Fares Al Khori Street

Saad Allah Al Jaberee Street

Al Azman Street

Fares Al Khori Street

Kostaki Homsi Street

Al Telal Street

Qastal al Harami

QASTAL AL HARAMI

AL TADRIBAH

AQIOL

Beit Dallal
28

Maronite Church

Al Zahawi Street

Al Telal Street

Forty Martyrs Armenian Cathedral

27 Beit Ghazzalah

26 Beit Ajiqbash (Museum of Popular Tradition)

AL JDAIDAH

QASTAL AL MOSHT

29 Baron Hotel

Baron Street

Al Khandak Street

Khan Outshan

Souk al Niswán

30 National Museum

Al Maari Street

Clock Tower

BAB AL FARAJ

Bab al Faraj

Abdoul Mounem Ryad Street

Bab Al Nasr Street

Al Nasr Gate

Bab Al Hadid Street

QASTAL AL MOSHT

AL JIBELAH

Central Bank

Bab Al Faraj Street

Municipality

Jumblatt Palace

Al Kawakbi Street

Commercial Bank

Al Motanabbi Street

AL AQABAH

Al Sejn Street

Al Mahmandar

AL FRAFIRAH

Hammam al Sultan

Hawl Al Qalaa Street

Bab Antakah Street

Kikan
25

Madrasa al Halawin
13

Khan al Saboun

Matbakh al Ajami

Great Mosque
14 15

16

17 Khan al Wazir

Khan Khayr Bey

Souk al Manadil

Souk Al Hal Street

Bab Antakya
24

23 Al Touteh

Khan Tutun as-Seghir

Khan Tutun al-Kebir

Great Mosque

Citadel
1

Al Souk

Madrasa Mokadamiyah
22

21

Al Bahramiah

20

Khan al Jumrok

Khan al Nahaseen
19

12 Hammam al Nahaseen

Souk al Attarin
18

National Hospital

Bimaristan Nuri

11 Al Adliah

2

Madrasa as Sultaniyah

Hammam al Nasri

4

AL JALLOUM

Khan as-Salihiyah

Khan al Burghul

Al Khosrofiah
3

Law Courts

8 Al Saffahieh

Mousalam Ibn Abdel Malik Street

9 Bimaristan Argon al Kamily

5 Emir Aq-Bogha al-Otrushi

Hammam al Jawhari

Karmiyeh

AL SIFAHIAH

AL AAJAM

Jisr Afnal Street

Bab al Qinnesrin
10

Al Tavashi

Al Qasilah Street

AL KALLASAH

Ibn Shadded Street

Aleppo

N

0   200 m
0   200 yds

QALAAT AL SHARIF

AL QASILAH

Bab Al Makam Street

6 Bab al Makam

7 Madrasa Faradis

AL QASILAH

Saad Al Ass Street

exists today dates from the end of the 12th century when Saladin's son al-Malik al-Zaher Ghazi made it the centre of his new city. He was responsible for building all the most remarkable features of the citadel, such as the 22-metre (72-ft) deep moat, the upper ramparts, the monumental bridge and entrance, and the stone-faced glacis which used Roman columns to help offset the pressure of the upper slope.

Approaching the citadel from the bridge gives an idea of how impregnable the citadel, with that deep moat, a stone glacis at a 48° angle and the **defence towers** must have appeared to invaders. The majestic entry bridge, built early in the 13th century but heavily renovated three centuries later, is a masterpiece of military architecture, combining aesthetics with military efficiency. Supported by eight arches and fronted by a 20-metre (65-ft) high defence tower now housing the ticket office, the bridge leads to a magnificent entrance portal. The solid tower of the entrance gateway is so big that it could easily be a citadel in its own right. Originally there were two towers which ended at the level of the machicolations, but the late 13th-century Mamluke Sultan al-Ashraf Khalil made several additions, and during the 16th century the arch and upper facade joined the two towers. There are five turnings and two more gateways to pass through before entering the citadel proper, more proof of the citadel's impregnability. The **front gateway** is sided by two serpents, the next two by lions, believed to protect the entrance with their mystical powers.

Inside the citadel, the most important sites are on either side of the paved causeway which runs north towards the mosque. First on the right is the **Byzantine Hall**, an old **cistern** and the remains of a **palace** built by al-Aziz in 1230. Behind it there is a restored 14th-century *hammam*. To the left, past

Map on page 204

The Citadel's Ayubbid gateway displays the contrasting stonework so typical of Syrian masonry.

BELOW: the mighty citadel

the 12th-century **Hammam of Nour ad-Deen** is the **Mosque of Abraham**, also attributed to Nour ad-Deen. The mosque was built over a church in which there was a stone believed to have been the one on which Abraham used to sit. Further along is the small **Great Mosque**, built in 1214 by al-Zaher Ghazi, which is magnificent in its simplicity, and very atmospheric with the wind blowing through the three huge pine trees in the perfectly proportioned courtyard.

Beneath the elegant minaret, a small café-terrace commands wonderful views over Aleppo and its surroundings. The café is housed in one wing of a **barracks** built in 1834 by the Egyptian general Ibrahim Pasha; the other wing was converted into a small **museum**.

Follow the path south from the barracks past a recently built amphitheatre, walking up towards the back of the entrance gateway. On the top is a courtyard paved in black-and-white stone with a door leading into the ornate **Throne Room**, built by the Mamlukes after the last Mongol invasion in 1400 led by Tamerlane and recently restored in all its rather kitsch splendour.

South of the citadel

To get away from the busy **souks** and the tourist buses queuing at the foot of the citadel, explore the less-visited *madrasa*, mosques and *khans* in the area south of the citadel. Immediately opposite the citadel's entrance are a few café terraces which are particularly pleasant late afternoon to have a cup of mint tea or a *narguileh* (waterpipe). Behind is the **Khan ash-Shouna**, an old *caravanserai* restored to house a handicraft market similar to the Takieh as-Sulaymaniyya in Damascus. Many items, such as the papyri and wooden inlaid boxes, are more likely to have been produced in Egypt than in Syria and prices are steep but

BELOW: Madrasa as-Sultaniyah.

usually fixed. The neighbouring **Madrasa as-Sultaniyah ②**, built in 1223, contains a superb polychrome marble *mihrab* in the prayer hall and the mausoleum of Saladin's son Al-Malek al-Zaher Ghazi, who developed the citadel.

On the other side of the street is the 16th-century **Al Khosrofiah Mosque ③**, the first Ottoman monument in Aleppo built under the supervision of the young master architect Sinan. Further east, next door to the grand 1930s Governorate building, is one of Syria's most touted *hammams* or steam baths. The **Hammam al Nasri ④** (also known as Hammam Yalbogha; opposite the citadel; daily 9am–midnight; for women only on Mon, Thurs and Sat from 9am–5pm) was built in the 14th century, but was extensively restored and rebuilt in the 1980s, mainly to suit the increasing numbers of tourists interested in visiting. One of Syria's grandest bath houses, it is a great place to be initiated into the delights of a day or a few hours in the *hammam*.

Behind the baths is the stern building of the Justice Ministry and south of that, at the intersection on the left, is the small **mosque and mausoleum of Emir Aq-Bogha al-Otrushi ⑤**, built in 1403. The intricately decorated high portal and facade are truly among the finest of all Mamluke buildings in Aleppo. A corridor in the northwest corner of the courtyard leads to the emir's simple, domed mausoleum. Follow the main road southwest which turns into Shari Makam. To the right is the 14th-century **Al Tavashi Mosque**, with a beautiful facade decorated with elegant colonettes, before arriving at the southern gate of the old city. This is the **Bab al Makam ⑥**, built in the 12th century by al-Zaher Ghazi and rebuilt by the Mamluke Sultan Qaytbey in 1493. Walk to the tree-lined square south of the gate and take the road leading southwest, where immediately to the left is the early 16th-century **Mausoleum of Kheir Bey**, a

Map on page 204

Light filters through the special windows in the dome of Hammam al Nasri.

BELOW: inside Hammam al Nasri.

Mamluke official who was transferred to Cairo before he could be buried in the tomb he had so carefully prepared for himself. Follow the street for about 1 km (½ mile), passing through the cemetery. Just where the cemetery ends, a small track on the left leads to the most stunning of all the mosques in Aleppo, the **Madrasa Faradis ❼** (el-Firdaus). This Qur'an school, literally School of Paradise, built in 1234 by Daifa Khatun, Saladin's daughter-in-law and niece, exudes an atmosphere of calm and spirituality. The entrance portal, decorated with stalactites, leads to the courtyard which is impressive for its simplicity and harmony. An arcade supported by fine ancient columns surrounds the courtyard on three sides, while the north side houses a large vaulted *iwan*. The prayer hall on the south side is covered by three honeycombed domes and has a particularly beautiful *mihrab* decorated with arabesques.

Taking the backstreets to the Great Mosque

From the citadel, take the little street just before the Madrasa Al Sultaniyah; at the first intersection turn right, and at the second intersection take a left to find, on the left hand side, the **Al-Saffahieh Mosque ❽** (open only at prayer times). Built in 1425, the mosque has a typical Mamluke black and white striped portal, decorated with stalactites, and a slender minaret.

Continue along the same street and after 100 metres/yards turn left, following the winding street southwards. The first *caravanserai* to the left is **Khan Labsi**, further on is **Khan as-Salihiyeh** and a third to the right is the 15th-century **Khan al-Qadi**, an atmospheric small *khan*.

Opposite is the **Bimaristan Argon al Kamily ❾** (open daily, knock when the door is locked), built in 1354 by the Mameluke governor of the same name and

TIP

Check with the guard at the Bimaristan of Arghun to see if there are any evening performances of the Whirling Dervishes scheduled.

BELOW: an example of the old wooden balconies that overlooked the narrow streets of the old quarter. Women could look out of these without being seen.

BIMARISTANS

The word *bimaristan* comes from two Persian words – *bimar* meaning patient and *stan* meaning house, so it is literally a house for patients. The Umayyad Caliph al-Walid is believed to have introduced the idea of a hospital combined with a medical college into Syria around AD 707. He appointed the best doctors to work in them and provided a large budget to be spent on the treatment of the sick. The Ayubbid ruler Nour ad-Deen particularly encouraged the study of medicine and opened several hospitals. It seems that the treatments were quite advanced for their time and the 12th-century traveller Ibn Jubayr was sufficiently impressed by what he saw to describe his visit to the *bimaristan*. Physicians arrived early every morning to do their daily rounds and prescribe the right drugs and diet for each patient. They believed that musical therapy and storytellers were an appropriate entertainment for the ill and that this alleviated their pain.

Both rich and poor patients were treated for free, and when patients recovered they were given clothing and five gold pieces to help them get by during the period of convalescence. The food in some *bimaristans* was reported to be so good that some people feigned illness in order to get a free and nutritious meal.

arguably the best preserved medieval psychiatric hospital in the Middle East. A superb honeycombed doorway gives way to the largest courtyard, surrounded by open cells, with a central fountain and an *iwan* where music and theatre performances are held. Just before the *iwan*, to the left, a passage leads off to a much smaller courtyard with tiny cells and very little light – this was reserved for the more severe cases of mental illness – and a larger one with slightly bigger cells. The aim of this arrangement was to create a calming atmosphere for the mentally ill through the flow of fountains and through music concerts held in the courtyards.

On the other side of the road is an olive soap factory, for which Aleppo is renowned. Continue along the street towards Bab al-Qinnesrin and look out to the right for the **Madrasa Asriya**, a restored 12th-century **madrasa** which now houses the offices of a German-Syrian cooperation project for the renovation and preservation of the old city. The 13th-century **Bab al-Qinnesrin** ❿ is the best preserved of Aleppo's old gates. Return north along the same street towards the main souk area. Beyond the crossroads that lead to the al-Saffahieh Mosque, continue straight and look on the right-hand side for a passage leading to the **Al-Adliah Mosque** ⓫ (all day). This is Aleppo's second oldest Ottoman mosque, after the al-Khosrofiah Mosque *(see page 207)*. Built in 1555 by Mohammed Pasha, the tranquil courtyard is lined with pine trees and the walls of its double arcade are covered in beautiful locally-produced blue tiles. The prayer hall beneath a large dome has an elegant *mihrab*.

Further to the right, opposite the Khan al Nahaseen *(see page 213)*, is the **Hammam al Nahaseen** ⓬ or **Hammam as-Sitt**, a 12th-century bath house now open to men only. Cross over the main souk, the Souk al Attarin, into the

Map on page 204

Olive oil soap is a speciality of Aleppo. It is made from water, soda and olive oil.

BELOW: the Mosque of al-Halawiyeh.

The ornately decorated minaret of the Great Mosque.

BELOW: courtyard of the Great Mosque.

narrow streets of a rope and spice souk: at the t-junction walk left around the back of the Great Mosque and then take the first street to the right. At the end of the street, past a little bakery selling delicious *fatayer* (little pasties stuffed with cheese and mint, with meat or with spinach) is the tourist entrance to the Great Mosque (*see below*).

Across the street a doorway leads to the **Madrasa al Halawin** ⓭ (daily until late afternoon). This 13th-century religious school was built over the 6th-century Cathedral of St Helena, in honour of the mother of the Emperor Constantine. For some centuries after the Great Mosque was built, Muslims and Christians apparently coexisted quite happily. But in the 12th century, after the crusaders attacked Aleppo and committed many atrocities against the Muslims, the Muslim ruler decided in revenge to seize the cathedral, along with several other churches, and make it a *madrasa*. The pleasant courtyard is flanked on three sides by student cells and on the western side by two large arches. All that remains of the original cathedral is a bricked-up domed hall with a semi-circular row of six fine Byzantine columns.

Back in the courtyard, the door to the right in the glass facade leads to the small prayer hall with a magnificent sculpted wooden *mihrab*.

The Great Mosque (Al Jamaa al Kebir)

The **Great Mosque** ⓮ (Jamia al Ayyoubi Street; tourist entrance opposite the Madrasa al Halawin; women are required to wear a hooded cloak; open daily; the prayer hall may be partly closed for restoration), also known as the Gami'a Zakariyeh or the Umayyad Mosque, may lack the grandeur and splendour of the Umayyad Mosque in Damascus, but being smaller it has a more intimate feel to

it. Women sit around resting from their day's chores, children chase pigeons across the courtyard, traders walk through from the souks while the devout pay the blind Qur'an reciters to sing a few verses for the good of a sick member of their family. Only 10 years younger than the Damascus Umayyad Mosque, it was started under Caliph al-Walid, but completed by his brother Caliph Sulayman in 715–717. Like his brother's mosque, Sulayman's mosque was also built on Christian foundations, specifically the garden and cemetery of St Helena's Cathedral. Nothing remains of the original Umayyad mosque, which burned down in 1169 and was rebuilt by Nour ad-Deen.

The **minaret**, a later (1090) addition by the Seljuq Sultan Tutush was spared, but has a noticeable bend due to an earthquake. Forty-five metres (148 ft) high, it is one of the highlights of Syrian medieval architecture, with an ornately decorated facade interspersed by bands of Kufic inscriptions. Some of the stones are believed to have been lifted from the nearby cathedral. The leaning tower, in danger of falling over, is now undergoing serious restoration and may have to be dismantled and rebuilt stone by stone.

As in the Damascus mosque, the **courtyard** is surrounded by arcades on three sides. Dazzling in the midday sun, it is adorned with several sun dials and a central fountain. The **prayer hall** has an elaborate 15th-century *mihrab*. To the left of the *mihrab* is the **shrine of Zakariah**, which is said to contain the body of St John the Baptist's father.

Khans and souks

Leave the mosque's courtyard from the opposite side to where you came in, and walk straight through the **Souk al Manadil** ⓯ with gold and silver jewellers.

Map on page 204

Shopkeepers put locks on the grille around the shrine of Zakariah, in the hope that this will help protect their shops: others leave flasks of water near the tomb believing that the blessed water will cure sick loved ones.

BELOW: Khan al Saboun (soap).

TIP

The son of a former *muezzin* from the Great Mosque, Ahmed Modallal, offers half-day tours or day tours of the city at reasonable prices and speaks perfect English. He is often in the courtyard of the mosque, but you can also book him in advance, tel: 6719, fax: 251 606.

BELOW: herbal remedies in a traditional apothecary.

To the right are several entrances to the vaulted **Souk al-Khourrag** with more jewellers and carpet sellers. Return to the Souk al-Manadil and before the cross-roads to the left is the impressive entrance to the early 16th-century **Khan al Saboun ⑯**, one of the great Mamluke monuments in Aleppo. Behind the intricately decorated facade, with a beautiful window, lies a courtyard with well-proportioned arcades partially hidden amongst the clutter of the warehouses and workshops. The olive soap *(saboun)*, for which Aleppo is famous, is no longer traded here but is found elsewhere in the city.

Back on the street, at the fountain take the next street to the left and walk outside the gate to reach a small square. Take a left along the Mamluke **Mosque of al-Fustuq**, built in 1349, and on the opposite side of the square is the 12th-century **Matbakh al-Ajami**, a small Zengid palace which used to house the Museum of Popular Tradition (now in the Jdaidah quarter, *see page 215*). On the eastern side of the square is the imposing portal of the finest *caravanserai* in Aleppo, the **Khan al Wazir ⑰**, built in 1682 by one of Aleppo's governors. Inside, note the six superbly decorated windows above the entrance – the upper one to the right with a minaret and the upper one to the left displaying a stylised cross supposedly represent the religions of the two artisans who decorated the *khan*. The vast courtyard planted with eucalyptus and fig trees has a small mosque at its centre, and is surrounded by two floors of rooms, now storage spaces and workshops. In the southwestern corner are a couple of antiques shops and souvenir stalls.

Outside, turn left back towards the souk, left again and then right to find the beautiful brick-vaulted **Khan Khayr Bey**. Turn right onto the covered main souk, the **Souk al Attarin ⑱** (Spice Souk), where shops sell herbs, herbal

KHANS (CARAVANSERAIS)

Both Damascus and Aleppo were important stops on the major trade routes between Eastern Europe, Africa, the Mediterranean and Near Eastern markets, and the *khans* or *caravanserais* were numerous. The word *khan* is originally Persian, meaning house or palace, although sometimes they are also called *caesarias*, from the Greek, meaning royal structure or a property of the state. *Khans* served as inns, often accommodating many travellers and hundreds of animals, but they were also places where tradesmen could do deals or store goods safely. Behind high protective walls and an ornate entrance portal lies a large courtyard, often with a central kiosk that served as a mosque, surrounded by arcades. Usually the ground floor is where the animals or goods were kept, while the travellers' cells were on the upper floor. *Hammams* (public bath houses) in the neighbourhood of the larger *khans* provided weary travellers with a much-needed bath, but they were also places to relax and enjoy oneself. The considerable revenues generated by *khans* were sometimes used for the upkeep of a charitable institution such as a *bimaristan (see page 208)* or *madrasa*. Many *khans* have long disappeared or fallen into ruins, but in Aleppo quite a few are still used as storage places for wholesalers or as workshops.

remedies, nuts and dried fruits, including famous Aleppan pistachio nuts, soap and pyramids of *za'atar*, a mixture of cumin, oregano, sumac and toasted sesame seeds. It is believed that this lively thoroughfare follows the Roman *decumanus*, which in turn followed the plan of the town built by the Seleucids in the 4th–3rd centuries BC. Take the fifth street to the left to reach, on the right, the **Khan al Nahaseen** ⓳ (Khan of the Coppersmiths), opposite the Hammam an-Nahaseen. This small 16th-century *caravanserai* was used as the warehouses and consulate of the Venetians during the 19th century. On the south side of the courtyard is the house of Adolphe Poche, born here in 1895, who died in the early 1990s. The consul for Austria-Hungary, the Netherlands and Belgium, Poche was an archaeologist who assembled a fascinating collection of antiques and archaeological finds which can still be seen at his **house** (permission must be obtained from the Belgian consulate at the Khan al-Kattin immediately south of the Khan al-Wazir). Almost next door is the **Khan al-Burghul**, with two courtyards shaded by vines.

Return to the Khan al-Nahaseen and walk along the northern wall, cross the alley with colourful fabric shops and find, on the left, the entrance to Aleppo's largest *khan*, the **Khan al Jumrok** ⓴ (Customs Khan), where taxes were levied on the goods that arrived in Aleppo. Covering some 6,400 square metres (68,900 sq ft) this vast *caravanserai*, built in 1574, housed 344 shops as well as the banks and consulates of England, France and the Netherlands. The *khan* has four entrances closed by heavy nailed wooden doors and, as elsewhere in the city, the inside of the main entrance portal has lovely carved windows. The complex has two vaulted rows of shops in the front and a little mosque at the centre which is now behind some more modern constructions.

Map on page 204

Coppersmith in the Khan al Nahaseen.

BELOW: textiles have always been one of Aleppo's most important industries.

Towards Bab Antakya and the City Walls

Back on Souk al-Attarin walk left towards the Bab Antakya. On the left after 150 metres/yards, is the **Mosque al Bahramiah** ㉑ (the courtyard is open during prayer times, although at other times someone is usually around to open the doors), built in 1583 by Bahram Pasha, then Governor of Aleppo. The original minaret was destroyed by an earthquake and rebuilt in Ottoman style in the 17th century. The *mihrab* in the prayer hall is beautifully decorated with arabesques, but this area is closed to non-Muslims. Behind the mosque, take the first right turn and find, further on the right, the **Bimaristan Nuri**, a hospital built in 1150 by Nour ad-Deen, whose more famous *bimaristan* is in Damascus. Its ruinous state makes it hardly worth the detour, but the narrow residential streets make for a quiet escape from the souk.

From the mosque take the second lane to the left, walking down the stairs to find, after 20 metres/yards to the left, **Madrasa Mokadamiyah** ㉒ (open at prayer times only), the oldest *madrasa* in Aleppo. Originally an old church, this was one of the Christian sites seized by the Muslims in revenge for the crusaders' siege of Damascus; it was converted into a religious school in 1168. The elegant portal is decorated with two medallions of arabesques.

Return to the Souk al-Attarin and find almost immediately to the right **Khan Tutun al-Kebir**, a two-storied *khan* with an elegant arcade on the second floor and, next door, the smaller **Khan Tutun as-Seghir**. Pass the *za'atar* sellers with their layered pyramids of spices and peep into a few of the smaller working *khans* as well as the 14th-century **Karmiyeh Mosque** (on the right) with a fine minaret, before arriving at the tiny 13th-century **Mosque al Touteh** ㉓ (Mosque of the Mulberry Tree). This Ayubbid mosque, which incorporates

BELOW: the classic Aleppo taxi.

stones from a Roman triumphal Arch, is built on the site of a 12th-century mosque believed to have been the first mosque in Aleppo. Note the fine Kufic inscription and entrelac decoration from the 12th century.

The souk ends at **Bab Antakya** ㉔, the 13th-century city gate erected by the Ayubbids, which was restored in the 15th century. It was through the earlier gate on this spot that the first Muslims entered Aleppo, but the gate is now occupied by masons and other workers, waiting with their tools to rent themselves out for the day. Coming from the souk, just before the gate, a broad stairway leads up to the walls, passing a *hammam* to the right. From the top of the walls there are excellent views over modern Aleppo, with its crop of satellite dishes and grand new mosques, symbols of affluence for modern Aleppan businessmen. A residential area starts here, built on the site of the Hellenistic village of Beroia. Note the small **Mosque of Kikan** ㉕, with two ancient basalt columns on either side of the portal and some ancient stones incorporated into its facade.

The Armenian Jdaidah quarter

The old Christian Armenian quarter, extending to the north beyond the old city walls, is a fascinating place to wander around, particularly on Sundays when the faithful come to its many churches. The picturesque, narrow paved streets are bordered by high walls, behind which are hidden opulent mansions, many currently undergoing restoration. The quarter developed during the late Mamluke period, when trade with Venice was in full swing. It attracted largely Maronite and Armenian Christians who acted as middlemen in the flourishing trade. At the time it was the **jdaidah** or new quarter, a name that it has kept. Most houses date from the 17th and 18th centuries and are typically Arab in design which

Map on page 204

A typical paved street in the Armenian quarter. Sunday is a good time to explore its alleyways.

BELOW:
a garden game of backgammon.

Finely sculpted window detail of the 17th-century Beit Ghazzalah.

means that they hide their sumptuous interiors and perfumed courtyards behind plain and often stern facades. The easiest approach to the area is from Tilal Street, a lively pedestrian shopping street of lingerie and perfume shops off Quwatly Street. The first larger street on the right, Saahat Farhat, leads to the late 19th-century **Maronite church** and, beside it, the modern **Greek Catholic church**. Before the churches turn right, and right again at the T-junction, to reach the **Greek Orthodox church**, with the tomb of a Russian consul in the courtyard and some icons of special interest. Further right is the 15th-century **Forty Martyrs Armenian Cathedral**, with interesting Armenian icons and paintings. Back at the T-junction, to the left is the **Syrian Catholic St Assia Church**, usually closed now that the community has moved out of the area.

Continue further east amidst wool and knitting shops until you reach, on the left at the end of the street, a door leading to the stunning **Beit Ajiqbash** ㉖, which now houses the **Museum of Popular Tradition** (Wed–Mon 8am–2pm, closed Tues). This mid-18th-century house, built by the wealthy Christian Ajiqbash family in traditional Arab style, is one of the most magnificent residences of Aleppo. Rooms are centred on a lavishly decorated courtyard with fruit trees and a central fountain, and a splendid sculpted *iwan*. The rooms contain a collection of weapons, old household goods, handicrafts, traditional costumes and beautiful inlaid furniture. Note the impressive painted and gilded ceiling in the grand reception room opposite the *iwan*.

Turn left on Jdaidah Street, also known as Al-Kayyali Street, and find on the left the large 17th-century **Beit Ghazzalah** ㉗, currently undergoing restoration. The frames around the windows of its courtyard are richly sculpted, as was fashionable at the time. 40 metres/yards further along is **Jdaidah Square** with

silver jewellers and a few antique shops, and to the left is Beit Sissi, a restaurant serving traditional Aleppan dishes. The narrow street to the right, al-Sissi Street, has first to the right **Beit Dallal** ㉘, a 17th-century house with a large marble paved courtyard, and further left **Beit Wakil**, now converted into one of Syria's most atmospheric hotels with a good restaurant-bar. The beautiful wood panels that adorned the reception room, now the hotel lobby, were sold in 1912 to the Berlin Museum where they form the Aleppo Room. Until recently the *salamlek* part of the house, now the hotel, was used as a home for the elderly, while the more lavishly decorated private quarters of the family, now the restaurant, were used as a Greek Orthodox orphanage. The bar is located in very deep cellars which probably date back to pre-Islamic times.

In the same street is the less decorated Beit Sayegh, now used as a small Armenian school. In the parallel Zabel Street, two other 18th-century houses – **Beit Basil** and **Beit Balit** – are now used as orphanages.

THE NEW CITY

There are very few sights in the modern city of Aleppo, with the exception of several recently built but rather ostentatious looking mosques and the fascinating National Museum. Central Aleppo tends to look rather run-down and turns into something of a red-light district at night. The old **Baron Hotel** ㉙ now at heart of it, continues to be a social centre for passing foreigners, although it is but a shadow of its former self. When the hotel was built in 1909 by the two Armenian Mazloumian brothers, it was a truly palatial hotel with central heating and well-equipped bathrooms. At that time the hotel was situated outside the city and was surrounded by a wood; duck shooting from the windows was a

Map on page 204

The Baron Hotel remains a favourite choice of romantic foreigners.

BELOW: buses are works of art.

favourite pasttime for visitors. During World War I the Baron was commandeered as the headquarters of the Turkish commander-in-chief Jamal Pasha and his sumptuous parties established the hotel's reputation. T. E. Lawrence, who often stayed in room No. 202, is probably the hotel's most famous guest, but there were many others including General Allenby, Zsa Zsa Gabor, the aviator Charles Lindberg, Freya Stark and Theodore Roosevelt. The hotel was nationalised in 1966 and the owner-manager Koko, the last of the Mazloumians, died in the 1990s.

Agatha Christie wrote part of Murder on the Orient Express *in the Baron Hotel.*

The large public park northwest of the hotel district makes for a pleasant change from the hubbub of the souks and downtown area. North of the park is the district of Al-Azizaiah where many of Aleppo's wealthy and mostly Christian families live.

National Museum

The collection of Aleppo's **National Museum** ㉚ (Baron Street, Bab al-Faraj, Wed–Mon 9am–6pm, 9am–4pm in winter, closed Tues; there is a small but useful guide book to the museum on sale at the ticket office) is every bit as important as its counterpart in Damascus, despite being housed in a rather uninspiring building with its artefacts often poorly displayed. The majority of objects were found in sites in northern Syria, with special emphasis on the period from the Iron Age up to the classical period. The building, in plan if not in atmosphere, follows traditional Arab design, with two storeys arranged around a central courtyard. The entrance follows a longstanding Syrian tradition of monumental entrances, being fronted by three huge caryatids, two gods and a goddess, supported by their rather unwieldy mythical animals. This is a reproduction of

BELOW: 3rd-century find in the National Museum (**RIGHT**).

part of the gateway to the temple at Tell Halaf, probably from the 10th century BC. Inside the museum, walk anti-clockwise for a chronological order.

The tour begins with finds from the **Jazirah region**, between the Tigris and Euphrates rivers in northeastern Syria. The votive offerings and beautiful friezes come from the fourth millennium BC Eye Temple at Tell Brak, the oldest temple so far discovered in Syria. Note the big-breasted naked clay figurines, most probably representing the mother goddess, and greenish Obeid pottery from the 5th millennium BC found in Tell Halaf. Among finds from the Bronze-Age site of Mari are a superb vase with a relief of intertwined serpents, several fine statuettes depicting their owners – including the statue of one Prince Lamji-Mari – at the temple in constant prayer to the gods, and a very beautiful alabaster head of a warrior. The larger pieces, mostly from the golden age of Mari, 21st century BC, are even more impressive, particularly the delicate limestone sculpture of the Lady of the Well-Spring and the black diorite life-size sculpture of Prince Ishtup-Ilum. Mari was important because of a library of more than 20,000 clay tablets discovered at the palace, some of which are on display here. The tablets give insight into the political, economical and social life of the time.

Beyond the Hama and Ugarit Hall is the **Tell Halaf Hall**, with finds from the Iron Age, including several rather crude black statues similar to the ones found at the entrance to the museum, as well as stone slabs from the Temple Palace, carved with mythological and battle scenes. More interesting is an outstanding collection of 9th century BC ivory carvings, some inlaid with precious stones, found at the Aramaic city of Arslan Tash, but probably Phoenician in origin. Upstairs is a fine collection of classical and Byzantine finds, including statues and pottery from Palmyra, and a hall displaying Arab Islamic Art. ❑

Amarite spring goddess, 18th century BC.

BELOW:
ram-headed sphinxes and holy tree, 9th century BC.

SECRETS OF THE ARABIAN SOUK

The souk is the heart and soul of the Islamic medina, and the best place to sample the traditional Arab way of life

In the souk's medieval maze of twisting, narrow alleyways, the buildings stand close together to protect people from the fierce heat of summer and from the rain and cold of winter. The shops are squeezed between the five key buildings: mosque, *madrasa* (Qur'anic school: often more than one), *hammam* (bath), *khan* (warehouse) and bakery. Traditionally, every area has its own speciality; most cities still have a gold souk, carpet souk, spice souk and fabric souk. Generally, luxury goods are clustered closest to the mosque, and more prosaic items are situated further out.

SCENTS AND ODOURS

Entering a souk is an assault on the senses. A cacophony of noises, a dazzling sea of colours and glitter, and 1001 aromas, from the sweetest of perfumes to the nauseating smells of hanging carcasses, dung and rotting skins. Once you have adjusted to the smells and the deceptive impression of chaos, you can spend hours exploring little alleys, chatting to shopkeepers, bargaining for a carpet, drinking tea or smoking a waterpipe.

The longer you spend in a souk, the more you come to appreciate its harmony. Undoubtedly time has a different value in the souk, and life seems generally more humane, but don't be fooled by the relaxed atmosphere: Arabs are fierce traders and it can be hard work to get a bargain.

▷ MAGIC CARPETS
Damascus and Aleppo are good places to buy Persian carpets. For centuries these two cities have been a channel for luxury goods from the east.

△ ORIENTAL SLIPPERS
Decorated leather or fabric slippers make great gifts. In Aleppo hard-wearing leather sandals are sold near the Umayyad Mosque.

△ GOLD, GOLD, GOLD
Jewellery represents financial security for many Arab women, who always keep it in cases of divorce.

◁ SWEET SMELLS
The perfumiers of the souk make divine scents, but also cure ailments and stimulate sexual powers.

FINDING THE BEST BUYS

Aleppo, the mother of souks, is famous for its pure olive oil soap which is still produced in the old city's little factories. The city is equally renowned for its silk and cotton fabrics, available at Souk al-Juh. Several places in the spice market sell *za'atar*, used in regional recipes. Also worth looking out for are woollen coats lined with sheepskin, and simple but well-made leather sandals on sale near the Great Mosque.

Damascus is renowned for its fine handwoven brocade, beautifully inlaid silver swords, hand-crafted musical instruments, hand-blown glass and finely inlaid woodwork, from boxes and chess games to tables and cupboards. The boxes of candied fruit, sugared almonds and stuffed dates in the spice market, and particularly in Ghraoui, make excellent presents. Damascus is also a famous source for carpets, antiques and embroidered cotton tablecloths.

In Lebanon, the souks in Sidon and Tripoli sell fine brassware, handblown glass and pottery, but the quality and prices are generally better in Syria.

△ SPREE TIME
One of the busiest but most atmospheric times to visit the souks is around 5–7pm, when locals like to shop.

◁ SPICE WORLD
The spice market sells everything from sweets, nuts, herbs and spices to dried chameleons and flies.

THE NORTHWEST

*Although little visited by tourists, the region around Aleppo
is packed with classical sites whose isolation and beauty bring
back a sense of romance to ruin-roaming*

Map
on page
227

The city of **Aleppo ❶** is an excellent base from which to venture to the region of the "Dead Cities". This evocative term refers to the bare mountainous limestone region in northwest Syria, scattered with the remarkably well-preserved ruins of many elegant country villas, towns, monasteries and churches, now abandoned. During the Roman and Byzantine periods, these communities were the centre of a thriving olive oil and wine industry, which relied on the careful conservation of winter rains and commerce with the Mediterranean world.

The wealth generated was reflected in sumptuously decorated and well-appointed civic and domestic buildings. Rich mosaics such as those displayed in the museum at Ma'arrat an Nu'man *(see page 177)* documented the lifestyles and preoccupations of the cities' inhabitants, with subject matter ranging from classical mythology to local scenes of harvesting. This thriving economy collapsed with the disruptions of the Muslim conquest but the monuments to daily life remain, largely unpillaged and undisturbed, except by earthquakes. The buildings, standing up to three storeys high, are of well-cut limestone, marrying Graeco-Roman architecture with an individualistic Syrian interpretation unique to this area.

The most rewarding and accessible sites are the Church of St Simeon, Cyrrus and Ebla (the latter more for its historic importance than for its ruins), all of which lie to the west of Aleppo (the best base for exploring the area as there is little in the way of accommodation near the sites themselves). However, there are various other concentrations of "Dead Cities", some of which are touched upon in the chapter "The Orontes Valley and the Desert Steppe" *(see pages 177)*, and almost any village hereabouts will have something of archaeological interest, such as a Roman tomb or sections of the old Roman road that linked Aleppo with Antioch.

Another feature of the region is its sizeable Kurdish population. Kurds comprise some 10 percent of Syria's total population, and they live mainly in the border regions with Turkey.

The stones speak

Though having less to see on the surface than some of the other Dead Cities, **Ebla** (Tell Mardikh) **❷** is of enormous significance in recent scholarship. Forty-five kilometres (28 miles) south of Aleppo on the north Syrian plain (turn off the main Aleppo–Hama highway), Bronze-Age Ebla was a major urban centre with international links at the time of the great cities of Sumer and Akkad in Mesopotamia. In 1975 Italian archaeologists discovered its archives, full of some 17,000 cuneiform tablets in the local language of the time (now called Eblaite) providing a repository of information for historians. Parts of the enormous tell

PRECEDING PAGES:
a rural landscape
north of Aleppo.
LEFT: sitting on the
worn steps of Ebla.
BELOW:
tombs at Cyrrhus.

St Simeon

St Simeon the Stylite demonstrated his outstanding piety from the day he entered a Syrian monastery at the age of 16. Issued with a spiked iron girdle tightened until it drew blood, he went one better by wearing it while buried in a hole in the ground for an entire summer with only his head sticking out. His special request for Lent was to be bricked up without food of any description in a wall.

But it was his next idea, which came to him in the year 423, that made Simeon a revered figure in early Christendom. In an age when opinionated religious figures generally became hermits, wisely retiring to deserts or mountain caves to evade martyrdom, Simeon lived for 30 years on top of an 18-metre (60-ft) stone column at the site now known as Kalat Seman and from there preached loud and clear to enormous congregations.

The top of Simeon's column was completely exposed to the elements, the only refinement being a low parapet in case he rolled about in his sleep. To be doubly sure, he slept with a chain attached to an iron collar around his neck. A monk climbed a ladder once a week to bring him communion and anything else he needed and, when not actually preaching, Simeon passed the day in prayer and constant prostrations. One of his followers started to count the number of prostrations on a particular day and gave up when he got to 1,244.

Not once in 30 years did Simeon leave his perch, not even when an ulcerated foot threatened his life and the Byzantine Emperor Theodosius sent a personal letter and a delegation of bishops begging him to come down for treatment. Never a big eater, he went without food altogether for 40 days and pronounced himself cured.

By the middle of the 5th century, Simeon's miracle-working had become legendary and he preached to a sea of pilgrims from all corners of Christendom, including from as far away as Britain. On controversial questions such as the nature of God the Father and God the Son, his line was strictly orthodox, but he did not shrink from offering the emperor advice on imperial policy. It was his intervention that cancelled an edict which would have allowed Jews to regain possession of their synagogues.

Reports of Simeon's imminent death in 459 brought huge multitudes to the hills around the column to hear his last words. His body was brought down on a ladder and transported to Antioch in great pomp for burial in a church that had been specially built for the purpose.

Simeon's example was so inspirational that hills all over northern Syria and far beyond soon sprouted similar pillars with a "stylite" installed on top. Simeon Stylite the Younger was said to have not yet cut his teeth before his parents, presumably, put him on one, and at the university in Beirut one of the professors lectured to his students from another. The movement never caught on in the west – the religious authorities in France brought a stylite down to earth by demolishing the column under him – but it remained popular in Syria until the Crusades. ❑

LEFT: sunset at St Simeon's.

have been excavated, revealing sections of the royal palace, sanctuaries, and city fortifications; the tablets, which form some of the earliest writings in the world, are slowly being translated and revealing that Ebla was the most powerful city in northern Syria during the 3rd millennium BC. The texts are also shedding a new light on many historical theories, including some aspects of biblical history. South of Ebla is a clutch of other Dead Cities, such as Ruweiha and Bara. A little far for a day trip from Aleppo, they are included in the chapter on the Orontes Valley and the Central Plains.

Map on page 227

Byzantine churches

West of Aleppo, highway 5 leads to a number of minor sites, the most interesting of which is **Qalb Loze ❸**, about 6 km (4 miles) off the road, close to the Turkish border. This church is one of the most impressive Byzantine churches in the country. Its isolation is puzzling (the surrounding village is entirely modern), though the most common theory is that it was built as a resting place for pilgrims on their way to Qala't Samaan. Also of note along this route is a beautifully preserved stretch of Roman road (about 40 km/25 miles from Aleppo).

In past steps – the Roman road from Aleppo, close to the Turkish border.

Of the multitude of sites, **Qal'at Samaan** (Church of St Simeon) ❹ (10am–6pm; winter until 4pm; admission charge) with its related monastery and pilgrimage centre, is perhaps the most striking. The hilltop setting is dramatic and the honey-coloured buildings are extraordinary not just for their beauty but for their numerous architectural innovations, such as the carving of acanthus leaves in such a way that they look as though they are rustling in the breeze – a decorative device that began here and was then copied throughout the Byzantine empire.

A great cruciform church was built around the pillar of the 5th-century ascetic

BELOW:
local inhabitants.

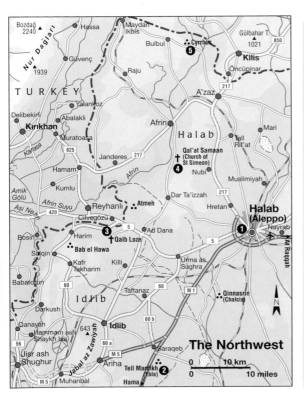

The Northwest

A man irrigates a field. Even in a region with relatively high precipitation, water has to be harvested and managed carefully. Water shortage is one of Syria's main problems.

BELOW:
in the fields.

Simeon Stylites, who chose to isolate himself from the world by living on top of a giant column for the final 40 years of his life *(see page 226)*. He was revered for his piety and wisdom all over the Byzantine world, attracting hordes of pilgrims, as well as many imitators. After Simeon's death, his column became the centrepiece of a magnificent church laid out like a cross. Apart from Haghia Sophia's in Constantinople, it was the biggest Christian building in the world until Europeans took to building cathedrals in the Middle Ages. Pilgrims were attracted in tens of thousands by reports of numerous miracles and regular sightings of "a resemblance of the saint's face flitting about here and there, with a long beard and wearing a tiara". Women, however, were not admitted. In his own lifetime, the saint had barred all women, including his mother, from crossing a circle of stones around the base of his pillar.

In due course, the immense wealth deposited at the saint's shrine necessitated fortifications that turned the church into a virtual castle. Its last significant appearance in history was in 985, when it was besieged and sacked by the Hamdanid princes of Aleppo, who killed or sold into slavery the remaining monks.

The remnants of St Simeon's pillar forms a popular plinth for photographs. It occupies the central courtyard, linking four basilicas in a cruciform pattern. Liturgical services would have taken place in the larger eastern basilica, with the south, west and north basilicas mainly used as ante-rooms for the many pilgrims. Other buildings of note in the immediate vicinity include a mortuary chapel beyond the northern basilica, and a monastery which would have served as lodging for more important visitors. Further off are the baptistry which would have had a walk-in baptismal font, where mass baptisms were

held, and down the Via Sacra a monumental arch, through which the pilgrims would have begun their ascent to the church. Beyond this arch is **Deir Seman**, the village which would have served the monastic community and the visiting pilgrims. Modern development sprawls between the ancient buildings, which include a pilgrims' inn, a market area, a law court and a chapel.

Map on page 227

Romantic Cyrrhus

The ruins of the classical city of **Cyrrhus** ❺ (modern-day Nabi Khouri) perched on the Turkish border about 80 km (50 miles) north or Aleppo, are not as well preserved as other such sites in Syria, but the location is one of the most romantic in its isolation and beauty, with rugged slopes dotted with ancient masonry, grazing sheep and olive trees. The approach to the site crosses two Roman bridges, one over the Afrin River and the second over the Sabun; both are still in use today. Cyrrhus was founded by the Seleucids in around 300 BC, then became a garrison town during the time of the Roman and Byzantine empires, and like other such towns in the region it was refortified by Justinian in the 6th century in his attempts to shore up the crumbling empire. But though its *raison d'etre* was primarily military it also became an important commercial centre and was on the caravan route from Antioch.

The Roman tower tomb with pyramid top, Cyrrhus.

As well as a theatre, citadel, walls and the remains of the Cardo Maximus which dissected the city, there are several interesting tombs, in particular that of the 5th-century chronicler of St Simeon, Theodoret. One of the most intriguing tombs is a two-storey Roman tower tomb with a pyramid top dating from the 2nd–3rd century situated outside the south gate; the tomb's lower storey is now occupied by a 14th-century Muslim saint. ❑

BELOW: the tumbled remains of Cyrrhus.

ALONG THE EUPHRATES

*The Euphrates is one of the great rivers of Asia.
Its fertile flood-plain has been settled for millennia, as the
huge number and range of ancient sites prove*

Map on page 234

Damascus

From Aleppo it is less than an hour's drive (about 70 km/45 miles) to the flood-plain of the great Euphrates River, a river which rises in eastern Turkey, flows southeast though Syria and eventually, after 3,600 km (2,230 miles), joins the Tigris in the marshlands of southeast Iraq. A crucial source of water for Turkey, Syria and Iraq, the river is an intermittent source of conflict between the three countries. Lake Assad, created by Syria in the 1960s, is just one of many reservoirs that harvest its waters.

Like the Nile Valley, the river's fertile flood-plain, nowadays a rather tatty green ribbon threading through the flat parched landscape, has been settled by man for millennia and is packed with the archaeological evidence of the towns and cities that once flourished here. The seemingly empty Jazirah, spreading north of the river, is particularly rich, for this region, up to the valley of the mighty Tigris in Iraq, was ancient Mesopotamia, the centre of the Babylonian, Sumerian and Assyrian civilisations. Many of the archaeological remains are little more than piles of dust and rubble from successive periods of habitation *(tells)*, destroyed by foreign forces, builders in search of stone, or earthquakes, revealing virtually nothing to laymen. Others, such as Ar rusafah, Mari and Dura Europas have yielded some of the finest exhibits in the archaeological museums of Aleppo and Damascus, though even these sites have largely been left to crumble, their exquisite finds being more important than the ruins in which they were found.

Following the river

Archaeological sites are just part of the region's appeal. The fertile areas close to the river are planted with wheat and cotton and agricultural scenes enliven the journey east; elsewhere the light bouncing off the parched land intensifies colours, especially of the women's neon-coloured clothing, delighting the eye.

The river's role as an important channel for trade and armies (it was a frontier for the Romans) has produced several fine castles, such as Qala't al Najim and Qal'at al Jabar, usually commanding crossing places. But one of the most intriguing forms of architecture are the beehive houses characteristic of this area and the region northwest of Aleppo *(see page 237)*. Built of mud-brick, making them cool in summer and warm in winter, they are usually grouped around a courtyard, with additional beehives added as a family's size and wealth expands.

This chapter explores the region from north to south. A good stop-over on the way is the modern administrative centre of Dayr az Zawr, from where a fast road connects with the Orontes Valley, Palmyra and Damascus.

PRECEDING PAGES: donkey-riding in the Euphrates Valley.
LEFT: moored at Lake Assad.
BELOW: pedestrian bridge across the Euphrates at Dayr az Zawr.

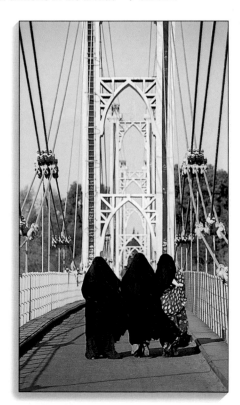

The castles and the lake

The hydro-electric dam at Madinat ath Thawrah produces electricity for the whole of Syria.

Lake Assad (Buhayrat al Asad) is the usual starting place for a tour the region, but 60 km (40 miles) north of here, just south of the main M4 highway from Aleppo into the Jazirah is the impressive **Qal'at Najim ❶** perched above the river. The castle was first built by the Umayyads to guard a bridge over the river, but the present structure is mostly 12th–13th century, and built by crusaders. Its excellent state of preservation invites exploration; you can climb up to the battlements for commanding river views.

From **Manbij**, 30 km (18 miles) west of the castle, a road cuts south to join the main road running along the south bank of the Euphrates, passing close to Lake Assad at **Madinat ath Thawrah**, site of the dam that created the lake. It is now the home to the families of the men who migrated here to work on the project, as well as the populations of assorted villages that had to move out of the way of the great new lake. The minaret in the centre of this unprepossessing town was moved here from the village of Maskanah.

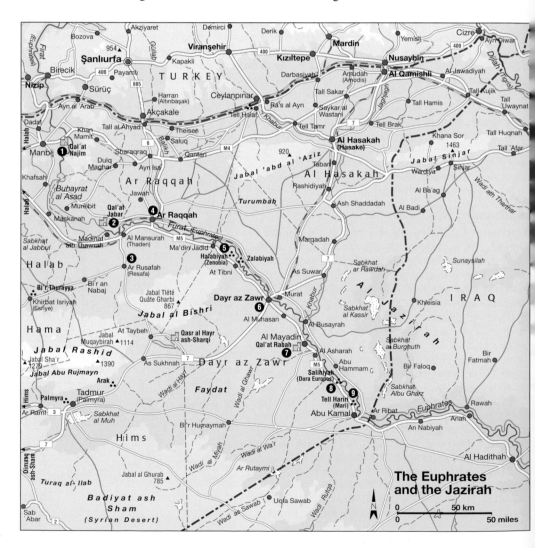

The Euphrates and the Jazirah

Crossing the dam to the northern side of the lake, a road leads on to **Qal'at Jabar ❷** (Wed–Mon 9am–4pm; closed Tues; admission charge) and lakeside beaches where locals come to picnic, especially on Friday. The castle, reached by a causeway, dates from the 11th century; it was held by the crusaders from 1104 but then recaptured by Arab forces under Nour ad-Deen.

City of Sergius

Turn right at **Al Mansurah** and cross a plain (paved road) for 28 km (17 miles) to arrive at yet another impressively fortified city apparently in the middle of nowhere, with sand drifting around its walls and towers. **Ar Rusafah ❸** was part of the Roman defences against the Sassanians and lies on a caravan route from Damascus, via Palmyra, to the Euphrates ford at Thapsacus. Its remarkable ascendancy in Byzantine times was due to the gruesome martyrdom and subsequent cult status of a Roman court official called Sergius, who refused to renounce his Christian beliefs during the persecutions of Diocletian in AD 305. After Constantine legalised Christianity, the city changed its name to Sergiopolis, a church was built over the spot where he was executed, and a century later work began on a great cathedral and monastery in his honour.

St Sergius eventually became the patron saint of Syria *(see below)*. In the 7th century the city was destroyed by the Sassanians, and though restored by the Umayyads, under whom it prospered, their successors were less conscientious about maintaining the elaborate water supply on which the city's existence depended. When in 1247 the Mongols broke through the walls they found a city occupied only by ghosts.

Much of the city is collapsed and buried, and pockmarked with treasure-

Map on page 234

BELOW:
Qal'at Najim.

THE CULT OF ST SERGIUS

Such was St Sergius's repute that pre-Muslim Arabs carried his icon on their caravan raids and afterwards gratefully showered a proportion of their booty on his shrine. The emperor Justinian and his wife Theodora added a magnificence.

But Sergiopolis's fame and treasures attracted unwanted attention. Chosroes I, the fearsome Persian king, sent word to Candidius, the Bishop of Sergiopolis, that only the immediate despatch of 90 kg (200 lb) of gold would save the lives of 12,000 Byzantine prisoners he had taken at Sura. Replying that he was unable to raise the sum at such short notice, the bishop sent off Justinian's cross and pledged the rest of the saint's treasures for a two-year stay of execution. This carried no weight with Chosroes, who sent 6,000 troops with orders to strip the city bare. They, however, found the walls far stronger than anticipated and were forced to withdraw empty-handed when they ran out of water.

Fifty years later, Chosroes II, whose Christian wife was having difficulty conceiving a child, penitentially returned the cross. The subsequent birth of a child was attributed to the saint's intervention and his shrine was duly submerged in presents from the Persian king.

Extracting salt from the waters of the Euphrates.

hunting holes made by the Bedouin. Of the main monuments emerging above ground are the finely decorated triple north gate, three Byzantine churches (the one east of the cisterns is thought to have contained the original tomb of St Sergius in the central apse), a *khan* (market) and the magnificent brick cisterns, which normally held enough water, collected from the winter rains, to last two years. When these cisterns ran dry during prolonged drought every drop of water had to be carried on donkeys or passed down a chain of slaves from the nearest point on the Euphrates.

Caliph's capital

The modern provincial centre of **Ar Raqqah** ❹, on the north bank of the river about 25 km (15 miles) east of the turning for Ar Rusafah, was historically important from Hellenistic to Ayubbid times, though the unappealing modern town suggests little past grandeur. Famed as the summer capital of Harun al-Rashid (the caliph immortalised in *A Thousand and One Nights*), it was, from the late 12th century, a centre for the glazed ceramic industry. Remnants of this past are not obvious, but can be found in the 12th-century Bab Baghdad (Baghdad Gate), the only remaining town gate, the 9th-century Qasr al-Banat (Palace of the Maidens), the Great Mosque, whose current form dates from Nour ad-Deen in 1165, and the **museum** (Wed–Mon 9am–6pm; until 4pm in winter; closed Tues).

Eighty-six km (53 miles) south of Ar Raqqah is the fortified garrison town of **Halabiyah** ❺, less than an hour's drive from Dayr az Zawr *(see opposite)*. About 20 km (12 miles) north of the main road, the city is perched on the edge of the river, the great stone walls climb the hill westwards to a citadel built at the apex of a triangle. Much of the interior is buried or collapsed, but

BELOW: to market in Ar Raqqah.

the magnificent walls, bastions and associated vaulted rooms are largely intact. Though most of what you see dates from the time of Justinian, the city was founded in AD 265, by Queen Zenobia, leader of the Palmyrans, who famously rose up against Rome. After capture by the Romans in 273, the city was reinforced in their stepped-up efforts to defend the empire from the east, but in 610 the Sassanian Persians sacked the city.

A couple of kilometres east of Halabiyah (though the only access is from the road running along the north side of the river) is the badly ruined sister city of **Zalabiyah**, which shares a similar history.

Map on page 234

Beehive buildings – sometimes homes, sometimes for storage – are a feature of this region.

A crossroads and a base

The best overnight base for exploring the southern region of the Syrian section of the Euphrates is **Dayr az Zawr ❻**. There is little of antique interest in this town, but it has an energetic and relatively prosperous feel, partly stemming from it being the hub of Syria's oil industry; other benefits for the traveller are the riverscape itself, where you will find pleasant café terraces and restaurants, and the town's role as a base for trips south and north. The town's **archaeological museum** (Wed–Mon 9am–6pm; closed Tues), is exceptionally good, with an interesting collection of material from the major sites of the region, particularly Mari and Dura Europos.

This is also a good point to cross the river and enter the most remote, but agriculturally rich region of Syria, the Jazirah, a landscape riddled with ancient tells, and well-watered by the Balikh and Khabur rivers, but the southern region of the Euphrates route still has some intriguing places of interest for visitors. It is possible to combine Dura, Qala't Rabah, and Mari in one trip.

BELOW: downtown Ar Raqqah.

The southern region

The small castle of **Qal'at Rabah** ❼, just off the main road south to Abu Kamal, some 45 km (28 miles) from Dayr az Zawr is the first site along the route. Built by the energetic Nour ad-Deen in the 12th century, it contains a five-sided keep established to guard the Euphrates.

Further south, the massive mudbrick walls of the riverside garrison and caravan city of **Dura Europos** (Salihiyah) ❽ are clearly visible from the distant road. A chance discovery by British soldiers on manoeuvres against troublesome Bedouin in 1920 led to the uncovering of a treasure-trove of wall paintings in a church (dating from AD 230) and synagogue just inside the Palmyra Gate. The frescoes (of the life of Christ and of scenes from the old Testament respectively) revolutionised our understanding of early Christian and Judaic traditions and revealed a fascinating mixture of Parthian and Western art. The Christian paintings have been removed and taken to the safety of museums (including the Louvre and Yale University), and the famous synagogue murals can now be seen in the National Museum in Damascus.

Standing in the stones of Dura Europos, a city named after Europos in Macedonia.

Dura was established as a military colony by the Seleucids in the early 3rd century BC; it came under first Parthian and then Roman control and was destroyed forever by the Sassanian Persians in AD 256. The frantic thickening of the city walls was achieved by filling in the buildings adjacent to them. This ensured the survival of the unique representational paintings in the synagogue, various temples, and the house-church which is the earliest Christian cult centre found in Syria.

BELOW:
an archaeologist
at work in Mari.

Twenty-four kilometres (15 miles) downriver, close to the border with Iraq, is the Sumerian city-state of **Mari** ❾ (known locally as Tell Hariri), founded,

it is thought, in the late 4th millennium BC. The 60-hectare (148-acre) mound is surprisingly low and unprepossessing, considering the discoveries it has produced, for it has yielded crucial information on the history of Syria/Mesopotamia in the 3rd and 2nd millennia BC. Thousands of cuneiform-inscribed clay tablets from the palace archives revealed the political, social, religious and economic systems of its inhabitants and neighbours.

The structures are predominantly mudbrick, dominated by the labyrinthine palace of its last ruler, Zimri-Lim. Mari was destroyed by fellow Amorite Hammurabi of Babylon in 1759 BC, when the rivalry between the two great Mesopotamian cities escalated into a power struggle.

The Jazirah

From Dayr az Zawr *(see page 237)* a bridge crosses to the **Jazirah**, which, along with the region north of Aleppo, is home to Syria's small Kurd population. It is also the site of the country's main oil resources, though new fields have also been discovered around Dayr az Zawr itself. After leaving the bridge the road strikes northeast across the plain then follows the course of Al Khabur river to Al Hasakah (about 180 km/112 miles from Dayr az Zawr). There is little for travellers to see, though it, too, is littered with dusty tells.

Tell Brak, north of Al Hasakah has the distinction of having been first excavated by Agatha Christie's husband, Max Mallowan, who unearthed its late 4th-millennium "Eye Temple", named after the many votive offerings depicting the form of an eye. Christie accompanied her husband and recorded her experiences in a book entitled *Come, Tell Us How You Live*, which humorously captures the dogged determination needed for investigating tells. ❑

Map on page 234

The meaning of the Arabic Al Jazirah is "the island", referring to its position between the Tigris and the Euphrates.

BELOW: girls of the Euphrates.

LEBANON

A detailed guide to the entire country, with principal sites clearly cross-referenced by number to the maps

At just under 10,500 sq. km (4,050 sq. miles), Lebanon is a slip of a country, yet it packs in more stunning scenery, classical sites and cultural variety than many much larger nations. It is ideal for exploring by car and in the space of about a week it is possible to take in all its diverse attractions, from the ancient Phoenician seaports of Tyre and Sidon to the Maronite monasteries perched high in the Qadicha Valley and the mighty temple of Jupiter at Baalbek. Experiences might include wine-tasting at a Bekaa Valley vineyard, skiing (in winter) in the Cedars, betting at the legendary Casino du Liban on the outskirts of Beirut or feasting on the ultimate Lebanese *mezze* while overlooking the pretty harbour at Byblos.

Any tour is bound to include Beirut, a capital associated with pleasure and strife in equal measure. Before the country's civil war the British writer Jan Morris described it as "the last of the Middle Eastern fleshpots... a tireless pleasure-drome incorrigibly prospering". Though still reconstructing itself, it is clear that post-war Beirut intends to regain its reputation as the nerve centre of the Middle East.

Until the withdrawal of Israeli forces in 2000, a 15-km (10-mile) strip in the extreme south of the country was out of bounds for visitors, and even nearby places such as Nebatiyé, Jezzine, Qana and Tibnine could be unsafe. In theory, this is no longer the case, but caution is still advisable and until peace is established between Lebanon and Israel it is sensible to monitor the media for news of border skirmishes. That said, the UN peace-keeping force is unlikely to allow anyone to stray into trouble.

Travellers in the south are bound to run into signs of the organisation Hizbollah. Though still synonymous in the minds of many people with hostage-taking and suicide bombing, Hizbollah has radically improved its public image in recent years *(see page 319)*, and needn't be feared by visitors. Mines left over from the civil war, however, are still an occasional hazard and for this reason expeditions off the beaten track, particularly hiking or camping, should only be done in the company of a guide. ❑

PRECEDING PAGES: hunter in the Bekaa Valley; springtime in the anti-Lebanon.
LEFT: a Levantine picnic.

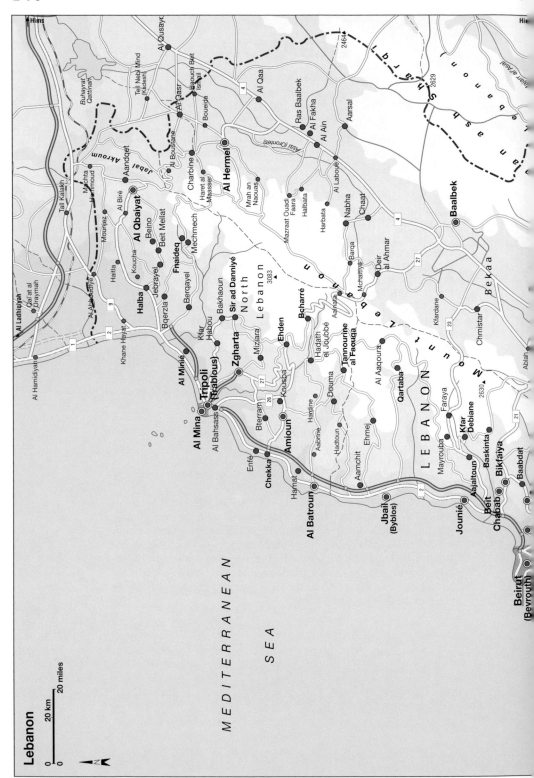

Lebanon

MEDITERRANEAN SEA

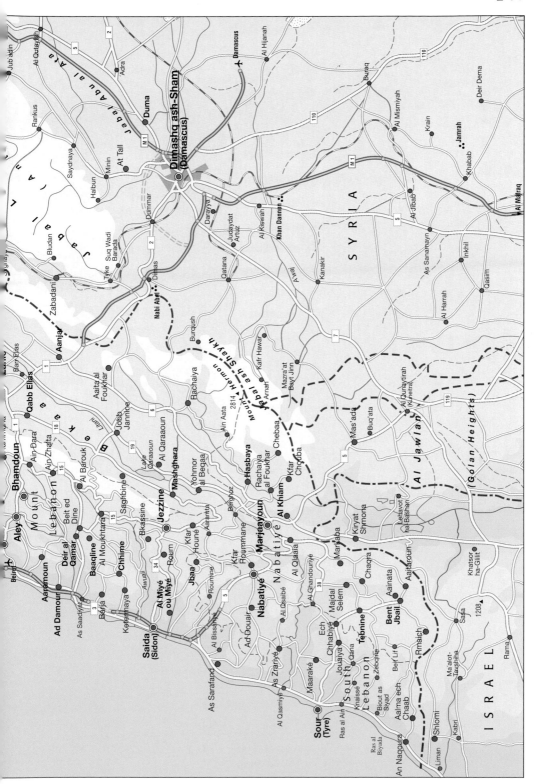

BEIRUT

Beirut has already come a long way since its years at the heart of Lebanon's civil war. Among its attractions are great shops, excellent restaurants and one of the largest casinos in the Middle East

Map on page 252

Beirut

The Paris of the Middle East, they called it, in the Switzerland of the Orient. Before the civil war, Beirut was the most glamorous, exciting city in the region, with snow skiing in winter, beautiful beaches in summer, ancient history, great shopping and wild nightlife. It was a playground for tourists from Europe, the United States and the Arabian Gulf, and was the banking and publishing capital of the Middle East, with an envious education system which attracted the brightest of the Arab world.

The civil war brought Beirut's glory days to an end, and the city is still physically and spiritually scarred. But since the end of the conflict in 1990, great strides have been made towards reconstructing both its buildings and its confidence *(see Rebuilding Beirut, page 101)*. Today, though many streets still bear the scars of war, Beirut is a vibrant, buzzing city, with one of the most diverse mix of communities and lifestyles imaginable.

Source of Roman law

Compared to the settlements at Byblos, Tyre and Sidon, Beirut is a relative newcomer, with its oldest relics dating from around 1900 BC. The first mention of Beirut in historical texts comes some 500 years later, on an engraved tablet found in Egypt, where a vassal king of Beirut pleads for assistance to fight off an invading army. Little is known of the city during the Hellenic period, with its real emergence only coming in the Roman era. The city fell to the Romans in the 1st century AD, and was used as a base for their east Mediterranean fleet because of its geographical position and protected ports. The settlement was made a colony, and members of two veteran legions were granted land.

Some 200 years later, the first law school in the Roman Empire was established here, bringing fame and prestige to the colony, with one 5th-century Greek poet describing Beirut as the "giver of law". Indeed two professors from the faculty were part of a team invited by Emperor Justinian to revise the entire Roman legal system, producing a new body of law which became the basis of all western legal systems. But the growing importance of the city was shattered in 551 by a huge earthquake. The law school was relocated to Sidon, and Beirut drifted into obscurity. In 635 it was taken by the Arabs, who faced little resistance.

In 1125 Beirut changed hands again, this time to crusader Baldwin I after a long siege. The city remained in crusader hands on and off until 1291, when it was taken by the Mamlukes. For several hundred years France and Cyprus repeatedly tried to retake the city, but failed.

PRECEDING PAGES: Beirut on the beach. **LEFT:** symbols of a warring past. **BELOW:** a garden city image revives.

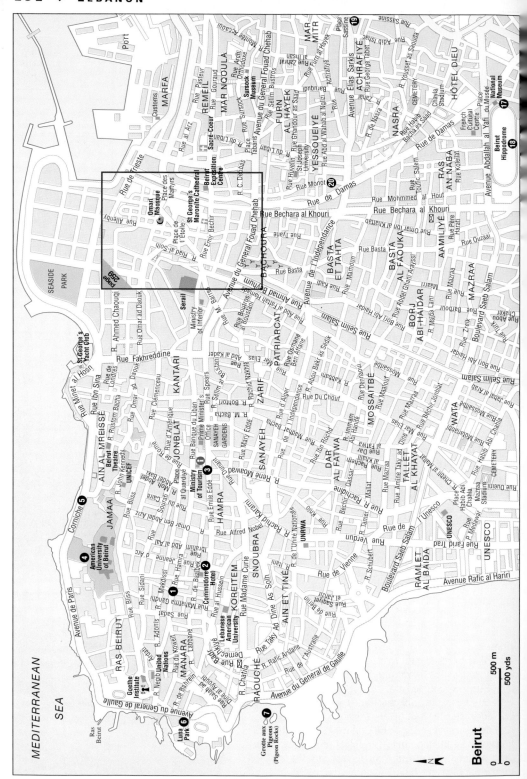

Beirut

MEDITERRANEAN SEA

The Ottomans' capital

In 1516, Beirut became part of the Ottoman Empire, whose interests lay more in taxing the emirs than outright political control. Fakr ed-Deen, Lebanon's first nationalist leader, who ruled between 1585 and 1635, took advantage of this regime to carve out a semi-autonomous state, and promote its prosperity. While in Sidon he encouraged trade with France, in Beirut he welcomed Venetian merchants, off-setting the power of the Ottomans. Fearing they would lose the city, the Ottomans arrested Fakr ed-Deen, and took him to Constantinople where he was executed, leaving Beirut to stagnate once more.

The city's next revival came early in the 19th century under Emir Bechir. But his alliance with Egypt led Britain to intervene in support of the Ottomans. A British fleet attacked Beirut in 1840, and Bechir was captured and also taken to Constantinople, where he died in prison. Some 20 years later, growing tensions between Lebanon's Druze and Christian community resulted in a massacre of 10,000 Christians on Mount Lebanon, and this led to the beginnings of urban migration to the city. The mountain-based Christians increased Beirut's commercial importance, and were supported by France, protector of the Maronites, which landed troops in the city.

In 1920, after the end of World War I, France was granted a mandate over the area which is today Lebanon and Syria, and carved out the state of Lebanon, making Beirut its capital. After independence in 1946, the city grew to become the commercial heart of the Middle East, with a thriving banking and service industry. But rising communal tensions, coupled with the arrival of some 300,000 mostly Sunni Muslim Palestinian refugees, whose leaders formed a state within a state, led to the 1975–90 civil war *(see below)*.

Map on page 252

Beirut tastes, but seldom absorbs. It is always contemporary, shifting and tacking to the winds of circumstance.

– JAN MORRIS
Beirut 1956,
Among the Cities

BELOW: café under the Corniche.

THE GREEN LINE

Beirut's rapid expansion during the 20th century was driven by successive waves of migration. Christians came from Mount Lebanon and settled in its foothills in east Beirut. Muslims came up from the south, and built homes in the west of the city. The beginnings of the civil war in 1975 led to a *de facto* division between the ostensibly Christian east and Muslim west. There were – and still are – many Christians in west Beirut and Muslims in the east, but for those outside the country this "Green Line" – *Khutut Tammes* in Lebanese – became a symbol of Lebanon's religious division and war. The line itself was a wasteland corridor, stretching from Beirut port in the north, through the middle of the city centre, along the Damascus Road to the southern edge of the city. It was unsafe to cross the line, except at a handful of recognised "crossing points" where civilians – in the constant gun-sights of militiamen – would risk their lives every day.

When the war ended, the barricades of the Green Line were the first to be pulled down. Today, redevelopment has disguised the site of the division in many places, especially in central Beirut. But a drive from the Solidere area to the National Museum at Mathaf passes along parts of the Green Line unchanged since the war.

The city was torn apart, and became the battleground for a host of militias fighting for ideology, territory or money. Large swathes of the city were destroyed, and tens of thousands killed. The 1989 peace deal brought the conflict to an end, and efforts to rebuild the city began. Today, though the scars remain, a futuristic metropolis is being built in central Beirut, and yet more archaeological treasures are being uncovered.

The rebuilding of Beirut gave archaeologists the opportunity to dig down under the very centre of a major Mediterranean city for the first time, to trace the relics of countless generations.

Across the delta

The city of Beirut lies on the flood plain of the Beirut River. The west is largely flat, while the east rises up to the mountains. During the war, the two sides were separated by the infamous Green Line, which was the scene of the most widespread destruction. To the south of city are the poor Shia Muslim suburbs which become know as the city's Belt of Misery, the result of rural migration to the city in the 1950s and 1960s. South of these suburbs is the new Beirut airport, and a modern highway now brings travellers over the poor suburbs directly into the city in minutes. At the northern end of the airport highway, in what was once the heart of the city, is one vast construction site, with new steel and glass office buildings appearing by the score.

For the visitor, the areas of interest are east and west Beirut, the northern beach suburb of Jounié, Jeita Grotto and the mountain ski area of Faraya.

Lebanon's Champs Elysées

BELOW:
a French feel
at La Mie Dorée.

When Beirut was ruptured by war, various suburbs competed to take the mantle of the city centre. **Hamra**, in west Beirut, was the most successful. Though other suburbs have a host of shops and restaurants, Hamra became the buzzing

heart of the city, home to ministries and *mezze* bars, banks and boutiques. With the vast majority of hotels in the district, Hamra is also the logical place to begin a walking tour.

Hamra Street (Rue Hamra) ❶ was once the Champs Elysées of Beirut, home in the 1960s to glitzy boutiques with the latest fashions from Paris. Today, it is a little tired and jaded, and only just beginning to recover its former glory. One block south of the western end of the street is the **Commodore Hotel** ❷. Though today just another faceless hotel, during the war it was home to the foreign press corps, a parrot which could imitate the whistle of incoming shells, and discreet staff who would convert bar tabs into laundry bills. Continuing east, you pass faded cinemas and bookshops to the Piccadilly junction, with a collection of very 1960s-looking outdoor cafés, with stainless steel tables and dark interiors. Three decades ago, these were a favourite rendezvous for artists and political radicals; today the cafés are more a focal point for tourists, as the artists have moved off to new venues such as the Ristretto, northwest of Hamra, and Café Rouda on the Corniche.

Further east along Hamra is the **Ministry of Tourism** ❸, with a useful information office (tel: 01 343073), in a complex of government buildings opposite Pizza Hut. A right turn here takes you to **Sanayeh Gardens**, a tiny park but one of the only green spaces in the city. Turning left instead, walk down past the remaining elegant late19th and early 20th-century houses to Bliss Street, home of the **American University of Beirut** (AUB) ❹.

AUB began life in 1866 as the Syrian Protestant College, founded by American Daniel Bliss. Today the campus is an oasis of greenery and quiet, and a sanctuary from the hustle of Beirut. The main entrance is through a 19th-century

The American University of Beirut evolved from the Syrian Protestant College, founded by American missionaries in 1866.

BELOW: eyes down.

*Roller-blading –
the modern way to
promenade.*

archway some 300 metres/yards to the left along Bliss Street. After showing some form of identification to the security staff, you will be allowed to enter the inner sanctuary and roam the campus. Here students sit quietly under trees studying or talking, and the cacophony of car horns becomes a distant memory. Past the main gate, and some 200 metres/yards to the right is a tiny **archaeological museum** (Mon–Fri 10am–noon and 2–4pm; free) with a collection of Phoenician glassware and early artefacts.

Continuing down through the campus, along shaded paths, you approach the north gate. This leads onto the Corniche, Beirut's busy seafront highway.

The Corniche

There is one place where all Beirutis meet at all hours of the day and night – the seafront **Corniche ❺**, which has long been a place to escape the city and catch some fresh sea air. From 4am it is packed with joggers; by lunchtime it is populated by office workers; in early afternoon the joggers return; and at sunset, couples and families come out for an evening stroll. As well as vendors of coffee, corn on the cob, fruit and sandwiches, the Corniche is where most of the city's famous beach clubs and expensive hotels can be found.

Walking right, with the sea on your left, takes you to the former hotel district. During the civil war, one of the fiercest battles was fought for control of this area, with snipers attacking each other from the tops of well-known hotels, the St George, Phoenicia and Holiday Inn. Today, most of the hotels are undergoing renovation, but the scars are still visible, particularly on the huge Holiday Inn.

All along the Corniche are beach clubs, where middle-class Beirutis pay some LL20,000 to swim and sunbathe during summer. The term "beach club" is

BELOW: early
evening on the
Corniche.

a little misleading, because none has a beach, just concrete terraces around a swimming pool. But these are the only places where women can sunbathe in bikinis without attracting unwelcome attention, and they make a welcome retreat from the city.

Map on page 252

If you take a left turn at the AUB gate, instead of a right, and walk west, past the elegant Riviera Hotel, and around the headland for 500 metres/yards or so you will reach **Luna Park** ❻, a permanent fairground. But just before this, a right turn takes you down to an excellent open-air seafront café, Café Rouda, which offers Lebanese food, accompanied by *nargeilehs* (water pipes). This is a wonderful place to relax in summer and watch the sun go down, though it can get busy. Next to Café Rouda is the Sporting Beach Club, which is the most easy-going of all the Corniche retreats. Here the emphasis is less on what you wear, and more on relaxation.

Beyond Luna Park, the Corniche begins to climb up a rocky outcrop. From the top, there is a fine view of **Pigeon Rocks** ❼. These vast towers of rock are Beirut's most famous natural feature, and before the war were the venue for spectacular cliff divers, with speedboats weaving between the columns below. Along the top of the cliffs are a number of restaurants, with spectacular views across the Mediterranean. Taking a sharp left here takes you to the suburbs of **Raouche** and **Verdun**, some of the most expensive in Beirut, and the home to most of the city's designer fashion boutiques.

Pigeon Rocks.

City centre renaissance

From Raouche, it is a short taxi ride to the pre-war heart of the city which is currently undergoing a massive reconstruction. Central Beirut was largely destroyed

BELOW: fresh from the oven.

during the war, and afterwards, in 1994, the government commissioned a company to pull down many of the remaining buildings, and begin to construct a futuristic new city on the scale of London's Docklands. The reconstruction gave archaeologists an unprecedented opportunity to dig down below the city, and unearth previous settlements. Items found include a vast Roman bath complex, a tiny Mamluke mosque, and many ancient artefacts.

TIP

Central Beirut is small enough to navigate on foot, but Solidere, the company overseeing its reconstruction, offers free guided tours by minibus (tel: 01 646120).

A useful landmark in the area is the ESCWA **building**. The recently completed brown glass and stone building is in **Riad al-Solh Square ❽**, dedicated to Lebanon's first prime minister, and his statue stands nearby. North, towards the sea, stands **Bank Street**, one of the few to survive the war nearly intact, largely because it was home to the country's largest banks, and thus considered sacrosanct by militias of all sides.

Fifty metres/yards along Bank Street is an opening to the left leading to an **archaeological site ❾** that has been turned into a park. Here are the remains of a Roman baths complex dating from the first century AD. The brick vaults once supported a permeable floor which allowed warm air to circulate around bathers. Stacked between the vaults are hundreds of heating bricks, which would have been warmed over fires before being used to heat the water. Above the baths and to the left is the **Serail ❿**, a vast Ottoman structure built in the 1890s as the seat of government. Since the end of the civil war, it has been extensively restored, and today once again serves as the home of the government.

BELOW:

an archaeological dig in progress in downtown Beirut.

Walking back down to Bank Street, cross the road, and continue straight down to the elaborate clock tower. This is **Nijmeh Square ⓫**, and surrounding it is the Lebanese parliament and various ministries in elegant late 19th-century and early 20th century buildings. Because of its importance to the country's

image, this was the first central area to be restored, and Solidere is encouraging many small antiques shops to set up in the streets around Nijmeh Square to bring back the atmosphere of a shopping souk.

Turning left from the clock tower, north towards the sea, you approach the east–west **Rue Weygand** ⑫. Immediately on the left and right stand two restored mosques. To your left is the **Omari Mosque** ⑬, which began life in the 12th century as the crusader Church of St John the Baptist, itself built on the site of a previous Roman Temple to Jupiter. In 1291 the Mamlukes converted it into a mosque, but its heritage is clear from the minaret, which was obviously a bell-tower, and the stonework, which is clearly crusader.

To your right is the **Emir Mansour Assaf Mosque** ⑭, which is a much later structure, dating from the 17th century. This also suffered during the war, but has now been largely restored. Ahead, across Rue Weygand, is the historic souk. Much of this was heavily damaged during the war. Some buildings have been torn down, notably in the area to the left, but some Ottoman-era buildings ahead and to the right were salvaged.

Many of the most interesting artefacts found during the reconstruction of the centre were located below this area, including Byzantine and Roman shops and mosaics, and countless jars and pots dating from as early as 3,000 BC. Ahead and to the left are remains of a tiny Mamluke mosque, built in 1517, which was found hidden between several buildings after they were demolished. With restoration work on the area ahead and to the right mostly complete, many new shops and cafés have begun to open, breathing life back into the city.

Turning right onto Rue Weygand and walking east takes you past Beirut's old opera house to a vast open area. This is **Martyrs Square** ⑮, the focus of the

Map on page 259

Downtown Beirut. The shiny new city is clean, organised and modern.

BELOW: the *minbar* (pulpit) from which the *imam* leads prayer in the Great Mosque.

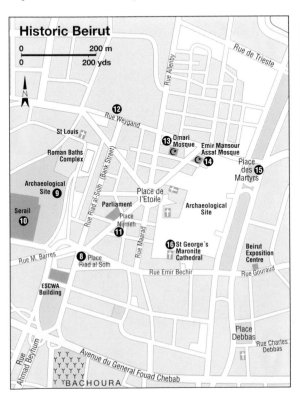

Historic Beirut

pre-war city, and at its centre, flanked by gardens and palm trees, once stood a bronze statue to nationalist leaders who were executed by the Ottomans in 1915.

Most of the pre-war buildings around the square have long been destroyed, and the monument itself is being repaired, soon to be returned. Walking right (south) to the end of the square, and turning right again (west), brings you back towards the ESCWA building. Immediately on your right is **St George's Maronite Cathedral ⓰**. Built in 1890, it was modelled on the church of Santa Maria Maggiore in Rome. Heavily damaged during the war, it is under restoration, though it is still used for services.

The crypts of the cathedral are now also a temporary home for many of the archaeological finds from the area. And the land immediately to the north of the church is itself the site of a major dig, with columns from a Roman arcade visible behind the church. Though under pressure from developers keen to rebuild in the area, archaeologists are still hoping to discover the remains of the Roman law school close by.

The Green Line was so devoid of human activity for 17 years that it began to resemble the green mark it was on military maps, with trees and plant life flourishing along the length of the city.

The Green Line

From the ESCWA building, take a taxi to "Mathaf", a road junction 2 km (1¼ miles) south, and home of the National Museum. This journey takes you along the infamous Green Line which once divided east and west Beirut, and on both sides of the road are many war-shattered buildings, some so full of bullet holes that they look like a honeycomb.

The position of Lebanon's **National Museum ⓱** (tel: 01 388833) right in the centre of the fighting led to massive destruction of its contents. The saving grace was that one farsighted official saw to it that many larger items were

BELOW: model looks at a fashion show in the Al Boustan Hotel.

Map
on page
252

encased in concrete to protect them from damage. The exterior of the museum, built in 1942 to an Egyptian design, has now been restored, but with the concrete still being chipped away from the relics inside, the museum will be closed for the forseeable future.

Before the war, the museum's collection included items from all the country's historical periods. On the ground floor were collections of Phoenician pottery, stones slabs with early inscriptions from the 1st millennium BC, and statues and mosaics from the Roman and Byzantine period. The first floor held many smaller objects, such as Stone-Age weapons found at Byblos, bronze figures and jewellery. The lower ground floor housed the most impressive items, such as huge sarcophagi found at Byblos, including the burial casket of Phoenician King Ahiram, bearing one of the world's first alphabetical inscriptions. Until the museum reopens, it remains unclear how many of the pre-war items still remain.

Behind the museum, to the southwest, is the **Beirut Hippodrome ⓲**, where horseracing takes place at weekends, and behind this is a large park which is slowly being restored after its destruction during the Israeli invasion of 1982.

The Christian quarter

From the Green Line it is not far to Christian **East Beirut**. The centre of the Christian quarter is **Sassine Square ⓳**, about 1 km (½ mile) northeast of the museum. The focus of the square is a black and white steel and concrete memorial to Bashir Gemayel, a Christian wartime leader who was elected president in 1982, but assassinated days later.

East Beirut is mostly residential, and with its French inspired buildings and pâtisseries, could easily be confused for a suburb of Marseille or Nice. Yet

Although the physical Green Line was removed in 1989, marking the end of the war, there is still a division in many people's minds. Some taxi drivers, for example, will refuse to take a fare from one side of the city to the other, and many Beirutis have never seen the other side of their own city.

BELOW: shopping in the Dune Centre.

The colonial-style Sursock Museum in East Beirut is a venue for modern art, with a permanent collection and visiting exhibitions.

behind its relaxed Gallic appearance, east Beirut is home to the most expensive restaurants, and the glitziest clubs. Most nightspots are around **Monot Street ⑳**, which is halfway between Sassine and the city centre. Beyond Monot is one of the prettier quarters of the Christian area, **Sursock**, full of fine century-old houses, and home to a small **museum of modern art**.

City outskirts and Mount Lebanon

Beyond central Beirut, to the northeast, are a number of places worthy of an excursion. Northeast on the Jounié Highway, 5 km (3 miles) from the city centre, is **Borj Hammoud ㉑**, the Armenian quarter, whose people are the descendants of the many thousands who fled from massacres in Turkey during World War I. Today Bourj Hammoud is the centre of the gold and jewellery trade and items can be purchased for very reasonable prices.

Travelling up from Borj Hammoud towards the mountains, the road passes through a number of pretty resort towns, popular summer retreats for rich Gulf Arabs. Some 17 km (11 miles) from, and 800 metres (2,620 ft) above Beirut is **Beit Meri ㉒**, a village with spectacular views over the city. Beit Meri has been settled since the Phoenician period and has a number of remains from the Roman and Byzantine era. These can be found at the east end of the main street, to the right of the roundabout, and include delicate mosaics in a 5th-century Byzantine church and the remains of several Roman temples.

A further 6 km (4 miles) deeper into the mountains is **Broummana ㉓**, another summer tourist resort, which sits on a narrow ridge, offering spectacular views across the city and valleys. The wooded areas around Broummana are recommended for summer walks and picnics, but expect to

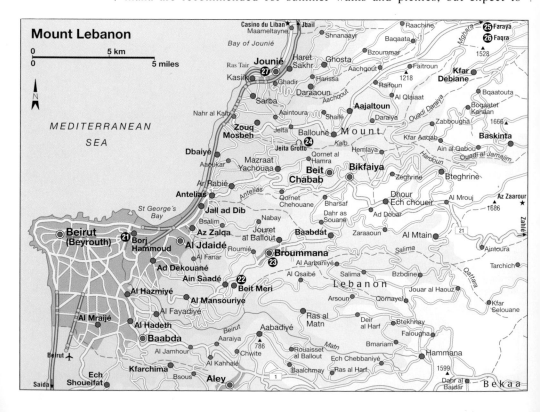

encounter a disproportionate number of north Europeans, for this is the retreat of the many expatriate workers.

Back on the coastal highway, and beyond the turning to Beit Meri, the route passes the mouth of **Nahr al-Kalb**, or Dog River, then goes through a tunnel cut through a headland and continues to the Christian town of Jounié, today almost an extension of the city. The headland through which the tunnel passes was throughout history a near impregnable barrier that conquering armies had to cross. Many armies that passed this way, travelling north or south, left their mark (now on the far side of the tunnel) to note their successful passage. There are 20 plaques in all, from those of the army of Egyptian Pharaoh Rameses II, through the Babylonian invasion of the 6th century BC, right up to British and French forces in World War II. Some of the carvings are in Latin, others Greek, Arabic, French and English. They can be found by turning right immediately past the tunnel, where they are lined along the face of the cliff, with many directly above the noisy road tunnel.

Map
on page
262

Spectacular Jeita grotto

Before entering Jounié proper, just beyond the tunnel there is a right exit from the highway signposted to Jeita. Turn here for one of the most fabulous sites in Lebanon, **Jeita Grotto** ❷ (9am–6 pm; admission charge). About 2 km (1¼ miles) along the road, another turning to the right leads down to the entrance. Here, buried in the mountainside, is a stunning series of vast caves with thousands of eerily shaped stalactites and stalagmites, discovered by an American hunter in 1836.

Used as a munitions store during the civil war, the upper and lower grottoes

BELOW:
gone fishing.

Map on page 262

Taking the cable-car up to Harissa.

BELOW: on White Sands Beach.
RIGHT: the Virgin Mary statue in Harissa.

have now been reopened to the public and are truly breathtaking – a complex of tunnels and cavernous chambers with many of the formations almost taking a human form in the half-light. The lower grotto floods in winter, but in summer visitors are carried through the moodily-lit interior in flat-bottomed boats, the whole scene like a setting from a Tolkien novel.

Playground resorts

Continuing past Jeita on the road up to the mountains, you arrive after 20 km (12 miles) at the village of **Faraya** ㉕, at an altitude of 2,000 metres (6,600 ft). In winter this is Lebanon's most popular ski resort, with 15 pistes and thousands of skiers, while in summer it makes a pleasant retreat from the heat of the city. With Faraya so close to the beaches of Jounié, it is possible to live out the Lebanese legend, and spend the morning snow-skiing on the mountain, and the afternoon water-skiing in Jounié bay. Faraya has several small hotels, and for those intending to stay longer, it is possible to rent chalets with open fires, notably in the cosy Soulouge complex (tel: 03 376969).

Some 3 km (2 miles) beyond Faraya is the village of **Faqra** ㉖, where there is a spectacular natural bridge, and ruins dating from Greek and Roman times, including the remains of a temple dedicated to Adonis.

Jounié ㉗, back down on the coast, was a simple fishing village around a spectacular bay before the war. But soon after 1975, many Christians from Beirut fled here, and it quickly mushroomed to become a city in its own right, and a playground haven from conflict. Today the entire coastline from the tunnel to the casino is one long urban sprawl, with a dizzying mix of nightclubs, bars, restaurants and boutiques. The prettiest part of Jounié is the old port, where small cafés and restaurants occupy the old stone buildings. There are also a number of beach clubs with moorings for the many expensive speedboats and cruisers owned by Beirut's elite.

Above the coast road, on a rocky outcrop, is the excellent restaurant, La Crêperie, with spectacular views from the terrace across the Bay of Jounié. Nearby is the ground station of a **cablecar** (10 am–midnight; admission charge) which climbs 800 metres (2,600 ft) to a huge 19th-century statue of the Virgin Mary in **Harissa**, a popular pilgrimage site. The ride up offers spectacular views over Beirut and Jounié, and is a cool escape in summer.

Home of the high rollers

At the northern edge of Jounié is the **Casino du Liban** (noon–4 am; tel: 09 930067). This was once one of the most famous casinos along the east Mediterranean coast, with spectacular shows featuring African elephants, waterfalls and the obligatory dancing girls. Since the end of the civil war, it has been reopened, and is trying to regain its pre-war reputation. It has three gambling rooms and five restaurants. Access to the roulette and blackjack tables requires temporary membership, which is free, but you will need identification and men must wear a jacket. The casino is well signposted at the northern end of Jounié, just beyond the seedy suburb of Maameltayne. ❑

BEKAA VALLEY

Highlights include the vast Roman city of Baalbek, the Umayyad remains at Aanjar, and the excellent wines produced by the vineyards of Kefraya and Ksara

Map on page 270

Beirut

T he Bekaa Valley has long been distinct from coastal Lebanon. A fertile tableland tucked between two towering mountain ranges, it is the north-ern point of a geological fault which stretches through the Dead Sea in Israel to the Great Rift Valley in Africa.

Because of its protected geography, the Bekaa has a stable climate, with some 250 days of sunshine a year, and less rain than elsewhere in Lebanon. As a result, it is the country's agricultural centre, with plantations of walnuts, apricots and tobacco, as well as citrus fruits and vegetables. During the civil war, the upper reaches of the valley were also the centre of the hashish-growing district, producing many hundreds of tonnes of the drug a year. At the end of the war, the government put an end to the industry, bringing much poverty to the area as a result.

Culturally, the Bekaa has a distinct atmosphere. Villages are small and iso-lated, there is little industry, and politics is dominated by powerful clans. Most of the population is Shia Muslim, though Zahlé is a Christian city, and the vil-lage of Rachaiya in the south has a large Druze population. Visitors come to the Bekaa for the vast Roman city of Heliopolis at Baalbek, the Umayyad city of Aanjar and the excellent vineyards of Ksara and Kefraya.

PRECEDING PAGES: spring flowers in the Bekaa Valley. **LEFT:** the Temple of Bacchus, Baalbek. **BELOW:** statue of St Charbel, Zahlé.

Vast tableland

From Beirut, the Bekaa valley lies on the road to Damascus, which climbs through a 1,540-metre (5,000-ft) pass over the Mount Lebanon range. There are few more inspiring sights than cresting the top of the range at dawn, and catching a first glimpse of the valley as the sun climbs over the Anti-Lebanon range. The valley stretches out ahead like a piece of baize, perfectly flat, and around 1,000 metres (3,280 ft) above sea level. As the mountain road descends, it approaches the busy trading town of **Chtaura ❶**, some 44 km (27 miles) from Beirut, which marks the junction with the north–south Bekaa highway. Chtaura is a utilitarian place, a stopping-off point for long-distance travellers, with a wide choice of roadside cafés and excellent Arabic sweet shops. At the centre of town, the road splits, with a turning left to Baalbek, right to Kefraya, and the road ahead leading to Aan-jar, and ultimately Syria.

South Bekaa

Ignore the left turn for Baalbek and turn right to reach the vineyard of **Kefraya** (daily, 8am–5 pm; tel: 08 840293), and the eastern side of the Chouf Mountain *(see South Lebanon, page 307).*

While Lebanon has a rich collection of Phoenician and Roman monuments, little remains of early Arab

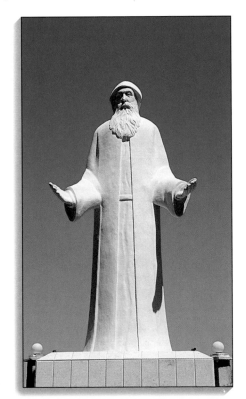

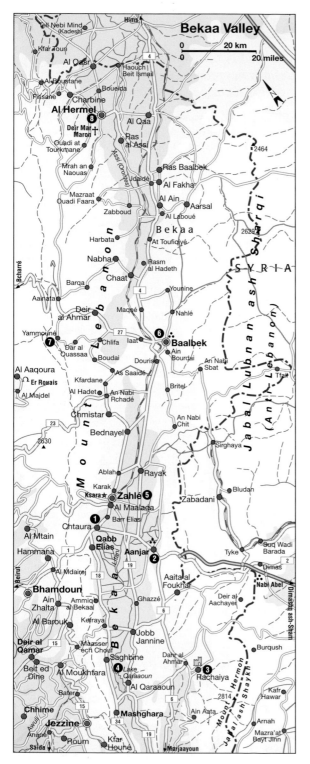

Bekaa Valley

0   20 km
0   20 miles

Tell Nebi Mind (Kadesh)
Hims
Kfar Zabad
Al Qasr
Haouch Beit Ismail
Al Boustane
Boueida
Fissane
Charbine
Al Hermel
Deir Mar Maroni
Al Qaa
Ouadi at Tourkmane
Ras al Assi
2464
Mrah an Naouas
Ras Baalbek
Udaide
Al Fakha
Mazraat Ouadi Faara
Al Ain
Aarsal
Zabboud
Al Laboué
Harbata
Bekaa
At Toufiqiyé
2629
Nabha
Rasm al Hadeth
Barqa
Chaat
SYRIA
Aainata
Younine
Deir al Ahmar
Maqné
Nahlé
Yammouné
Chlifa
Iaat
Baalbek
Dar al Quassaa
Boudai
Douris
Ain Bourdai
An Nabi Sbat
Al Aaqoura
As Saaide
Tfail
Er Rouais
Kfardane
Britel
Al Majdel
Al Hadet
An Nabi Rchadé
Chmistar
An Nabi Chit
Bednayel
Sirghaya
2630
Ablah
Rayak
Karak
Bludan
Ksara
Zahle
Al Maalaqa
Zabadani
Chtaura
Barr Elias
Al Mtain
Qabb Elias
Hammana
Aanjar
Tyke
Suq Wadi Barada
Al Mdairej
Dimas
Aaita al Foukhar
Nabi Abel
Bhamdoun
Ammiq
Ghazzé
Deir al Aachayer
Ain Zhalta
al Bekaal
Al Barouk
Kefraya
Deir al Qamar
Maasser ech Chouf
Jobb Jannine
Burqush
Saghbine
Dahr al Ahmar
Beit ed Dine
Al Moukhtara
Lake Qaraaoun
Rachaiya
Bater
Al Qaraaoun
Kafr Hawar
Chhime
2814
Mount Hermon
Jezzine
Mashghara
Ain Aata
Arnah
Anane
Roum
Kfar Houné
Marjaayoun
Mazra'at Bayt Jinn
Saida

civilisation. At **Aanjar** ❷ (daily 8am–8pm; admission charge), 56 km (35 miles) from Beirut, this imbalance is redressed. In the shadow of the Anti-Lebanon range are the remains of a city, built by the Umayyads, a dynasty which lasted not much more than 100 years yet conquered as far west as Spain.

With its copious supply of water (in Arabic *Ain Jarr* means river source) and its position on the trade route between Beirut and Damascus, as well as the route north, Aanjar was built for the Caliph Al Walid I around AD 700. Unlike the other ancient cities of Lebanon, which have seen waves of inhabitants, Aanjar was a "new town" built from scratch. It prospered for less than a century, then fell into disuse. In more recent times, a village has established itself nearby, largely populated by Armenians who fled the Turkish genocide during the World War I. The Aanjar ruins were discovered only in the 1940s, with excavation beginning some 10 years later.

The ancient city was laid out as a perfectly rectangular grid, 350 metres/yards from east to west, and 385 metres/yards from north to south, surrounded by heavily fortified walls, and bisected by two 20-metre- (65-ft-) wide avenues. The design of the city borrowed heavily from the Byzantines, with a pattern of alternating red bricks and yellow stone. Much was also recycled from the Roman-Byzantine period, either in design, or quite literally in the building materials themselves.

The site is now entered from the north, through one of four towering gateways that once protected the city. To the left, past the entrance, are the *hammams* (public baths), similar in design to the Roman baths in Beirut, with heating blocks and water channels, and separate rooms for warm and cold bathing.

The main street, leading south, would once have been flanked by shops. The remains of some 600 have been found by archaeologists, indicating the city's importance as a trading centre.

Beyond the east–west crossroads, marked by a tetrapylon recycled from

Roman times, the remains of the **mosque**, with a small column in the fore-court, lie to the left. Beyond the mosque are the partially reconstructed remains of the **Grand Palace**, which would have served as a summer retreat for the caliphs. Decorated with intricate carvings of owls, doves, lilies, grapes, seashells and eagles, the palace had a square central courtyard, flanked by delicate fluted columns, very different from the heavy-handed architecture of the Romans. Crossing the main north–south street into the southwest quarter, you enter the residential and commercial quarter, where most of the shops were excavated, along with well-preserved houses. Built in the Arab style, the latter featured one large room opening onto a small courtyard, flanked by a number of small sleeping quarters.

Beyond the city ruins, and back into the village, are some good restaurants, specialising in fresh fish which is locally farmed.

Slopes of Mount Hermon

Along the main road east of Aanjar, turn right at the village of Masnaa, just before the Syrian border, and take the road south. Looming ahead and to the left, and visible from much of the country, is Mount Hermon, which borders Lebanon, Syria and the Golan Heights.

The mountain has been a site of worship and homage since the earliest of times, with the remains of ancient stone temples on its peaks. Like the Greeks' Mount Olympus, Hermon was believed by the Phoenicians to be the home of the gods, including Baal, lord of the sky. From its highest peak of 2,814 metres (9,232 ft), it is possible to see into Galilee, across to the Mediterranean and deep into Syria. Many rivers begin their journey here, including the River Jordan, which flows down to the Dead Sea. The height and strategic position of Mount Hermon has given it great military importance in recent times. In the 1967 Arab-Israeli wars, Israel captured its southern peak along with the nearby Golan Heights, and still holds both, making the mountain off-limits for tourists, except on the Israeli side, where a number of ski resorts have been built.

Rachaiya: Birthplace of the nation

Near the base of the Bekaa Valley, the village of **Rachaiya** ❸ stands on a hillock in splendid isolation. It is composed almost entirely of stone-built houses topped with the traditional red-tiled roofs, having escaped the ugly developments seen elsewhere. Home to a large Druze community, much of the village was destroyed in the 1920s when the Druze staged a revolt against the French occupation. Its greatest moment in history came in 1925, when it was used as a prison for nationalist leaders opposed to French rule: French marines locked up the president of the republic and the prime minister here. But after a national strike, the French backed down and Lebanon was given its independence. One of the first acts of the new state was to declare Rachaiya a national monument.

The small castle above the village was built in the Middle Ages for the princes of Rachaiya, and today it

Map
on page
270

The Beka'a is I think the boundary between the Levant and Asia. Where the tiled roofs end and the flat roofs become general, and the Christian churches have no bells, is the beginning.
— FREYA STARK
Beyond the Euphrates,
1951

BELOW: Aanjar.

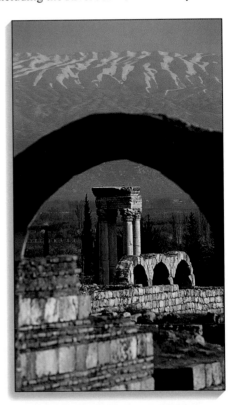

Shrine to St Charbel in Zahlé, where Christian images abound. A bronze statue of the Virgin Mary watches over the town from a 54-metre (180-ft) high hill-top tower.

BELOW:
Lake Qaraaoun.

offers breathtaking views over the village and the valley. Turning west here takes you along a beautiful scenic route to **Lake Qaraaoun ❹**, an artificial body of water which was created in 1959 through the damming of the Litani River. Today the lake is the site of a bird sanctuary, and there is a visitor's centre, along with a number of good restaurants.

North Bekaa

Back at Chtaura, by taking the left fork you begin to head northeast. As you leave town, the modern buildings give way to vineyards, at the centre of the Lebanon's wine producing industry. Some 7 km (4 miles) north of Chtaura, the city of **Zahlé ❺** appears on the left, tucked into the lee of the Jabal Sannine mountain range along both banks of the Baroudi River. This is Lebanon's fourth largest city, and a summer resort for many Lebanese. At the base of the valley, on the banks of the river, are dozens of open-air restaurants, which are famed for their *mezze*.

A Christian city on the edge of the mostly Muslim valley, Zahlé is politically important. It suffered heavily during the civil war, in 1981 it was besieged by Syria, and it was the site of the first confrontation between Syria and Israel ahead of the 1982 Israeli invasion. On its northern outskirts is **Ksara**, one of the country's most important wine producers. The vineyard was established by Jesuit monks in 1857, and is famed not only for its wine but also its *arak* – the fiery aniseed spirit known by many different names around the Mediterranean. Ksara vineyard is open to the public (daily 10am–2pm; tel: 08 801662), and the cellars are a cool retreat from the summer heat, with each tour followed by a satisfying wine-tasting session.

Just beyond Ksara, some 2 km (1¼ miles) from the centre of Zahlé, is a small turning on the left to the village of **Karak**, which has a 14th-century Mamluke mosque in a well-tended garden. Below the mosque is a historic site said to house the tomb of Noah. According to Lebanese legend, when the waters of the flood subsided, Noah landed on Mount Sannine and saw the first rainbow at Aanjar, indicating the end of the flood. He then came and lived in the Bekaa, and began the local wine industry, living for 350 years. Noah was said to be a giant, and his "tomb" – which is probably a Roman aquifer – is more than 40 metres (130 ft) long by 2 metres (6 ft) wide. If you ask a member of staff at the mosque, he will tell you that his body was so long, it had to be bent double in order to fit in the casket.

Baalbek

For most visitors, a trip to the Bekaa Valley has just one objective: to see the remains of the Roman city at **Baalbek ❻**, some 30 km (18 miles) north of Zahlé, 86 km (53 miles) from Beirut. Heliopolis, "the City of the Sun", was built on a gigantic man-made acropolis rising above the surrounding plains, and represents one of the most audacious construction projects in the history of architecture. The site was chosen by the Romans in the first century AD for its strategic position on two trading routes. Here, over more than 200 years, successive emperors spared no effort to construct the greatest temple complex ever built in the Roman world.

On the approach to Baalbek along the floor of the valley the six remaining columns of the Temple of Jupiter are visible on the horizon long before arriving; for much of the year they are framed by the snow-capped Anti-Lebanon

Maps:
Area 270
Site 276

The cellars of the Ksara winery make use of extensive caves built around a natural grotto once used by the Romans.

BELOW:
arak distillery.

TIP

Baalbek Festival is
held each July/August.
For information on
events and booking,
tel: 01 373151.

mountain range. Baalbek is the largest Roman temple ever built, and these are the tallest Roman columns in the world. Yet, despite its scale and importance, because of Lebanon's troubled recent history Baalbek sees few visitors and it is sometimes possible to explore the ruins virtually alone.

Baalbeck's history

There is evidence that Baalbek was first inhabited around the 2nd millennium BC, and, with two nearby rivers, became an important point on the caravan route between Tyre, Damascus and Palmyra in Phoenician times. Here, a cult developed to the Phoenician god of the sky, Baal, with one Roman historian describing ritual worships that involved "decadent immorality", with sacrifices of women and children and frequent orgies.

There is little record of the site during Babylonian and Persian times, but in the Hellenic period, beginning in 332 BC, the settlement was named Heliopolis. The Romans, arriving around 30 BC, valued its important strategic position and its religious importance as a cult centre, and established a city to reinforce Roman culture and power in the east. Over the next 200 years or so, successive emperors oversaw the construction of the vast temple complex.

At its peak, Roman Baalbek was an extraordinarily opulent and ornate city, with pilgrims travelling from across the empire to consult the oracle of the Temple of Jupiter. The temple complex was dedicated to a trinity of gods, in the Graeco-Roman tradition. The largest temple was in honour of the Roman god Jupiter, a development of the Phoenician god Baal. The second temple, today called Bacchus, was probably dedicated to the Roman Venus, the Phoenician Atargatis. And a third temple, which once stood on a hill overlooking the town

BELOW: soldiers
at ease in the
Temple of Bacchus.

but has now almost disappeared, was dedicated to the youthful Roman god Mercury, the Greek Hermes.

Though the city was a splendid outpost for Rome, by the time the complex was complete, in about AD 220 , the empire had already started to crumble, and Christianity had overtaken imperial cults. Even before that, the complex was vandalised by early Christians. In the later Roman and early Byzantine periods, when paganism was outlawed, part of the courtyard and the facade of the Temple of Jupiter was demolished and a Christian basilica built. In 634 Heliopolis was taken by the Arabs and transformed, over several hundred years, into a fortified city, with the steps of the original temple complex torn away and used in the construction of high city walls. A fortress was built on the southeastern corner by the Mamlukes, and still stands today, while other parts of the complex were destroyed and used in the construction of a nearby mosque. Arab control of the city continued until Ottoman times, and the crusaders, who so dominated the cities along the Mediterranean coast, never breached its walls.

The first archaeological interest in the ruins came in the 16th century, but it was not until 1898 that a German expedition excavated the two huge temples, followed by a French expedition in the 1920s, which tore down the Christian church to reveal Phoenician remains beneath.

In the steps of emperors

The **temple complex** (8am–8pm; admission charge) is today entered from the east. After passing the ticket stall , you climb a narrow modern staircase, which is probably one-20th the width of the original. The acropolis, or high city, above is not a natural feature, but was man-made using vast stones brought from a

Maps:
Area 270
Site 276

The scale of Baalbek is breathtaking. Even the smallest temple in the complex at Baalbek is larger than the Parthenon in Athens.

BELOW:
decorative detail.

quarry to the south of modern Baalbek. At the top of the stairs, you enter the **propylaeum** **A** – or entrance to the sacred interior. Several of the original 12 columns of Aswan granite have been reconstructed, while the two towers which once flanked the broad staircase bear little resemblance to their original state, having been heavily fortified under successive Arab rulers. The right (north) tower is the best preserved, while little remains of the left. At the base of several of the columns are inscriptions dedicating the temple to the gods.

Passing through the propylaeum brings you to a 50-metre (160-ft) deep hexagonal **forecourt**. This would have been open to the sky, but surrounded by a columned walkway. To the left and right *exedrae* – walled recesses where scholars and worshippers would rest and contemplate – still remain. The walls here clearly indicate the original Roman work and the later Arab fortifications above. Continuing west in the footsteps of Roman pilgrims, you pass into the **Great Court B**, more than 100 metres (330 ft) along each flank. This too was once lined with columns and a covered walkway. The *exedrae* here are decorated with carved flowers and masks, though the entablature above, and the majority of the 84 columns which would have supported it, have long since disappeared. Within and between the *exedrae* are niches which once held statues, several of which have been recovered and stand in the Beirut National Museum.

To the left and right are the remains of two **pools** where sacrificial animals were washed. These were decorated by the Romans with images of nymphs, tritons and griffins. Between the pools is a reconstructed sacrificial altar atop a tower, and, to its east, the base of a second tower – thought to have been four storeys high – which would have allowed spectators a clear view of sacrifices. The origins of the pool and the altars are much older than the rest of the site,

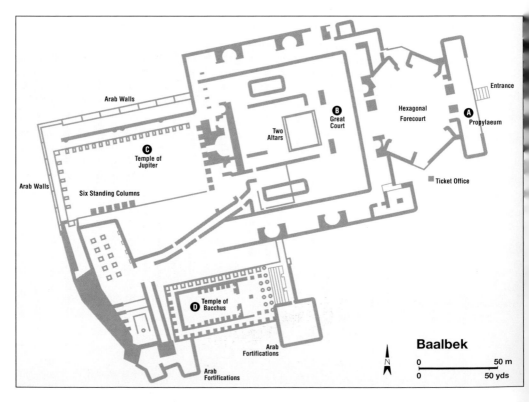

dating from before the 1st millennium BC, when it was a Phoenician place of worship. After the arrival of Christianity in the Roman Empire, a church was built in the middle of Great Court around AD 400. The church covered the two towers and extended up the steps of the temple ahead, which were cut to make way for its foundations. A decision was taken by French archaeologists in the 1920s to remove the church, allowing access to the Phoenician remains below, after which the high altar was carefully rebuilt.

Jupiter rises

Ahead at this point stands the magnificent **Temple of Jupiter ⊙**, completed in AD 65, the largest Roman temple ever constructed. The proportions are breathtaking: 88 metres (288 ft) long, 48 metres (157 ft) wide, the 54 columns each 22 metres (72 ft) high and 2 metres (6 ft) in diameter, and formed of three vast drums of stone, held together by pouring molten lead along grooves on their surface. Above the columns was a 5-metre (16-ft) high entablature, and a roof of Lebanese cedar.

The whole temple stands on yet another platform, 7 metres (23 ft) above the towering acropolis, itself 13 metres (42 ft) above ground. Though the roof has long since gone, and only six columns remain, the elaborately carved entablature can be seen above the remaining columns, covered with carvings of lions' and bulls' heads linked by garlands. The steps leading up to the temple are largely complete, but they bear the scars of the foundations of the 4th-century church.

Within the temple, little remains. In 1759 there were nine columns, but an earthquake that year left just six standing. The remains of another eight columns were taken to form part of the Santa Sophia church, now a mosque, in Istanbul.

In spite of Baalbek's massive proportions, there are plenty of delicate details, such as this nymph decorating a fountain.

BELOW: exploring the Great Court.

Maps:
Area 270
Site 276

In a quarry south of Baalbek is one block of stone which never made it to the site. Known as "the Stone of the Pregnant Woman", it is estimated to weigh at least 1,200 tonnes and moving it would need an estimated 40,000 men.

Beyond the temple, down the steps on the far side, it is possible to see some of the finely-cut blocks of stone which were used to raise the acropolis to its breathtaking height. They are some of the largest blocks of stone in the world, up to 30 metres (100 ft) in length, 4 metres (13 ft) high and 4 metres (13 ft) wide, each weighing more than 1,000 tonnes. Yet the joints between the blocks are accurate to the millimetre, and archaeologists puzzle over how such blocks were moved and placed – a feat that would be hard to recreate today, even with the latest technology.

For love or wine?

From the southern edge of the Temple of Jupiter, there is a fine view of what has long been called the **Temple of Bacchus ❿** – the Roman god of wine – because of the elaborate carvings of grapes. Modern scholars now believe it was in reality dedicated to Venus, the Roman goddess of love. It is a magnificent sight. The best-preserved Roman temple in the Middle East, and one of the finest decorated temples from the ancient world. Completed in about AD 150, it may look small compared to the Temple of Jupiter, which predates it by some 90 years, but is actually larger than the Parthenon in Athens.

It was built with eight columns front and back, and 15 along each side, and almost all of them remaining. Its preserved cella walls and peristyle, or walkway, are possibly the most intact examples to have survived from classical times. You approach the temple from the east, climbing more than 5 metres (6 ft) up the original broad flight of stairs. To the left are the remains of a Mamluke defensive tower, built some 1,000 years after the temple, when the city became an Arab fortress.

BELOW: the Temple of Bacchus.

Before you is the grand entrance portal. Above, the central keystone at the top of the archway was hanging dangerously for many hundreds of years before German archaeologists restored it to its original position in the late 19th century. On its lower face is carved an eagle carrying the rod of Mercury.

Inside the cella, the walls are well preserved and you can see the alcoves where statues would have been placed. Above are fine carvings of gods and mythical creatures mostly of Greek origin. The interior is also covered with graffiti from the 19th century. On the right wall is a plaque commemorating Kaiser Wilhelm's visit in 1898, during the German phase of excavation. To the rear, more broad stairs lead to a high altar, where a carved image of Venus probably once stood, much as the image of Christ does in a modern church.

Back outside, a walk around the exterior of the temple offers a view of the elaborate carvings and their intricate detail. To the left of the entrance, and to a lesser extent elsewhere, small sections of the peristyle ceiling remain, with images of Tyche (the Greek goddess of chance), Mars (the Roman god of war), Dionysus (the Greek god of wine, known as Bacchus to the Romans), and Diana (the goddess of the hunt).

Leaving the Temple of Bacchus, the exit from the site is through an ancient 120-metre (390-ft) tunnel, which passes under the acropolis. All around stand stones and relics which long ago toppled to the ground. On a hilltop in the distance, at the foot of the Anti-Lebanon range, are the remains of yet another temple, the third in the trilogy, which was dedicated to the youthful god Mercury, or Hermes to the Greeks. But all that remains of this today are the broad stone steps. The site is also in an area of the town controlled by Hizbollah, and is currently off-limits to tourists.

Maps:
Area 270
Site 276

Baalbeck is the triumph of stone; of lapidary magnificence on a scale whose language, being still the language of the eye, dwarfs New York into a home of ants.

— ROBERT BYRON

The Road to Oxiana, 1937

BELOW: exhibit in the museum at Baalbek.

Across the road from the site exit, and in a fenced off section, is the tiny 3rd-century BC circular **Temple of Venus**, though it was more likely dedicated to Tyche. The circular cella has five concave bays, though it suffered heavily as a result of earthquakes. Despite its poor condition, it was used as a church for many years.

Back at the entrance to the temple complex, and to the right, are the remains of the **Great Mosque**, which was built around AD 800 using stone taken from the temple; it was destroyed by a massive flood in 1318.

Resthouse of the famous

Walking up from the temple complex to the main road, you will reach the Palmyra Hotel. This was purpose-built in 1874 to cater for the growing number of tourists visiting the site. It was commandeered in World War I by the German army, and again in the World War II by the British. General de Gaulle stayed here, as did General Allenby, the World War I conqueror of Syria. Its classy reputation continued after the war, when guests included Brigitte Bardot and Jean Cocteau. The hotel has changed little since it was built, with dark cavernous rooms, and faded late 19th-century furniture. Some of the staff seem almost as old, and can be persuaded to show off the visitor's book containing many famous signatures.

Before the civil war, Baalbek was the site of a vast annual arts festival, which attracted a host of famous stars, including Ella Fitzgerald, Miles Davis, Duke Ellington and Rudolf Nureyev. The festival was relaunched in 1997, and has since seen performances by Lebanon's most famous diva, Fairuz, along with a smattering of foreign stars such as Herbie Hancock and Vanessa Mae.

BELOW: home farm in the valley.

Sacred lake of Yammouné

There are two principal roads north out of Baalbek: one leads to the Cedars resort, over the Mount Lebanon range, and the other leads north to the Syrian border. The road to the cedars passes through barren land which was once the heart of the hashish-growing district, but which is today sparsely planted with tobacco and potatoes. After the villages of Iaat and Deir al Ahmar, at the base the mountains, a left turn leads to the village of **Yammouné ⑦**, lying in a miniature version of the Bekaa Valley, accessed by a single road to the north.

Foreign visitors are rare, but the people are very hospitable, and just south of the village is a tiny pond, rather grandly called **Lake Yammouné**. This was the final destination of pre-Christian pilgrims to Afqa (on the other side of the mountain, *see page 287*) who would walk the many kilometres over its peaks, then plunge into the waters of the lake (then much bigger). The pool is said to be the source of the Nahr Ibrahim River, which emerges at Afqa; it is also supposed to be possible to walk under the mountain for the 4 km (2½ miles) that connect the two. Beyond Yammouné, the road climbs up to the Cedar range and brings you within a few kilometres to the town of Bcharré *(see North Lebanon, pages 285–303)*.

Refuge of St Maron

Back at Baalbek, the right-hand route leads to the Syrian border. As the road goes north, the two mountain ranges to the east and west fall away and the land becomes more arid as it approaches the Great Syrian Desert. After some 20 km (12 miles) the road crosses a rusting railway line which once led to the station of Ras Baalbek. At this point take a left along a narrower road leading to the isolated town of **Al Hermel ⑧**. After 4 km (2½ miles), there is a yet smaller turning on the left, which leads both to the source of the famed Orontes River, and an ancient monastery. Follow the track about 1 km (½ mile) to its end, where the monastery cut from the rock appears on the right. This is **Deir Mar Maron**, said by the Maronites to be the refuge of St Maron, the founder of their sect, who died at the beginning of the 5th century. The lower levels of the monastery are accessible, though it would be helpful to bring a torch.

There is a series of rooms, one more than 15 metres (50 ft) in length. The upper levels require climbing equipment to explore, as the ancient stairs have long since fallen away. Down the track just beyond the monastery is **Ras al-Assi**, the source of the Orontes, which bubbles with fresh cool water even at the height of summer.

Back on the road to Al Hermel, to your right, 2 km (1¼ miles) from the monastery, is a Phoenician **pyramid** on top of a hill. The structure is 26 metres (85 ft) high, made of black basalt and limestone and decorated with hunting scenes. It is thought to date from the 2nd century BC and to be a memorial to a king killed during a hunting expedition. Beyond the monument after another 1 km (½ mile) the road reaches a small bridge over the Orontes, where there is an excellent restaurant and trout farm. You can choose your fish from the water, and have it expertly cooked in a flash. ❏

Map on page 270

During the civil war Al Hermel was at the centre of a lucrative hashish industry. The number of abandoned palaces in the Al Hermel area testify to the wealth generated by this illegal production.

BELOW: banana plantation.

NORTH LEBANON

Rich in culture and beauty, this region offers dramatic mountainscapes, holy valleys, the picturesque port of Byblos, and the enticing souks of Tripoli

Map on page 286

The area north of Beirut is the most diverse in the country, and the one least touched by the civil war. A rich green plain stretches along the coast from Beirut to the Syrian border some 110 km (68 miles) north. Above, climbing to 3,100 metres (10,200 ft), is the Mount Lebanon range, spiritual home of the Maronite Christians. At its peak stand the Cedars of the Lord, a tiny patch of ancient trees which has enormous symbolic value for the Lebanese.

The key areas of interest are Byblos – the site of ancient ruins dating back 7,000 years, Tripoli, with its magnificent crusader castle, the rich green Qadicha Valley and, at its head, the cedars.

Valley of the gods

North of Beirut on the coastal highway – just beyond the vibrant Christian metropolis of **Jounié**, with its opulent casino, brash lifestyle and lethal drivers – the road gives way to a quieter, more rural landscape. Some 13 km (8 miles) north, the highway passes high over a small river, the **Nahr Ibrahim**, and just beyond is a road to the right signposted to Afqa. Immediately the road begins to climb and the spectacular valley of the Nahr Ibrahim appears to your right. In ancient times this was the valley of Adonis. Greek mythology has it that in the 5th century BC Adonis was born of the incestuous love between King Cinyras of Byblos and his daughter Aphrodite, the goddess of love. Charmed by the beauty of the newborn Adonis, Aphrodite fell in love with the child, put him in a box and handed him to Persephone, queen of the underworld, for safekeeping. But Persephone herself became infatuated with Adonis and refused to return him. Zeus, king of the gods, was called in to arbitrate, and ruled that Adonis should spend a third of the year with Persephone and a third with Aphrodite, with the remaining third at his own disposal.

As Adonis grew, he and Aphrodite became lovers, and exchanged their first kiss at Afqa (a translation of ancient Greek for kiss) in the Nahr Ibrahim Valley. But moments later, Adonis was charged by a wild boar and bled to death. In spring, the Nahr Ibrahim River is said to run red with the blood of Adonis.(In fact the soil high above the river is rich in iron deposits, which give it a faint pink tinge.) In pre-Christian times, the valley was the centre of a pilgrimage to Adonis, culminating in a festival of free love as participants re-enacted the lust of the gods.

Travel inland for 21 km (13 miles) and you reach the head of the valley at the village of **Al Majdel**, where the road splits, leading left to Al Laqlouq and right to Afqa. Along the right fork, the route narrows and twists, with waterfalls crashing to the left. It then

PRECEDING PAGES: Khan al Khayyatin, Tripoli. **LEFT:** Qadicha Valley. **BELOW:** contrasting icons.

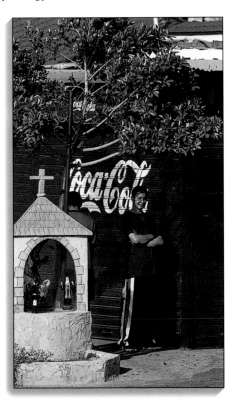

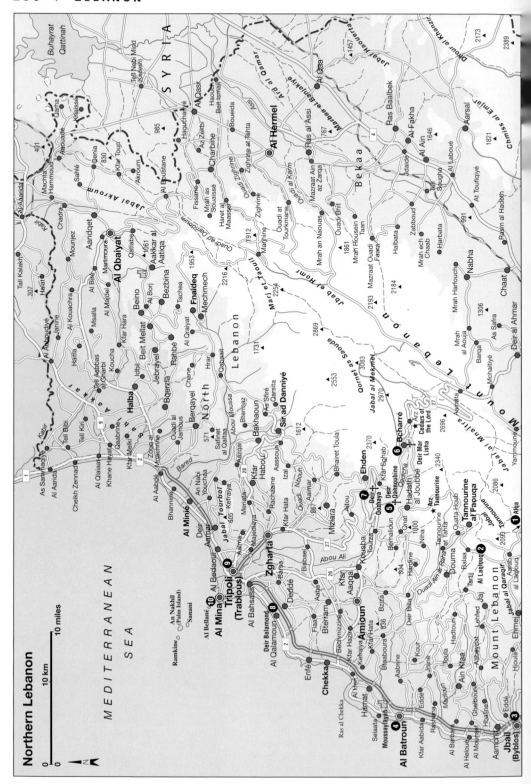

Northern Lebanon

begins to climb again, and after 2 km (1¼ miles), a wall of rock appears on your left. This is the waterfall of Afqa, and the site of the fatal kiss. In spring, the meltwater cascades down to wash under the Roman bridge to your right. Behind the waterfall is a deep grotto, which is accessible for most of the year.

Below the grotto, on the far side of the road, are the remains of a Roman temple to Aphrodite – or Venus, as the Romans called her – constructed with granite columns brought from Aswan in Upper Egypt. This was once the focus of the pilgrimage, but the first Christian emperor of Rome put a stop to pagan worship, leading to the destruction of the temple, and little remains today.

Just before the waterfall, a road to the left leads to the village of **Afqa ❶**, and at the far end of this, a small dirt track leads to the **Afqa Nature Reserve**.

Mountain retreat

Back to the junction of Al Majdel, the left fork leads high up into the mountains, to **Jabal Tannourine**. After 8 km (5 miles) it passes through the village of **Laqlouq ❷**, one of several popular skiing areas in the country. At an altitude of 1,750 metres (5,740 ft), the resort (tel: 09 904184) has a skiable area of some 600,000 sq km (231,700 sq miles). There is one modest hotel (the Shangri-La, tel: 03 441112), and out of the ski season, the centre is a retreat for nature lovers, who can rent bicycles or wander under the trees.

Beyond Al Laqlouq, the road narrows and approaches the mountain town of **Tannourine al Faouqa**, home of one of the country's mineral water producers. Close by are the Arz Tannourine – Tannourine Cedars – one of the small patches of the fabled trees still in existence. From here it is possible to continue along the narrowing road to the town of Bcharré and the Cedars of the Lord; this is one of the slowest but most scenic routes to the area.

Ancient claims

Back down to the coast, and 7 km (4 miles) from the Afqa turning, the busy coastal highway brings you to the town of **Byblos ❸** – Jbail in modern Arabic – some 41 km (25 miles) north of Beirut. This is perhaps the most popular tourist destination in Lebanon, and certainly one of the prettiest, its yellowing stone buildings with roofs of red tiles in sharp contrast to the deep blue Mediterranean. The town is littered with the relics of the many previous inhabitants, including a Byzantine church and a fine crusader castle. After a walk among the ruins, the town's pretty fishing port is the perfect place to relax and watch the sun set over the Mediterranean as the fishing boats return with their day's catch.

There is evidence that Byblos was first settled in the 5th millennium BC, its people living in circular stone huts, and making a living from fishing and small-scale agriculture. The hinterland was at that time covered with rich forests of pine and cedar, and progressively these began to be exported by ship to Egypt, bringing wealth to the settlement. The first evidence of the people now known as Phoenicians dates from 1900 BC, and the burial casket of King Ahiram dating from 1200 BC carries the first recorded inscriptions of the Phoenician alphabet.

Map on page 286

TIP

The Aqfa Nature Reserve is a good base for camping, rock-climbing, walking and picnicking.

BELOW: on the quay in Byblos.

Byblos is one of the prettiest tourist destinations in Lebanon.

Building on its trade, Byblos flourished for many hundreds of years until it was invaded in 875 BC by the Assyrians. The later arrival of first the Persians, and then Greeks brought yet another revival, with Byblos becoming a centre for the trade in papyrus between Greece and Egypt. Unlike Tyre, Byblos voluntarily became an ally of Alexander the Great, and thrived as a Greek city-state.

But by the 1st century AD, the rich timbers of the hinterland had almost been exhausted, and Byblos, now under Roman rule, began its long drift into obscurity. In 1104, it saw a modest revival under the crusaders, who built an impressive castle, but the departure of the last crusaders saw its decline gather pace. During the most recent civil war, Byblos was virtually untouched by the fighting, remaining in the area of the country under permanent Christian control, and serving as a refuge from the fighting in Beirut.

Walking through the past

Byblos is a perfect place to explore on foot, with all sites within easy walking distance and an array of cafés and restaurants along the way. The best point to begin and end a tour is at the port, from which Phoenician trade and warships once sailed, and which today is home to a tiny fishing fleet.

Walking south along the port, past the stone walls interspersed with granite columns long ago imported from Egypt, turn left immediately after the Byblos Fishing Club, and begin to climb uphill along the cobblestones, past a Greek Orthodox church on the left. After some 500 metres/yards the magnificent crusader **castle** emerges to the right, and a few metres further stands the entrance to the 5-hectare (12-acre) **archaeological site** (8am–8pm, admission charge), which includes relics spanning six centuries.

BELOW: the castle at Byblos.

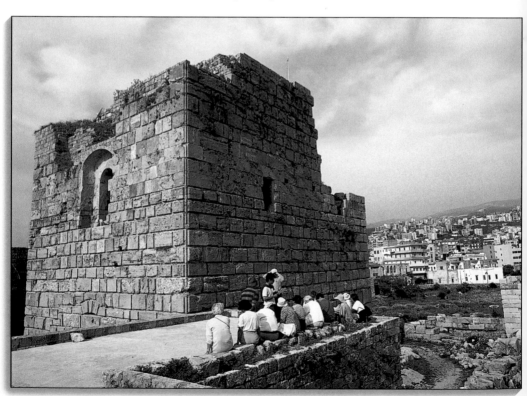

Map on page 286

The crusader castle, the most recent monument at the site, dates from 1109. Many of the huge blocks of stone used in its construction were recycled from earlier settlements, and are some of the largest in the Middle East. As well as the impressive keep, look out at the base of the structure for the vast water cistern, which once supplied its moat. Views from the walls are spectacular – north across modern Byblos and south across the archaeological site – and offer a good way of getting your bearings before beginning a walking tour of the much older monuments.

To leave the castle, climb down to the basement and step out into the vast site, where relics from many previous settlements have been discovered and preserved, though the whole area is sadly overgrown. Turn left after leaving the castle and follow the worn path heading inland. On your left (north) is the ancient Phoenician city wall dating from the 3rd millennium BC, which is 25 metres (82 ft) thick in places. Close to the castle, on the left, is an ancient entrance through the wall. Through here several steps lead to a passage lined with stone blocks. Beneath your feet notice the traverse grooves, each worn by a series of vertical gates that used to defend the city.

Regaining the path, and continuing inland (east), you come to a fenced off area containing an obelisk temple dating from around 2100 BC. The presence of this temple reflects the extent to which trade with Egypt had led to an adoption of Egyptian beliefs. The 30 or so obelisks pointed to the divine sun, with many placed to win favour from the gods.

This is not the original location of the temple: it was moved by archaeologists to give access to the **Temple of Reshef** (look behind you towards the sea), which was discovered below the obelisk temple, and dates from around 3000 BC.

The word Bible derives from "Byblos".

BELOW:
the Roman theatre.

TIP

It can be difficult to distinguish particular monuments at the archaeological site, so to make a visit worthwhile it is best to hire a guide at the ticket office for around LL15,000.

Towards the sea, past the Temple of Reshef, there is a deep depression which was the site of a sacred lake, and, close to it, the **Bir al-Malek** or King's Well, which supplied the ancient city with water until the Hellenic period. Stone steps, which were rebuilt many times over the centuries, lead down to the deep well. Ahead, and to the left are the remains of yet older dwellings, dating from the early 3rd millennium BC.

Dominating the site ahead is an Ottoman period house, which is a useful marker. To its left are the much older relics. To its right – after a fight through the undergrowth – is a perfectly preserved Roman theatre, one-third its original size (much of the stonework was pillaged by the crusaders for the much later castle). The site of the Roman theatre, which dates from around AD 200, is also not original, having been moved to access older monuments. Beyond the theatre and to the right are some spectacular Phoenician burial caskets dating from the 2nd millennium; these were excavated from a series of tunnels dug below the site. Behind the burial chambers it is possible to peer over into the shafts cut by archaeologists to access the tunnels. The burial casket of King Ahiram, with the first example of the Phoenician alphabet, was uncovered here, and now rests in the National Museum in Beirut. The tunnel in which his casket was found bears an inscription in the ancient alphabet to ward off intruders: "A warning: Your death is below."

On the way back towards the castle there is a well-preserved Roman colonnade on the left and, on the right, the **Temple of Baalat Gebel**, the oldest in Byblos, which dates from the 4th millennium BC. This was heavily damaged during the Amoraite period, was rebuilt by many successive generations and still was in use up to Roman times.

BELOW:
the Church of St John the Baptist.

Souks, churches and the port

Leaving the site of ancient Byblos, once again through the crusader castle, you arrive in the town's souks. More than anywhere else in Lebanon, the shops here are geared to foreign visitors, with an array of souvenirs and refreshments.

Leaving the souks to the left, walk back towards the port. Immediately on the right is a kitsch **wax museum**, with scenes depicting life through the ages. Further down on the left is the Church of **St John the Baptist**. Originally built by the crusaders in 1115, it has seen much destruction and change. Some parts, including the nave, are original. The open-sided baptistry dates from about 1200, while the northern door is 18th-century. At the far end of the church, on the right, are some vine mosques – all that remains of a Byzantine church which was originally on the site.

Continuing back down the hill, you again arrive at the **port**, which is at its most scenic just before sunset. After a hard day's exploring, there are few more perfect places to relax over a cold local Almaza beer, and watch the sun sink behind the crusader wall and towers. Around the port are a number of excellent restaurants and cafés.

The northern coast and the Qadicha valley

The coast north of Byblos is easily the most beautiful stretch in the country, less developed and more rugged than elsewhere. As the coast road rises, you will see several beaches tucked into the bottom of the cliff, with a growing number of hotels and beach clubs. Sixteen kilometres (10 miles) north of Byblos is **Al Batroun ❹**, settled by the Phoenicians in about 870 BC and now home to a small Maronite fishing community. There are several pretty churches, including

Map on page 286

TIP

Among the restaurants and cafés around the port is the Byblos Fishing Club, once a stopping-off point for celebrities cruising the eastern Mediterranean. The owner, Mexican playboy Pepe Abed, is a tourist attraction in his own right.

BELOW: in the wax museum.

High places are often holy places, as at Qadicha, a word that comes from a Semitic root meaning holy.

BELOW: typical landscape of Northern Lebanon.

the 18th-century church of **St George**. Just past Al Batroun a major right turn off the main highway leads up to the mountains, to the Maronite holy valley of **Qadicha** and the high cedars of Bcharré.

The drive to Bcharré, about three hours from Beirut, takes you through some of the most spectacular landscape in the country. Sleepy villages set among olive groves and vineyards dot the route as it climbs higher above the ever-visible Mediterranean, and then, suddenly, on the left, the seemingly bottomless Qadicha Valley appears, its cliff walls punctuated by cascading waterfalls.

For more than 1,000 years, the Qadicha served as a sanctuary for the Maronites, who came here to escape persecution soon after the crusaders departed, living in hermit caves along the walls of the gorge. The valley is now holy to the Maronites, and is dotted with monasteries and churches; it often resounds to the soft sound of church bells.

At the eastern end of the valley, the village of Bcharré appears on the opposite wall. Before the road twists to the left, and just before the "Mississippi" restaurant, a small turning to the left, which soon becomes a precarious narrow road, plunges more than 1,000 metres (3,300 ft) down to the valley floor. Near the base of the valley, and clinging to the far wall, is the **Mar Lisha monastery** (8am–7pm; free) dating from 1112. No longer used as a monastic residence, it is these days part-church, part-museum, and used by monks and nuns only for services on Sundays.

From here the road snakes along the tranquil green valley, between orchards of mulberry and apple and passing a fish farm and restaurant. After this it becomes a dirt track – a good point to park the car and take a walk, with the Qadicha River bubbling to your left. Surrounding this stretch are many hermit

caves where the early Maronites sheltered. A three-hour walk will bring you to the monastery of **Qannoubine** ❺. Between 1440 and 1800, this was the seat of the Maronite Patriarch – which now resides in Jounié – and 17 previous patriarchs are buried below the chapel.

Map on page 286

Struggle of the Maronites

The Maronites take their name from St Maron, a hermit who lived close to what is now Hama in Syria, and was buried there in AD 433. Some 200 years after this hermit's death, the Byzantine Emperor Heraclius passed by and learned from monks a solution to the long-standing Christian doctrinal dispute over how Christ could be both human and divine at the same time. The monks presented a compromise whereby Christ had two natures, but one will.

Hoping this would put an end to the doctrinal dispute which had split the empire, Heraclius rushed back to Constantinople. His efforts to promote the theory were in vain, but the doctrine of the monks led to the creation of the Maronites as a distinct Christian sect. The Maronites flourished after the arrival of the crusaders, but after their defeat retreated to the Qadicha to escape persecution from the Muslims.

Under the Ottomans, tension rose between the Maronites and Druze, their fellow inhabitants of the Mount Lebanon range, leading to a Druze slaughter of 10,000 Maronites in 1860. When France carved out Lebanon from Syria in 1920, it created a country for the Maronites, ensuring they had numerical superiority over the Muslims. The country prospered as they leaned on their strong links with the West and their entrepreneurial skills. But the faster birth-rates of Muslims, coupled with the arrival of some 300,000 mostly Muslim Palestinian

TIP

Many of the monasteries and chapels of this region have developed from remote hermits' caves. Some of these are therefore only accessible on foot. For instructions on how to reach them, enquire at the tourist office in Bcharré *(see page 294)*.

BELOW:
Deir Qozhaya, near Ehden.

refugees, chipped away at their numerical strength, leading the Muslims to seek more political power, a key factor in the 1975–90 civil war. Today, having effectively lost the war, the Maronites have reduced political power, and many of their leaders are in exile.

Gibran, the people's prophet

Rising from the valley floor, the road loops around the neck of the Qadicha, and approaches the village of **Bcharré ❻**. This is the birthplace of Lebanon's most famous writer, Khalil Gibran (1883–1931), who spent most of his life in the United States, from where he wrote and painted. On marriage, from *The Prophet*, he wrote:

> *Love one another, but make not a bond of love;*
> *Let it rather be a moving sea, between the shores of your souls;*
> *Fill each other's cup, but drink not from one cup;*
> *Give one another of your bread, but eat not from the same loaf;*
> *Sing and dance together and be joyous, but let each one of you be alone;*
> *Even as the strings of a lute are alone, though they quiver with the same music;*
> *Give your hearts, but not into each other's keeping;*
> *For only the hand of life can contain your hearts;*
> *And stand together, yet not too near together;*
> *For the pillars of the temple stand apart;*
> *And the oak tree and the cypress grow not in each other's shadow.*

Beyond his paintings and philosophy, Gibran also wrote scathingly of his country and its religion, leading to his excommunication from the Maronite church in 1930. A year later, at the age of 48, he died, and was returned to Bcharré,

BELOW: Bcharré.

where he is buried in a monastery above the village. Part of the monastery is a **museum** (9am–5 pm; closed Mon in winter; admission charge), and contains a collection of Gibran's paintings and original manuscripts.

Map on page 286

Cedars of the Lord

Climbing north out of Bcharré, another 10 km (6 miles) or so brings you to the **Cedars of the Lord**, a patch of several hundred trees, with around a dozen thought to be more than 1,500 years old. The trees are best viewed at dawn or dusk in winter, with snow on the ground, and shrouded in mist, and also when the tacky souvenir stalls, which sell items made of fallen branches, are closed. At the centre of the grove, one dead tree has been carved to represent Christ on the cross, and close by is a tiny chapel, where on 6 August, the Maronite patriarch celebrates mass.

On every flag and Lebanese aircraft, banknote and official building is a depiction of the cedar tree, which is the country's national symbol. Once the source of the wealth of the Phoenicians, there are only a tiny number left, and in some parts of the country these are almost worshipped. Mentioned in the Bible, Lebanese cedar wood was used in the construction of the Pyramids of Egypt, and in the temple of King Solomon in Jerusalem because of its strength and durability. Lebanese cedar resin was used to embalm many Egyptian Pharaohs. Unfortunately successive exploitation by the Assyrians, Babylonians, Greeks and Romans decimated the forests, leaving today on a few tiny patches.

The oldest and most famous, but not the largest, grove is at an altitude of more than 2,000 metres (6,500 ft) above Bcharré. Efforts have long been made to preserve the trees. Queen Victoria, for example, paid for a wall around

A museum dedicated to Khalil Gibran can be visited in the monastery above Bcharré, where he is buried.

BELOW: souvenirs of the cedars.

The Cedars

The cedar is Lebanon's national symbol, depicted on everything from the national flag to locally-produced cigarettes. In antiquity, forests of the fabled trees covered much of what is now Lebanon, and logging was a source of wealth for successive civilisations. Evidence of efforts to preserve the cedars has been found dating from the time of Roman Emperor Hadrian, in the form of inscribed stones near Tannourine, indicating which trees should be preserved, and which could be cut for timber. In more contemporary times efforts were stepped up to preserve the remaining groves. Since the end of the civil war, these have included preserving weak trees and planting new ones. Today, there are seven groves remaining.

The oldest and most famous grove is the Cedars of the Lord, at an altitude of more than 2,000 metres (6,500 ft) above Bcharré in the north. There are some 620 trees, a dozen of which are more than 1,500 years old. Many saplings have been planted, but the trees grow slowly at such a high altitude, taking about 40 years to produce fertile seeds.

One of the most interesting – yet tragic – groves is at Tannourine, inland from Batroun. At a lower altitude than Bcharré, the area has many thousands of trees. During the civil war, members of one militia planted landmines around parts of the grove – without making a note of where the mines were buried. As a result, much of the grove is inaccessible today, not only to visitors but also to conservationists who need to address problems created by insects. Many trees are dying but the landmines make spraying with insecticide from the air the only option.

Further south in the Chouf Mountains are two other large groves, centred on the town of Barouk, on the road between Damour on the coast and the Kefraya vineyards. There have perhaps fared best of all the Lebanese cedars, after the recent establishment of the 550-sq-km (212-sq-mile) nature reserve in the area. Visitors are excluded, and as a result, many animals which were dying out from the area are now returning, including deer, badgers and wild cats.

There have also been some rather unconventional efforts to save the cedars. In 1994, the International Society of Lebanese Cedars – a Japanese organisation based in Kyoto began efforts to revive trees near Bcharré. Tree specialist Yasuda Yoshinori sought to use a treatment developed to protect Japanese pine trees, dubbed the "Pine Reviver".

Yoshinori visited Bcharré, but was forbidden from treating the trees because the stuffy Lebanese Ministry of Agriculture mocked his evil-smelling potion (which comprised garlic and chicken droppings as well as a number of chemical enzymes). "We tried very hard to convince them the treatment was safe, but they remained unimpressed," Yoshinori told a Beirut newspaper. "I knew I had to do something drastic to convince them. We were sitting in a restaurant, so I took a sample of the Pine Reviver and drank it." Yoshinori was finally given permission to treat 30 trees. A year later, after the treatment had proved to be an unqualified success, he was allowed to treat the grove, which is now thriving. ❏

LEFT: Lebanon's precious cedars.

this grove in the 19th century. Today many saplings are being planted, but the trees grow slowly in the high altitude, taking, for example, around 40 years to produce fertile seeds.

Map on page 286

Face of god

From Bcharré, it is possible to choose from several routes back down to the coast. As well as the Batroun route, which is the shortest, there is a new highway that leads to Tripoli, passing through the summer retreat of **Ehden**, a good base for visiting another important monastery, **Deir Qozhaya ❼** (accessible by car from Aarbet Qozhaya). Monastic life was established here in the early Middle Ages and by the 16th century it had its own portable printing presses, imported from Europe, on which it produced the *Book of Psalms* in 1585 and 1610. The grotto near the entrance was used to imprison the insane, who were brought here for safe-keeping; the chains used to constrain the incarcerated can still be seen.

Back down on the coast, past Al Batroun, the old road and the new highway split approaching a vast mountainous outcrop, **Ras al Chekka**, known to the Greeks as the Face of God. The coast road climbs around the outer edge, the most scenic route, while the new highway passes by the dramatic Moussaylayha Castle, precariously perched on a rocky platform to the right of the highway just before a road tunnel. As soon as you are in sight of the tunnel, take a right, which leads down to a gully where the castle stands. Moussaylayha Castle has the appearance of a Crusader outpost, but is not referred to in any crusader chronicles, and is believed to have been built in the Middle Ages to protect travellers. The small river and grassy area below the castle is an ideal picnic spot,

TIP

Below the cedar grove is a small resort, which hosts skiers in winter and walkers in summer. One local hotel, the Alpine (tel: 06 671057), organises skiing, trekking and parascending. It is run by Elie, a Lebanese-Australian disc-jockey.

BELOW:
Moussaylayha castle.

and the area would be picturesque, were it not for the nearby six-lane highway.

Back on the highway and immediately beyond the road tunnel, quickly pull off the highway to the right. Here is a most unusual optical illusion. Drive forward up the slip road from the highway – which is clearly a small upward slope – and park your car, applying the handbrake. Now slowly release the brake, and hold your breath, as the car appears to roll uphill. Though clearly an optical illusion, it has been professed miraculous by many.

Beyond the tunnel, and down to the left after the Ras al Chekka headland are some attractive beach clubs, notably the oddly named **Benny Beach** (8am–8pm; admission charge). The water here is clear, and it is a fine place to spend a day swimming and relaxing, though the sun sets behind the headland at around 4pm, making an early start essential. The views out to sea from the beach clubs are somewhat overshadowed by the nearby industrial town of **Chekka**.

Some 25 km (15 miles) north of Byblos, rising high up on the right, is **Deir Balamond** ❽, a Greek orthodox monastery dating from the 12th century. It began life as a French Cistercian abbey, managed to retain its bell-tower after the fall of the crusaders, and now serves as one of Lebanon's better universities. With its Orthodox domes and crosses and the spectacular view from the top over the Mediterranean, it is reminiscent of churches on the Greek islands.

Tripoli: three cities, many invaders

The northern city of **Tripoli** ❾ is the most conservative and Middle Eastern in Lebanon. It has fine souks and a huge castle. It also has Lebanon's best preserved relics from the Middle Ages, with a host of mosques, religious schools and baths built by the Mamlukes. For sightseeing, the city can be divided into

BELOW: from Tripoli you can take a boat trip to Palm Island.

two, A Mina – the port – which occupies a narrow peninsula jutting out to sea, and Al Madina – the medieval city on the banks of the Abou Ali River, the local name for the Qadicha which flows down from the cedars.

The earliest settlements in Tripoli date from the 8th century BC, when the headland – Al Mina – was settled by the Phoenicians. Some 400 years later it became the federal capital of three Phoenician cities, Sidon, Tyre and Arwad (now in Syria). Each community had its own quarter, leading the Greeks to call it *Tri-Polis* or three cities. Under Greek and Roman rule, the city was home to many fine temples, but a huge earthquake in AD 543 destroyed much of this. The crusaders laid siege to the city of Al Mina in 1102, and began building the vast castle inland. After seven years Al Mina fell, and its library of 100,000 volumes – the finest in the Muslim world – was burnt to the ground.

For 180 years, Al Mina was held by the crusaders, who developed an important silk-weaving industry, and schools of medicine and philosophy. But in 1289, after a month-long siege, it fell to the Mamluke Sultan Qalaun. The fall of the city was precipitated by the flight of the Venetian and Genoese fleet based there, which left overnight, abandoning its residents. Qalaun razed Al Mina, to prevent the crusaders ever returning, and built inland instead at Al Madina, under the castle.

The city thrived under the Mamlukes, and in 1516 was taken by the Ottomans. During the most recent civil war, the city escaped most of the destruction until the Syrian army laid siege to it in 1983, when it was one of many brief bases of the PLO. Today Tripoli is Lebanon's second largest city, and the administrative capital of the north, with a population of some 350,000, comprising mainly Sunni Muslims.

Map on page 286

Narguileh *for sale in Tripoli. The pipes should cost no more than US$20. Fragrant fruit tobacco is widely available.*

BELOW: festive flags fly in Tripoli.

Tripoli's sights

The destruction of Al Mina by the army of Sultan Qalaun left little for the tourist to see today. However Al Madina has a wealth of medieval monuments, as well as the awesome castle. Approaching the city from the south, the best way to get your bearings is to drive to the castle. Beyond is the Abou Ali (or Qadicha) River, and on the nearside is an array of Mamluke buildings, running left to right, and the modern centre of the city at Al Tal Square. The areas of interest are all within walking distance of one another, and run along a north–south line of about 1 km (½ mile). The city is famous for its souks, which spread across the centre of the town.

Though the **Citadel**, or castle of Raymond de Saint-Gilles (9am–5pm; admission charge) was built by the crusaders in the 12th and 13th centuries, most of the structure still standing is the work of the Mamlukes and Ottomans, with little more than the foundations and the lower walls original. The northern entrance passes through a series of gates – first an Ottoman gate, over a moat, and then through an angled Mamluke gate, designed to prevent assault with a battering ram, and finally through a pointed crusader arch. Beyond this, the passageway is lined with Roman sarcophagi, leading to the inner citadel. Down steps to the left (east) are vaulted chambers, while ahead are the foundations of a crusader church with an octagonal crypt.

Climbing the walls of the castle offers fine views over the city and surrounding countryside, with the Mount Lebanon range in the distance. From the western wall it is possible to see the other points of interest in the city. To the left is the green-domed Taynal Mosque; ahead is the Great Mosque, with an open square courtyard and rectangular minaret; slightly to the right is Al Tal Square.

Interior of Tripoli's Ottoman Hammam al Jdid, the "New Bath", which is the largest in the city.

BELOW: inside the Taynal Mosque.
RIGHT: the Great Mosque.

The **Taynal Mosque** was built by the Mamlukes in 1336, on an original 12th-century church. It is one of the best preserved of the Mameluke buildings, and the features of the original church can be clearly seen, including a partially-preserved nave, with columns of granite brought by previous settlers from Aswan in Upper Egypt. Some 80 metres/yards from the mosque, in the direction of the castle, is the Ottoman **Hammam al Jdid**, or "new" bathhouse, built around 1740.

Continue along the main street, and parallel with the castle, set back on the left after another 200 metres/yards, is the **Great Mosque**. This was converted from the 12th-century crusader church, St Mary of the Tower, as is evident from the minaret, which clearly began life as a bell tower. Outside the east door of the mosque is the **al-Qartawiya Madrasa**, a theological school built on the site of the church baptistry, with its handsome black and white facade and elaborate honeycombed ceilings.

Map on page 286

Souks and traders

Leaving the mosque by the north door, you are facing three *madrasas*, or religious schools, from the 14th and 15th centuries. A left turn takes you to a useful **tourist information office**, but instead turn right and walk parallel to the castle. Immediately on your right is one of the still active Turkish baths, the **Hammam an Khoury**, and within 50 metres/yards, on your left is the **Khan al-Sabun**, or soap trading house. This was originally an Ottoman barracks, converted under Fakr ad-Deen in the 17th century. Turn right and then left towards the river, again parallel to the castle, and within 200 metres/yards to your right is the newly restored **Khan el-Khayatin**, dating from 15th century but built

Though the Qartawiya Madrasa is the most ornate, there are at least half a dozen madrasas (lodging houses-cum-schools for theological students) clustered around the Great Mosque, all of them dating from the 14th century.

BELOW: ready-to-wear in the souk.

Map on page 286

on earlier Byzantine and crusader foundations, which has long been home to tailors. Immediately opposite, is the **Khan al-Misriyyan**, the run-down home of Egyptian traders. If you continue walking towards the river you will see, after another 50 metres/yards on your left, Al Attar Mosque. Here, double back and take a left (walking directly away from the castle), and follow the road to the commercial centre of the city, **Al Tal Square**. Here, around the clock tower, are shops, cafés and hotels.

Al Mina and the islands

From Al Tal Square, it is a short taxi ride to **Al Mina ⑩**, the Phoenician city. Relics were destroyed after it fell to the Sultan Qalaun, and little of historical interest remains. However, the peninsula is a good place to escape from the city, and it is interesting for railway buffs as it is home to a long-abandoned Tripoli railway station. Parked in the yard are half a dozen huge rusting steam locomotives, with plates dating them to the beginning of the 20th century. The yard is occupied by a handful of Syrian soldiers who seem to find the arrival of tourists bemusing; whistling a jolly tune as you arrive may prevent them from being startled.

Just beyond the abandoned station, is **Lion Tower**, the last remaining of a series of Mamluke defence towers, built in 1440, with a beautifully decorated west portal of black and white stone; its name comes from a carved relief of lions that once topped the entrance. Further south along Al Mina is a seafront corniche, a good place to relax over an Arabic coffee. From here it is also possible to take organised boat trips out to a number of small islands, the nicest of which is **Palm Island**. Though infested with rabbits, the tiny island is a wonderful place to swim (bring walking shoes because the rocks are very sharp).

The road beyond Tripoli leads to the **Aakkar**, a quiet and rural area of Lebanon, which is today mostly a transit point for traffic to and from Syria, but is also one of the most unspoilt and attractive regions in the country, having few of the ugly developments that have sprouted elsewhere. As well as beautiful scenery, it is home to one of the more remote crusader castles, which is worth seeking out.

From Tripoli take the road towards **Al Qbaiyat**, but turn right at the crossroads in the centre of **Halba**. Follow the narrowing road through Jebrayel, Beit Mellat, Beino and Al Borj. Then, about 1 km (½ mile) before the village of Aakkar al-Aatiqa, the road passes over a small stream, with a dirt road to the right. Take this, and park near the farmhouse; ahead, high up to the right, is the **castle**. Much of it is in ruins, which can be explained by its many previous occupants. In chronological order, these were Fatimid Arabs, the crusaders in 1109, Sultan Nour ad-Deen, the crusaders again in 1170, Sultan Baybars in 1271, the Ottomans, and Fakr ad-Deen in the 17th century. The climb up 700 metres/yards to the castle is not an easy one, but the view from the top is spectacular, across to Syria and Crac de Chevaliers. The **keep** is still intact, and has an entrance so high it would be impossible to enter without ropes. Around the base of the hills runs a pretty stream, and this would be yet another ideal place for a picnic. ❑

BELOW: along the craggy coast.

Where to Go Skiing

Compared with Europe, the US and Australasia, the skiing in Lebanon is modest. The resorts have a relatively short season (Jan–Apr), a small number of lifts and a limited area of groomed pistes. At weekends the crowds can be oppressive, and most lifts close by 4pm. Yet when the skiing is good, it is wonderful. The Middle East sun can be baking hot, the sky a clear deep blue, the snow crisp and fresh, and the views down to the Mediterranean magnificent.

While many Lebanese go up to the mountains during the season to take advantage of the skiing, an equally large crowd goes up every weekend simply to party and spend the afternoons sunbathing at the terrace cafés. Those that do venture onto the slopes generally ski the way they drive – hurtling along with little regard for those around them while glued to their mobile phones.

Most skiing Beirutis go to Faraya for the weekend, or to the Cedars for a longer break. All resorts have shops renting skis for about $7 a day, while a lift pass costs up to $30 a day, depending on the resort. Beirut travel agents and hotels can arrange for a day or weekend skiing, or you can hire a car and drive yourself, though you will need chains in mid-winter.

Faraya-Mzaar: Nearest to Beirut, Faraya is just inland from Jounié, 46 km (28 miles) from Beirut and less than an hour's drive. The pistes are at altitudes of between 1,900 and 2,500 metres (6,000–8000 metres) and there are 17 slopes, from two nursery runs to several long tracks of more than 2km (1¼ miles), and a number of deep bowls and crazy black runs. There are several small hotels, and chalets can be rented. It also has the best *après ski* in Lebanon, with two nightclubs and the excellent and inexpensive Chez Mansour eatery nearby.

Faqra: Some 3 km (2 miles) beyond Faraya is Faqra, which has a small private ski resort with seven runs and three lifts. Faqra is self-consciously exclusive, and attracts a rich cigar-smoking crowd. Pistes are very quiet, but you will need to get an invitation to come.

Laqlouq: In the mountains behind Byblos, this resort (pronounced La'lou) is just 62 km (40 miles) from Beirut, but access roads are much narrower than at Faraya, and the journey can easily take two hours. The resort is quiet and not subject to weekend crowds. Skiing takes place between 1,650 and 1,920 metres (5,400–6,300 ft), on nine slopes with nine lifts. There are several hotels.

Cedars: Some 122 km (76 miles) from Beirut is the Cedars, the highest skiing resort in Lebanon at an altitude of between 2,100 and 3,100 metres (6,900 and 10,000 ft). It has the longest skiing season, often running into late April. There are four long runs and nine lifts. It also has the most breathtaking views, and on a clear day it is said you can see Cyprus from the top of the south run.

Kanat-Bakish/Zaarour: These are two of many small resorts in the Metn mountains inland from Beirut. Each has half a dozen pistes, and a couple of lifts. The skiing is unpretentious, but the facilities limited. ❑

RIGHT: refuge from the snow.

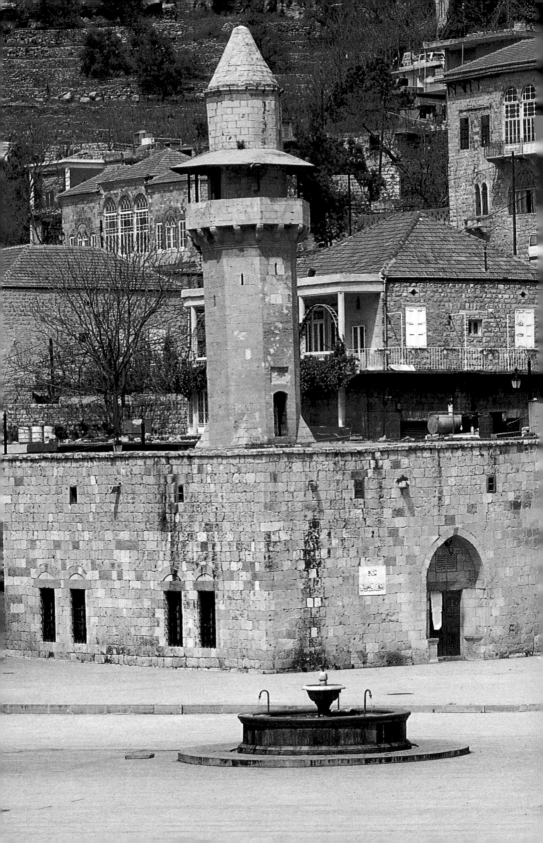

STORE: 0349   REG: 01/66   TRAN#: 8639
SALE   03/03/2004   EMP: 01827

INSIGHT SYRIA INSIGHT GD
                    ST T   23.95
Order#:31495

            Subtotal   23.95
            VIRGINIA 4.5%   1.08
1 Item   Total   25.03
            VISA   25.03
ACCT # /S XXXXXXXXXXXXX5184
            AUTH: 183300
NAME: BARAKAT/MHD/W

CUSTOMER COPY

03/03/2004 03:32PM

BORDERS®

Merchandise presented for return, including sale or marked-down items, must be accompanied by the original Borders store receipt. Returns must be completed within 30 days of purchase. The purchase price will be refunded in the medium of purchase (cash, credit card or gift card). Items purchased by check may be returned for cash after 10 business days.

Merchandise unaccompanied by the original Borders store receipt, or presented for return beyond 30 days from date of purchase, must be carried by Borders at the time of the return. The lowest price offered for the item during the 12 month period prior to the return will be refunded via a gift card.

Opened videos, discs, and cassettes may only be exchanged for replacement copies of the original item.

Periodicals, newspapers, out-of-print, collectible and pre-owned items may not be returned.

Returned merchandise must be in saleable condition.

BORDERS®

Merchandise presented for return, including sale or marked-down items, must be accompanied by the original Borders store receipt. Returns must be completed within 30 days of purchase. The purchase price will be refunded in the medium of purchase (cash, credit card or gift card). Items purchased by check may be returned for cash after 10 business days.

Merchandise unaccompanied by the original Borders store receipt, or presented for return beyond 30 days from date of purchase, must be carried by Borders at the time of the return. The lowest price offered for the item during the 12 month period prior to the return will be refunded via a gift card.

Opened videos, discs, and cassettes may only be exchanged for replacement copies of the original item.

Periodicals, newspapers, out-of-print, collectible and pre-owned items may not be returned.

Returned merchandise must be in saleable condition.

BORDERS®

Merchandise presented for return, including sale or marked-down items

Returned merchandise must be in saleable condition.
may not be returned.
Periodicals, newspapers, out-of-print, collectible and pre-owned items
replacement copies of the original item.
Opened videos, discs, and cassettes may only be exchanged for
via a gift card.
the item during the 12 month period prior to the return will be refunded

SOUTH LEBANON

The cities of Tyre and Sidon are steeped in history, with an abundance of ancient monuments. Above, in the rolling Chouf Mountains, are villages almost untouched by the modern world

Map
on page
308

Beirut

South Lebanon is easily the most varied and exciting part of the country. Geographically, it is the greenest region, mixing the beautiful southern coast of beaches and banana, orange and lemon groves, with pine-forested mountains. It also has one of the richest histories of any region in the world. More than 2,000 years before Columbus "discovered" America, the educated and entrepreneurial Tyrians were colonising the Mediterranean, and had circumnavigated Africa. Today the region has a rich melange of peoples, from the mysterious Druze of the Chouf Mountains, to the Sunni Muslims in Sidon, to the olive growing Shia Muslims of the hills around Nabatiyé. Considering its history and beauty, south Lebanon sees very few visitors on account of its recent troubled history. But the vast majority of the south is now safe to visit, with caution only required close to the Israeli border.

There are three principal areas of interest, the Phoenician cities of Sidon and Tyre, and the pretty Chouf villages of Beit ed Dîne and Deir al-Qamar.

Chouf: birthplace of independence

Leaving Beirut on the southern highway, the modern developments quickly give way to a narrow coastal tableland of banana plantations and groves of citrus fruit. On the left, the Mount Lebanon range comes into view, with the aqua-green Mediterranean just below the highway on the right. Along the side of the road are traders tempting drivers with freshly caught fish or stalls piled high with locally-grown fruits and vegetables.

Some 20 km (12 miles) south of Beirut a side road leads off to the Chouf Mountains, a wild and beautiful region of Lebanon with pine forests and olive, apple and grape plantations. Since the Middle Ages the Chouf has been home to a mixed population of Maronite Christians and Druze – an offshoot of Shia Islam *(see page 63–4)*. Life in the area has changed little over the past two centuries. Under the Ottomans, it enjoyed semi-autonomy, giving rise to the country's first nationalist leaders, Emir Fakr ed Deen, and Emir Bechir al-Chehab.

Some 15 km (9 miles) up from the coastal highway, is the village of **Deir al-Qamar ❶**, renowned as Lebanon's prettiest village, and home to the largest Christian community in the Chouf. It was from here that Emir Fakr ad-Deen sought to bring under his control the many feudal factions of Lebanon to create a nation in the early 17th century, and this village was the country's first capital.

Around the square are buildings of his dynasty, and that of his successor, Emir Bechir, including a 17th-century Fakr ad-Deen mosque, and an 18th-century

PRECEDING PAGES:
Deir al-Qamar.
LEFT AND BELOW:
the sea castle and
harbour at Sidon.

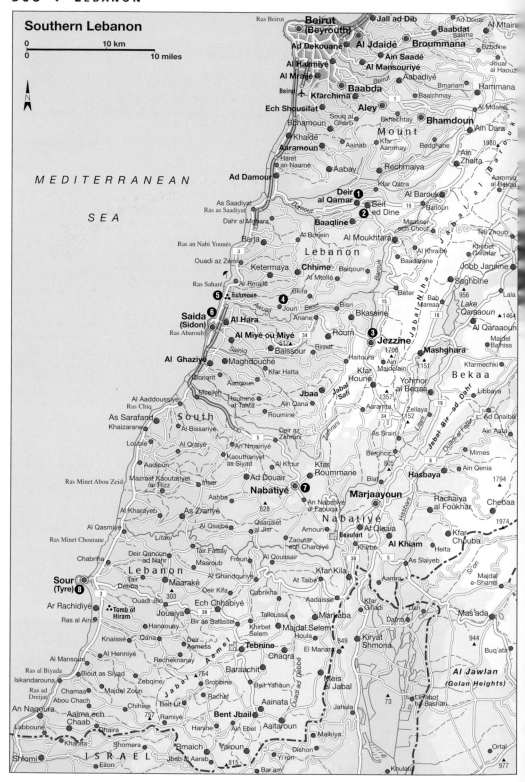

Southern Lebanon

0   10 km

0   10 miles

M E D I T E R R A N E A N

S E A

I S R A E L

Palace of the Chehabs. The mosque of yellow stone dominates the square, and was built atop a Mamluke ruin. Above the mosque, and to the left, is the palace of Fakr ad-Deen's brother Younis. On a higher level north of the square is a former Jesuit monastery, while on the south side of the road is the serail, which now serves as a town hall. All the buildings were built in Mamluke style, with ornate arches and stones carved to appear as wooden nails, used to decorate the grand entrances. Though now in private hands, most buildings around the square can be visited, their owners often only too pleased to welcome tourists.

The palace of Beit ed Dîne

In the early 19th century, Emir Bechir moved the seat of government 5 km (3 miles) south to the village of **Beit ed Dîne** ❷. Here he built a magnificent **palace** (9am–5 pm, admission charge). Designed and built by Italian architects between 1788 and 1840, the palace sits on a rocky spur overlooking carefully tended terraces, and is divided into three courts. On entering, a carved stone archway leads into the grand Dar al-Baraniyeh courtyard, around which were lodgings for travellers. In one corner is a museum devoted to daily life in the 18th century. On the far side of the courtyard a vast double stairway leads to the middle lodgings, or Dar al-Wousta. This was the administrative heart of the palace, surrounding yet another courtyard.

In the centre of this courtyard a fountain is dedicated to Kamal Jumblatt – the political leader and father of the current feudal lord of the Druze, MP Walid Jumblatt – who was murdered in the early years of the civil war *(see page 65)*. Across the courtyard, through another magnificent archway, is the Dar al-Harem, the private apartments of the emir. The palace was briefly used by Emir Bechir, but soon after its construction he was deposed by the English, in collusion with the Ottomans, and forced into exile.

Emir Bechir had three sons, and a palace was built for each of them. On a hill overlooking Beit ed Dîne Palace stands one of these smaller, yet no less lavish residences, built for Emir Amin. It has now been converted into the Mir Amin Palace Hotel (tel: 05 501315–8), an attractive place to stay, with lovely views over the valley, though its standards of food and service do not match it self-appointed five-star description.

Some 10 km (6 miles) south of Beit ed Dîne, is the town of **Al Moukhtara**, the unofficial capital of the Chouf and home of Walid Jumblatt, who lives in a splendid palace which it is possible to visit on most days. Another 20 km (12 miles) south along the spine of the Chouf mountain range is **Jezzine** ❸, once one of the country's main tourists attraction because of two 40-metre (130-ft) waterfalls and its cool maintain air. Between 1982 and the summer of 1999, Jezzine was under the control of Israel, and almost impossible to visit. But in June 1999 it was handed back to Lebanon, after a series of Israeli military defeats. It is perhaps the prettiest settlement in the country after Deir al-Qamar, and because of its wartime isolation has been spared the ugly developments seen across much of the country.

Map on page 308

TIP

The palace at Beit ed Dîne is the venue for an international summer festival of music, held every July. Tel: 01 373600/01 373800 for festival details.

BELOW: fountain in the splendid palace at Beit ed Dîne.

Hester's house

Beit ed Dîne suffered heavily during the Israeli invasion of Lebanon in 1982, but has been carefully restored by Jumblatt. The government is trying to wrench control of Beit ed Dîne from the Druze leader and remove all monuments to his father from the town.

Back on the highway, and past another headland, a long sandy beach comes into view 38 km (24 miles) south of Beirut. **Remailee** (admission charge) is one of the best beaches in the country and makes a pleasant stopping-off point on the road south. The approach to the beach crosses an abandoned railway line, which before the war linked all the coastal cities.

Some 5 km (3 miles) further south, just before crossing the Awuali River, there is a clearly marked turning on the left to **Joun ❹**, which is about 12 km (7½ miles) east of the highway. Here, from 1818–39 lived Lady Hester Lucy Stanhope (*see below*) and on the edge of the village is her tomb, shaped like a pyramid and hidden among olive groves. It was heavily damaged during the civil war, but villagers are today happy to direct tourists to the remains.

Temple of Eshmoun

BELOW:
the ruins of Hester
Stanhope's house.

At the crossing of the Awuali River, just past a forest of palm trees, and in the middle of a Lebanese army checkpoint, is a small road to the left, which has no signpost. A turning here takes you to the Phoenician temple of **Eshmoun ❺** (8am–7pm; free). Set amid orange groves, the temple was built in the 6th century BC by the kings of Sidon in honour of the gods of their town. Little remains of the Phoenician temple today, with many of its most interesting finds, including a giant altar and ornate friezes, long since taken to the museum in Beirut. But amid the ramshackle collection of carved stones that remain are inscriptions dating from the 5th century BC, describing the temple's builder as Bodashart, king of the Sidonians. There are also monuments and mosaics from later Byzantine and Roman periods.

AN ENGLISH ECCENTRIC

Lady Hester Stanhope was born in 1776, the daughter of Viscount Charles Stanhope, a radical and eccentric English politician and inventor. She was also the niece and confidante of William Pitt, who, in 1783, became England's youngest-ever prime minister at the age of 24.

The death of Pitt in 1806, coupled with the deaths of her fiancé and brother in 1809 – both fighting in the Spanish war – left her broken-hearted, and led her on a trip to the East from which she would never return.

With her personal physician by her side, she made her way south to Malta, before travelling on to Syria. In Palmyra, she was hailed as a queen and prophet, and before leaving issued a letter to the keeper of the ruins "authorising" him to charge Europeans to visit the site. She then moved to Joun, on the Lebanese coast, and took up residence in the house of a local trader. He assumed her to be a temporary guest, and when she refused to leave, he protested to the Ottoman sultan in Constantinople, who offered a curt reply: "Obey all wishes of the European princess."

Over time, she gradually became a recluse, receiving only a trickle of curious European visitors. Local people were never quite sure if she was a prophet or a mad woman. She died in poverty in Joun in 1839.

Sidon: First born of Canaan

Beyond Eshmoun, the road reaches the outskirts of **Sidon** (Saida) ❻, 43 km (27 miles) south of Beirut. Sidon was once the most significant of all Phoenician cities, having grown wealthy through trade, and in ancient times it was renowned for its powerful sea fleet. It is said that this was where glass was invented, and the rare purple dye murex was extracted and exported. One of the oldest towns on the Levantine coast, it was a centre of trade as early as 1700 BC, exporting silk dyed with murex and cedar wood to the Egyptian pharaohs. In the Book of Genesis, it is identified as the northern border of Canaan.

In the 9th century BC, it fell to the Assyrians, then in 539 BC, to the Persians. The city continued to prosper, with the Persians making use of the Sidonian fleet of warships to control the eastern Mediterranean. But in the 4th century BC the city was sacked and burnt, and later surrendered to Alexander the Great in 332 BC. In the 1st century AD it passed to Roman control, marking the beginning of its long decline which was noted by St Paul as he passed by on his way to Rome. In 667 AD it was captured by the Umayyads and ruled from Damascus, with its name changed to Saida. Then in 1111, the city fell to the crusaders after a 47-day siege. They built the picturesque Sea Castle, as well as a fortified residence for the Knights of the Hospitallers of St John *(see page 190)*. But in 1289, they too were ousted, this time by the Mamlukes, and the fortified residence was converted into the Great Mosque. Under the rule of Emir Fakr ad-Deen in the 17th century, the city saw a renewed period of prosperity, when it became the main port of his empire.

In more recent wars, control of the city passed from the Palestinians to the Syrians in 1976, then to the Israelis in 1978, and again in 1982, when they

Map on page 308

TIP

Shortly after turning off for the temple of Eshmoun there is a pretty picnic site on the left by the river.

BELOW: Astarte's throne in the Phoenician temple of Eshmoun.

occupied the town for three years. Today, with a population of some 100,000, it is the municipal capital of south Lebanon, but its prosperity is yet to fully recover from the war.

Sidon, true to Phoenician form, was built on a promontory with an island offshore, allowing use of several natural harbours. This tiny island is today entirely occupied by the crusader Sea Castle, constructed on the base of many previous defensive settlements. Arriving in the city, the road splits 44 km (27 miles) from Beirut, with the right hand fork leading to the most interesting part of the city. Its most famous monuments, the crusader Sea Castle, the Great Mosque and the Khan al-Franj, are all clustered on the headland within easy walking distance of each other.

The **Sea Castle** (8am–7pm; admission charge) was erected in 1228 by the crusaders, destroyed by the Mamlukes in 1289, then later rebuilt and extended by the Arabs. It was constructed of local yellow stone interspersed with columns of grey granite brought from Aswan in Upper Egypt. From the shore a modern bridge to the island leads through an archway decorated with carved crusader figures of lions and men. Through the outer gate, a sand-strewn passageway leads to an inner temple with pointed arches and a vaulted vestibule. Ahead and to the right are the remains of a finely-cut corner pillar of clustered columns from which arches and vaults would have sprung. To the far left and far right are two towers; the larger south tower was restored by the Arabs, while the smaller north tower has a tiny mosque set high up on its roof. Walking left to the south tower, a modern stairway leads to its high and spacious upper chamber, which would have been agreeably cool in summer. Stairs give access to the roof, from where it is possible to see the city's four harbours of ancient times.

TIP

For those in need of rest and refreshment, the excellent Resthouse next to the castle has a Lebanese restaurant in a refurbished 17th-century *khan*, with a lawn and lovely views.

BELOW: Sidon is a seafaring town.

Returning to the mainland from the castle, and following the coast to the right, past a mosque with a yellow minaret and busy fruit and fish markets, you will reach the vast square stone **Khan al-Franj** (8am–7pm; free), or French trading house . This was built for French merchants in 1610 by Emir Fakr ad-Deen, with taverns, workshops and stables on the ground floor and living quarters above. The *khan* was badly damaged during the war, and is now being restored by local craftsmen.

Along the waterfront another 400 metres/yards to the south, the **Masjid al-Kabir**, or Great Mosque (sunrise–sunset; free but permission required). This was originally the church of the Knights Hospitallers of St John. Built in the 13th century, it was converted to a mosque after the fall of the crusaders. Its imposing high walls were not enough to protect it during the civil war, but it has since been carefully restored.

Just past the mosque, turn inland for 200 metres/yards to reach **Qalaat al Mezzeh**, or the Castle of St Louise, another crusader structure but in poor condition. Back along the waterfront, a further 200 metres/yards south is a small man-made hill. Dating from Phoenician times, this is all that remains of the murex dye trade, which was once the source of Sidonian power *(see page 315)*. Inland from the seafront monuments some attractive souks can be explored between Khan al Franj and the Great Mosque.

Road to Nabatiyé

Three kilometres (2 miles) south of Sidon a vast statue of the Virgin Mary appears on a hilltop to the left. This marks the Greek Catholic village of **Magh-douché**, which can be reached from a turning at this point. It is said that this is

Map on page 308

Sidon is a great place to eat fresh fish.

BELOW: a market stall in Sidon.

Sarafand has been famous for glass-making since ancient times. Its name may derive from the Hebrew word saraph, *meaning to melt.*

BELOW: Sarafand.

where Mary came after the crucifixion of Christ, awaiting his resurrection. Another 5 km (3 miles) south the road splits at a roundabout dominated by a colossal Soviet-style sickle commemorating the death of a Lebanese guerrilla in the war against Israel. The inland fork leads to Nabatiyé.

Nabatiyé ❼ is a ramshackle town built over two hills, with a population of some 50,000. It is the largest town close to the border with Israel, and home of Hizbollah, the Shia Muslim guerrilla group and political party *(see page 319)*. Every year the town hosts a festival of Ashoura (the exact date changes from year to year according to the Muslim calendar). Here the Shias commemorate the martyrdom of the Imam Hussein, the son of Ali, killed in 680 at the battle of Kerbaa; it was his death which led to the creation of the Shia faith. The Ashoura festival is not for the squeamish, as it culminates in a procession of thousands of young men dressed in white shrouds lacerating themselves with blades to re-enact Hussein's suffering.

Just beyond Nabatiyé, a small road to the right leads to the village of **Arnoun**. Above this village is **Beaufort Castle**, perched on a sheer escarpment 710 metres (2,330 ft) above the Litani River. The crusader structure was built in 1139, but fell to Saladin 51 years later after a long siege. In 1240, the Arab Sultan of Damascus, Ismail, returned it to the crusaders, but the Arab forces inside refused to leave, leading to yet another siege. In 1260 it was sold to the Knights Templar – said to be the bravest but also the most roguish of the crusaders.

In 1268 it was taken by the Mamlukes, and in the 17th century it was occupied by the forces of Emir Fakr ad-Deen. From 1978, Palestinian guerrillas shelled northern Israel from here, and in 1982 Israel destroyed much of the castle during its invasion of Lebanon, and held it as a military position until the

Israeli withdrawal from southern Lebanon in 2000. The departing Israelis were accused of employing "scorched earth" tactics and blowing up substantial sections of the castle's walls.

Back on the highway, 16 km (10 miles) south of Sidon the road passes the ramshackle village of **Sarafand**, which is connected to a sister village of the same name on the hill to the east known in the Old Testament as Zarephth.

Map on page 308

Ancient Tyre

Around the next headland the city of **Tyre** (Sour) ❽ looms in the distance, some 80 km (50 miles) south of Beirut. At one time, Tyre was the most important commercial centre in the Mediterranean. Tyrians were great explorers, travelling to the Atlantic, circumnavigating Africa and founding colonies in Carthage, Cyprus, Rhodes and Crete. The city's merchants were among the most successful in the known world, and its citizens were said to be the most flamboyant.

In legend, Tyre was founded by the Phoenician god Melkart. He is said to have anchored two small offshore islands together, and taught the inhabitants to build boats and to use the stars to navigate the seas. During a stroll along the beach his dog is said to have bitten into a murex shell, staining its mouth purple and leading to the beginning of the fabric dyeing industry. Commercial production of the dye began during the Phoenician era and continued for more than 1,000 years. Along with cedar wood, the dye was the bedrock of Phoenician wealth.

Ancient Tyre had strong trade links with New Kingdom Egypt around 1400 BC, but its zenith came under King Hiram I, in around 1100 BC. He signed trading agreements with kings David and Solomon, exchanging cedar wood used in

Tyre the crowning glory, whose merchants are princes.

—THE BIBLE, Isaiah 23:8

BELOW: inscription in the Roman necropolis, Tyre.

THE MUREX INDUSTRY

Anybody who was anybody in ancient Rome would only ever be seen in one colour: Tyrian Purple. The famous dye of the classical world was named after its centre of production, the city of Tyre. Tyrian Purple was made from a fluid extracted from small molluscs – called murex – which were found in abundance off the Phoenician coast in antiquity. One hundred shells were needed to produce just one gram of dye, ensuring that only the wealthiest could afford to wear the colour. Indeed, as late as AD 300 a kilo of murex-dyed silk was traded for three kilos of gold.

But production was also a smelly, messy process. The molluscs were gathered in deep water using narrow-necked baskets. The dye sack was removed on land – downwind from populated areas – and then boiled in huge vessels, changing the colourless liquid to purple. As well as having an obnoxious odour, the process produced mountains of shells. The shores of Tyre, Sidon and other cities were littered with the stinking by-products, with Murex Hill in Sidon the only visible remains today.

Under the Roman Empire, production sites were also established in Crete, Sicily and Anatolia, where murex was also found. But such was the scale of the industry that today the murex is almost extinct.

Finely carved embellishments at Tyre.

the construction of Solomon's Temple for political control of parts of the northern Galilee. From Tyre, ships also sailed to Africa and Arabia, returning with gold and ivory, and founding the city of Carthage near present day Tunis.

The city of Tyre was strong, and survived a 14-year siege by Nebuchadnezzar of Babylonia which began in 586 BC. During the siege, the Tyrians destroyed a causeway which had connected the offshore islands to the mainland, and retreated behind the city's walls, said to be 50 metres (160ft) high.

But having weathered Babylonian advances, Tyre fell to Alexander the Great some 200 years later. He rebuilt the causeway during a seven-month siege, and stormed the city, slaughtering most of the population. Under the Greeks, Tyre's wealth and power again grew, with one Greek writer noting that the houses of Tyre were more opulent than those in Athena. Later, in AD 34, the city became one of the first refuges of the early Christians, with St Paul visiting the city in AD 58, according to the Acts of the Apostles. The Arabs were the next to arrive, succeeded by the crusaders who eventually fled in 1291 when the city returned to Arab control under Saladin.

Roman roads and colonnades

There are two vast excavation sites in Tyre, both of them spectacular. The road into the city leads to the headland, where there is a pretty and relaxed port, with a notable floating fish restaurant. On the south side and slightly inland is the **Al-Mina** site. (8am–8pm; admission charge). Divided in two by a road, only the right-hand site is open to the public. Here most of the remains are Roman, though a few houses dating from Phoenician times have been unearthed.

At the centre of the site are three well-preserved colonnaded **Roman roads**,

BELOW:
the Triumphal
Arch, Tyre.

with tesselated surfaces still present, and partially reconstructed columns made of marble imported from Greece almost two millennia ago. The splendour of the imperial Roman city is easily imagined as you walk towards the sea with the intact remains of Roman houses to your left and right. At the edge of the site, looking across the sea, the tops of many Roman columns are visible at low tide.

To the left (south) of the site are the remains of vast Roman **baths**, and the **cistern** used for the production of murex dye. Turning around, and facing inland, the main colonnade was once connected to the **Al-Bass site** (8 am–8 pm; admission charge), which lies directly in front of you, about 1 km (½ mile) east. Unless you are feeling particularly energetic, walking to the Al-Bass site can be gruelling, especially in summer. At its south entrance the Roman avenue resumes, then to the right appears a truly vast Roman **hippodrome** dating from the 2nd century AD. Part of the grandstand remains intact, and it is possible to climb the ancient seating, or shelter from the sun underneath. The centre of the horse track is also intact, marking out the path where charioteers once raced. Walking north again to the avenue, you pass under an elaborate archway then enter the **necropolis**, or city of the dead, where there are literally hundreds of ancient sarcophagi or burial chambers, dating from Phoenician, Roman, and Byzantine times. Most remained intact until the civil war, when some were broken open and they still carry the scars.

Beyond the ruins, Tyre's other attractions include its perfect white southern beach, which runs south of the Resthouse Hotel.

Ancient Qana

South and inland from Tyre is the area of Lebanon that is patrolled by United Nations peacekeepers. For more hardy and adventurous visitors, there are some

Map on page 308

Poster in aid of Hizbollah in Tyre.

BELOW: to quench your thirst – a juice bar in Tyre.

Map
on page
308

The remains of an ancient wine press at Qana, where Christ is believed to have turned water into wine.

BELOW: memorial to the Qana massacre.

interesting sites here Some 10 km (6 miles) inland from the coastal city, on the road to Qana is the tomb of Phoenician King Hiram, a huge sarcophagus topped with a pyramid-shaped cover, standing on the right-hand side of the road. A further 4 km (2½ miles) east is the village of **Qana**. In the Gospel According to St John, Christ turned water into wine at a marriage in the village of Cana. There are several modern villages which claim to be that site. On a rocky ridge east of this one are metre-high engravings, which date from the 1st century, depicting the 12 apostles, along with a series of ancient stone jars, which have led to regular pilgrimages to the site.

But in recent history Qana has become synonymous with a less pleasant deed. In April 1996 Israel shelled a UN camp at the village, killing 107 Lebanese refugees. In the centre of the village stands a monument to the victims who died in the attack.

Tebnine Castle

Continuing inland from Tyre, the road draws close to the former Israeli-occupied zone of southern Lebanon. Although Israeli troops and their South Lebanon Army allies withdrew from the area in July 2000, the area is still being cleared of mines, and for the time being it is sensible not to go much beyond Tebnine, 20 km (12 miles) inland from Tyre. This is home to a battalion of Irish UN soldiers, and yet another Crusader castle, some 1,000 metres (3,300 ft) above sea level. Built in 1104, it fell to Saladin in 1219, and was subsequently destroyed, then rebuilt by the Arabs. Inside the castle are several enormous vaulted chambers which have been fully restored. From the top, you can see over to the crusader fortifications of Beaufort. ❑

Hizbollah

For many in the west, Hizbollah is a shadowy "Iranian-backed" terrorist group which kidnapped westerners during the Lebanese civil war, and routinely launches missile attacks on Israel. In Lebanon the view is somewhat different. Hizbollah is seen by many Lebanese as a heroic group of plucky "resistance" fighters, who battled against Israel's long military occupation of southern Lebanon, flying the nationalist flag somewhat like the French Resistance during World War II.

Hizbollah – literally "Party of God" in Arabic – began in the early 1980s as a Shia Muslim militia sponsored by Iran, with the somewhat ambitious aim of turning a country which is one-third Christian into an Islamic republic. In 1982, Israel launched a massive invasion of Lebanon – ostensibly to stop Palestinians launching attacks on northern Israel from southern Lebanon. Most of the people of south Lebanon are Shia Muslims, and Israel's brutal invasion and occupation of the area radicalised the population and provided a fertile recruiting ground for Hizbollah. The party began to redefine its goals, and spearheaded attacks against occupying Israeli troops.

Its actions attracted many supporters, and the party used money from Iran to reinforce this support, building schools and hospitals and rebuilding homes destroyed in Israeli attacks. At the same time Hizbollah splinter groups – notably Islamic Jihad – began kidnapping foreigners in Beirut *(see page 69)* and were involved in suicide bomb attacks on western embassies and peacekeeping forces.

When Lebanon's bitter civil war finally came to an end, the 40 or so rival militia organisations which had battled for 15 years were all disarmed, except Hizbollah. The Lebanese government (and more importantly its powerful neighbour Syria) allowed Hizbollah to remain armed so it could continue waging a war against Israel's occupation.

Since then, Hizbollah has evolved politically and militarily. In southern Lebanon, the armed wing fought an increasingly effective war against the Israeli occupation, resulting in withdrawal in 2000. In Beirut the political arm of Hizbollah modified its radical goals, contenting itself with joining the political process. In 1992 it put candidates up for parliament, and won almost a dozen seats.

The public image of Hizbollah in Lebanon has thus changed radically. Today teenage children dubbed "Islamic scouts" complete with striped neckerchiefs and woggles – can be seen collecting money from motorists, even in Christian areas, while the organisation's television station offers a beguiling message of tolerance and coexistence.

Hizbollah today denies any involvement in the kidnapping of westerners, and the bombing of US and French peace-keeping troops in the early 1980s, blaming incidents on "other elements". Indeed, the organisation goes out of its way to create a friendly image. At the entrance to the Roman ruins in Baalbek stands a huge Hizbollah sign welcoming tourists. And in the southern city of Tyre there's a Hizbollah souvenir shop selling everything from key-rings, calendars and T-shirts to souvenir prayer mats and huge yellow flags incorporating the organisation's kalashnikov logo. ❑

RIGHT: memorial to a Hizbollah suicide bomber.

INSIGHT GUIDES
Travel Tips

CONTENTS

Getting Acquainted

The Place

Area: approximately 185,000 sq km (about 71,500 sq miles).
Situation: Syria is bordered on the north by Turkey; on the west by the Mediterranean, Lebanon and Israel; on the east and southeast by Iraq; and on the south by Jordan.
Capital: Damascus.
Major rivers: Euphrates, Tigris and Orontes.
Population: around 17 million.
Language: Arabic. French and some English are also spoken by the better educated.
Religion: Muslim (87 per cent): Sunni (75 per cent), Shia (12 per cent); and some Druze. Christian (10 per cent): Syrian/Greek Orthodox and Armenian; and around 2,000 Jews.
Time zone: GMT+2 hours.
Currency: Syrian lire (SL).
Weights and measures: metric.
Electricity: 220 volts, 60 cycles. Most hotels have Continental-style electrical outlets.
International dialling code: Syria 963. Damascus 11, Aleppo 21.

Geography

Almost trapezoidal in shape, with its longest distance north to south at approximately 750 km (466 miles), and its widest distance from west to east at approximately 850 km (528 miles), Syria is a crossroads of different geographical features. The country's coastal zone, along the Mediterranean Sea from southern Turkey to northern Lebanon, is a small plain extending eastwards and ending at the Jabal An-Nasayriyah mountain range. These begin in southern Turkey and extend southwards into northern Lebanon. The Crusaders used them to their advantage by building several fortresses for coastal observation and communication with the Byzantine empire.

Northeast of the mountain range is the fertile Aleppo district which extends to the northern part of the Euphrates river. Running due east of them is a short, fertile plain which eventually blends into the Homs Desert.

South of the mountains, along the Syria-Lebanon border, is the Anti-Lebanon mountain range which includes Syria's highest peak, Mount Hermon (Jabal Sheikh) with an altitude of 2,814 m (9,230 ft). Mount Hermon looks over the Golan Heights, a series of hilly plateaux of basaltic rock that form Syria's border with Israel.

East of the Golan Heights is a fertile plain known as the Haurun region. Southeast of the Haurun is Jabal Druze, a mountain range of basaltic rock and home to Syria's Druze population.

Extending northeast from the Haurun region Syria's landscape converts into rugged, yet beautiful desert steppes. In the middle of these is the Roman city of Palmyra (Tadmur), an oasis of palm trees and local agriculture. Southeast of the steppes is flat, arid desert. East of Palmyra and diagonally bisecting the Great Syrian Desert is the Euphrates river, which originates in Turkey and extends through Syria into Iraq. Northeast of the Euphrates, towards Iraq, is the Jazirah region, fed by the tributaries of the Euphrates. This is the northern arc of Mesopotamia or the Fertile Crescent.

Though Syria's total land mass appears to be dominated by desert steppes, several fertile agricultural areas exist: the Jazirah region; along the Euphrates; and the region of Lake Assad, west of Aleppo; the northern area along the Turkish border; the Jabal an-Nusayriyah area, and the Haurun district near the Jordanian border.

Climate

Syria's diversified topography provides various climatic conditions. The coastal region is hot and humid in summer and cold and wet in winter with an average annual rainfall of 50–100 cm (20–40 in). It snows heavily in the Anti-Lebanon mountains in winter.

When visiting Syria in winter be prepared for cold and wet conditions. Travellers to the desert regions are often surprised to encounter heavy rain, sleet and some snowfall.

Economy

Very little privatisation exists in Syria. Most major economic institutions (such as transport, communications, power and utilities) are state controlled.

The economy is mainly agricultural. Since most of the rain falls in winter, not the normal growing season, the country is heavily dependent on its rivers (the Euphrates provides 80 percent of the nation's agricultural water) and irrigation systems. These systems enable Syria to grow a variety of

Temperatures

	Summer high	Summer low	Winter high	Winter low
Damascus	39°C/102°F	19°C/66°F	12°C/54°F	3°C/37°F
Aleppo	39°C/102°F	20°C/68°F	10°C/50°F	0°C/32°F
Latakia	38°C/100°F	22°C/72°F	10°C/50°F	0°C/32°F
Dayr Az-Zawr	41°C/106°F	23°C/73°F	12°C/54°F	3°C/37°F

crops: barley and wheat, grapes, olives, some vegetables and citrus fruits, which are exported. Cotton, grown in the Jazirah area, and other textiles are also exported.

Natural resources include phosphates, some oil and natural gas (from the Iraqi border region) which Syria exports. Some revenue also comes from allowing oil pipelines to cross the country. However, Syria is still dependent on aid from the major oil-producing Arab countries.

In recent years, as *rapprochement* with the west has progressed, Syria has begun to realise the economic potential of tourism, and has attempted to attract visitors through advertising, some restoration of sites and provision of facilities at the more popular sites. Syrian artisans, renowned for many centuries for their distinguished craftsmanship generate revenue through the sale of silk brocade, oriental carpets, and metalwork in brass, copper, gold and silver.

Government

Syria is officially known as the Syrian Arab Republic. Its government is a unitary, multi-party republic with an elected president and one legislative house of 250 members known as the People's Assembly. The Ba'ath Party, designated as "the leading party of the society and state", nominates the president for a seven-year term. The nomination is then approved by the People's Assembly and confirmed by an absolute majority vote in a national referendum.

The president appoints the vice presidents, the prime minister, other cabinet members, provincial governors and the judges for the High Court. He also has the power to dissolve the People's Assembly and to assume the Assembly's legislative functions until it is reconvened. In addition, he is commander-in-chief of the armed forces.

Elections for the People's Assembly are held approximately every four years.

Concept of Time

The hardest adjustment for many Westerners is the Syrian concept of fate and time. The locals joke about this among themselves with the expression IBM: *Insha-allah, Bukra, Mumkin* ("God willing, tomorrow, possibly"). Any and everything can be put off, because it is not as important as right now. It takes some time to get used to this.

Culture & Customs

As with most of the Middle East, Syria is a family-oriented society. This is evident upon arrival at Damascus International Airport, where after passing through customs one immediately encounters throngs of family members waiting for loved ones. Also, in the evening, it is delightful to see families gathered along the roadsides eating and playing games. Small parks are scattered throughout the major cities, and these are popular for family outings as well.

Syrians express this familial feeling through friendliness and hospitality. It is not uncommon for shop owners to offer customers tea or coffee, or even a meal, while bargaining over goods. Westerners who get to know Syrians will be amazed how well they are treated.

Syrians often ask about one's family and will boast about their own, especially their children. They also freely debate religion and international politics. The average Syrian is up to date on international political activities and opinions, but tends to avoid commenting on domestic politics.

Planning the Trip

What to Bring

Most things are available in the main cities of Syria. There are no major department or grocery stores, however, as most shops are family owned and specialised.

Pharmacies are common and most pharmacists speak English and are very helpful. Larger hotels often have a small store for toiletry needs. If not, the receptionist will direct you or even have someone take you to a suitable store.

If you need special medication, bring it with you.

What to Wear

For spring, summer and autumn you should pack light cotton clothing, plus a sweater or light jacket for the evening. Hats, sunglasses and sunscreen are essential.

When visiting tourist areas outside the cities, shorts and sleeveless shirts for both men and women are generally not a problem. These are not permitted when visiting historic mosques, however, and women must cover their heads in mosques. Shorts are also not recommended for women in the markets or around towns. It is not uncommon for local women to sun themselves scantily clad at beaches or swimming pools, but leave dressed in the traditional *abiya*.

For winter, heavier cotton and wool clothing and jackets are required. Winter evenings can be very windy and cold.

Evening attire ranges from casual to dressy, depending on the setting.

In general, wear shoes and clothing that are comfortable and sturdy and expect to get dusty and dirty (it's the desert). If planning to tour the castles and archaeological sites bring a small, but strong flashlight with extra batteries.

Getting There

BY AIR

Damascus Air services to Syria are mainly through Damascus International Airport. Upon arrival, you need to proceed to immigration before baggage claim and customs. Once through customs you'll have to fight through throngs of people waiting for loved ones; it is in this area that you will find the various options for travelling into the city.
Aleppo The airport in Aleppo mainly handles domestic flights. The few international flights coming into this airport are used by travellers on business in the region.

BY SEA

Arrival by sea is through the ports in Tartus and Latakia. This route is used mainly by merchant seamen, and seldom by tourists (except in large pre-arranged tour groups).

BY LAND

Border Crossings

From Turkey Entry into Syria is through either the crossing at Idlib or Kassab. If going to Aleppo, the east or directly to Damascus cross at Idlib. This crossing is also where all the tour buses and most service taxis cross. Expect longer delays

A Tour of the Levant

If you are planning a wider tour of the Levant and want to avoid border hassles, fly into Amman, Jordan, visit Syria, if possible go to Lebanon, return to Syria and then to Jordan. After this, cross over to Israel and eventually depart from Jordan. This is usually the least expensive, as well as the smoothest course.

Tipping at the Border

It has to be said that tipping, known as *backshish*, often proves helpful on the Syrian side of any of the border crossings. Slipping a SL50 note into your passport where your Syrian visa is stamped should expedite processing. Usually you're not questioned about this, but don't be embarrassed if confronted by the

(approximately 1½ hours for both sides) if travelling in a large tourist bus. A service taxi takes less time.

If travelling to the coastal area, cross at Kassab; this is a more scenic route. Because it is seldom used, the actual time required for crossing is shortened. You may be asked to drink tea or coffee on both sides of the border. If you're not in a hurry, enjoy the hospitality.

From Jordan Entry is through one of two crossings: Nassid (a relatively new border crossing) or Der'a. Most tour buses and Jordanian-based service taxis cross at Nassid. This crossing has has more modern facilities, with immigration and inspections generally faster.

Der'a is used mainly by the Syrian-based service taxis, with the advantage that the drivers are more familiar with the immigration and customs agents.

By car

For the courageous (see driving conditions, *page 330*), driving in Syria is fun. You must have all of the appropriate data pertaining to your car: registration from your country of origin, engine size and bore and stroke ratios, which should be in the vehicle owner's manual; for some reason these are important. Ensure you have these before departing for your travels. Syrian insurance is required and can be obtained at the border.

Entry Regulations

A valid passport and entry visa are required. Everyone enters Syria on

immigration agent. Just apologise if you have offended the agent and state that it is a tip for all the hard work he has performed on this busy day. If the agent doesn't want the tip he'll give it back.

Syrian government employees are paid extremely little, and these extra tips supplement their income.

a three-month single or double-entry visa ($60). When applying, push for the double-entry one; that way, you can visit a neighbouring country and re-enter. Syria seldom issues multiple-entry visas or visas at the airport and borders.

If your stay is to be longer than 15 days, to include days of entry and departure, you must have an extension, which can be obtained at the Immigration Office in any major city (around SL250/$5). Take along at least five passport pictures. If you do not obtain this extension, you will face a fine upon departure and may be detained. In Damascus the Immigration Office is near Al-Assad Bridge in the Baramki district.

Warning: If you have previously travelled to Israel, and wish to visit Syria, renew your passport. Syrian embassies will issue visas if you have visited Israel, but you will be denied entry. Some overland travellers attempt to circumvent this by not having the Israelis stamp their passports (they usually stamp a blank piece of paper to keep in the passport). But when they enter Jordan, the Jordanians stamp their passports, so that later when they attempt to cross into Syria, they are rejected as they could only have entered Jordan from Israel. Don't try to outsmart the Syrians: they have been doing this for years.

It has even been known for immigration to deny entry to diplomats who are posted to Syria and have travelled to Israel for official business with the full knowledge of the Syrian government. They usually end up

Airport Porters

Upon arrival at the airport you will be mobbed by porters. These have no uniforms and generally look like disreputable villains trying to pinch your luggage. The cost for using one is about SL25.

The same happens when leaving the country. There are no porters at the border crossings

crossing to Cyprus, where they are issued a new passport, and then returning to Syria. The only exceptions to this rule are foreign dignitaries with prior approval.

Customs

Arrival: You can bring $5,000, one carton of cigarettes and 1 litre of alcohol into Syria without declaring them.
Departure: You can leave with up to $2,000 and up to SL2000 ($40) without declaration. There is a departure tax at the airport of SL200 ($4). After receiving your seat assignment go to the tax kiosk at the end of the airline booths, where the officer will give you a tax stamp. Do not paste the stamp into your passport; the officer in the departure gate area will do this.

Animals

If you are just visiting Syria it is not wise to bring pets. Animals, especially dogs, are not treated well. Immunisations and quarantine are not required, even though rabies and other diseases exist among the wild dogs in the desert.

Health

No immunisations are required for Syria, but hepatitis A & B exist here. Malaria is not a problem, but an up-to-date tetanus shot is advisable. If planning an extensive trip in the desert, treatment against rabies is often recommended.

The larger and more popular hotels and restaurants tend to adhere to Western standards of cleanliness, but be sure your food

has been thoroughly cooked, especially meat, and avoid goat's milk (longlife milk is available). Avoid potential stomach problems by not eating fruit or vegetables that have not been peeled.

Shwarma stands, in abundance on street corners, are easily identified by their lamb and chicken meat shaped into cones and roasting on an open gas fire. Be careful when selecting a stand; look for one where custom is brisk or ask a local to recommend one.

Water is usually safe to drink in the major cities (although bottled water does exist). In older hotels, let the water run for about 30 seconds before using it, so that rust is cleared from the pipes.

Money Matters

The exchange rate for Syria is officially set at SL46 to US$1. This is the rate that travellers receive at the Syrian Commercial Bank (the only bank operating in Syria). But more favourable rates (sometimes as high as SL53 to $1) can be found in neighbouring Turkey, Lebanon and Jordan *(see below)*.

Upon arrival at the airport, in order to meet immediate expenses, it is sensible to change at least $50 into Syrian currency (a bank is located to the left of the exit doors).

Best exchange rates

When entering from Turkey, the best places to change money are at the local banks or exchange houses in Antioch (Antakya). A less favourable rate can be found at the banks on the Turkish side of the border. In Lebanon, banks in the town of Chtaura, the largest town closest to the Lebanon-Syria border, provides the best rates. The banks on the Jordanian side of the border and the small rest stops located about 3 km (1¾ miles) from the border will also provide a fair rate, though rates tend to be better in Amman.

Some local merchants will also provide a more favourable rate and may also claim to take hard currency and personal cheques for purchases. Don't rely on this. All

Public Holidays

The government and most businesses follow the Gregorian calendar, except for religious observances.
● **1 January** New Year's Day
● **8 March** Revolution Day, the day that the Ba'th party emerged as the prominent Syrian political party in 1963
● **March/April** Catholic Easter*
● **March/April** Orthodox Easter*
● **17 April** National Day
● **1 May** May Day
● **6 May** Martyrs' Day
● **1 August** Army Day
● **6 October** Liberation War of October, celebrating the 1973 October War with Israel
● **16 November** Correctionist Movement
● **25 December** Christmas Day

Muslim Holidays
In addition to the above, there are Muslim feast days which are governed by the Hegira calendar and are therefore moveable. They move forward by 11 days every year (12 in a leap year).
● **Eid Al-Fitr** End of Ramadan, the Islamic month of fasting. During Ramadan, Muslims fast during the day and business hours are shortened (except for Christian businesses)
● **Eid Al-Adha** Feast of the Sacrifice commemorating Abraham's sacrifice of a sheep.
● **Al-Hijira** New Year's Day
● **Mouloud** (Birthday of the Prophet)

these things are illegal and it is not worth getting caught.

CREDIT CARDS

All hotels and car rental agencies are required to take hard currency or credit cards, but will charge at the official rate.

Neither the Syrian Bank nor hotels provide cash on credit cards, but it can be obtained at banks in Turkey, Lebanon and Jordan.

Practical Tips

Media

The media is government controlled.

RADIO

Voice of America: 1260 KHz 7–9am and 7pm–midnight.
BBC World Service: 1332KHz 5am–1am.

TELEVISION

Syria has only two television stations. Channel 1 has Arabic programmes from 8am to 1am. Channel 2 also operates from 8am until 1am, with some English and French programmes early afternoon, news in French at 8pm, news in English at 10pm, and various French and English-speaking pro-grammes and films after 10.30pm.

Satellite TV is officially illegal in Syria, but you wouldn't know this judging by the plethora of satellite dishes on every building block. Most hotels will have some form of satellite TV.

NEWSPAPERS

Syria has an abundance of Arabic-language newspapers and magazines, but very few international French and English publications, which are found mainly in hotels and some book stores (they are usually several days old). The Syrian government publishes the *Syrian Times*, an English-language daily full of anti-Israeli slogans and pro-Arab, specifically pro-Syrian, rhetoric.

BOOKSTORES

These are abundant in Damascus (most are located near the Cham Palace Hotel), but they offer little variety in English-language books and literature. They mainly carry English-language study books and trashy novels.

The major hotels (Meridian and Sheraton, for example) also have bookshops, which stock maps and books on Syria and Jordan.

Postal Services

POST OFFICES

A central post office is found in all cities. Though a few small post boxes can be found elsewhere in cities, it is best to take mail to the central post to cut down on delays. Expect at least two weeks for delivery to Europe and three to the United States. The central post offices are the only means of sending parcels, apart from express mail services (*see below*). Parcels are normally inspected before being posted, so take them unwrapped along with the required wrapping material.

EXPRESS MAIL

DHL
Next to the *Tishreen* newspaper building in the Al Midan district of Damascus.
Tel: 2130207/08/09.
Fax: 2247486.
Federal Express
Hamra Street, downtown Damascus.
Tel: 2226250/4420/4451.
Fax: 2226214.

Telephone Codes

● **Aleppo**	21
● **Damascus**	11
● **Dayr Az-Zawr**	51
● **Homs**	31
● **Latakia**	41
● **Palmyra**	31

Telecommunications

TELEPHONES

Public telephones can be found along main streets of major cities and are generally reliable. But in smaller cities, the public phones tend to be located at the central post office.

INTERNET

Currently Syria does not have an Internet provider, but the Internet can be accessed through the larger international providers by connecting through Turkey, Lebanon or Jordan. You will have to pay the long-distance charges to that particular link. Before departure contact your Internet provider and ensure that your service works in those areas. See also computers in hotel rooms under *Security and Crime (see page 327)*.

Medical Services

Shami Hospital in Damascus is the best option for foreigners, and also the most expensive by Syrian standards. Most of the staff there have trained and worked in the west. The hospital is located across from Tishreen Park on Jawaher al-Nehru Street. Every taxi driver in the city knows how to get there.

Security & Crime

The Syrian government prides itself on maintaining calm and security. There is great embarrassment when it fails to provide security for its citizens and visitors, so police and security personnel are prevalent and highly visible in the streets.

Petty theft
The biggest problem that visitors face is petty theft. Take care with valuables, cameras and important papers. Foreign passports sell for a lot of money on the black market and are susceptible to theft. Not all hotels provide room safes or safe deposit boxes (although they will

often hold your valuables under the counter for you).

If a theft occurs report it at once to your hotel and the local police. Report passport loss to your consulate. Having a copy of your passport should speed up the process of getting a new one, so keep a photocopy .

Pickpocketing

For some reason, pickpocketing in Aleppo and Latakia is on the rise. The best way to avoid being a victim is to carry your cash in a front pocket and your passport around your neck, under your shirt in a pouch of some type. Women should keep a close hold on their bags.

One particular scam is for one thief to grab your valuables or bag then quickly hand them/it to another person. If you are able to chase and stop the first thief, he will detain you by denying he stole anything, and then keep you busy with questions in an attempt to "help" while the other is getting away.

If you feel that you have been victimised and the accused denies it, don't be afraid or embarrassed to call for the police. There are usually one or two officers standing around.

Credit card fraud

In Syria only hotels and car rental agencies accept credit cards. Ensure that you destroy all of the carbon copies of credit card receipts and double check your balances when you return home.

Computers/technical equipment

Syrians (including officials) are both fascinated and suspicious of computers and technical equipment. If you have such equipment with you (and be sure to register it with customs when you arrive), expect it to be tampered with if left in the hotel room.

Tourist Information

Larger towns and cities have tourist offices with staff who usually speak English, but the quality of information supplied is not great. You will be better off enquiring about local sites and events at the reception of your hotel.

There is a good list of websites providing information on travel, hotels and tourist sites at: www. mysite.com/syria/yrll.html

Religious Services

ISLAMIC

Islam is the official religion of Syria. Mosques predominate throughout the country, and one will find a mosque at each border crossing.

Non-Muslims should not enter mosques during prayer time, which is announced from the minarets. If visiting a mosque, shoes must be removed and women must be covered (head covers and robes can be rented at the doorway of the more popular tourist attractions). A tip at the door is appreciated.

CHRISTIAN

Orthodox

A large **Syrian Orthodox** Christian community exists in Syria. The church is similar to the Greek orthodox, with the same calendar and holidays, and services are held partly in Greek.

Damascus is also home to the **Greek Orthodox Patriarchate** (located across from the old Roman Arch in the old city on Bab Sharqi Street (the Biblical Street called

Business Hours

Banks 9am–2.30pm daily. Closed Friday.
Government offices 9am–2.30pm.
Shops 9am–8pm. Most stores are closed according to the owner's religious affiliation:
● Muslim-owned shops in the old city of Damascus are closed on Friday, except for a few establishments catering for Westerners.
● All Jewish shops are closed on Saturday.
● Gold shops owned by Armenians are shut on Sunday.

Straight). Services are held on Friday at 8.30am and Sunday at 8.30am. Communion is on Sunday.
St Nicolas Church
Abdullah Bin Massoud Street in west Mezzeh.
Services (in Arabic) are on Sunday at 8.30am.
Holy Cross Church
Al Manama Street, near Bilal Square.
Services (n Arabic with some Greek) are on Friday and Sunday at 9am.

Catholic in Damascus

Franciscan Church
At the corner of Al-Majles An-Niyaby Street and Maysaloun Street.
Services (in Arabic) are on Sunday at 8.30am.
St Anthony's Church
Abed Street, west of the Parliament Boulevard.
Arabic services: Sunday 8.30am.
English services: Sunday 11am.
Ananais Church
At the end of Hananya Street, about 2 m (6 ft) beneath the present street level. As a historical site, this church is open daily, and anyone may attend Sunday services at 8.30am.
Russian Church
Just off of Jawaher Al-Nehru Street. Services (in Arabic) are on Sunday at 8.30am.

Female Travellers

Unlike in other Middle Eastern countries, foreign women don't

Souk Al-Hamidiyah, Damascus 9am–8pm daily. Most shops are closed on Friday
Businesses 9am–2.30pm and 6–8pm.
Most businesses are closed on Friday, with the following exceptions:
● on Monday all hair salons and barber shops are closed.
● on Wednesday most museums, historic sites and many tourist attractions are closed.
● on Thursday most pharmacies are closed.

Embassies/Consulates

The following diplomatic missions can be found at these adresses:
Australia, 47 Farabi Street. East Villas, Mezzeh.
Tel: 6132424. Fax: 6116734.
Canada, Lot 12, Mezzeh.
Tel: 6116851. Fax: 6114000.
United Kingdom, Mohammed Kurd Ali Street, Maliki.
Tel: 3712561.Fax: 3731600.
USA, No. 2, Al-Mansour Street.
Tel: 3331342. Fax: 2247938.

draw much attention (such as whistling, cat calls and pinching) from young Syrian males. However, it does occur occasionally. Discretion is always advised. Walk with friends or travelling companions, and stick to the more populated areas. Feel free to defend yourself and cause a ruckus, which will draw unwanted attention to your attacker. Syria is a conservative country, and no local wishes to draw that type of attention to himself.

Photography

Syria has many historical sites worth photographing, but the environment can be difficult. The best film speed for outdoor use is 100. But indoor and night-time desert shots require faster film speeds. Use of a UV haze filter in combination with a yellow filter is recommended for daytime desert photos; this should eliminate evidence of the static discharges in the desert atmosphere.

Care should be exercised when taking photographs. Photography of security zones, restricted areas and anything military is strictly prohibited. These areas are not always clearly marked.

Disabled Travellers

Hotels, restaurants and historic sites do not usually have facilities for the disabled.

Getting Around

From the Airport

There is an information booth in the arrival area of Damascus International Airport, where you can enquire about transport into the city centre (about 20 km/12 miles away). But here are the basics:

From the Airport by Taxi

Several taxi service booths are located in the area immediately upon leaving baggage claim and Customs. Transtour and Orientour seem to be the most popular companies, but all of the vendors will haggle for your attention.

If using a taxi tell the vendor your destination, and expect to pay about SL500 ($10). You will be issued with a receipt indicating your taxi number, and someone will usually lead you to the taxi and load your bags.

From the Airport by Bus

A bus service booth is also available in the arrival area. The fare to the city centre is about SL25, and never pay more than SL35. The bus leaves approximately every half hour for the al-Bahsa district in Damascus. From there you will find yellow taxis, the usual mode of travel in the city, to take you to your destination. The bus operates from 5.30am to 9pm.

By Rail

Travelling around Syria by rail is inexpensive, but confusing and long. There are two stations in Damascus. If travelling to Aleppo, Tartus, Latakia, Dayr az-Zawr or Amman, Jordan, you must first go to the old train station (Muhata al-

Qadim) which is, confusingly, actually the new train station.

Schedules vary and change often. If you ask your hotel for a train schedule they will discourage you from using the train. But if you insist, it is best to visit the station a day or two beforehand, to arrange your timing, because the departure times do not keep to a proper schedule.

The trip to Aleppo takes eight hours by train, but 4½ by bus or taxi. Thus taking the train is usually the most problematic means of transportation (plus this station is used for those travelling to Mecca for the *haj*, so can be busy).

If travelling by rail to the Bludan or Zabadani region in the Anti-Lebanon Mountains, you must go to the downtown train station near Marjai Square, called Muhata al-Qitar (literally "Train Station") but also known as the Hejaz railway station. This is actually the old train station that has serviced the region for over 100 years. It uses the same steam engine and wooden passenger cars that were around when Lawrence was in the area. You can visit the station and drink tea in one of the historic old passenger cars standing off to the side. The proprietor is a retired engineer and loves to sit and chat about the old days.

Trains depart four days a week for Zabadani at 9am. Be early, as the service may leave before the scheduled time. On Friday morning the station is packed with Damascenes going off to the mountains for the weekend. The trip to Zabadani takes about three hours by train (whereas it is 30–45 minutes by car!).

If you want to go to Zabadani or Bludan, your best bet is to take a service taxi.

By Bus

In the past, bus travel between cities was only in large, dilapidated and very packed Scania buses. But in the mid-1990s the government raised a ban on importing buses into the country. Thus inter-city bus travel, which seems complicated to the uninitiated but is actually simple, has blossomed. For Syrians this is the most economic means of inter-city travel.

In Damascus go to the central bus station at al-Abbassiein Square and just look and listen for the drivers who will call out their destination and the number of seats available. Don't expect orderly queues with scheduled arrivals and departures, as no real organisation exists – in fact, there isn't even an information booth.

If you have problems, just ask someone for help but don't get taken for a ride. The drivers will try to push you into a bus once they know your destination. They will try to get a full bus, so for a quick departure and less expensive ride look for a bus that is nearly full – otherwise you may have to wait around until the driver is satisfied. Don't worry if you miss any given bus, as another will come along shortly. Establish the price with the driver before you set off on your journey. You shouldn't have to pay more than around SL200 ($4) for any given trip.

The buses come in all shapes and sizes, but are generally slightly larger than Microbuses. They are air-conditioned, but the driver doesn't usually turn it on. Space can be limited, so if you have a lot of luggage you may have to take one of the larger buses. The station operates 24 hours daily. The driver will stop at any time upon request.

Every major city has a central bus station, so the same holds true when returning to Damascus or travelling to another city. Upon your arrival take either a Microbus or a taxi to your destination in the city.

By Pullman Coach

These large, air-conditioned Pullman buses are a more luxurious way to travel between cities. The central Pullman station is in the Harista district of Damascus.

The buses usually depart every half hour to all major points: Homs, Hama, Aleppo, Latakia, Tartus and Dayr az-Zawr. Departure times may vary depending on the destination. The buses do not have to be full for departure. Cost should be about SL250 ($5).

Since the Pullman coach station is different from the other, less expensive bus station, be sure to specify your preference to the taxi driver or hotel concierge.

By Service Taxi

Intercity

Every city has a service taxi station. These taxis are normally only permitted to travel from city to city and stop at the central station. They are usually old, large, yellow American automobiles.

Like the central bus station, the service taxi stations are disorganised and operate 24 hours daily. The drivers will stand around and yell out their destinations and number of passengers needed to fill the taxi, and they will wait until the vehicle is full. You can rent the entire taxi for yourself, however, but you'll have to pay the full cost: about SL2500 ($50) to any large city. The driver will take hard currency, but not in full view of everybody.

Your hotel can arrange a service taxi to pick you up, but this will be slightly more expensive. Sightseers can also arrange, through their hotel, a service taxi for an entire day (costing about SL5,000/$100), which will take you to any destination you desire. You may have to pay for the driver's accommodation if staying overnight at your destination. You should try to arrange this well ahead and demand a clean car.

To bordering countries

The central taxi station in Damascus also provides service taxis to Lebanon, Turkey and Jordan. The central station in Aleppo provides service taxis to Turkey as well.

If travelling to Jordan by service taxi you must go to the central taxi station in Damascus, where you will find taxis from both Jordan and Syria going that way. The Jordanian

Taxis Over Borders

Before crossing the border a taxi driver will usually stop and buy something at a rest stop, and when you reach customs you'll be surprised to find merchandise in the boot that was not there when you left Damascus. Yes, they're smuggling. If questioned, just account for your own luggage; everybody at the border seems to cooperate with one another and no problems occur.

When travelling to Turkey this type of exchange will generally not occur. Syria doesn't have the same cordial relations with Turkey as it does with Jordan, either on a governmental or individual level. When crossing into Turkey, you may find that you are treated rather well, but the Syrian driver is not.

taxis are the cleanest; they are white and generally newer than the Syrian ones. You may be able to get a better price from them as well since the driver will want to return home. Another advantage of using Jordanian taxis is that the driver will be more familiar with Jordan and its capital, Amman.

Once you have met the driver and determined your price, he will literally run off with your passport to register it with customs and the police; don't worry, he'll return. This is actually for the safety of the passenger. The Jordanian drivers will also use the new border crossing, which is much faster.

Taxis and Microbuses

The best mode of transportation within the cities are the yellow taxis. They are usually faster, safer than Microbuses and very inexpensive (about SL20 for a 4km/2½-mile ride).

A more exciting mode of transportation within the cities is the ubiquitous Microbus. These are small passenger vans that recently replaced the older, larger buses. They normally seat nine to 10, but the Syrians can pack in 15.

They operate from the central Microbus station in each city and travel throughout their assigned district in that particular city. There are over 16,000 Microbuses throughout the country. Their assigned districts are clearly indicated in Arabic, not English. There are no fixed bus stops, so anyone standing along the street is a potential passenger. They move about at dangerous speeds and weave in and out of the already congested traffic looking for a fare, which usually causes traffic jams and minor accidents.

If you don't know the city (there are no route maps or schedules), and if you don't speak Arabic, using these buses can be confusing. But it is inexpensive (SL10 to go anywhere in that district or to the central Microbus station), and it's a good way to experience what life is like for the average Syrian.

So if you're looking for an interesting ride, stand on the street, wave your arm and tell the bus driver where you want to go. The Syrians seem to enjoy having foreigners ride on the Microbuses with them and will often try to help (sometimes they're too helpful). If you get really confused just tell the driver to stop or wait until it reaches the central bus station and then grab a taxi.

Travel Agencies

The following agencies deal mainly in traditional bus tours and are located in the "Souk of the Travel Agents" on Al Fardoos Street, near the Cham Palace Hotel, in downtown Damascus.

Atlas Travel
Tel: (11) 2215275.
Fax: (11) 2221807.

Cham Tours
Tel: (11) 2232300.

Orient Express
Tel: (11) 2223848.
Fax: (11) 2243737.

Driving

Driving conditions in Syria are dangerous compared to Western standards. The roads in the cities are usually congested, and drivers tend to use their horns more than their brakes. Night driving and country driving are also hazardous: people often fail to use their lights, and the major highways between cities, which are not lit, are full of slow-moving farm tractors and fast-moving lorries and cars. Sheep crossings occur haphazardly and are supervised by children.

So if you are faint of heart, renting a car in Syria is not recommended. Hiring a car and driver is better – you can sit back, relax and enjoy the scenery.

Car rental agencies
Eurocar/Transtour
Located at Damascus Airport, Sheraton and Meridian hotels.
Tel: (011) 2120624.
Fax: (011) 2111304.
Hertz
Located at the Cham Palace hotel, downtown Damascus.
Tel: (011) 2232300.
Fax: (011) 2226181.
Orient Tours
Mezzeh autostrad, near Jalaal Sports City.
Tel: (011) 6114467.
Fax: 6114050.

Sahara Travel & Tourism
Tel: (11) 2226221.

Silk Road
Tel: (11) 2226221.

Sanadiki Travel
This company provides a selection of standard sight-seeing bus tours, but specialises mainly in study tours, walking and hiking trips, religious tours and business conferences. It is located near the Al-Assad Bridge in Abou Ramaneh.
Tel: (11) 2238900.
Fax: (11) 2245207.

Where to Stay

Choosing a Hotel

As there are no youth hostels or campsites in Syria, your only option for accommodation is hotels. These are ranked from one to five stars, with the very best given a five-star deluxe rating.

The cheapest (one- and two-star) can be filthy and bug-ridden so do check out rooms before you pay. Three-star hotels usually have hot water and ensuite facilities. Top-of-the-range hotels in Damascus and Aleppo have international-standard facilities, but tend to be characterless. it is usually most economical to book rooms in these as part of a package tour.

By law hotels should display prices in the lobby, but in practice these are often out of date in smaller establishments. Double rooms have twin beds only, not doubles. Breakfast is not provided in the less expensive hotels.

Before booking it is worth checking how you will be expected to pay. International hotels will, of course, accept credit cards and travellers' cheques, but one and two-star establishments may require payment in Syrian pounds.

Hotel Listings

ALEPPO

Chahba Cham Palace
Damascus Street, just before entering the old city.
Tel: (21) 249801.
Fax: (21) 235912.
One of the hotels from the Cham chain,and probably the most luxurious hotel in Aleppo with clean rooms and a good swimming pool.
$$$

Amir Palace
Al-Mutanabbi Street.
Tel: (21) 214800.
A little rundown, but one of the better hotels in the city, with quite good facilities. **$$–$$$**

Al Boustan
Bab al-Faraj
Tel: 021- 217104
Medium level hotel, with quite good service, en suite bathrooms and air-conditioning.

Tourism
Al Walid Street
Tel: (21) 210156
Medium level hotel with central location. Comfortable, with air-conditioning, en suite bathrooms and televisions. Popular, so best to book. **$$**

Al-Faisal
Baron Street.
Tel: (21) 217768
Behind the Baron (*see below*), very clean and inexpensive. **$**

Baron Hotel
Baron Street.
Tel: (21) 210880.
A relic from the days of T.E. Lawrence, this is one of least expensive places to stay, but it is a little run down these days. It's nice just to visit, have a drink at the bar and look at the famous signatures in the old registry book. **$**

Afamia
Off Baron Street
Tel: 217078
Basic but clean rooms with fan. **$**

BUSRA

Bosra Cham Palace
Tel: (15) 790488.
New and seldom used hotel with swimming pool and tennis court. The rooms are modern and clean. Apart from a hostel, this is your only option in Busra. **$$–$$$**

DAYR AZ-ZAWR

Al-Furat Cham Palace
On the city's outskirts along the river about 5km (3 miles) west of town.
Tel: (51) 225418

Fax: (51) 225950
Modern rooms, a swimming pool and tennis courts. **$$$**

Concord
Al Hurriya St
Tel: (51) 225 411
Good amenities, including a pool, bar, restaurant and air-conditioning. On the outskirts of town. **$$$**

Raghdan
Khaled Ibn al Walid St
Tel: (51) 222053
Medium level hotel with air-conditioning, pool and comfortable rooms. **$$**

DAMASCUS

Semiramis Hotel
Near Victoria Bridge
Tel: (11) 2213813
Very close to the old city, with an excellent Chinese restaurant. **$$$$**

Meridian Hotel
Shukri Al-Quwatli Street
Tel: (11) 3718730
Fax: (11) 3718661
Centrally located, but rooms need renovation; has large banquet hall, several restaurants, an excellent French bakery and pool. **$$$–$$$$**

Sheraton Hotel
Umayyad Circle
Tel: (11) 3734630
Very central to everything in the city, and across from Tishreen Park. Expect all the usual mod cons, including a swimming pool, tennis courts, large banquet hall, several restaurants and a pub that serves a good hamburger. Some rooms have recently been renovated. **$$$–$$$$**

Cham Palace Hotel
Downtown
Tel: (11) 2232300.
Fax: (11) 2212398.
Has a rotating restaurant atop the building, swimming pool and excellent Japanese restaurant. **$$–$$$**

Jalaa Cham Hotel
Tel: (11) 664946
Pleasant small hotel in Mazzé area of town. Access to nearby pool. **$$**

Ebla Cham
Along the road from the airport.
Tel: (11) 2241900.
Fax: (11) 5410070.

Recently built with rooms that range from simple to very lavish suites. Most hotels within the Cham chain have fitness centres that include a fitness room, sauna and small gym. **$$**

Fardous Tower
Near Maysaloun Street, downtown.
Tel: (11) 2246546.
Fax: (11) 2247009.
Not the most luxurious hotel in town, but rooms are air-conditioned and clean. **$$**

Afamia Hotel
Behind the central post office.
Tel: (11) 2219152
Clean and close to the old city. **$–$$**

Al-Majad Hotel
Behind the Ambassador Cinema.
Tel: (11) 2323300.
Has a great view of the city and beautifully decorated Oriental ceilings. Inexpensive, but clean. **$–$$**

Omar Khayam Hotel
Off Martyrs Square
Tel: (11) 2211666
Moderately priced and close to the Old City. The 1920s Art Deco style makes this one of the more characterful places to stay. **$$**

Orient Palace Hotel
Tel: (11) 2220501
Opposite the Hejaz railway station. Once comfortable older-style hotel with shabby colonial-style furnishings. Nonetheless, a pleasant and characterful place to stay. **$$**

Sultan Hotel
Moussallam Baroudy Road
Tel: (11) 2225768
A modest but clean and pleasant

Price Guide

Prices are per night for a double room, excluding the 10 per cent tax.

£	Up to $50
££	$50–100
£££	$100–175
££££	$175+

Note: a hotel's price does not necessarily equate to quality

hotel situated near the Hejaz railway terminal. **$–$$**

Venicia Hotel
On Al-Bahsa Street.
Tel: (11) 2316631.
Inexpensive and very close to the Old City. Television and fridge in each room. **$–$$**

HAMA

Apamee Cham Palace
Tel: (33) 227429
Fax: (33) 233195
Luxury hotel overlooking the Orontes river. Swimming pool and tennis courts. **$$$**

Noria
Qouwatli Avenue
Tel: (33) 511715
Comfortable, well-appointed and good value. Can get booked out with tour groups, so best to book. **$$**

The Cairo
Tel: 33 237206
Fax: (33) 511 715
Excellent budget option which is clean and good value. En suite available. **$**

LATAKIA

The two luxury hotels on the coast north of the city, the Cote Az-Zour and Meridian, have great potential, but both tend to be shabby and therefore disappoint.

Cham Cote Az-Zour
About 10km (6 miles) north of the city along coast.

Price Guide

Prices are per night for a double room, excluding the 10 percent tax.

$	Up to $50
$$	$50–100
$$$	$100–175
$$$$	$175+

Note: a hotel's price does not necessarily equate to quality

Tel: (41) 228691.
The advantage to this hotel is that from the ground-floor seaside rooms you can walk straight out on to the beach. Most of these rooms are equipped with kitchenettes (those on the west side are completely furnished, while those on the east are not). Book these rooms early in the year, though, as they fill up quickly during the summer months. Sea side **$$$**, garden side **$$**.

Meridian
Situated in woodlands about 7km (4 miles) north of the city along the coast.
Tel: (41) 229000
The hotel has its own beach, swimming pool, tennis courts and restaurant. But the rooms are looking dated. **$$**

Riviera
14 Ramadan St
Tel (41) 421803
Large, comfortable rooms equipped with full range of amenities.
$$–$$$

Zenobia Hotel
City centre
Tel: (41) 425703
Though it lacks the coastal views, Zenobia is recommended. The Argentinean owner has brought some of his home flavour to the hotel. **$**

New Omar Khayam
Al Jalaa Street
Tel (41) 228219
Good, clean budget option. **$**

MA'LULA

Asfir Hotel
Beside the monastery
Tel (12) 770250
Pleasant hotel with 4-star hospitality. Excellent restaurant and bar, a playground for children and a spectacular view of the village. **$$$**

PALMYRA

Cham Palace
Tel: (31) 37000
Just as you enter the city from the west.

Tel: (31) 910156
The most expensive hotel in Palmyra. it is old and rundown and the service is poor. It claims to have a swimming pool, but there is no water in it. **$$$**

Zenobia
Tel: (31) 910107
Probably one of the most famous hotels in the area. It too is old and rundown. Rooms are shabby, and air-conditioning seldom works – not a good thing in the middle of the desert. **$$**

Heliopolis Hotel
This is one of the better places to stay. A new up-and-coming hotel, but located off the main street of the city. It may be difficult to find, so ask around for directions. Rooms are very clean, service is great, but the parking is limited (though the staff will find additional spaces for you). **$–$$**

Orient Hotel
Tel: (31) 910131
Modern hotel which represents one of the better deals in town. Clean rooms. **$**

Tower Hotel
Main street
Tel: (31) 910116.
Fax: (31) 910273
Also one of the better deals.Clean, rooms with en-suite bathrooms. **$**

SAFITA

Safita Cham Hotel
Tel: (321) 25980
Small hotel overlooking the rolling valleys of this mountain resort. Swimming pool. **$$$**

Where to Eat

Types of Restaurant

Generally the best restaurants are attached to hotels, and you'll find Chinese, French and Italian restaurants in Aleppo and Damascus. Elsewhere it is standard local fare, usually without a menu. Street stalls sell cheap, filling snacks, but check they are clean and food is well cooked.

Restaurant Listings

ALEPPO

Though every hotel has its own restaurant, here are some favourites among the expatriates.

Baron Hotel
Baron Street
There is a pleasant quiet outdoor restaurant around the side, towards the back of the hotel. The food is well cooked and inexpensive. **$$**

Pullman Shahba Hotel
University Street
Excellent Italian restaurant which is rated as one of the best in Aleppo. Expensive. **$$$**

Sissi House Restaurant and Pub
Jdaidah Quarter
Tel: (21) 219411
Considered to be the Aleppo's best restaurant. Serves mainly Arab and some European cuisine in an 18th-century house with central courtyard. Book ahead and go by taxi. **$$**

Price Guide

Prices are per head for a meal with half a bottle of wine, but not including the 10 per cent tax.

$	$10–15
$$	$15–20
$$$	$20–25

Yasmeen House
Tel: (21) 224462
Traditional Arab cuisine served in attractive 18th-century merchant's house with central courtyard. Good food matches the lovely setting **$$**

Al Andalib
Baron Street
Roof-top restaurant serving basic grills. Good location makes up for the average food. **$**

Ali Baba
Yarmouk Street
Mezze and grilled meats. **$**

Beit Wakil
Jdaidah Quarter
Near the Sissi House restaurant, again occupying an old house. Good quality Arab cuisine in atmospheric setting. **$**

DAMASCUS

The Golden Dragon
In the Semiramis hotel.
Chinese restaurant with good food and pleasant ambiance. **$$$+**

Arabesque
In the old city, down the side street at the Greek Patriarchate along Straight Street.
Excellent Arab and European cuisine; some consider this the best Arab restaurant in Damascus. **$$–$$$**

Old Damascus Restaurant
Behind the Citadel in the old city. Wonderful Middle Eastern ambience. **$$–$$$**

Old Town Restaurant
In the old city, the next side street east of the Greek Patriarchate along Straight Street.
Tel: (11) 5428088.
Serves French and European cuisine. Reservations recommended. **$$–$$$**

Casablanca
Near the house of Ananais near the East Gate.
An old Damascene home converted into a restaurant. Arab cuisine. **$$**

La Cahumiere
Malki area, near Saudi Embassy.
French cuisine, with a reputation for excellent fried squid. **$$**

The Chavalier
Also near the Saudi Embassy in the

Malki area.
French cuisine. **$$**

Umayyad Palace Restaurant
Tel: (11) 2220826
Situated in a narrow alleyway on the south side of the Umayyad Mosque. Offers a delicious lunch and dinner buffet amidst an eclectic assortment of antiques and plenty of atmosphere. Live music and whirling Dervishes every evening. Moderately priced, but no alcohol is served.**$$**

The Piano Bar
On Hanaia Street
Tel: (11) 5430357
Serves European cuisine in a lovely outdoor area. Spaghetti, fish, chicken, soups and salads. Good place for cold beer. Atmospheric bar. **$$**

Ali Baba
Fardoos Street
Good *mezze* and grilled meets. **$**

Sahara
On the Mezzeh highway.
Arab food with European entrées. **$**

LATAKIA

As well as the hotel restaurants, there are several smaller restaurants with quite tasty food.

Plaza
Corniche
Upmarket international and Arabic restaurant with good fish. $$–$$$

Restaurant Spiro
Recommended for good fish and chicken. **$$–$$$**

Mamma
8 Azar Street
Excellent pizza and pasta option. **$**

PALMYRA

Food at the hotel restaurants is not very inspiring, but the best of the bunch are probably the restaurants at the **Villa Palmyra** and the **Cham Palace** and the terrace restaurant of the **Zenobia** hotel. Otherwise, the best options are in the main street, in front of the archaeological museum. Cost per head at these is around $10–15, and most do not serve alcohol.

Shopping

What to Buy

The old cities of Damascus and Aleppo, in particular the souks clustered around the Umayyad mosques of the two cities, are the places to look for traditional Syrian goods and crafts, such as damascened metalwork, textiles, inlaid woodwork, carpets and rugs. There are literally hundreds of shops throughout these areas, and all are worth an initial glance. Shopping is a long, drawn out affair, in which you will be offered copious amounts of tea, coffee or soft drinks, to lubricate the haggling process. Never buy at the first place you stop; you can always return.

Opening hours are generally dictated by the owner's religion *(see Business Hours, page 327)*.

Where to Buy

DAMASCUS

In addition to the traditional souks there are a few upmarket shops specifically aimed at the tourism industry, for example Azem Ecole, located in the old Madrasa Abdullah al-Azem near the Umayyad Mosque. This sells antiques and traditional crafts, including hand-woven brocades.
Gold Souk

Sweet Gifts

If you are looking for inexpensive presents, you might try gift-boxed Syrian sweets, including candied fruit, which are among the best in the Arab world. Souk al Bzouriah in Damascus is a good place to buy them.

The Gold Souk in the Old City is famous throughout the world. Most gold shops are owned and operated by Armenians. Some Syrians claim that the Armenians are the keepers of the country, because their craftsmanship is exceptionally detailed and spectacular. Therefore their goods are in demand and contribute to the economy of the country. Their work in gold lives up to this reputation. The souk is closed on Sunday.

Souk Al-Hamidiyah

This busy shopping area (for tourists and locals alike) begins to the right of the entrance to the Citadel. It was originally built by the Romans as the western thoroughfare to the Temple of Jupiter (the current Umayyad Mosque). Over the years it developed into a market area and was later expanded and covered by the Ottomans towards the end of the 19th century.

Arts and Crafts Souk

Located near the Army Museum, it contains some small shops selling traditional and modern artifacts. All are for sale.

ALEPPO

Aleppo has one of the best souks in the Arab world.

Gold Souk

This spans Souk al Manadil and Souk al-Khourrag. Also good for silver.

Souk Al Attarin

Wonderful selection of herbs, spices, nuts and natural remedies.

Khan al Nahaseen

This coppersmiths souk has a wonderful range of metalwork, from highly decorated trays and coffee pots to huge utilitarian vessels for cooking

Khan ash-Shouna

Huge range of crafts from all over the Arab world

Language

Useful Phrases

Hello *Har'haban* (reply is *Har'habtein* or *Ahlein*)
How are you? *Shlonak* (shortened from shuu-lone-ak, which literally really means How is your colour?)
I'm fine *Tamaam*
Welcome *Ahlan wasahlan* (reply is *Ahlan beek,* Same to you)
What is your name? *Shu ismak?*
please *Min fadlak* (to men)/*Min fadlik* (to women)
Goodbye *Ma'assalami*
Thank you *shukran*
Yes *aiwa/na'am*
No *la*
God willing *inshallah*
I do not understand *Ana mish fahem* (to men)/*Ana mish fahma* (to women)

Vocabulary

airport *mataar*
boat *merkab*
bridge *jisir*
car *sayaara*
embassy *safaara*
Good health *Sah-tein* (said before eating)
hospital *mashfa* or *mustashfa*
hotel *fundaq*
post office *maktab al-bareed*
restaurant *mataam*
square *sahta*
street *shaaria*

Directions

left *ala yassaar*
right *ala yamein*
straight ahead *Dughri*
Slow down *shway*
Stop here *waqif hoan*
North *Shamaal*
South *Jannub*

East *Sharq*	
West *Qharb*	

Numbers

0	*zifer*
1	*wahid*
2	*ithnain*
3	*talata*
4	*arbaa*
5	*khamsa*
6	*sitta*
7	*saba'a*
8	*tamanain*
9	*tisa'a*
10	*a'shra*
11	*ithnasher*
12	*haddasher*
13	*talatasher*
14	*a'rbaatasher*
15	*khamstasher*
16	*sitasher*
17	*sabatasher*
18	*tamatasher*
19	*tisatasher*
20	*a'shreen*
21	*wahid wa a'shreen*
22	*ithnain wa a'shreen* and so on
30	*talatain*
31	*wahid wa talatain* and so on.
40	*a'rba-ein*
50	*khamsein*
60	*sittein*
70	*saba-eain*
80	*tama-nein*
90	*tisa-ein*
100	*miya*
200	*mitayn*
300	*talata miya* and so on
1,000	*alf*
2,000	*alfayn*
3,000	*talat alaf* and so on

Pronunciation

q = a hard qaf sound in the back of the throat.

kh= similar to the ch in the Scottish loch.

g/a The most difficult sounds for Westerners to make are the ghayn and ayn.

The ayn is a sound made by forcing air through muscles constricted in the back of your throat. The ghayn is a hard guttural g similarly forced through muscles in the throat.

Further Reading

Islam

The Life of Muhammad by Muhammad Haykal (American Trust Pub.)

Life of Muhammad by Muhammad, Ishaq, translated by A. Guillaume (Oxford)

The Venture of Islam by Marshall G.S. Hodgson (Chicago).

Islam and the West, by Bernard Lewis. A view on the relationship by the Professor of Arabic at Edinburgh University.

History and Civilisation

Syria: Cradle of Civilisations by Alain Cheneviere (Stacey International). Comprehensive history of the archaeological sites.

Ancient Iraq by Georges Roux (Penguin).

A History of the Crusades by Steven Runciman (Cambridge). Exhaustive (three volumes) but very readable account.

The Crusades through Arab Eyes, Amin Maalouf (Al-Saqi). This account is based on the records left by Arab chroniclers.

Seven Pillars of Wisdom by T.E. Lawrence (Anchor Books). Lawrence's account of the Arab Revolt of World War I.

A History of the Arab Peoples by Albert Hourani (MJF Books). A landmark history of the Arabs, by the 20th-century doyen of Middle East studies.

Syria 1945–1986, Politics & Society by Derek Hopwood (Unwin Hyman).

The Struggle for Syria, by Patrick Seale (Tauris; Yale University Press). Excellent history of modern Syria.

The Arabs in History by Bernard Lewis (Harper).

A History of the Middle East by Peter Mansfield (Viking). A very readable introduction for the layman.

Assad: The Sphinx of Damascus by Moshe Ma'oz (Grove Weidenfeld). Respected biography of Syria's late ruler.

The Middle East Since 1914, by Ritchie Ovendale (Longman). This useful reference book helps disentangle the complex history of the region in the 20th century.

Women

The Hidden Face of Eve, by Nawal El Saadawi. Introduction to understanding women in the Muslim world by leading female Arab writer.

Travel

Monuments of Syria by Ross Burns (I.B. Tauris Ltd).

Travels in Arabia by Charles M. Doughty. (Deserta Doughty). Classic 19th century travelogue.

Crusader Castles by T.E. Lawrence, (Hippocrene Books, Inc,). After World War I Lawrence embarked on a tour of the Crusader castles. These are his impressions.

Heart–Beguiling Araby – The English Romance with Arabia, by Kathryn Tidrick (I.B. Tauris). A must if you nurture romantic ideas about the Arab world.

The Desert and the Sown, by Gertrude Bell (Virago). Vivid account of Bell's journey from Jerusalem to Alexandretta at the beginning of the 20th century.

Letters from Syria, by Freya Stark (John Murray). Travels by well-known early 20th-century woman Arabist.

Come Tell me How You Live, by Agatha Christie. The famous crime writer accompanied her archaeologist husband on a trip through the Jazirah region in the 1930s. These are her (often amusing) observations.

Mirror to Damascus by Colin Thubron (Heinemann, London). Entertaining account of Thubron's impressions of Syria during the 1960s

Food/Cooking

A New Book of Middle Eastern Food, by Claudia Roden. Interesting and easy cookbook by one of the best writers on Middle Eastern cuisine.

Getting Acquainted

The Place

Area: 10,500sq km
(4,050 sq miles).
Capital: Beirut.
Longest river: Litani (145km/
90 miles).
Population: just below 4 million
(1998 estimate).
Language: Arabic, but English and
French fluently and widely spoken.
Religion: Islam and Christianity,
with a small community of Druze,
an offshoot of Islam.
Time zone: GMT+2 hours (winter) or
3 hours (summer).
Currency: Lebanese lira (known as
Lebanese pound) and US dollar.
Measures: metric.
Electricity: mainly 220 volts, but
some areas still have 110 volts.
International dialling code: 96.

Geography

Lebanon was created in 1920 by
France and Britain, and gained
independence in 1943. It is 225 km
(140 miles) from north to south,
and 50 km (31 miles) at its widest
point east to west. It is bounded to
the north and east by Syria, with
the Mediterranean to the west, and
Israel to the south.

Most of the population lives on a
coastal plain running north to south,
and flanked on the east by a
mountain range running the length of
the country. At the north this is called
Mount Lebanon; it becomes the
Chouf in the centre, and Mount Amil
in the south. The highest peak is
3,000 metres (985 ft) in the north.

East of this range is the fertile
Bekaa Valley, stretching
north–south for the length of the
country. Beyond this, the eastern

border with Syria is marked by the
north-south Anti-Lebanon mountain
range, with the highest peak at
Mount Hermon, at 2,800 metres
(920 ft) in the south.

There are no navigable rivers, but
Lebanon has the most abundant
water supplies in the region, and is
the only Arab country self-sufficient
in water. Much of the coastline is
rocky, though there are some sandy
beaches. Strong currents at some
beaches, however, make swimming
at one of the many beach clubs a
safer bet.

Climate

The coastal strip is hot and humid
in the summer, with the beach
season lasting from May to
October. Temperatures often exceed
33°C (92°F) in Beirut, with humidity
of more than 90 percent in August.
Winter on the coast is cool and
rainy. It doesn't rain often or for
long periods, but when it does the
streets of Beirut flow like rivers.

The mountains, where many
better-off Beirutis head for the
summer, have cool and refreshingly
breezy summers, but the winters
can be extremely harsh, with heavy
snowfalls and treacherously icy
mountain roads. The rush to the
mountains in winter is less to
escape coastal rain than to invade
the ski slopes, especially those
around Faraya and the Cedars. The
Bekaa Valley has very hot, dry
summers and cold, wet winters.

Economy

Before the 1975–90 civil war,
Lebanon was a small but
prosperous trading nation, with
20 percent of national income also
coming from tourism. Sixteen years

of conflict brought that to an end,
and despite massive private and
public sector investments since the
war, the country is only now
beginning to recover.

The clearest evidence of the
recovery is new infrastructure, such
as the airport, roads and reborn
Beirut city centre. Much attention
has been focused on the tourism
industry, with many new five-star
hotels and restaurants.

There is a huge diversity of
incomes, with the tiny country home
to some of the richest and poorest
of the Middle East, living almost
side by side. The average Lebanese
income is three times that of Syrian
neighbours, and twice that of an
average Jordanian, but this is far
below the pre-war level.

Government

Lebanon is one of the Middle East's
few nominal democracies, though
most people vote according to
religion, and overwhelmingly for
members of semi-feudal political
families. There are few political
parties in the Western sense.

The head of state, the president,
is traditionally a Maronite Christian
and in theory is elected by the
members of the 128-seat
parliament. In practice, the choice
of president over the 57 years of
the country's independence has
been influenced more by regional
and international powers, notably
Syria and the US.

The president invites a Sunni
Muslim to be prime minister and
form a cabinet, which is equally
split between Christians and
Muslims, who are themselves
subdivided into a quota of sects to
reflect the demographic strength of
each sect.

Average Temperatures in Beirut

● January	13°C/56°F	● July	27°C/81°F
● February	14°C/58°F	● August	28°C/82°F
● March	16°C/61°F	● September	26°C/79°F
● April	19°C/67°F	● October	24°C/75°F
● May	22°C/72°F	● November	20°C/68°F
● June	25°C/77°F	● December	16°C/61°F

MPs, half of whom are Christian, half Muslim, are elected every four years while the president serves a six-year term. Only three women are currently members of parliament.

Culture & Customs

Culturally Lebanon is schizophrenic, from the very Muslim cities of Tripoli and Sidon, to a European lifestyle in cosmopolitan parts of Beirut. Beirut is also a magnet for Gulf Arabs, who represent the largest number of tourists each summer. With its long history as a trading centre, the city has a reputation as a den of wild living and sin for many Arabs.

The Lebanese are highly hospitable, friendly, generous and educated. Most speak English or French and are culturally tolerant. Those in rural areas, even the poorest, are renowned for their generosity – to turn it down is an insult. All Lebanese are much more religious than Westerners.

Women in Society

Women can be divided broadly into two groups. In the cosmopolitan business and living environment of Beirut, many have almost the same lifestyles as those in the West. They drive, go to university, have careers and a social life similar to any European woman.

Outside Beirut, women are often uneducated wives and mothers. They are expected to stay at home until marriage, when responsibility for them is transferred from their father to husband. A marriage of different religions, or an illicit love affair, can result in the family disowning the girl, and murder – or "honour killing", as it is termed in Arabic – is not unheard of. Few rural women are educated, and most are veiled as soon as they reach puberty. Christian rural women are generally not veiled, and have relatively more freedom.

Planning the Trip

What to Bring/Wear

If you forget anything, don't worry. Thousands of foreign goods are imported, and sold in almost all supermarkets (prices are similar to European ones). Medication of all sorts is sold without a prescription..

In terms of clothes, much depends on where and when you intend to visit. Lebanon is always humid, even in winter, so cotton clothes are best. In winter, warm clothes are required for the mountains, waterproofs for Beirut (particularly waterproof shoes because of heavy downpours). In summer loose cotton clothes are the most comfortable.

In Muslim and rural areas, such as Tripoli, Sidon, the Bekaa Valley and the south, women should keep shoulders and upper arms covered and not wear shorts. In Beirut, however, and in Christian areas such as Jounié and the Metn, anything goes. However little a female tourist wears, she will be overdressed compared to the locals. Even so a bra should always be worn. It is common to see women in shorts and very short tank tops. In beach clubs, the tiniest bikinis are acceptable, but going topless is not.

Entry Regulations

Visa regulations have relaxed in recent years, and visitors from most Western countries, including Europe, the US, Australasia and Japan, can obtain a three-month entry visa on arrival at Beirut Airport for $38. Shorter term – and therefore cheaper – visas are also being introduced.

Alternatively, visas are issued in those countries with Lebanese embassies, usually with a minimum of fuss since Lebanon is trying to attract tourists.

Warning: if you have a passport with Israeli entry stamps, you will not be allowed into Lebanon because of Israel's recent occupation of parts of the south of the country. This may change if the peace process makes progress, but in the meantime you'll need to get your passport renewed. If you want to embark on a wider tour of the Levant, but fear border problems, see page 324 for the best itinerary.

From Syria

It is not possible to obtain a visa to enter Lebanon in Syria, or a visa to enter Syria in Lebanon, making prior planning essential before beginning any land trip.

Extension of stay

Extending a three-month visa is not difficult but, since the wheels of bureaucracy grind slowly, leaving a renewal until the last few days may result in a fine for not having the application filed in time.

Customs

Customs procedures on arrival and departure are very relaxed, with Western travellers rarely checked. Tourists are by law allowed to bring in two bottles of alcohol, 500g of tobacco (400 cigarettes, or 20 cigars), as well as 100 ml of perfume. But given that the local tax on alcohol and cigarettes is very small, it is almost the same price to buy the items in Beirut.

There is no restriction on bringing into the country, or exporting, any amount of local or foreign currency, and Beirut is a regional centre for changing money. Importing or exporting pornography or narcotics is illegal, and imported videotapes and DVDs may be confiscated and checked. Any Israeli-manufactured items will be confiscated, and the holder questioned.

On departure, exporting antiquities, defined as items more

than 300 years old, is prohibited. There are also restrictions on the export of olive oil by air, because it is flammable.

Animal Quarantine
Animals brought into the country must have a valid health certificate. Rabies is rare. Lebanon is not a pet-loving society.

Health

No special inoculations are required, though an anti-tetanus jab is recommended. Tapwater is not safe, but bottled water is widely available. Hotel and restaurant food are usually safe, but food bought along the roadside in rural areas should be treated with caution.

Prescription and non-prescription medicine is widely available from pharmacies. Healthcare at Beirut hospitals such as the American University Hospital and Hotel Dieu is very good, but health insurance is essential. The only effective ambulance services are private or a volunteer service operated in the evenings by the Red Cross.

Money Matters

The official currency is the Lebanese lira (LL), confusingly also known as the Lebanese pound. Lebanese banknotes, which have both Arabic and Roman numerals on them, are divided into 100,000, 50,000, 20,000, 10,000, 5,000 and 1,000 notes, and 500, 250, 100 and 50 coins.

The Lebanese lira is fairly stable. Shops and hotels frequently give a confusing mixture of Lebanese currency and dollars in change, but it is possible to insist on one currency or the other.

CHANGING MONEY

Many transactions are conducted in US dollars, which are accepted by all save government offices. This removes the necessity to buy Lebanese currency on arrival. However, should you wish to do so,

you will find a branch of the Canadian Lebanese bank at Beirut Airport.

All areas have *bureaux de change* as well as dozens of banks. Most moneychangers are concentrated in Hamra Street in Beirut, where it is possible to change any amount of the major, and often minor, currencies.

Getting There

BY AIR

Beirut International Airport is serviced by some 30 major carriers, with good connections to Europe, the Arab Gulf and the Asian subcontinent. The airport has one terminal that is used by all the airlines. Two domestic airports are planned, in the north and the Bekaa.

Airlines
The national airline is:
Middle East Airlines (MEA) offices
Headquarters, Beirut Airport.
Tel: (01) 629 125/250.

Airport/City Links
The airport is situated about 5km (3 miles) from Beirut city, connected by a new highway. The new metered airport taxis are about $30 to the city centre, much more expensive than an ordinary cab. A walk of just 600 metres/yds outside the perimeter of the airport will reveal taxis willing to go to Beirut for as little as $10 (after hard bargaining) or even LL2,000 ($1.35) if shared with others. Alternatively, a public bus runs every half hour during the day from the airport to the city; this costs LL500.

Porter service
A free porter service is theoretically provided for passengers as they

Airport Numbers

Airport information:
(01) 628 000
Airport general number:
(01) 629 065/6
Customs: (01) 629 160/65
General security (immigration and visas): (01) 629 150/1/2

Tourist Information

The network of tourist information offices outside Lebanon is still fairly limited.
Paris
124 Faubourg St Honoré
75008 Paris
Tel: 43 59 10 36
Fax: 14 35 91 19 9
London
90 Picadilly
London W1V 9HB
Tel: 020 7 409 2031
Fax: 020 7 493 4929

enter or exit the airport. However, suitcases are delivered to cars and taxis with greater loving care if a dollar or two is forthcoming.

BY SEA

Before and during the civil war there was a regular sea connection with Cyprus. This has been suspended, but during the summer months several cruise companies have added Beirut to their Eastern Mediterranean schedule, with ships regularly arriving from Greece and Cyprus, usually via northern Syria.

BY LAND

It is possible to enter and leave Lebanon across the Syrian border to the north and east. The Israeli border will remain closed until a peace agreement is signed.

There are a number of buses and taxis that travel from Beirut to Damascus, and Amman in Jordan. The fare between Beirut and Damascus is 500 Syrian pounds, LL15,000 or $10 for one seat one way in a five-seat cab. The fare from Beirut to Amman is LL20,000 or about $13. Buying two seats or the whole taxi is worth it for greater personal comfort. The taxis travel 24 hours a day and some pick up and drop off passenger wherever needed (*see also Entry Regulations, page 337* for visas if travelling overland from Syria).

Practical Tips

NEWSPAPERS AND MAGAZINES

Many popular US, British, French, German and Italian newspapers and magazines can be found in bookstores and on street corner stands. As the publishing capital of the Middle East, Lebanon also has a host of newspapers and magazines in English and French, as well as Arabic.

Useful publications for visitors include:

The Daily Star: an English-language daily with local, regional and international news, published six days a week. It also has information on cultural events, including concerts, theatre and films. Star Scene on the back page is an eye-opening section on how the local elite spends its time. Website: www.dailystar.com.lb.

L'Orient le Jour: this serious-looking French-language daily newspaper has been left behind by the switch to English. Nevertheless, it has good coverage of local politics and world news.

The Guide: the Lebanese version of London's *Time Out* magazine featuring comprehensive listings of shops, cafés, bars and restaurants, cinemas and theatres, as well as sports and other events. It also carries reviews and features on where to shop, and what to buy. Though it has a cover price of LL5,000, it is available free in many hotels and cafés.

Monday Morning: a weekly glossy news magazine with a long history. Occasionally it carries interesting political interviews, but these are alongside many pictures of young socialites, as well as many pictures of the magazine publisher and his family.

Lebanon Opportunities: this business monthly focuses on local property, finance and economic news. Interesting and professionally produced magazine, as well as a great place to find your dream holiday villa in the mountains or by the sea.

RADIO

Lebanon has a range of domestic stations broadcasting in Arabic, French and English. These tend to consist of back-to-back music 24 hours a day on FM. Only a small number are licensed to broadcast news. Stations worth tuning into include:

Radio Liban (96.2 FM): the state broadcaster transmits Arabic programmes and music, but has news bulletin in English and French. 12.30pm in French, 1pm and 2pm in English, 6pm in French.

Pax Radio (96.2 FM): classic rock and pop, with all programmes in English.

Fame FM (99.9 FM): a youth station playing techno and rave. All programmes are in English.

FML (99.0 FM): Radio Mount Liban, an alternative station playing rock and pop and alternative music. Broadcasts around the clock, with programmes in English and French.

Nostalgie (88 FM): a French station playing continuous music, mostly French, with many older titles.

Radio One (105.5 FM): modelled on the British equivalent, and even using the same jingles, Radio One plays hits and chart music. Programmes are in English.

Voice of Lebanon (93.3 FM): transmits Arabic programmes and music, but news is in English at 8pm.

TELEVISION

Arab and international satellite and cable stations are available in all major hotels. Lebanon also has

Many international stations can be received in Lebanon. The BBC World Service is found at 1323 kHz on the AM band.

many privately owned and liberal domestic channels transmitting in Arabic, English and French, as well as one state broadcaster. Detailed listings are found in local newspapers, notably the English-language *Daily Star*.

TeleLiban: the state-owned broadcasting station with a mix of foreign and local programmes, including regular foreign films. There is also a separate channel, TL le Neuf, that transmits in French in the evening, with news at 8pm.

Future TV: owned by ex-Prime Minister Rafik Hariri, broadcasts mostly in Arabic, but there are also English and French films until very late. News in French is at 5.30pm, and in English at 5.45pm.

LBC: Lebanese Broadcasting Corporation began life as a Christian channel during the war, but now has a much wider audience. It transmits in Arabic, French and English, with local Arabic productions or dubbed Mexican soap operas, as well as US films. There is no news in English or French, but CNN news is at 1.30pm every day.

Lumière: the official Christian channel, transmitting religious programmes and services.

Manar: this station belongs to Hizbollah, the political-guerrilla movement in south Lebanon. It features a mixture of religious programmes, talk shows in Arabic and footage of Hizbollah raids on Israeli forces.

MTV: the M stands for Murr (the family of the Deputy Prime Minister), not music as in its international namesake. It transmits much programming from France, including game shows, with several English-language comedies and dramas. It has no serious political programmes, and no foreign-language news.

NBN: National Broadcasting Network is transforming itself into a 24-hour all-talk station. Part of its plan is to buy in British and American factual programmes and documentaries.

Postal Services

POST

Lebanon's postal service was destroyed during the war, and it is only now making a recovery. Post boxes are slowly reappearing, but letters can be posted at one of the small number of post offices (open 8am till 1.30pm). Mail to Europe and the US takes about two weeks, but it's getting faster.

The only reliable way to receive mail is to have it sent to a post office box – most businesses and hotels have one. Mail from Europe and the US takes about two weeks.

Post Offices

The main post office in Beirut is at: Riad Al Solh Square. Tel: (01) 646 540/1.

New post offices are constantly being opened throughout the Greater Beirut area. They include:
1st floor, Matta building (above Star Stationery), Makdissi Street, Hamra.
Tel: (01) 354 706.
Place Sassine, Achrafié.
Tel: (01) 321 657.
Corniche Al-Mazraa, next to the Internal Security Building, Mazraa.
Tel: (01) 314 090.
American University of Beirut, Bliss Street. Tel: (01) 345 000.

COURIERS

DHL
Park Building, Sami Al Solh Avenue, Badaro, Greater Beirut.
Tel: (01) 390 900/1/2, (01) 391 800/1.
Hamra Street, Hamra, Beirut.
Tel: (01) 746460/1/2/3.
Federal Express
Emile Eddé Street, Hoss Building, ground. floor, Hamra, Beirut.
Tel: (01) 345 393, (01) 342 856, (01) 345 385.

Telephone Codes

Aley	05
Baalbek	08
Bekaa	08
Beirut	01
Chouf	06
Hazmieh	04
Jbeil	09
Jounié	09
Kesourwan	09
Lebanese mobile	
phones	03
Metn	04
north	06
Sidon	07
south	07
Syria	02
Tripoli	06
Tyre	07

Telecommunications

TELEPHONES

Lebanon's fixed-line telephone system was virtually destroyed during the war, but has been rebuilt from scratch, and is therefore of better quality than those in most neighbouring countries. Almost all hotels have good quality international telephone lines, but expect to pay some $3 a minute for a call. Mobile phones can be hired at leading hotels.

Local calls can be made from most shops for LL500. All calls within Lebanon are charged at the same price, around 12 cents a minute.

Scattered across Beirut are a number of small callback shops offering international calls for as little as $1 a minute, but the government is trying to close these down. Alternatively MCI International phone cards offer calls for about $1.50 a minute. These are sold at most newsagents, with values of $35 for 260 units and $55 for 520 units.

There are also the following direct-dial numbers for British Telecom, AT&T and MCI, allowing use of domestic phone cards, or collect calls.
British Telecom: (01) 425 044, (01) 425 495.

AT&T: (01) 426801, (01) 425 967.
Telstar (Australia): (01) 425 900.
MCI: (01) 425 036, (01) 428 710.

INTERNET

Beirut is packed with Internet cafés where you can send and receive email for around $4 an hour.

Security & Crime

Personal crimes, such as muggings and pickpocketing, are virtually unknown in Lebanon, and the country's wartime reputation is very much out of date. Foreigners can walk the streets at any time, day or night, and be much safer than in any Western city. The biggest danger for tourists is traffic, because of the appalling driving habits of most Lebanese.

All tourist areas are safe to visit, though the British and US embassies still suggest – unnecessarily – that visitors visiting Baalbek and Tyre travel only as part of organised groups.

There is no overall regular police force in Lebanon, and therefore don't be surprised to see young soldiers patrolling the streets. These are conscripts, often speaking English, and doing military service after graduating with a degree in finance or business studies.

Equally, if you are driving,

Emergency Numbers

Emergencies: 112
from any telephone in the country, in case of a fire, theft, and accident.
Police: 160
Medical emergencies: Red Cross 140 (*see also page 341* for local services)
Fire Brigade: 175 or
Doura (01) 445 000.
Sidon (07) 720061.
Jounié (09) 914 617.
Tripoli (06) 431 017.
Information: 120
mainly for telephone numbers and addresses.

many highways are dotted with checkpoints, where it is necessary to slow down, and turn on the interior light of the car. Foreigners are usually stopped only out of curiosity. Identification documents should nevertheless be carried at all times.

Medical Services

Lebanon has very sophisticated healthcare facilities and they are some of the best in the region. Many doctors have trained in the US and France. However, there is effectively no ambulance service, with only a Red Cross volunteer service at night. Though of high quality, the healthcare is expensive, and insurance is essential before arriving.

Many pharmacies are open late, and provide medication without prescription. The staff are often very knowledgeable, and also speak English or French.

HOSPITALS

The best hospitals in Beirut are the American University Hospital in Hamra, and the Hotel Dieu in Achrafié.

Beirut
AUH, American University Hospital
Abdul Aziz Street, Hamra
Tel: (01) 350 000
(01) 340 460/70
(01) 344 704
(01) 345 325.
Hariri Medical Centre
Gefinor, Hamra
Tel: (01) 739 142
Hotel Dieu De France
Hotel de Dieu Street, Achrafié
Tel: (01) 386 941/2/3/4
(01) 387 000/1
(01) 387 350/1/2
Trad Hospital
Mexico Street, Hamra
Tel: (01) 362 373
(01) 366 130/31
(01) 366 429

Tripoli
Al Munla Hospital
Tel: (03) 322 111

Public Holidays

With 18 official religions, Lebanon seems to have more public holidays than anywhere in the world, celebrating various Muslim and Christian festivals as well as national holidays.
● **1 January** New Year's Day
● **9 February** Mar Maron Day. Saint Maron was the founder of the Christian Maronite faith, and lived and died in Syria. Celebrated in Christian areas of the country, including East Beirut, the Metn and parts of north Lebanon.
● **March/April** Easter. Both the Orthodox and Catholic Easters are celebrated. They are one week apart, with public holidays on both occasions for Good Friday, Easter Sunday and Monday.
● **1 May** Labour Day.
● **6 May** Martyrs' Day, a commemoration of the hanging in 1916 of Syrian and Lebanese nationalists by the Ottomans in Beirut and Damascus.
● **1 November** All Saints' Day is widely celebrated in Christian areas.
● **22 November** Lebanese Independence Day: most businesses are closed.
● **25 December** Christmas Day, celebrated across the country, though Armenian Christians mark 6 January as Christ's birthday.

Islamic Holidays
Lebanon follows the Western calendar for all business and government events. However, the Muslim calendar (based on a lunar cycle of 12 months of either 29 or 30 days) is used to mark Muslim religious occasions. This difference makes the Muslim year

Sidon
Hammoud Hospital
Tel: (07) 721 021
Tel: (07) 720 152

Chouf
Ein Wouzein Hospital
Tel: (05) 501 515
Tel: (05) 501 311

11 days shorter than the Western year, so dates of Muslim holidays change every year.
● **Eid Al Fitr**
Feast of breaking the fast, which celebrates the end of Ramadan (the Muslim holy month) and lasts about three days. During Ramadan, many men and women abstain from eating, drinking and sex during daylight hours, but feast *(Iftar)* in the evenings. During the breaking of the fast, families visit friends and relatives, and give to charity.
● **Eid Al Adha**
Feast of the Sacrifice commemorating Abraham's sacrifice of a sheep instead of his son. The Eid is held 70 days after Ramadan, and lasts for four days. Many Muslim families slaughter a sheep and share the meat with relatives or donate to the poor.
● **Al-Hijria**
Islamic New Year.
● **Ashoura**
A Shia Islamic holiday is celebrated mostly in south Beirut, south Lebanon and the Bekaa Valley. The Shia commemorate the loss of Hussein, son of Ali, who was married to the Prophet's daughter and was the founder of the Shia sect. The commemoration lasts 10 days, but only the last (the 10th day of the first month of the Muslim calendar) is a public holiday. It is marked in Nabatiyé and south Beirut by parades of men self-flagellating with blades to re-enact the suffering of Hussein. Not for the squeamish.
● **Mouloud**
Prophet's Birthday

RED CROSS

Phone if you need an ambulance during the night.
Central office
Tel: (01) 924 020
Beirut
Tabaris, Achrafié
Tel: (01) 448 100, (01) 448 200.

Jounié, Greater Beirut.
Tel: (09) 830 799.
Jal El Dib, Greater Beirut.
Tel: (01) 523 809.
Baalbek. Tel: (08) 370 889.
Sidon. Tel: (07) 722 532.
Tripoli. Tel: (06) 620 748.

BEIRUT PHARMACIES

Kaddoura
Gefinor building, block B, Hamra.
Tel: (01) 739 593/4
Madina pharmacy
Hamra Street, Hamra
Tel: (01) 343 043, (01) 349 349
Mazen (24 hours)
Wajih Sinno building, Corniche
Al-Mazraa. Tel: (01) 313 362
Hotel Dieu
Hotel Dieu Street, Achrafiyé
Tel: (01) 614 760.

Money Matters

CASH MACHINES

There are ATMs (cash machines) in
most major streets, but several
banks accept only their own cards.
Below is a brief list of those that
take major credit cards.

Byblos Bank ATMs take Visa,
MasterCard, Cirrus, Visa Electron,
Maestro and Plus. Machines are
found at these branches:
Hamra: Makdissi Street.
Hamra, Sadat Street, near LAU's
lower gate.
Doura: Doura roundabout.

Furn El Chebbak: Furn El Chebbak
main road.
Hazmieh: facing Tele Liban.
Antelias: facing the Armenian
Patriarch.
Jounié: Jounié souk, near Amwaj
Centre.
Zouk Mosbeh: Jeita main road,
facing the *Daily Press*.
Tripoli: near ABC Centre.

British Bank ATMs accept Visa,
MasterCard, Global Access and
BankerNet. Machines can be found
at the following branches:
Doura: Doura highway, Ghantous
building.
Hamra: Makdissi Street.
Jounié: Neameh building.
Mazraa: Corniche Al-Mazraa, Arayssi
building.

Banque Audi ATMs accept
BankerNet, Visa-Electron, Plus,
Visa, MasterCard and American
Express. Branches are at:
Achrafiyé: Sofil Centre.
Doura: Banking Centre.
Hamra: Bliss Street.
Jounié: Fouad Chehab Boulevard.
Sidon: Riad El-Solh Boulevard.
Tripoli: Azmi Street.
Verdun: Rachid Karame Street.
Zouk: Val De Zouk Centre.

Religious Services

Lebanon has 18 officially
recognised Muslim and Christian
communities.
   Muslims in Ras Beirut, Tripoli
and Sidon are predominantly Sunni,

whereas in the southern suburbs of
Beirut, the south and Bekaa Valley,
they are mainly Shia. Only Muslims
are allowed in mosques.
   The Christians, living mostly in
east Beirut, Jounié, the Metn,
Mount Lebanon and North Lebanon,
are mainly Maronite, but with large
communities of Orthodox and
Catholics.
   Below is a brief selection of
Christian services, mainly in
Achrafiyé, which is a predominantly
Christian quarter.

St Maron Church (Maronite)
Mar Maroun Street, Gemaizeh,
Beirut. Tel: (01) 446 249.
Sunday Mass is at 8am, 10am,
11am and 6pm until June, and after
June it is at only 8am and 10am. All
masses in Arabic.

St Francois Church (Latin)
Opposite Cinema Saroulla, Hamra
Street, Hamra, Beirut.
Tel: (01) 351 727, (01) 351 626.
Sunday Mass in Arabic at 9.30am,
in French at 10.30am and in
English at noon.
Santa Church (Latin)
Goro Street, Gemaizeh, Beirut.
Tel: (01) 447 003.
Sunday Mass is at 6.30am in
French, 8.30am in Arabic and
10.30am in French.
St Elie Church for Armenian
Catholics
Debbas Square, Tabaris-Achrafiyé,
Beirut.
Tel: (03) 736 798, (03) 668 746.
Sunday Mass is in Arabic at 10am

Business Hours

Banks
Most banks open Mon–Fri
8am–2.30pm, Saturday
8am–noon. Some close a little
later, however: for example,
Byblos Bank at 3.30pm on
weekdays and 1.30pm on
Saturday, and the British Bank
closes at 5pm weekdays and at
noon on Saturday.

Businesses and Shops
Almost all outlets, from computer

hardware to lingerie, are open
every day except Sunday from 8am
to 7pm. Some open for only half a
day on Saturday and a few close
around 6pm on weekdays. Small
grocers are usually open until late
at night, ensuring no one ever runs
out of Almaza (a local popular
beer) or cigarettes.
Several shops that sell food and
household products open on
Sundays, as well as a handful of
big supermarkets, such as

Spinneys (which sells products
made by the British supermarket
chain Tesco) and Monoprix, a
franchise of the French giant.

Government offices
These are open every day except
Sunday from 8am to 2pm. Some
ministries open 9am–4pm or 5pm.
It's best to check by phone first –
government personnel are usually
delightfully polite but maddeningly
unhelpful.

and in Armenian at 11am.

Saint Antoine de Padoue (Maronite)
Pasteur Street, Al-Madawar,
Gemaizeh, Beirut.
Tel: (01) 447 736.
Sunday Mass is in Arabic at
8.30am, 10am, 11.30am and
5.30pm.

Saint Demetrius Church (Roman
Orthodox)
Sassine Street, Achrafiyé, Beirut.
Tel: (01) 216 885.
Sunday Mass on is in Arabic at
9:30am. This Church has the most
beautiful cemetery annexed to it
that can be seen from the street. If
in the area, make sure to stop by
and look at it, particularly when it is
lit at night.

Saint Nichan Church (Armenian
Orthodox)
Army (Jeish) Street, Al-Serail, Riad
Al-Solh, Beirut.
Tel: (01) 981 102.
Sunday Mass is in Armenian at
9.30am.

First Armenian Evangelical Church
(also for Protestants)
Mexico Street, Hamra, Beirut.
Tel: (01) 343 182.
Sunday Mass is in Armenian at
10am.

Disabled Facilities

Beirut Airport is accessible for
disabled travellers, but very little
else. The downtown area of Beirut,
currently being rebuilt, is being
designed to cater for disabled
people. Beyond that, only a tiny
number of streets are designed to
accommodate the disabled. In
Byblos, the local council is making
an effort to make beach and
changing facilities accessible, and
the Marriott and Mayflower hotels
have special facilities for the
disabled.

For further information contact
the Lebanese Association for the
Disabled. Tel: (01) 650 417.

Photography

Most people will not object to
having their picture taken, though it
is always best to consult them first.

Embassies

Australia
Farra Building, Bliss Street,
Hamra, Beirut.
Tel: (01) 789 010, (01) 789
018.

Canada
Coolrite Building, Jal El-Deeb
Highway, Greater Beirut.
Tel: (04) 521 163/4/5.
Fax: (04) 521 167.

UK
Villa Tohmeh, Number 8 Street,
Rabieh.
Tel: (04) 417 007, (04) 405
070, (04) 403 640
Coolrite building, Jal El Dib
Highway, Beirut.
Tel: (04) 405 033, (04) 402
035,

US
Awkar, Beirut.
Tel: (01) 402 200, (01) 417
774, (01) 403 300.

However, do not try to photograph
anything of a government nature,
such as soldiers or military bases,
the port or airport. If you do, you
could find yourself being arrested.
Photography is also prohibited in
the National Museum and Jeita
Grotto.

Standard 100 ASA film is fine for
taking photographs almost
everywhere and is widely available.
A 36-shot roll of film costs about $3
in Beirut, and there are numerous
one-hour developing shops.

Getting Around

Public Transport

BUSES

Lebanon has one state and one
private bus company, of which both
connect the suburbs of Beirut for a
one-way fee of LL500. The main
bus terminal (Charles Helou) is
close to the port. Buses are a
novelty and rarely crowded. Myriad
ill-maintained minibuses also
perpetually ply for traded.

SERVICE TAXIS

Service taxis (pronounced "ser-
vees") travel along established
routes, picking up and dropping
passengers as they go.

If you merely stand in the street
and look around, several cars will
stop and enquire where you are
going. The official fare for a service
taxi anywhere in Beirut is LL1,000,
with the car taking three passengers
in the back, and an uncomfortable
two in the front.

The destinations of service taxis
in Beirut (going clockwise) are
Hamra, Riad al-Solh Square,
Charles Helou Station, Doura,
Achrafiyé (Place Sassine), Badaro
and Cola junction.

The central-point interchange for
most service taxis is the Mathaf
junction, near the museum. It is
also possible to connect with taxis
going north by taking a service to
Doura, or with those going south by
picking up a service to Cola.

With all taxis and service taxis,
foreigners are seen as fare game to
be ripped off. So be quite prepared
to wave on five cars asking a
ridiculous sum of money, and you will

Tourist Information in Lebanon

Ministry of Tourism
550 Central Bank Street, Hamra,
Beirut.
Tel: (01) 343 073,
(01) 340 940–4.
Fax: (01) 340 945/ (01) 343 279.
E-mail: mot@lebanon-tourism.
gov.lb

Tourist Information Centre
To pick up brochures and specific
information on all regions, the
Tourist Information Centre is
adjacent to the Ministry of Tourism

be guaranteed eventually to find one
driver who is prepared to accept the
official fare. Many drivers speak
English or French (as well as on
occasion German, Swedish,
Spanish, Portuguese and Italian).
   Service drivers not going in your
direction will roll their eyes or throw
their heads back and drive off
without saying a word. This is local
habit, not a sign of rudeness.

TAXIS

Lone women should not take a cab
on the street at night, but call one of
the respectable companies listed
here:
Lebanon Taxi
Hamra, Beirut.
Tel: (01) 340 717/8/9.
Beirut Taxi
Australia Street, Raouche,
Beirut.Tel: (01) 805 416/418.
City Taxi
Al-Ghazalieh, Achrafiyé, Beirut.
Tel: (01) 397 903.

Driving

There is no better reflection of the
Lebanese personality than the
nation's driving habits. Few laws
are enforced: it's a free for all.
Motorists lean on their horns, drive
on the pavements and do anything
to get where they are going, with no
regard for other road users. But if
they do happen to catch the eye of
someone they have been abusing
with a horn for half an hour, they

and can be contacted at:
550 Central Bank Street, Hamra,
Beirut.
Tel: (01) 343 073
or (01) 340 940–4.
Fax: (01) 340 945
or (01) 343 279.

Tourist Police
For any problems or complaints
linked to tourism services such as
hotels, restaurants or travel
agents, contact the Tourist Police,
tel: (01) 343 209.

are exceptionally polite.
   Driving yourself is only for the
brave, and can be both frightening
and liberating. There is no regard
for seatbelt laws, no speed limits,
few traffic cops and no enforced
drink-driving laws, and insurance is
not yet compulsory.
   Those brave enough to venture
on Lebanese roads need to carry
an international driving licence
issued in their home country. They
should also note two idiosyncrasies
of driving Lebanese-style:
● An arm hanging out of the driver's
window (left-hand side) may mean
many things: "I don't want to fill the
car with smoke"; it's less sticky in
the breeze; or there's nowhere else
to put it. It rarely means "I am
turning left".
● One-way streets are used for

Beirut Travel Agents

Afif G. Abdul-Malik
CLTC, Jeanne d'Arc Street,
Hamra.
Tel at office: (01) 341 676,
(01) 341 677;
home: (01) 345 588.
Beirut's oldest travel agency and a
one-man band. Honest, efficient,
offering old-style service and very
cheap prices.
CIS Commodore
near Commodore Hotel, Hamra.
Tel: (01) 354 229/347 699.
Ghazi Travel Agency
Bliss Street, Hamra.
Tel: (01) 342 546/348 555.

travelling one way at a time, though
not necessarily the way indicated by
the no-entry signs.
   Short-term visitors are better
advised to hire a driver with their
car (around $75–$100 a day).

CAR RENTAL

Lebanon is awash with car rental
agencies, with cars available from
around $25 a day. All companies
require a deposit of about $500,
which is usually lodged using a
separate and returnable credit card
slip. Many of the smaller agencies
have vehicles of dubious condition,
so inspect an offered car for body
and mechanical damage before
leaving the agency.

Avis
● Army Street, Kurban-Daouk
building, Hamra-Kantari, Beirut.
Tel: (01) 371 013.
Email: avis@avis.com.lb
● Amine Gemayel Street, Soufi
Garden, Achrafiyé, Beirut.
Tel: (01) 614 914,
● Commodore Hotel building,
Commodore Street, Hamra, Beirut,
Tel: (01) 749 997/8, (03) 716 606.
● Summerland Hotel, Jnah, Beirut,
Tel: (01) 858 000 ext 5020.

Budget
● Minkara Centre, Mme Curie
Street, facing Bristol Hotel.

Nawas Tours
Sadat Street, Hamra.
Tel: (01) 740 275.
Nour Travel
Hamra.
Tel: (01) 340 375/6.
Pan Asiatic
Gefinor Centre, Hamra.
Tel: (01) 361 230.
Saad Tours
Pavilion Centre, Hamra Street,
Hamra.
Tel: (01) 346 232/352 194.
Silk Road Travel and Tourism
Mme. Curie Street, Hamra.
Tel: (01) 742 712/3.

Distances from Beirut

● **North**
Batroun: 49km (30.5 miles)
Byblos: 38km (23.5 miles)
The Cedars: 130km (81 miles)
Jeita Grotto: 20km (12.5 miles)
Jounié: 19km (11.75 miles)
Tripoli: 85km (52.75 miles)
● **Mount Lebanon**
Aley: 17 km (10.5 miles)
Beit ed Dîne: 45 km (28 miles)
Beit Meri: 16 km (10 miles)
Broummana: 20 km (12.5 miles)
Faqra: 45 km (28 miles)
Faraya: 40 km (25 miles)
● **South**
Sidon: 48 km (29.75 miles)
Tyre: 63 km (39.25 miles)
● **Bekaa Valley**
Aanjar: 58 km (36 miles)
Chtaura: 50 km (31 miles)
Zahleh: 54 km (33.5 miles)
Baalbek: 85 km (52.75 miles)

Tel: (01) 740 741-(01) 741 740.
● F. Minkara, Hayek Square,
Sin El Fil.
Tel: (01) 480 626, (01) 502 202.
● Transorient Travel and Touring, Al
Khazen Building, Kaslik.
Tel: (09) 641 300, (09) 641 304.
● Riviera Hotel, Avenue de Paris,
Manara, Beirut.
Tel: (01) 602 273, (01) 373 210.

City Car
●Kalaa St, Al Oraifi Building, Hamra
region, Beirut.
Tel: (01) 803 308, (01) 805 19
Email: citycar@citycar.com.lb.

Hala Rent a Car
● Sami El Solh Avenue, Beirut.
Tel: (01) 601 331, (03) 272 817.
● Ain El Mreisseh, Beirut.
Tel: (01) 369 280.

Lenacar
● Saarti Building, Fouad Chehab
Avenue, Sin El Fil, Beirut.
Tel: (01) 480 480, (01) 502 200.
● Regency Palace Hotel, Adma,
Greater Beirut.
Tel: (09) 934 900/9
Email: lenacar@cyberia.net.lb.
● Beirut International Airport, desk
in the arrival lounge

Where to Stay

Choosing a Hotel

The standard of hotels in Lebanon is
generally fairly high. The number of
luxury hotels in Beirut is rising
rapidly, as the city seeks to regain its
reputation as a key business and
leisure base in the Middle East.
Outside Beirut and neighbouring
Jounié the number of hotels
declines considerably. In the south
of the country there are very few
hotels at all. However, with
distances so short this shouldn't
present too much of a problem.

Hotel Listings

BEIRUT

Most of the five-star hotels in Beirut
have been built in the past few
years, and are therefore equipped
to modern standards, with new
decor and fittings. But as a result,
most have little to distinguish them,
save their location.

Summerland International
Jnah
Tel: (01) 858 000
One of Beirut's landmark hotels,
the 151-room Summerland is just
south of central Hamra on a
sprawling complex, and is the only
hotel with its own sandy beach, with
watersport facilities and two
swimming pools (one with a
waterfall). During the war the
Summerland was completely self-
contained, with its own massive
supplies of water and gasoline, and
huge generators. It even had its
own militia to ensure those
escaping the war could have a
peaceful stay. At one point it was
used as the seat of government
when the city was divided. Today it

is a little faded, but maintains its
high prices, and has several good
restaurants. **$$$$**
Vendome Inter-Continental Intíl
Ain El Mreisseh
Tel: (01) 369 280
(01) 369 619, (01) 365 553
(03) 212 791, (03) 883 486
Fax: (01) 360 169
E-mail: beirut@interconti.com.
One of the first glitzy hotels to be
refurbished after the war, the
Vendome is on the seafront
Corniche, in the former hotel
district, and opposite some fine
beach clubs. In the past few years
its suites have played host to
visiting heads of state. On the roof
is one of the best restaurant-bars in
the area, Sydney's (named after its
wartime manager), which is open
24 hours a day for drinks and food.
The French restaurant, Au Premier,
is expensive but magnificent. The
Vendome has the highest
occupancy rate in the country so
they must be doing something right.
The owners plan to reopen the
nearby Phoenicia Hotel. Very
expensive. **$$$$**
Bayview
Ain El Mreisseh
Tel/fax: (03) 331 001/2
E-mail: bayview@dm.net.lb
Rebuilt horseshoe-shaped hotel on
the seafront Corniche giving every
room a sea view. The Bayview is
down the hill from downtown
Hamra, in the old hotel quarter,
making a car or frequent taxis
essential as there is not much to
do near the hotel, save go to the
beach. It has a good, but pricey,
restaurant on the top floor with a
spectacular view of the
Mediterranean. **$$$**

Price Guide

Prices are per night for a double
room, On top is a five per cent
government tax, plus usually a
16 percent service charge.

$	Up to $50
$$	$50–100
$$$	$100–175
$$$$	$175+

Le Bristol
Mme Curie Street, Hamra
Tel: (01) 351 400, (01) 346 390
(03) 223 138- (03) 236 643
Fax: (01) 351 409, (01) 602 451
E-mail: bristol@dm.net.lb.
Now under Starwood management, the old warrior of Beirut luxury is undergoing a multi-million-dollar facelift. The 162-room hotel retains its character and a sense of elegance with chandeliers and silver service. Le Bristol is very much a downtown hotel, located between the shopping districts of Verdun and Hamra. The roof-garden restaurant offers international and regional cuisine, and the Le Gourmet Café one the best selections of pastries, chocolates and cakes in town. **$$$**

Meridien Commodore International
Commodore Street, Hamra
Tel: (01) 350 400
Fax: (01) 345 806/7
E-mail: mail@commodore.com.lb.
The Commodore was famed for many years as the retreat of foreign correspondents during the war, complete with a parrot which could imitate the sound of an incoming shell. Located in the middle of downtown Hamra, the hotel has now been refurbished, and has 209 luxury rooms, 22 suites and one king-sized suite. Playing on its journalist theme, the News Bar features a carpet depicting British and foreign newspapers, in a bar room littered with journalists' paraphernalia such as old typewriters. The Commodore also features a reasonable Japanese restaurant (Benihana), French cuisine (La Brasserie) and the Lebanese La Casbah. There are also a fitness club and a business centre. **$$$**

Coral Beach
Jnah
Tel: (01) 895 000
Slightly to the south of central Beirut, but with a superb location on the beach, the Coral Beach has an excellent swimming pool, and rooms have a view over the sea. It is less than 5 km (3 miles) from the airport, making it popular with business travellers and aircraft crews. **$$$**

Cadmos
Tel: (01) 374 892/7
(03) 658 000/1
Fax: (01) 374 898/9
E-mail: harb01@cyberia.net.lb.
On the Beirut Corniche, in the old hotel quarter, the recently built Cadmos is away from the hustle of downtown, and well located with superb sea views. It is also across the road from a number of fine beach clubs including the St George (itself being rebuilt as a luxury hotel), and the recently opened Le Plage. The Cadmos includes the Sesto Senso Italian restaurant, a piano bar and Café Mer, unsurprisingly with a view of the sea. **$$$**

Holiday Inn Dunes
Dunes Centre, Verdun Street
Tel: (01) 792 111
Fax: (01) 792 333
Located in the glitzy shopping district of Verdun, slightly away from the central Hamra area, the newly opened Holiday Inn sits above the Dunes boutique shopping centre, which also features a cinema and bowling alley, making it a great place to be based for shopping trips if you have the cash for Verdun prices. **$$$**

Gabriel Sofitel
Independence Avenue, Achrafiyé
Tel: (01) 203 700/800
(03) 208 824
Fax: (01) 320 094
E-mail: legabriel@inco.com.lb.
One of the few hotels on the east of town, the Gabriel is a recent luxury establishment mostly for business travellers. Though away from the hustle of Hamra, it is close to the oh-so-fashionable restaurant district of Monot, and the expensive French-style boutiques of Achrafiyé. **$$$**

Marriott International
St. Elie Boulevard, Jnah
Tel: (01) 840 540
Fax: (01) 840 345
E-mail: marriott@marriott.com.lb.
The Marriott has become one of the hotels of choice for business travellers, located just 4 km (2.5 miles) from the airport, on the highway midway between the airport and downtown. It has been built as

part of a cinema-shopping complex, but its location puts it close to many of the poorer suburbs of the city, makes a car essential. **$$$**

Riviera
Corniche Al Manara
Tel: (01) 602 273/4/5
(03) 617 591/2
Fax: (01) 602 272
E-mail: info@rivierahotel.com.lb.
Located on the Corniche, downhill from central Hamra, the Riviera is in a superb location, with a tunnel under the seafront highway leading to what is called a "beach club" but which in reality is a vast concrete area of deckchairs and swimming pools next to a marina. The Rivera also has a Japanese restaurant, The Michiko, as well as La Terrazza Italian. The beach club is open to the public (for LL20,000 a day), and a favourite retreat of Beirut's beach-loving elite, giving it the unofficial title "Silicon Valley". **$$$**

Cavalier
Hamra Street
Tel: (01) 353 001, (01) 602 060
Fax: (01) 347 681
A little faded but with a good reputation for service. The hotel has its own bar, Charlie Brown's, and was a favourite of journalists during the war. **$$–$$$**

Casa d'Or
Hamra
Tel: (01) 347 850, (01) 348 300
Clean, basic and modern hotel in the centre of the Hamra shopping district, the Casa d'Or offers excellent services and modern facilities at a reasonable price. All rooms have cable TV, 24-hour room service and cooking facilities. The bar/restaurant is limited, but there is a pleasant roof terrace to while away the long, hot summer days if you don't mind the sound of aircraft as it is directly under the flight path for the airport. **$$**

The Mayflower
parallel to Rue Jeanne d'Arc
Hamra.
Tel: (01) 340 680/1/2/3, (01) 347 080, (03) 219 789
Fax: (01) 342 038
Email: mayflo@dm.net.lb
This is a cosy hotel with a lot of character, unlike most of the new

hotels in the city. It has a fine reputation for service in the middle of the Hamra shopping district, and sits above the Duke of Wellington, one of several faux-British pubs in the area offering draft beer by the pint, and packed to the gills with British expatriates during happy hour. The hotel also features a tiny rooftop swimming pool. **$$**

San Lorenzo
Rue Hamra
Tel: (01) 348604/5
The San Lorenzo is very central and cheap, but is above a brothel, and is far from the cleanest hotel. **$**

West House Residence
Artois-Abdul Aziz Street, Hamra
Tel: (01) 350 450/1/2/3.
Fax: (01) 352 450
Very basic, but clean and available for longer stays. The West House is usually populated by students during term time. **$**

AROUND BEIRUT

Beit Meri

Al Bustan International
Tel: (04) 425 258/9, (04) 870 400 (04) 972 980, (04) 872 753
Fax: (04) 972 439
Glitzy hotel in this hill town, with spectacular views of city and sea. It has its own arts festival every year, and is one of the most luxurious retreats in the country, with an English country club feel. Very expensive. **$$$$**

Broummana

Printania Palace
Tel: (04) 960 416/7/8/9
Fax: (04) 960 415.
Located in another hill town above Beirut, the Printania is on a ridge with views both out over the city to the sea, and inland over the mountains. **$$$**

Jounié

Portemilio Suite Hotel
Kaslik.
Tel: (09) 933 300/1/2/3/4, (09) 900831
Fax (09) 931 866
Email: portemilio@Lebanon.com.
In Kaslik, the beach club capital of Jounié, just north of Beirut, the Portemilio has an outdoor pool, three restaurants and fine views of the Bay of Jounié and mountains. It is also close to many shops and expensive boutiques, but the drive from Beirut can be tortuous given the awful traffic on the northern highway. **$$$**

Mount Lebanon

Coin Vert
Faraya
Tel: (09) 321 260/1
Fax: (09) 720 812
Faraya is a ski resort half an hour from Beirut. There are few hotels, so most people travel to the resort for the day, or rent a chalet for the season. The Coin Vert is a clean, basic hotel, located in the village below the resort, and has a reasonable reputation. **$**

THE NORTH

Byblos

Byblos-Sur-Mer A
Port of Byblos, Jbeil, Greater Beirut
Tel: (09) 584 000, (03) 303 010
Fax: (09) 944 859
E-mail: byblos.mer@inco.com.lb
Fine hotel located near the beautiful historical fishing port that is the hub of Byblos. Byblos-Sur-Mer has its own beach club and is an excellent location from which to explore the country away from the traffic and pollution of Beirut. **$$**

Cedars

Alpine Hotel
Tel: (06) 671 057
Fax: (06) 671 057
One of the friendliest hotels in the country, run by a delightfully crazy Lebanese-Australian who also owns a pop music radio station. The Alpine is in the centre of the Cedars resort, which offers skiing in winter and walking in summer. But the hotel also runs paragliding, climbing, four-wheel drive tours and horse riding. The recently refurbished rooms are cosy and warm in winter. The service is also second to none. Bookings are essential in the ski season. **$–$$**

Tripoli

Auberge Chateau les Oliviers
Tel: (06) 615 024, (06) 610 222 (03) 228 432
Fax: (06) 610 222
Just south of the city centre, this is an enormous house that has been converted into a country house-style hotel. Many of the rooms have national themes, with Spanish and Chinese rooms on the ground floor. There is a restaurant, nightclub and swimming pool, and the hotel is littered with antiques collected by the owners. **$$–$$$**

BEKAA VALLEY

Baalbek

Palmyra B
Tel: (08) 370 230, (08) 370 001
Fax: (08) 370 3025
Infinitely famous faded hotel which serves visitors to the Baalbek ruins. Previous guests have included Charles de Gaulle and Brigitte Bardot (not on the same night).But though rich in history, the hotel is tatty and faded, and you are often lucky to have water in the summer, or heating in the winter. Certainly worth stopping off for lunch even if you don't stay, just to look at the guest book from bygone days. **$–$$**

Zahlé

Monte Albergo
Tel: (08) 800 342 (08) 810 912/3/4
Fax: (08) 801 451
Email: malbergo@inco.com.lb
Website: www.montealberto.com
Offering spectacular views across the Bekaa Valley, the Monte Albergo is one of the finest hotels outside

Price Guide

Prices are per night for a double room, On top is a five percent government tax, plus usually a 16 percent service charge.

$	Up to $50
$$	$50–100
$$$	$100–175
$$$$	$175+

Beirut, located on a rocky outcrop above the town of Zahlé. Though the decor is very 1960s (don't miss the revolving restaurant), it is clean and well equipped, with a vast Lebanese restaurant and outdoor terrace, and only five minutes' walk down to the pretty river. **$$**

THE SOUTH

Chouf
Mir Amine Palace
Beit ed Dîne
Tel: (05) 501 315/6/7/8, (03) 377 967/8
Fax: (05) 501 315
The Mir Amine is in the former palace of an 18th-century prince. When the beautiful building, set in extensive grounds with a swimming pool, was converted into a hotel it was tastefully designed, with the decor in the rooms both elegant and simple. But the hotel suffers from poor service and ageing facilities which cannot match its high price. **$$$**

Tyre
Rest House
Tel: (07) 740 677
Effectively the only hotel on the southern coastal plain, serving the historic cities of Tyre and Sidon, the Rest House is next to one of the finest stretches of sand in the country, and has a private beach. It also has an excellent restaurant serving Lebanese food, but no alcohol. **$$**

Where to Eat

Types of Restaurant

Beirut has, without doubt, some of both the best and the most expensive restaurants in the Middle East. Alongside the ubiquitous American theme eateries, there are many fine places serving Lebanese and international food, with a particular emphasis on French and Italian menus.

Most Lebanese-Lebanese restaurants serve *mezze*, plates and plates of delicious dips, pickled vegetables, oriental salads, cooked and raw meat, all eaten with flat Lebanese bread and arak (the coarse spirit distilled from grains, rice or sugar cane). A smaller number of restaurants (such as Walimah and Chef in Beirut) serve traditional Lebanese home cooking, which centres on rice, soups and boiled meat and vegetables.

As this is a former French colony, the Lebanese elite are obsessed with all things French, which has resulted in an array of French restaurants of varying quality. There are also many Italian eateries, and the latest fashion is a rash of Japanese sushi bars.

While there are restaurants scattered across Beirut (few are outside the capital), the focus in the city is in the Monot suburb in the east of the city, where at least one third of the fashionable restaurants are found. Beirut's restaurant scene is very fickle, but local magazine *The Guide* (equivalent to London's *Time Out*) offers helpful reviews of all venues.

Though food and hygiene standards are as good as in the West, service can vary from excellent to appalling (and this often bears no relation to the price).

Alcohol is served everywhere, and in generous quantities. The local beer is Almaza, but foreign beers and spirits are available everywhere. Given that wine has been made in Lebanon for some 4,000 years, it's not surprising some of the wines are excellent, particularly the reds; these come from the Bekaa Valley vineyards of Kefraya, Ksara, Nakad and Musar, which are all open to visitors. As in much of the rest of the Mediterranean world, the local spirit is aniseed-flavoured arak.

Restaurant Listings

BEIRUT

Al Dente
Abdul Wahad Al-Inglizi Street
Achrafiyé
Tel: (01) 202 440/1
(01) 217 126, (03) 208 821
Al Dente is a luxurious Italian restaurant professing to serve food that is "done right", and if their seven-course meals are anything to judge by, they do not lie. It is the darling of the *crème de la crème* of Lebanese society, for its prices are not suitable for anybody else. Aside from being a gastronomic pleasure, it is also beautifully located in one of Achrafiyé's loveliest buildings, and the small hotel upstairs, the Albergo, has charming rooms. **$$$**

Avanti
Berkeley Hotel Building, Jeanne d'Arc Street, Hamra
Tel: (01) 340 600, (01) 750 111
One of Beirut's first eat-as-much-as-you-like restaurants, it offers a blend of Italian fare. It is quiet, cosy and reasonably priced, and you pay a flat price for all food and drink. **$$**

Babylone
Abdul Wahad al Inglizi Street
Tel: (01) 219 539
Yet another of the French bistro restaurants owned by one of Lebanon's biggest restaurant chains, Idarat, though that is not to take anything away from it. The decor and food are good, and after about 9pm diners give way to Lebanon's young and moneyed party crowd. **$$**

Blue Elephant
Searock Hotel, Raouche
Tel: (01) 788 488
Part of a small chain that began life
in London, the Blue Elephant offers
excellent Thai food, with many of
the ingredients flown directly from
Thailand. But as a result meals can
be expensive, though it is a perfect
escape from the local stranglehold
of French/Italian eateries. **$$$**

Blue Note
Rue Makhoul, Hamra
Tel: (01) 743 857
Beirut's best jazz club, with live
music many nights of the week. But
even better is the food and service.
The steaks, pastas and Lebanese
dishes are truly excellent, and the
service is first rate. Tucked away in
a Hamra back street, the Blue Note
has survived the mass exodus of
diners to the east of the city, and
the food is world class. **$$$**

Caracas
Caracas Street
Tel: (01) 741 634, (01) 743 105
Excellent food, oddball colourful
decor, and one of the few
restaurants in town where you can
almost guarantee the moneyed
middle-class diners eating quietly at
9pm will be dancing on the tables
at midnight. Caracas is
understandably packed Thursday to
Saturday, especially when they start
passing out free shots. **$$$**

Casablanca
Qaddoura Building, Ain El Mreisseh
Street
Tel: (01) 369 334, (03) 856 111
Casablanca is one of the new breed
of restaurants that have spent as
much money on design as on food.
It is gothically decorated with
abundant candles and rich colours.
Food is good, and a mix of
Lebanese and international cuisine,
but the prices are not cheap. At the
weekend local bands often play,
adding to the atmosphere. **$$$**

Chef
Abed Ansa Building, Gouraud
Street, Gemaizeh
Tel: (01) 446 769
Truly excellent. The Chef is a small,
simply decorated lunchtime
restaurant. Walking in would make
any guest hesitant, for it has no
claims to classy decor. Instead, it
offers excellent Lebanese home
cooking, at ridiculously cheap
prices. Sit down anywhere, order a
refreshing glass of orange juice,
and delve into a hot healthy plate of
mulukhieh (spinach stew), a local
favourite. The service is superbly
fast, largely as a result of
multilingual waiter Cherbel, who has
become an institution in his own
right. Not to be missed. **$**

Chase
Sassine Square, Achrafiyé
Tel: (01) 202 390
Espace 2000, Zouk Mikael
Tel: (09) 210 883/6/7
City Complex, Tripoli. Tel: (06) 442
469/70, (03) 777 570
The Chase serves everything, and
does it well. Whether it is a
delicious ice-cream dessert or a fat
steak, this place has it. Their main
branch on Sassine Square, in the
heart of east Beirut, is regularly
filled every night till 3am. In the
summer it has a pleasant terrace
where you can watch the crazed
drivers go by. Its coffees seriously
contribute to summer insomnia in
the city. **$$**

Ciao
46 Université Street Joseph Street,
Achrafiyé
Tel: (01) 326 481/2
A recently opened Italian pizzeria,
Ciao is an excellent place to dig into
fine pizza and pasta. Located in a
wonderfully restored building in the
Monot district of the city, it has
reasonable service and meals are
not too expensive. **$**

Price Guide

A government tax of five percent
is added to bills, and often a
service charge of up to 16
percent, on top of which waiters
will also expect a tip, so don't
think the menu price is what you
will pay.
Prices are per head for a meal
with half a bottle of wine: if
available

$	up to $15
$$	$15–30
$$$	over $30

Circus
243 Monot Street, Achrafiyé
Tel: (01) 332 523, (03) 366 200
E-Mail: info@circus.com.lb
From the outside the Circus looks
like a municipal library. But inside
it's like the vast set from a futuristic
movie. As you walk in, staff pull back
the acres of curtain to reveal a
restaurant/bar on several levels,
with decor of steel and glass, and
ancient movies projected on the
walls. If you can afford the prices,
the food, which includes ostrich and
kangaroo as well as conventional
dishes, is also not bad. **$$$**

City Café
Sadat Street, Hamra
Tel: (01) 802 288
This café has long been a lunchtime
choice for Lebanon's high society. It
has a reasonable menu, and
equally reasonable prices. But, with
its clientele of the power-dressing
elite guaranteed, it seems to have
given up on service, which is some
of the worst in the city. **$$**

Entrecote
Rue Abdul Wahad al Inglizi
Achrafiyé
Tel: (01) 334 048.
While most Beirut restaurants will
pretend to be French, this one really
is, and it is part of a chain that
began on the Champs-Elysée in
Paris. The menu is very simple:
steak, *frites*, and that's it, though
you may be able to get a little herb
butter for your steak. With most of
east Beirut dreaming of being
French, the high popularity of the
restaurant is hardly surprising. **$$$**

Kababji
Saroulla, Hamra
Tel: (01) 351 346
(03) 269 100, (01) 342 863
(03) 265 100
The Kababji chain is the nearest
you will get to Lebanese fast food.
Whether you are eating in or taking
food out, the menu is delicious, the
restaurants spotlessly clean and
the prices very reasonable. Kababji
is the ideal place to try out a variety
of local dishes but, with its modern,
stainless steel decor, the
restaurant is not recommended for
those looking for ancient Arabic
charm. **$–$$**

Maharaja
Sporting Club Beach, Manara
Tel: (01) 743 915
One of two Indian restaurants in Beirut, where diners do not yet seem to have discovered the delights of Indian food. Maharaja offers amazingly presented food, with vegetables carved into roses, in a dining hall with a 4m (13ft)-high scale model of the Taj Mahal. There are magnificent views over the Mediterranean too. **$$**

Mijana
Abdul Wahab Al-Inglizi Street
Achrafiyé
Tel: (01) 328 082, (01) 334 675, (03) 208 823
In the fashion of Al Dente (*see page 31*), and owned by the same people, the Mijana is a posh Lebanese eatery specialising in endless traditional *mezze*, with arak and *narguilehs* (water pipes). With its high prices, and proximity to the city's banks and parliament, it is a favourite of the power elite. In a finely restored Ottoman house in the Monot district, it offers a great chance to dress up and indulge in the best of Lebanese food,**$$$**

Modca
Hamra Street, Hamra
Tel: (01) 345 501
A hangover from the 1960s, Modca is a stainless steel and plastic café on the crossroads in the centre of Hamra. Thirty years ago it was a hangout for artists and writers. Today it is still popular because of its central location, and a great place for people watching. **$**

Monot
83 Monot Street, Achrafiyé
Tel: (01) 326 956, (03) 326 956.
The restaurant that launched 100 others, Monot is a French-feeling bistro at the very heart of the new restaurant district. It offers excellent salads and grills, but is hugely popular so getting a table can be trying. **$$**

Pacifico
Monot Street, Achrafiyé
Tel: (01) 204 446.
An excellent Mexican-Cuban restaurant famed for its cocktails and wild nights. Staff, for some reason, wear doctors' white coats,

and the ceiling is decorated with the vast wooden propeller of an aircraft. The food is very good, though, if you can get in the door, and exotic cocktails are ridiculously cheap during happy hour. **$$**

Ristretto
Mahatma Ghandi Street, Hamra
Tel: (01) 739 475, (01) 739 476
Simply the best breakfasts in Beirut. The Ristretto offers great coffee, pancakes and omelettes, and the service is excellent. Or stay for lunch, and enjoy the French bread sandwiches with fresh fillings. Located in downtown Hamra, this small, modern café is an institution among those Lebanese who grew up in Europe and the US, and have now returned. The friendliest host in town. **$–$$**

Sochimodo
Verdun 730 Centre, Verdun
Tel: (09) 222 211, (03) 444 553/4/6
Sochimodo is actually four restaurants in a shopping centre, offering anything from pizzas to sushi to Lebanese food. The salad bar is famed, and the service is not bad too. **$–$$**

Sirena
Bliss Street, Manara.
Tel: (01) 374 840/1, (03) 629 807
One of Beirut's two Indian restaurants, offering a refreshing break from Italian-French eateries. Indian food has yet to catch on in Lebanon, perhaps because it is seen as the food of "domestic staff", so Sirena is always almost empty. But the food is good. **$**

Sushi Bar
Monot Street, Achrafiyé
Tel: (01) 338 555, (01) 337 888.
Making the most of the new-found popularity of Japanese restaurants, Sushi Bar offers reasonable but expensive food, but has become more a place to be seen in than to eat in, and is populated with anyone who is anyone in Beirut. As a consequence, the service is geared towards piling food down guests as quickly as possible to get fresh bums on seats. **$$$**

Time Out
Liban Street,Achrafiyé
Tel: (01) 331 938, (01) 323 084.

Ostensibly a "private club", Time Out is hidden away in a converted Ottoman house with a range of lounges where it is possible to take tea, or sit and sip gin and tonic while reading *Country Life*. In the evening in summer, the terrace is a popular place for the moneyed elite to look down on the world. Delightful place. **$$**

Walimah
Makdissi Street, Hamra
Tel: (01) 745 933, (01) 343 128,
In a similar vein to the Chef (*see page 349*), Walimah is one of a tiny number of restaurants to offer home-cooked Lebanese food, as opposed to *mezze*. It serves a different menu every day, and is located in a fine old house with high ceilings, wooden tables and tasteful music. It has a small, enchanting garden. **$$**

Vieux Quartier
Akawi Street, Achrafiyé
Tel: (01) 334588, (01) 336640
A restaurant built as much on its reputation as its food and service. Vieux Quartier is *the* place of the elite, with politicians to be seen lunching there every day of the week. The menu is simple, but well cooked in a French style, and the service is suitably deferential. But you should expect to pay upwards of $50 a head even for lunch. **$$$**

Wimpy
Hamra Street, Hamra
Tel: (01) 345 440/1
Elsewhere in the world the Wimpy may be seen as a chain of burger bars. But in Beirut the café is an institution, along the lines of the Modca (*see opposite*), largely because it was a hangout for intellectuals in the 1960s. It is centrally located, and offers reasonable food, but has perhaps the worst service in the city. **$**

BYBLOS

Byblos Fishing Club
Byblos port
Tel: (09) 540 213
Byblos Fishing Club was once renowned as a stopping-off point for celebrities cruising the eastern

Mediterranean, a fact supported by hundreds of framed photos of diners including Frank Sinatra, Marlon Brando and Brigitte Bardot. The owner, ageing Mexican playboy Pepe Abed, is a tourist attraction in his own right. **$$–$$$**

El Molino
Tel: (09) 541 555, (03) 372 562
Byblos port.
A charming Mexican restaurant offering great dishes and a breathtaking view over the old port. Cosy yet efficient, it is an alternative from the array of Lebanese restaurants in Byblos. **$$**

Kababji
Jounié highway
Tel: (09) 217 100/300, (09) 218 100, (03) 270 088.
One of the popular chain serving fast food, Lebanese-style (see entry under Beirut for more details). **$**

JOUNIÉ

Chez Sami
Maameltein
Tel: (09) 910 520.
Some of the best local seafood in the country, served in a charming old stone-built house. In summer there is a pretty terrace outside overlooking the sea. **$$**

Crèperie
Kaslik
Tel: (09) 912 491, (09) 914 886
Jouniéis awash with restaurants, but most are awful. The exception is La Crèperie, housed in a classically beautiful Ottoman house with superb views across the bay offered by its position atop a small cliff. The service is immaculate, with penguin-attired waiters and waitresses. It serves great steaks and wines, as well as Lebanese dishes, but is worth a visit just for the view. **$$**

SIDON

Rest House
Seafront
Tel: (07) 722 469
In a restored 17th-century *khan*, which was disassembled, moved

---

Price Guide

A government tax of five percent is added to bills, and often a service charge of up to 16 percent, on top of which waiters will also expect a tip, so don't think the menu price is what you will pay.
Prices are per head for a meal with half a bottle of wine if available:

$	up to $15
$$	$15–30
$$$	over $30

and rebuilt down the road in the 1890s, and just next to the Crusader Sea Castle, this is a fine Lebanese restaurant, with excellent *mezze* and pleasant service. **$$**

TRIPOLI

Chase
City Complex.
Tel: (06) 442 469/70
(03) 777 570.
Popular all-rounder serving everything (see entry under Beirut). **$$**

TYRE

Rest House
Seafront
Tel: (07) 740 677
Like its sister in Sidon, the Resthouse offers a full Lebanese *mezze* meal in traditional style on the seafront. This one, however, is under a hotel, but the food is just as good, though the restaurant does not serve alcohol. **$$**

ZOUK MICHAEL

Chase
Espace 2000, Zouk Michael
Tel: (09) 210 883/6/7, (03) 777 573
Another branch of the popular eatery (see entry under Beirut).**$$**

Culture

Dance

Caracalla
Ivoire Theatre, near Antoine's Library, Sin El Fil, Greater Beirut.
Tel: (01) 490 380.
Lebanon's most famous dance troupe, Caracalla, led by founder/choreographer Abdul Halim Caracalla, has performed across the world, with a colourful mixture of both contemporary and traditional Lebanese dancing to traditional music.

Theatre

Seeing something of a revival, the local theatre scene is invigorating, but mostly in Arabic, with a mixture of social satire, farce and musicals.

Al-Madina Theatre
Clemenceau, Hamra, Beirut
Tel: (01) 371 962
Colourful, stylish local productions of serious drama, as well as poetry readings and Sufi music.

Monot Theatre
Achrafiyé, Beirut
Tel: (01) 202 422
Small, intimate stage, with plays mostly in Arabic, but occasionally in English and French, by local artists.

Ivoire Theatre
Sin El Fil, Beirut
Tel: (01) 490 380
Home of the Caracalla dance troupe (*see above*).

Piccadilly Theatre
Hamra, Beirut
Tel: (01) 340 078/9
One of the oldest and more traditional theatres which is home to popular farce and satire in Arabic, and routinely sells out.

Arts Festivals

Beirut Film Festival
Tel: (01) 493 492, (01) 502 409.
Fax: (01) 481 785.
E-mail: beyfilm@ifp.com.lb.
The country's biggest film festival takes place in October with a collection of international, regional and local films, as well as a competition for young local filmmakers. There is a heavy French participation, with leading French actors and directors attending in 1999.

Bustan Festival.
Tel: (01) 425 258/9, (03) 752 000-9, (04) 972 980/1/2.
Fax: (04) 972 439, (04) 871 569.
E-mail: albustan.festival@inco.com.lb
The annual festival takes place at a hotel of the same name in the summer hill retreat of Beit Mery, usually in February. It a European festival in style, with foreign and local artists in attendance. Each year the festival has a different theme, usually a country.

Ayloul Film and Theatre Festival
Moukarzel Building, Military Hospital Street, Greater Beirut.
Tel: (03) 750 285.
Fax: (01) 347 031.
E-mail: ayloul@cyberia.net.lb
Festival of mostly student theatre, dance and films which takes place every September.

Beiteddine Festival
Beiteddine, Chouf.
Tel: (01) 346 274/5.
One of several arts festivals featuring mostly international artists which take place in the summer, and in 1999 boasted a performance by Placido Domingo.

Baalbek Festival
Baalbek, Bekaa Valley.
Tel: (01) 373 150/1/2.
Lebanon's most famous international summer arts festival, regularly featuring local diva Fairouz, and international artists, which in recent years included Vanessa Mae, Charles Aznavour, Herbie Hancock and Nina Simone.

European Film Festival
Cinema Empire, Centre Sofil, Ashrafieh.
Tel: (01) 328 806, (01) 204 080.
Held in November, screening a collection of European films, mostly in French.

Beirut International Jazz Festival
Feghali Centre, Barbar-Abu Jaoude St, Bauchrieh, Beirut.
Tel: (03) 302 451.
Fax: (01) 875 890.
Held in May, featuring local and international artists.

Jounié, Greater Beirut,
Tel: (09) 937 300
Espace
Zouk, Greater Beirut
Tel: (09) 212 516, (09) 217 999
Circuit Planete, Zouk and Kaslik
Zouk, Greater Beirut
Tel: (09) 211 004/636
Kaslik, Greater Beirut
Tel: (09) 912 503/4
Presidence
Zouk, Greater Beirut
Tel: (09) 210 961
St Elie
Antelias, Greater Beirut
Tel: (04) 406 706
(04) 418 835

Baalbek
Roxy Cinema
Tel: (08) 871 057

Sidon
Scheherazade Cinema
Tel: (07) 720 699

Tivoli
Broummana
Tel: (04) 961 667

Tripoli
Les Salinas
Tel: (06) 540 970
Circuit Planete
Tel: (06) 614 097
Rivoli
Tel: (06) 433 249

Cinema

Lebanon has by far the best cinema in the region, with tens of cinemas offering everything from the latest Hollywood blockbusters to obscure Czech and French arthouse movies, and all in modern multiplexes. Most films start at 3.30pm, 5.30pm, 8pm or 10pm.

Beirut
Concorde Square, Hamra
Tel: (01) 738 439
Bourj Hammoud
Tel: (01) 260 382
Circuit Planete, Abraj
Tel: (01) 426 641/3.
Empire Dunes, Dunes Shopping Centre, Verdun
Tel: (01) 792 123/4.

Elite, Marriott Hotel, Jnah.
Tel: (01) 840 286
Elysée, Achrafiyé
Tel: (01) 320 153/7
Empire Sofil, Achrafiyé
Tel: (01) 328 806, (01) 204 080
Empire Sodeco, Sodeco Square
Sodeco. Tel: (01) 616 707
Freeway, Sin El Fil
Tel: (01) 485 590/1
Sagesse, Sagesse Street
Achrafiyé, Beirut
Tel: (01) 201 453, (01) 336 075
Vendome, Achrafiyé
Tel: (01) 443 992

Greater Beirut
Les Ambassades
Zouk, Greater Beirut
Tel: (03) 678 688, (09) 217 490
La Cite

Beirut Art Galleries

Agial
63 Abdul Aziz Street, Hamra.
Tel: (01) 345 213, (03) 634 244.
Changing collection of Lebanese and European artists. Open Monday to Saturday 10am–6pm.

Galerie Epreuve diArtiste
Victor Cassir building, 16 Sursock Street, Achrafiyé.
Tel: (01) 593 911.
Changing local and foreign exhibits. Open Monday to Friday 9am–6:30pm, Saturday 10am–7pm.

Maraya Reflets d'Art Gallery
Sami El Solh, opposite the Lebanese University for Fine Arts.
Tel/fax: (01) 390 555.
Rotating collection of works by local artists.

Cultural Centres

BEIRUT

British Council
Azzar Building, Yamout Street
Hamra
Tel: (01) 740 123/4/5
Fax: (01) 739 461.
E-mail: dto.enquiries@bc-Beirut.
sprint.com
The British Council has a
reasonable library, and video club.

Centre Culturel Francaise
Cite Bounnour, Damascus Street,
near the National Museum
Tel: (01) 644 850/1/2
(01) 615 859.
By far the most active foreign
cultural centre, the CCF, on a huge
campus, has an extensive library,
French café with outdoor terrace,
cinema and school offering
language courses.

Institute Cervantes
Commodore Street, Hamra
Tel: (01) 352 448, (01) 347 555,
(01) 347 755
The Spanish Cultural Centre has a
large library, and offers language
classes at various levels.

Goethe Institute
Gideon Building, Bliss Street
Hamra/Manara
Tel: (01) 860 149, (01) 740 524,
(01) 745 058.

Italian Institute of Culture
Najjar Building, Rome Street, Hamra
Tel: (01) 935 800/1
(01) 749 801/2/3
Haret el Mir, Zouk Mikael
Tel: (09) 215 552, (09) 222 534

The Russian Cultural Centre
Tel: (01) 309 889
Rashid Karame Street, Verdun.

Tripoli

German Cultural Centre
Al Mina Street
Tel: (06) 600 228
The German cultural centre shows
local and foreign theatre
performances, and holds monthly
film screenings in German with
English subtitles.

Nightlife

Nightclubs & Pubs

Beirut
Alecco's
Sodeco Square
Achrafiyé
Tel: (01) 612 100/200
Offers a variety of Western and
Arabic dance music. Elegant
evening clothes are commonplace,
and the skimpier they are the easier
it will be for you to fit in with the
wild crowd.

Blue Note
Makhoul Street
Hamra
Tel: (01) 743 857
A mix of delicious Lebanese cuisine
and the best jazz around, plus great
food too.

Greater Beiruit
B018
Next to the Beirut Forum
Doura
Tel: (03) 800 018
This place is definitely unique in the
Middle East. Designed to resemble
a graveyard, the club has deep red
curtains and tables shaped like
coffins. Built underground, it has an
electronic roof that opens up
allowing dancing under the stars. A
mixture of acid jazz, sensual
oriental beats and a few hardcore
rave numbers ensure non-stop
dancing till 6am. Anything can be
worn to B018, literally.

Amor Y Libertad
Debs Centre
Kaslik
Tel: (09) 640 881
(03) 640 881
Popular nightclub/restaurant with
Spanish beats from live bands.

Belly Dancing

Lebanon is famous for its *tarab*
evenings, complete with
traditional celebration music,
mezze (plates and plates of
delicious dips, pickled
vegetables, oriental salads,
cooked and raw meat, all eaten
with flat Lebanese bread), lots of
arak, and, of course, belly
dancers.

The music tends to be
rhythmic and sensual to help the
dancers gyrate and shake as
much as possible in their glitter
and tassels.

Several traditional Lebanese
restaurants include a belly
dancer in their evening
programmes, but most only have
a show when they have a special
offer on their menu or during
celebrations.

Where to go
Next to the Dog River on the way
to Jounié is a strip of land with
several restaurants that have a
belly dancing show every day.
The strip is called Nahr Al-
Founoun, which literally means
the river of the arts. Definitely
worth a visit.

Gambling

Casino du Liban
Maameltein
Jounié
Greater Beirut
Tel: (09) 932 932
Fax: (09) 932 779
(01) 604 555
E-mail: casino@cdl.com.lb
Recently reopened, the casino
decorates the Jounié bay. Some
come to play the 300 slot machines
in jeans and sneakers, others in
diamonds and dinner jackets
gamble away in the gaming rooms,
where formal attire is a
requirement. The vast casino also
has several restaurants, bars and
nightclubs.

Shopping

The Guide, the Lebanese version of London's *Time Out* magazine, carries reviews and features on where to shop, with suggestions on what to buy. Though it has a cover price of LL5,000 in bookstores, it is readily available free in many hotels and cafés.

Art & Antiquities

By regional standards, Lebanon has little to buy in the way of arts and antiquities. But there are many locally produced fabrics, blue glass and pots.
Exporting antiquities, defined as items more than 300 years old, is prohibited.

Where to buy
One of the best places to browse and buy what is available is Hawd Al Wilaya Souk in Bourj Abu Haidar in Beirut. Items made from brass, wood decorated with seashells, old furniture, old carpets, and other oriental artefacts are on sale.
Beirut's Gemaizeh Street also has a few shops that sell antiques, but these are mostly expensive, and rarely Lebanese.

Basketware

Some 15 shops sell traditional wicker baskets in Al-Helweh, on the old road to Amsheet.

Pottery

Pottery can be seen being made in Sidon in the south.

Copperware

Souk Al Nahasseen (coppersmith market) in Tripoli is the best place to buy brass and copper. Here imported copper plates are fashioned to local designs.

Furniture
For those not wishing to leave Beirut, locally produced furniture and items are available at the Artisanat chain, though the prices are high. Branches of the store are found at:
● Clemenceau, opposite the French business school.
Tel: (01) 364 880.
● St Antoine Building, Al-Akawi, Achrafiyé.
Tel: (01) 580 618.

Alternatively, there is a branch in Tripoli:
● Thaqafeh Street, next to Red Shoe, Tripoli.
Tel: (06) 443 531.

Clothing

Beirut is the fashion capital of the Middle East, with miles and miles of expensive French and Italian boutiques in Verdun, Hamra, Kaslik, Jounié, Mar Elias and Furn El Chebbak. There are also cheaper chain stores such as Max Mara, Armani, Donna Karan and the new Mango and Zara.
Jounié and Kaslik are home to *haute couture*. But don't expect to find much locally produced in Lebanon.

Leather

Locally fashioned leather is popular and widely available, notably, on Commodore Street, in the Hamra area of Beirut; at Jadoun on the Bliss Street, Hamra, Beirut; and in Tripoli and Sidon.

Bookshops

Beirut has a wide range of good bookshops, including:
● Librarie Antoine
(a chain store)
Elias Sarkis Avenue, Achrafiyé.
Tel: (01) 331 811.
● Horsh Tabet
Sin El Fil, Greater Beirut.

Tel: (01) 481 072/8,
(01) 486 538/9,
(01) 887 409.
Hamra Street, Hamra.
Tel: (01) 341 470/1.
● Bou-Khalil Drugstore
Baabda.
Tel: (01) 455 192/3.
● ABC
Dbayeh,
Greater Beirut.
Tel: (01) 404 749,
(01) 405 341,
(01) 406 503.
● Metro Superstore
Maameltein,
Greater Beirut.
Tel: (09) 932 964,
(09) 935 638.
● Books and Pens
Jeanne d'Arc Street,
Hamra.
Tel: (01) 342 066.
● Librarie Internationale
Verdun Street,
Verdun 730 Centre.
Tel: (01) 788 675/6.
● Librarie Naufal
Forest building, Horsh Tabet,
Sin El Fil,
Greater Beirut.
Tel: (01) 499 074.
Naufal building, Al-Mamari Street,
Hamra.
Tel: (01) 354 394,
(01) 354 898.

Jewellery

Most of the gold sold in Lebanon is imported from Italy and Germany, and reworked by local jewellers. Designs tend to be predominantly classical European, but there is a small market of oriental designs, mainly Pharaohic and Phoenician, that have been fashioned to suit more modern tastes.
The centre of the jewellery trade is Beirut's Armenian suburb of Bourj Hammoud.

Sport

Watersports

Lebanon is littered with beach clubs offering sunbathing, water-skiing, jet-skiing and sailing. Most charge about $15 for a changing room and plastic sun lounger from which to see Lebanese *Baywatch* wannabes.

Rafting

Rafting and Kayaking Club of Lebanon Ali Awada. Tel: (03) 678 398. On the Ibrahim, Al-Assi, Litani and Bared rivers.

Skiing

Lebanon has a short skiing season from January to April, but a number of resorts are very close to Beirut. Skiing is expensive, costing some $30 for a day pass, with most resorts having fewer than 20 lifts. Weekends are very busy, and the Lebanese ski the same way they drive. Faraya is the place to be seen, and wear the latest in French ski fashion. The Cedars resort is less crowded, but a good three-hour drive from Beirut.
Faraya-Mzaar Tel: (09) 341 034/5, (03) 771 211/2.
Laqlouq
Tel: (03) 256 853, (03) 441 112.
Cedars Tel: (06) 671 073/2.

Horse Racing

Beirut Hippodrome Omar Beyhum Street, near the National Museum, Greater Beirut. Tel: (01) 632 515. Fax: (01) 632 535.
Pure Arabian horses race in front of an average of 3,000 people at noon on Saturday in summer, and Sundays in winter. Horses are trained daily 6–8am.

Language

Lebanese Arabic

Most Lebanese natives speak at least a few words of English or French, and many are fluent in either. If you are having trouble explaining something to a person, ask a passerby. It is rare to be in an area where nobody speaks English.

Lebanese Arabic is distinct from that spoken elsewhere in the Middle East, having a softer tone, and with fewer of the hard ghh sounds prevalent, for example, in the Arabian Gulf.

The Arabic character, the qalf, is only pronounced by the Druze people of the mountains, with most speakers replacing the character with a gloteral pause (as in the Cockney pronunciation of bottle as boíl). This can make seeking directions complex. For example, the Bekaa valley is pronounced by most Lebanese as the Beíaa valley.

Useful words

Yes *Ay* (as in hay), or *naam*
No *Laa*
please *minfadlak* (*minfadlik* to a woman)
thank you *shukran, yislamo*
airport *mataar*
boat *safeena*
bridge *jisr*
car *sayara*
embassy *safara*
hospital *mustashfa*
hotel *ootel*
post office *al-bareed*
restaurant *mataam*
square *saa-ha*
street *shareh*
right *yameen*
left *shmel*
and/or *oo/aawo*

big/little *kabeer/zeer*
good/bad *mneah/mish mneah*
possible *mumkin, yimkin*
impossible *mish mumkin*
here/there *hone/honeek*
hot/cold *sukhon/baarid*
many/few *kteer/aliil*
up/down *faouq/taht*
more/enough *kameyn/bikafi*
breakfast *ftoor*
dinner *aasha*
today *el yom*
tomorrow *bookra*
yesterday *mbeareh*
morning *is-soboh*
noon *id-dohor*
afternoon *baad id-dohor*
at night *belayl*
next week *il osbooa il gayy*
next time *marra tayneh*
after a while *baad shwaay*
I/you *ana/inta*
he/she *hooweh/hiyyeh*
they/we *hinne/ihna*
money *masari*
change/no change *frattah/mafi frattah*
the bill *al-hisab*
this/that *hayda/ haydak*
How much? *Adey?*
How much do you want?
to a male   *adey biddak?*
to a female   *adey biddik?*
all/half *kuull/noos*

Common Expressions

Hello, welcome *Ahlan wa sahlan*
Good morning *Sabah el-kheir* (reply *sabah al noor*)
Good evening *Masa el-heir*
Goodbye *Ma salemeh*
What is your name?
to a male   *Shoo ismak?*
to a female   *Ahoo ismik?*
How are you?
to a male   *Kee fak?*
to a female   *Kee fik?*
I am fine
Ana mneah (m), *Ana mneaha* (f)
How much is this ...? *Adey haida?*
Where do I find...?   *Wayne fee?*
Why?   *Laysh?*
I don't want   *Maa biddi*
I want   *Biddi*
Do you want anything?
to a male   *Biddak shee?*
to a female   *Biddik shee?*

Numbers

2	tnain
3	tlaiteh
4	arrba
5	khamsee
6	sitteh
7	sabba
8	tmenee
9	tissa
10	ashra
11	hdaash
12	tnaash
13	tlaitaash
14	arrbataash
15	khamstaash
16	sitaash
17	sabbataash
18	tamantaash
19	tissaataash
20	ashreen
30	tlaiteen
40	arrbaeen
50	khamseen
60	sitteen
70	sabbaeen
80	tamaneen
90	tissaeen
100	meeyeh
1,000	

Days & Months

Sunday *Yom al-ahad*
Monday *Yom al-tnayn*
Tuesday *Yom al-tleteh*
Wednesday *Yom al-arbaa*
Thursday *Yom al-khamees*
Friday *Yom al-joumah*
Saturday *Yom al-sabbit*
January *Kanoun al-tani*
February *Shibatt*
March *Azaar*
April *Nissan*
May *Ayyar*
June *Hozeiran*
July *Tammooz*
August *Aab*
September *Aylool*
October *Tishreen al-aowal*
November *Tishreen al-tani*
December *Kanoon al-awal*

Further Reading

For general books about the region, Islam and ancient history, consult the reading list on page 335.

Travel

The Hills of Adonis, by Colin Thubron. An account of Thubron's travels and adventures through Lebanon prior to the civil war.

Lebanon's Civil War

The Making of Modern Lebanon, by H. Cobban. The complex history of Lebanon made clear.
Pity the Nation: Lebanon at War, by Robert Fisk. Compelling and thorough account of the civil war written by the Middle East correspondent of the London Times.
An Evil Cradling, by Brian Keenan. What it felt like to be one of the Westerners taken hostage in Beirut.
A House of Many Mansions – The History of Lebanon Reconsidered, by Kamal Salibi. Explores the causes of the civil war.

Other Insight Guides

Other Insight Guides highlighting destinations in this region, include titles on Israel, Egypt and Jordan:
The expanded and updated *Insight Guide: Egypt* not only covers in detail Egypt's many ancient and Islamic sites but also explores its heady mix of African, Arab and European influences. Includes background essays on topics ranging from food to popular culture, as well as a comprehensive places section and detailed listings.

From Syria, it is easy to visit neighbouring Jordan. Written by a team of Amman-based experts, *Insight Guide: Jordan* helps you make the most of a visit.

Feedback

We do our best to ensure the information in our books is as accurate and up-to-date as possible. The books are updated on a regular basis, using local contacts, who painstakingly add, amend and correct as required. However, some mistakes and omissions are inevitable and we are ultimately reliant on our readers to put us in the picture.

We would welcome your feedback on any details related to your experiences using the book "on the road". Maybe we recommended a hotel that you liked (or another that you didn't), as well as interesting new attractions, or facts and figures you have found out about the country itself. The more details you can give us (particularly with regard to addresses, e-mails and telephone numbers), the better.

We will acknowledge all contributions, and we'll offer an Insight Guide to the best letters received. Please write to us at:

Insight Guides
58 Borough High Street
London SE1 1XF
United Kingdom
Or send e-mail to: **insight@apaguide.demon.co.uk**

ART & PHOTO CREDITS

Index

Numbers in italics refer to photographs

INSIGHT GUIDES

The world's largest collection of visual travel guides

A range of guides and maps to meet every travel need

Insight Guides

This classic series gives you the complete picture of a destination through expert, well written and informative text and stunning photography. Each book is an ideal background information and travel planner, serves as an on-the-spot companion – and is a superb visual souvenir of a trip. Nearly 200 titles.

Insight Pocket Guides

focus on the best choices for places to see and things to do, picked by our local correspondents. They are ideal for visitors new to a destination. To help readers follow the routes easily, the books contain full-size pull-out maps. 120 titles.

Insight Maps

are designed to complement the guides. They provide full mapping of major cities, regions and countries, and their laminated finish makes them easy to fold and gives them durability. 60 titles.

Insight Compact Guides

are convenient, comprehensive reference books, modestly priced. The text, photographs and maps are all carefully cross-referenced, making the books ideal for on-the-spot use when in a destination. 120 titles.

Different travellers have different needs. Since 1970, Insight Guides has been meeting these needs with a range of practical and stimulating guidebooks and maps